CHEAP SLEEPS EUROPE

KATIE WOOD

RESEARCHERS
Sarah Gear and David Johnston

ROBSON BOOKS

This edition first published in Great Britain in 2005 by Robson Books, The Chrysalis Building, Bramley Road, London W10 6SP

An imprint of **Chrysalis** Books Group plc

First published by HarperCollins Paperbacks in 1992

British Library Cataloguing in Publication Data
A catalogue record for this title is available from the British Library.

ISBN 1 86105 714 8

Printed by Creative Print & Design (Wales), Ebbw Vale

CONTENTS

CHEAP SLEEPS EUROPE 2005/06

KATIE WOOD was born and educated in Edinburgh, where she read Communications then English at university. After a short spell in Public Relations she spotted the gap in the market for a guide on training round Europe on a budget. *Europe by Train* allowed her to combine her two greatest loves, travelling and writing, and the first edition of this now-classic book was published in 1983. Since then she has written some 35 guidebooks on topics ranging from family holidays to the environmental and social impacts of tourism. Her books have been universally praised for their practical, down-to-earth approach and the quality of her research.

A fellow of the Royal Geographical Society, Katie has travelled to over 100 countries and now freelances in travel writing for numerous national newspapers and magazines.

Also by Katie Wood and published by Robson Books:

Europe by Train 2005/06

For my wonderful sons, Andrew and Euan House

INTRODUCTION

You've opened this guide because you are about to turn that dream of travelling around Europe on a shoestring into reality. Seasoned travellers will tell you that getting from A to B is the easy bit. It's finding a budget bed for the night that causes real headaches. Well, I hope that investing in this book will be an instant cure. You'll keep more of those precious pounds (or euros) tucked in your pocket and save two other equally precious commodities as well: time and effort.

Originally the title was to be 'Where to find good, clean accommodation in Europe for travellers on very low budgets'. But the publisher was having trouble fitting this on to the cover and asked for something a little more snappy, hence *Cheap Sleeps Europe*. But be under no illusion. Cheap definitely does not mean grotty, or disreputable or risky. There are no 'double-duty' red light hotels here. Nor any seedy, down-at-heel dives that one's parents would be aghast at. We've included many great cheap hotels (around £20/$34 per person) with real character and in good locations; clean campsites; hostels to check out – including those affiliated to Hostelling International (HI) – and private rooms in houses. If you want to be cocooned in the big slick hotel chains with their fancy mini-bars, hairdryers, trouser presses and sanitary-wrapped toilet seats, this book is not for you. For one thing, I can find you a room at a quarter the cost with twice the character and for another, I believe that to experience a country to the full you need to 'live local'.

One of the most frustrating aspects of searching for new accommodation when on the move is the time it wastes. We have set out to give you plenty of choice at each location, so if one place is full or unsuitable you can quickly settle on another.

Overall, our listings are compiled from careful research, personal experiences, readers' recommendations and the expenditure of much shoe leather.

We've also included a new chapter on using the internet to find and book accommodation, along with as many useful websites as we could, to make planning a trip before you go even easier, and booking accommodation on the road as easy as finding an internet café.

Within these pages you will find 'the best for the least' to help you make informed selections quickly and easily. So does *Cheap Sleeps Europe* live up to its promise?

'I just had to put on paper our thanks for giving us so many great choices' ...'I saved enough to treat myself to a slap-up meal in Siena'...'A terrific help every day! Where do you find these places every year?'... 'The whole town was full up, so we followed your advice and ended up with a lovely room in a private house overlooking the lake. The owner even got up early to cook us her version of a full English breakfast...'

These are typical of the many comments from readers. Well, on reflection, that last one is less than typical, but does show how surprising things, even at the lower end of the accommodation scale, can turn a simple overnight stay into a treasured memory. Of course, on the other side of the coin, it can get tricky when popular places are bursting at the seams, or you're short of cash, or you turn up late in the day. So here are some tips to bear in mind:

1. In busy areas try to plan ahead and book in advance. Failing this, get your accommodation organised as early in the day as possible. Choices get fewer as the sun goes down.

2. Always try to check the room out before you hand over any cash.

3. Negotiate the price down whenever you can. For example, ask for a room without a view, or without breakfast, or share a double or triple room. In off-peak times, it may be possible to play a couple of competing hotels off against each other for the best deal.

4. Bear in mind that accommodation standards vary country by country. As a general rule, standards and facilities escalate as you go further north, but then, so do prices.

5. Remember that the quiet little place your aunt told you about can be somewhat different when the lads from an out-of-town football club are resident. Trust your intuition. If you sense something is 'not quite right' or not your style, move on, if you can.

If you are planning to travel by train (and in Europe this is about the cheapest, sanest and easiest way to get around), take a look at my companion guide *Europe by Train 2005/06*. It's an essential reference manual with lots of advice on how to use rail routes easily and cheaply.

We make every effort to ensure accuracy, but by its very nature, much of the information herein is susceptible to change. Currency conversions are based on rates of €1=£0.67, £1=$1.70, but nothing stays the same for very long. Hotels get new owners, staff come and go, rates, dates and conditions change. Do play safe and double check before booking in to avoid inconvenience or disappointment.

Oh, one more thing, if you come across a real gem or a stinker, or disagree with my comments, do drop me a line and tell me. Meantime, get cracking and get packing ... turn the page and let yourself go. Bon voyage!

Katie Wood
January 2005

NB: When the price for a double room is listed in the book, the price listed is for two people and not per person (unless stated otherwise).

USING THE INTERNET

The internet has revolutionised travel, and when it comes to booking accommodation or researching your next holiday destination, it has become an indispensable tool. Whether you want to plan ahead and get all your rooms reserved before you leave, or prefer to nip into an internet cafe along the way and book via email, the web provides a cheap and easy way to find and communicate with your hotel of choice.

You'll find tourist information websites, hotel websites and email addresses listed for everywhere that has one in this book. For a bit of extra help, in case you prefer to find your own hotel, or end up staying somewhere not covered here, we have listed some of the best budget accommodation websites on the net:

GENERAL ACCOMMODATION SITES

www.cheapnights.com, lists accommodation by city and type. Prices clearly displayed. Provides links to booking sites for each property listed.

www.inyourpocket.com, covers Eastern Europe. Provides accommodation details listed by country. Web links and booking facilities. Also provides excellent tourist information.

www.eurocheapo.com, accommodation arranged by city. Provides tourist information, some web links and hotel reviews.

www.cityvox.com, accommodation listings, reviews and tourist information for Belgium, Italy, France, the Netherlands, Germany, Greece and Switzerland. Some web links.

www.tripadvisor.com, worldwide accommodation listings and tourist information. Reviews and links to hundreds of websites.

BED AND BREAKFAST

www.bedandbreakfastineurope.com, city-specific links to B&Bs.
www.bbeurope.net, B&B listings across Europe. Web links provided.

YOUTH HOSTELS

www.iyhf.org, Hostelling International homepage. Links to sites worldwide. Buy the HI hostelling card online here.

AUSTRIA (Österreich) (00)43

Austria has a well-deserved 'must-see' reputation among travellers from all over the world. Its snow-capped Alpine peaks, its forests, castles and onion-domed churches all go to make up some of the most spectacular scenery in central Europe. Combine that with the country's musical heritage, its great classical and modern composers, and consider Vienna, one of Europe's most charming and intriguing cities, and it's easy to see why Austria has won the hearts of so many.

BACKGROUND

The ubiquitous Habsburgs seized Austria in 1282 and ruled until the end of the First World War. Their lengthy reign was characterised by intermittent violence with the Ottoman Empire.

Defeat in the Austro-Prussian War led to a decline in Austria's political influence, and by 1867 the Habsburgs were forced to acknowledge the power of the Hungarians, with whom they formed the dual monarchy of Austria-Hungary.

By this time, Vienna was the place to be in Europe, home to the great classical composers Schubert, Mozart, Beethoven, Salieri and, later on, Strauss.

Austria's success story faded in the twentieth century as the country fought on the losing side in two World Wars. The assassination of its Archduke Ferdinand in Sarajevo triggered the First World War, in which Austria fought with the central Axis powers against the British Empire, and Hitler's 1938 Anschluss (annexation) forced the stricken country into a pact with Germany for the Second World War.

After the war, Austria was occupied for 10 years before it regained its independence from the victorious Allied forces. It has made a spectacular economic recovery, and is now stable, progressive and confident. This cosmopolitan country is becoming a leading player in the development of the European Union.

ACCOMMODATION DETAILS

The standard is high, with impeccable levels of cleanliness. Finding moderately priced accommodation on arrival is relatively easy in most places throughout the year. However, as the student hostels and HI hostels do not open until July, late June can be a particularly bad time for those looking for inexpensive accommodation in the cities. Finding somewhere cheap to stay in Vienna is always tricky, while Salzburg becomes very crowded during its summer festival (late July–August). However, as there are reasonably cheap rooms available, and plenty of hostel beds, you can save yourself frustration on arrival (and probably money as well) by taking the trouble to book ahead. If not, it might be advisable to take a tent, even if only for use in emergencies.

Hotels are graded from one star up to five stars. In general, hotel prices are higher in the cities (especially Vienna) and in the Alpine resorts, so may be beyond your budget in most places. Away from the main tourist towns and resorts, a double in a one-star hotel generally costs from €35 (£23), but in the more popular tourist areas prices for a similar room start at around €60 (£40). As hoteliers try to fill their rooms outside the peak-season months of July–August, prices may be reduced: in May, June and September by 15–25%, and by up to 40% for the rest of the year.

Pensions, seasonal hotels and *Gasthäuser* are cheaper than hotels. These are graded from one star up to four stars, with a two-star pension being the rough equivalent of a one-star hotel. Outside Vienna, prices for doubles are normally under €35 (£23). But these tend to fill up quickly during the busy periods.

Private rooms and *Gasthäuser* can be booked through some Tourist Offices, or through private organisations which control a number of rooms. Alternatively, simply approach the owner of any house or farmhouse displaying a sign saying *Zimmer frei*, or showing a stylised white bed on a green background. In the cities and resorts expect to pay from €26–34 (£18–23) for doubles. Elsewhere, €15–18 (£10–12) for a single, and €22–30 (£14.50–20) for doubles is the normal price range. Travellers staying only one night may be liable to a small surcharge. The overnight price usually includes a continental breakfast.

At some **farms** it is possible to rent apartments. Most sleep from three to five people, but occasionally larger apartments are available. Assuming you fill all the bed space, you can expect to pay €15–18 (£10–12) each per night in the summer. During the winter months prices rise slightly, adding perhaps another €2 (£1.30) per night to the bill. The minimum length of stay permissible in farm accommodation seems to vary between regions. In the Tyrol it is only possible to pre-book for a week at a time, but in other areas stays of one night seem quite acceptable. If there is a train station nearby, farm accommodation can make a good base for exploring the surrounding area.

There are about 100 **HI hostels** spread over the country, covering all the main places of interest. Many are only open for the period between April/May and Sept./Oct., while some open only during July and August. Providing there is space, stays of longer than three days are allowed. The large city hostels can be very institutional, with a midnight curfew. The rural ones are more easy going, but may have a 10pm curfew. In general, prices vary from €14–18 (£9.50–12), usually with breakfast. Higher prices are sometimes charged at the large city hostels, which attract groups by providing a range of facilities that may be of little interest to the budget traveller. It is advisable to have an HI card. While some hostels may let you stay for a €2 surcharge (£1.30), those in Vienna are for members only, as is the main hostel in Innsbruck.

You will also find **independent hostels** in the main towns. These are mainly seasonal (May/June to Sept./Oct.). Unfortunately, their curfews are usually just as restrictive as those of their HI counterparts. Prices for dormitory accommodation are similar to the HI hostels, but some of the independents also offer singles and doubles, with prices around €15 (£10) per person. Similar prices are charged for accommodation in the various student residences that are let out July–Sept. Some are run by students themselves, with a much more relaxed atmosphere.

It is easy to recommend **camping** in Austria, as the campsites are among the best in Europe. Charges at the 450 sites are reasonable, given that they are immaculately maintained and have all the necessary facilities. Approximate rates are €5 (£3.30) per person, and about €4 (£2.70) per tent. The International Camping Carnet is not obligatory, but holders qualify for reductions at most sites. All the main towns have at least one campsite, and there are plenty of sites in the countryside. Except in Vienna and Linz, the city sites are all within walking distance of the centre. One site in Vienna stays open all year round, but elsewhere even the city sites only open between Easter/May and Sept./Oct.

Freelance camping is allowed, but you must first obtain the consent of the local *Bürgermeister*, or the landowner. Avoid lighting fires in or around woodland. Camping rough is a useful option for those planning to do a bit of walking along the excellent network of hiking trails. Be sure to have a good quality sleeping bag, as it gets very cold at night.

For anyone planning to hike extensively in the Alps, there are about 700 **mountain huts**, with 25,000 sleeping places (beds, or mattresses on the floor to put your sleeping bag on). Even if all the places are filled, it is unlikely that you will be turned away. All the huts have rudimentary kitchen facilities and many even serve meals. Joining one of the clubs might save you money in the long run. The largest is the Österreichischer Alpenverein, which offers its members discounts of 30–60% on the normal overnight prices of €8–20 (£5.30–13.30), plus reduced prices on various cable-car trips and outings. Membership costs about €25 (£16.50) for under 26s, €35 (£23) otherwise. If you are going hiking in the east of the country, it might be better to get in touch with the Österreichischer Touristenklub.

ADDRESSES

AUSTRIAN NATIONAL TOURIST OFFICE
30 Saint George Street, London W1R 0AL (tel. 020 7629 0461, *www.austria-tourism.co.uk*).

AUSTRIAN YHA
Österreichischer Jugendherbergsverband, Schottenring 28, A-1010 Wien (tel. (0)1 533 5353, *www.oejhv.or.at*, *oejhv-zentrale@oejhv.or.at*).

CAMPING
Camping Fuerher, Stein 1, A5221 Lochen (tel. (0)6217 20538, *www.camping.at*).

FARM ACCOMMODATION
Regional lists available from the Austrian National Tourist Office.

MOUNTAIN HUTS

Österreichischer Alpenverein, Wilhelm-Greil-Straße 15, A-6020 Innsbruck (tel. (0)512 59547, *www.alpenverein.at*).

Austrian Alpine Club. The UK branch is at 2 Church Road, Welwyn Garden City, Herts, AL8 6PT (tel. 01707 324835, *www.aacuk.uk.com*).

Kitzbühel (0)5356

TOURIST OFFICE

Tourismusverband, Hinterstadt 18 (tel. 62155–0, *www.kitzbue hel.com*). Open Mon.–Fri. 8.30am–6pm, Sat. 8.30am–12pm and 4pm–6pm, Sun. 10am–12pm and 4pm–6pm (off-season: 8.30am–12.30pm and 2.30–6pm, Sat 8.30am–12pm). The Tourist Office charges no commission for finding rooms. Just outside the door is a free telephone you can use to make reservations for local accommodation. From Kitzbühel Hbf go straight down Bahnhofstraße, left along Josef-Pirchl-Straße and then right at Hinterstadt. From the other train station, Hahnenkamm, walk down Josef-Herold-Straße into Vorderstadt, go left, then left again into Hinterstadt. Of the two train stations, Hahnenkamm is the closest to the town centre, but not all trains stop at the station. Arriving from Innsbruck or Wörgl the train reaches Hahnenkamm before Kitzbühel Hbf; coming from Salzburg the train reaches Kitzbühel Hbf first.

ACCOMMODATION

The prices quoted below are for the summer (high) season (July–Aug.) and are based on two people sharing a room. Supplements for single rooms are shown where applicable. All prices below are only valid for stays of three days and upwards. Most of the establishments listed below are either in the town centre or on the fringes of the town (exceptions are noted). As the town is small you will have no trouble getting to accommodation just outside on foot. Try to book in advance. Accommodation can be found relatively easily outside the winter season, as there are literally thousands of rooms available in and around Kitzbühel, though you will have to pay higher prices to stay in the town itself.

PENSIONS

CHEAPEST PRICE FOR B&B AROUND €15 (£10) PER PERSON
Linda, Brennerfeld 2 (tel 74450). Cosy.
Astlingerhof, Bichlnweg 11 (tel. 62775). Single supplement €2.50 (£1.70). Out from the centre, off Jochbergerstraße (main road to Aurach and Jochberg).
Arnika, St Johannerstraße 31A (tel. 62338). Single supplement €1.50 (£1). Out of town on the road to St Johann. An easy walk from Kitzbühel Hbf. Turn right at the end of Bahnhof-straße.

CHEAPEST PRICE FOR B&B AROUND €17–18.50 (£11.50–12.50) PER PERSON
Jodlhof, Aschbachweg 17 (tel. 63004). Just outside the town, near the hospital (Krankenhaus).
Eugenie, Pulvertürmweg 3 (tel. 66469, *a.engl@utanet.at*). Shared bathroom.
Schmidinger, Erhenbachgasse 13 (tel. 63134). Shared bathroom/WC.
Caroline, Schulgasse 7 (tel. 71971). Off Josef-Herold-Straße.
Erlenhof, Burgstallstraße 27 (tel. 62828). Just outside the town in Ecking. Single supplement €4 (£2.70).
Neuhaus, Franz-Reisch-Straße 23 (tel. 62200, *info@motorrad pension.at*). Single supplement €2.50 (£1.70).
Hebenstreit, Jodlfeld 1 (tel. 63022). Single supplement €4.50 (£3). Just outside the town, near the junction of Unterleiten-weg and Aschbachweg.

PRIVATE ROOMS

FROM €18 (£12) PER PERSON
Haus Obernauer, Obernaurach 237, bei Aurach (tel. 75805, *r.obernauer@tirol.com*). 1 mile out of Aurach (4 miles from Kitzbühel).
Haus Pankratz, Achenweg 12 (tel. 64063). Apartments also available. Breakfast extra.
Alpenblick, Pulverturmweg 7 (tel. 62458). Breakfast included.

Schmidinger, Ehrenbachgasse 13 (tel. 63134, *a.schmidinger@kitz.net*). Single supplement €2.50 (£1.70).
Landhaus Resch, Alfons-Petzold-Weg 2A (tel. 74118). Single supplement €1.50 (£1).
Landhaus Eva, Marchfeldgasse 34 (tel. 64768, *dr.bart@kitz.net*).

FARMHOUSE ACCOMMODATION

CHEAPEST PRICE AROUND €20 (£13.30) PER PERSON
Unterhausberg Ried Ecking 20 (tel. 65637, *hausberg@tirol.com*).
Hamos, Oberaigenweg 112 (tel. 64762).
Reiterhof, Malernweg 14 (tel. 64209). Single supplement. Just outside the town on the road to Högl.

CAMPING

Schwarzsee, Reitherstraße 24 (tel. 62806, *office@bruggerhof-camping.at*). €7.80 (£5.20) per person, and €7.70 (£5.10) per tent. Open all year round. As the name suggests, this campsite is near the Schwarzsee, which is a fair distance from the town centre. An easy walk from the Schwarzsee train station.

Salzburg (0)662

TOURIST OFFICES

Fremdenverkehrsbetriebe der Stadt Salzburg, Auersperg Straße 7 (tel. 889870, *www.salzburginfo.at*). Head office of the city Tourist Board. The Tourist Board runs six information centres in the city. A list of hotels and a list of private rooms are available from these offices, or online at their website.
Information Mozartplatz, Mozartplatz 5 (tel. 88987-330). In the centre of the Old Town. Open Mon.–Sat. 9am–6pm, Sun. (Easter–Oct., Christmas only) 9am–8pm.
Information Hauptbahnhof (tel. 88987-340). In the train station (platform 2A). Open daily 8.30am–8pm all year round.
Information Salzburg-Mitte, Münchner Bundesstraße 1 (tel. 88987-350). Open daily Easter–Oct. (closed Sundays during winter). For traffic arriving from Munich.

Information Salzburg-Süd, Park and Ride Parkplatz, Alpenstraße (tel. 88987-360). Open daily Easter–Oct. (closed Sundays during winter). For traffic arriving from Carinthia and Steiermark.

BASIC DIRECTIONS

Salzburg Hbf and the bus station are right next to each other. From these stations, Rainerstraße heads down to Mirbellplatz, another important bus terminal. Continuing straight on down Dreifältigkeitsgasse you arrive at the junction with Linzer Gasse just before the Staatsbrücke crosses over the River Salzach. Crossing the bridge and heading left along the riverside you can turn right at the next bridge (Mozartsteg) into Mozartplatz. The walk from the train station to Mirbellplatz takes about 10 minutes, from the station to the Salzach about 15 minutes, and from the station to Mozartplatz about 20 minutes. Buses 1, 2, 5, 6, 51 and 55 all run from Salzburg Hbf to the Staatsbrücke, buses 5, 51 and 55 continue on to Mozartsteg.

FINDING ACCOMMODATION

Accommodation can be very difficult to find during the city's summer festival (late July–Aug.). All the hostels fill rapidly at this time. Unless you have a tent you may have to spend around €35 (£23) on a private room (assuming there are any available), or even more on a hotel. Prices in some hotels fall slightly outside the peak season (May–Oct.).

HOTELS

CHEAPEST DOUBLES AROUND €35 (£23)

Junger Fuchs, Linzergasse 54 (tel. 875496). Singles start around €22 (£14.50). Prices fall slightly off-season. Left off Mirbellplatz at Schrannengasse, then right down Wolf-Dietrich-Straße into Linzer Gasse, or a bus to the Staatsbrücke and walk up Linzer Gasse.

Sandwirt, Lastenstraße 6A (tel. 874351). Take the rear exit from the train station on to Lastenstraße and head right. A few minutes' walk. Singles €20 (£13.30).

Elisabeth, Vogelweiderstraße 52 (tel. 871664, *info@pension-elisabeth.at*). Take the rear exit from the train station on to Lastenstraße, left, then sharp right at Weiserhofstraße, then left along Breitenfelderstraße into Vogelweiderstraße. Just under 10 minutes' walk. Bus 15 runs to the town centre from Vogelweiderstraße.

Merian, Merianstraße 40 (tel. 8740060). Take the rear exit from the train station on to Lastenstraße, head right, then left down Merianstraße. About 8 minutes' walk. Bus 15 runs from the stop on Bayerhamerstraße to the town centre.

CHEAPEST DOUBLES AROUND €45 (£30)

Ganshof, Ganshofstraße 13 (tel. 833630). Bus 27 from Mirbell-platz to the first stop on the street, then a short walk in the direction the bus was going.

Samhof, Negrellistraße 19 (tel. 874622). Singles start around €18 (£12). Bus 33 from Salzburg Hbf stops by the junction of Samstraße, Negrellisstraße and Maxstraße. The hotel is a short walk away.

Hotel Kolpinghaus, Adolf-Kolping-Straße 10 (tel. 4661, *www.kol pinghaus-salzburg.at*). Provides extra rooms in the summer months in their own youth hostel. Town centre.

CHEAPEST DOUBLES AROUND €55 (£37)

Dietmann, Ignaz-Harrer-Straße 13 (tel. 431364). Prices fall slightly off-season. Bus 77 from Salzburg Hbf runs along the street but the hotel is only 10 minutes' walk from the station. Head left down Rainerstraße, then right at St Julien Straße, which runs into Ignaz-Harrer-Straße.

Pension Jahn, Elisabethstraße 31 (tel. 871405). Next to the station. Can be booked through the tourist information website listed above.

CHEAPEST DOUBLES FROM €60 (£40)

Billroth, Billrothstraße 10–18 (tel. 930300, *office@billroth-hotels.at*). Bus 51 from Salzburg Hbf to the stop on Alpenstraße just past the junction with Billrothstraße. Under five minutes' walk from the bus stop.

Wallner, Aiglhofstraße 15 (tel. 845023). Bus 29 from Mirbellplatz runs along the street, the bus stop is about 200m beyond the hotel.

Itzlinger Hof, Itzlinger Hauptstraße 11 (tel. 451210). About 8 minutes' walk from Salzburg Hbf. Follow Kaiserschützenstraße away from the station, right down Fanny-von-Lehnert-Straße to the end, left, then right at Itzlinger Hauptstraße. Bus 51 runs along the street to the town centre.

Edelweiss, Kendlerstraße 57 (tel. 824883). Bus 27 from Mirbell-platz stops almost outside the hotel.

Wastlwirt, Rochusgasse 15 (tel. 820100, *info@wastlwirt.com*). Bus 27 from Mirbellplatz runs along Rochusgasse, stopping about 300m past the hotel.

Zur Post, Maxglaner Hauptstraße 45 (tel. 8323390). Buses 1 and 2 from Salzburg Hbf stop a short distance beyond the hotel.

Noppinger, Maxglaner Hauptstraße 29 (tel. 834034). See Zur Post, above, for directions. Close to the bus stop.

Lilienhof, Siezenheimer Straße 62 (tel. 433630). Take bus 77 from Salzburg Hbf to Innsbrucker Bundesstraße, then change to bus 80 which runs down Otto-von-Liliental-Straße. The hotel is on the corner of the junction with Siezenheimer Straße, a short walk from the bus stop.

PRIVATE ROOMS

Prices for private rooms start around €20 (£13.30) per person. Prices are set according to the location of the house and the facilities available in the room. All the owners below offer basic rooms with the use of the shower/bath. Try to phone or email in advance and check the price, as they change from area to area. Moosstraße is a fertile area for private rooms and those listed here are just a selection. There are many more to be found in this street.

Haus Elisabeth, Rauchenbichlerstraße 18 (tel. 450703, *info@ haus-elisabeth.net*). Cosy. Apartments also available.

Josefa Fagerer, Moosstraße 68D (tel. 824978). Singles and doubles. Bus 15 from Mirbellplatz along Moosstraße until the stop just around the corner on Firmianstraße. Then a few minutes' walk, back on to Moosstraße, then left. Baby beds.

Helga Bankhammer, Moosstraße 77 (tel. 830067, *helga.bank hammer@telering.at*). Doubles only. Directions as Josefa Fagerer. A 5-minute walk from the bus stop.

Haus Reichl, Reiterweg 52 (tel. 826248, *haus.reichl@telering.at*). 5 minutes' drive south from the train station.

Maria Langwieder, Törringstraße 41 (tel. 433129). Singles and doubles. Bus 29 from Mirbellplatz. Baby beds.

Elisabeth Mayerhofer, Moosstraße 156B (tel. 826299). See Josefa Fagerer, above, for directions.

Haus Kellner, Moosstraße 186a (tel. 824921). Breakfast included. Singles available.

HI HOSTELS

Jugendgästehaus Salzburg, Josef-Preis-Allee 18 (tel. 842670, *jgh.salzburg@jgh.at*). Dorms €13.30 (£8.90). Quads €17.40 (£11.70) per person. Doubles €22 (£14.50) per person. With breakfast. Midnight curfew. Very popular with school groups. Advance reservations either by email or over their website advised. Otherwise arrive between 7am and 9am, or as soon as possible after 11am, when the reception re-opens. Bus 5 or 51 to Justizgebäude (the first stop on Petersbrunnstraße after crossing the river), then a 5-minute walk along Petersbrunnstraße, then left down Josef-Preis-Allee. Kitchen facilities available, plus laundry room. Family rooms. Wheelchair access. Fans of *The Sound of Music* will love it here as it is played every day...!

Jugendherberge Aigen, Aignerstraße 34 (tel. 623248, *hostel. aigen@salzburg.co.at*). B&B in dorms €14 (£9.50). Open all year round. Bus 5 from Salzburg Hbf to Mozartsteg, then bus 49 along Aignerstraße to about 350m beyond the hostel. Family rooms.

Jugendherberge Eduard-Heinrich-Haus, Eduard-Heinrich-Straße 2 (tel. 625976, *hostel.eduard-heinrich@salzburg.co.at*). B&B in dorms €14 (£9.50). Bus 51 from Salzburg Hbf to the third stop on Alpenstraße, at the junction with Hans-Sperl-Straße and Egger-Lienz-Gasse. About 6 minutes' walk from the bus stop, down Egger-Lienz-Gasse, right at Henri-Dunant-Straße, and then left. Family rooms. Open all year.

Jugendherberge Haunspergstraße, Haunspergstraße 27 (tel. 875030, fax 883477). B&B in dorms €15 (£10). Curfew 11pm. Open July–end Aug. A 5-minute walk from Salzburg Hbf. Left a short distance from the station, then right along Porsche-Straße, right again at Elisabethstraße, then left at Stauffenstraße into Haunspergstraße. Family rooms.

Jugendherberge Walserfeld, Schulstraße 18 (tel. 851377). Open from July–end Aug.

HOSTEL

International Youth Hostel, Paracelsusstraße 9 (tel. 879649, *www.yoho.at*, *yoho@yoho.at*). Dorms €14 (£9.50), double rooms €19 (£12.50). Very noisy and extremely popular with Americans. A short walk from the Hauptbahnhof. Open all year.

CAMPING

Schloß Aigen, Weberbartlweg 20 (tel. 633089). €4.60 (£3.10) per tent, €4.60 (£3.10) per person. Open May–Sept. Bus 5 from Salzburg Hbf to Mozartsteg, then bus 49 along Aigener-straße to the stop Glaserstraße. From the stop, a 10-minute walk along Glaserstraße, then left up Weherbartlweg. The closest train station is Bahnhof Aigen, on Aigenerstraße, a 20-minute walk from the campsite.

Gnigl (Ost), Parscherstraße 4 (tel. 643060). €4 (£2.70) per tent, €5 (£3.30) per person. Open mid-May–mid-Sept. Bus 29 from Mirbellplalz along Linzer Bundesstraße to the stop near the junction with Parscherstraße (after the bus crosses over the railway) then a 200m walk. Bus 27 from Mirbellplatz to the first stop on Eichstraße is 400m from the site.

Stadtblick, Rauchenbichlerstraße 21 (tel. 450652). Around €2 (£1.30) per tent, €6 (£4) per person. Open year round. Bus 51 from Salzburg Hbf to the stop on Kirchenstraße by the junction with Rauchenbichlerstraße, then a 5-minute walk to the site. Facilities for people with disabilities.

'Nord-Sam', Samstraße 22A (tel. 660494). €5 (£3.30) per tent, €4.50 (£3) per person. Open Apr.–Oct. Bus 33 from Salzburg Hbf to the first stop after Samstraße passes under the railway lines.

Kasern (Jägerwirt), Carl-Zuckmayer-Straße 26 (tel. 450576, *campingkasern@aon.at*). €3 (£2) per tent, €4.50 (£3) per person. Open Apr.–Oct.

HI HOSTEL NEARBY

Traunerstraße 22, Traunstein (tel. 861 4742). Open only to visitors aged 26 and under. In Germany, on the line from

Munich to Salzburg. About 40 minutes from Salzburg by local train. If you are leaving Munich in the late afternoon during the summer you might consider staying here, then getting into Salzburg early next day.

Vienna (Wien) (0) I

TOURIST OFFICES

The main Tourist Information Office is at 1 Albertinaplatz, open daily 9am–7pm. Visit the website (*www.info.wien.at*) for more information or call 25555 to book a hotel in advance. You may also book accommodation at any of the other Tourist Information Offices in the city.

Westbahnhof. Open daily 6.15am–11pm.

Südbahnhof. Open daily 6.30am–10pm. The Südbahnhof and Westbahnhof both have room-booking facilities.

Flughafen Wien-Schwechat. In the airport arrivals hall. Open daily June–Sept. 8.30am–11pm; Oct.–May 8.30am–9pm.

Reichsbrücke landing stage. If arriving by boat, go to the DDSG information counter. Open Apr.–Oct. 7am–6pm.

Autobahn A1 (west motorway). At the Wien-Auhof services. Open Apr.–Oct. 8am–10pm; Nov. 9am–7pm; Dec.–Mar. 10am–6pm. For traffic from Innsbruck, Salzburg, Prague and České Budějovice (via Linz) and Germany.

Autobahn A2 (south motorway). Exit: Zentrum, Triester Straße. Open July–Sept. 8am–10pm; Mar.–June and Oct. 9am–7pm. For traffic arriving from Graz, Klagenfurt, Ljubljana and Italy.

Florisdorfer Brücke/Donauinsel. Open late Mar.–Sept. 9am–7pm. For traffic arriving from Brno, Moravia and Prague (via Moravia).

Youth Information Centre. 1 Dr-Karl-Renner-Ring/Bellaria-Passage (U2 & U3 Volkstheater station). Open 12pm–7pm. Will assist with finding rooms as well as information on other aspects of the city.

VIENNA'S STATIONS

The vast majority of people travelling to Vienna by train arrive at one of the two main stations, either the Westbahnhof or the

Südbahnhof. Any train passing through Salzburg, Innsbruck, Switzerland or Germany arrives at the Westbahnhof. Trains from Budapest and Romania going on to these places stop also at the Westbahnhof. Of the two daily trains running from Budapest to Vienna, one (via Gyor) goes to the Westbahnhof, the other (via Sopron) goes to the Südbahnhof. Trains from Graz, Klagenfurt, Poland, Brno, Bratislava, Italy, Greece, Sofia, Belgrade and Zagreb stop at the Südbahnhof, as do trains from Budapest continuing on to any of these destinations. The only other railway station you are likely to arrive at is Franz-Josefs Bahnhof. This station receives international trains from Berlin, Leipzig, Dresden, Prague and České Budějovice, as well as local services from Krems-an-der-Donau. Wien-Nord and Wien-Mitte deal with local commuter trains only, but Wien-Mitte is the main bus station and the city air terminal.

FINDING ACCOMMODATION IN SUMMER
Finding a cheap bed can be a problem during the summer months. Late June is particularly bad. By this time, large numbers of independent travellers are arriving but the extra bed space created by the conversion of student accommodation into temporary hotels and hostels is available only July–Sept., so reserve by letter or email well in advance. Failing this, phone ahead 24 hours in advance.

HOTELS AND PENSIONS
A continental breakfast is included in the overnight price at all the hotels below, unless indicated otherwise. At a few hotels a buffet breakfast is provided. Be warned – many hotels and pensions in Vienna place surcharges of up to 200% on telephone calls!

CHEAPEST DOUBLES AROUND €40 (£26)
Auhof, Auhofstraße 205 (tel. 877 5289). Without breakfast. Far out in the west of the city. Singles €18 (£12).
Auer, Lazarettgasse 3 (tel. 406 2121). U6: Alserstraße.
Auge Gottes, Nüssdorferstraße 75 (tel. 319 4488). A student residence run as a hotel during the summer vacation (1 July–30 Sept.).

CHEAPEST DOUBLES AROUND €45 (£30)

Cyrus, Laxenburgerstraße 14 (tel. 602 2578, fax 604 4288). Singles start at the same price. Near the Südbahnhof.

Matauschek, Breitenseerstraße 14 (tel. 982 3532). S-bahn: Breitensee (change at Penzing).

Esterhazy, Nelkengasse 3 (tel. 587 5159). Without breakfast. A 10-minute walk from the Westbahnhof.

CHEAPEST DOUBLES AROUND €50 (£33)

Hargita, Andreasgasse 1 (tel. 526 1928, fax 526 0492). Without breakfast. A 5- to 10-minute walk from the Westbahnhof.

Quisisana, Windmühlgasse 6 (tel. 587 7155, fax 587 715633). Windmühlgasse runs between Mariahilferstraße and Gumpen-dorferstraße.

Praterstern, Mayergasse 6 (tel. 214 0123, *hotelpraterstern@ aon.at*). Without breakfast. Near Wien-Nord station. S-bahn/U1: Praterstern (Wien-Nord). Singles available.

CHEAPEST DOUBLES AROUND €55 (£37)

Aüersperg, Aüersperg 9 (tel. 406 2540, *office@albertina-hotels.at*). Buffet breakfast. U2: Lerchenfelderstraße. Open 1 July–30 Sept.

Stadt Bamberg, Mariahilferstraße 167 (tel. 893 4287). A short walk from the Westbahnhof.

Fünfhaus, Sperrgasse 12 (tel. 892 3545). A 5-minute walk from the Westbahnhof to the junction of Hernalsergürtel and Alserstraße.

Lauria, Kaiserstraße 77, Apartment 8 (tel. 522 5353, *panda_vienna@hotmail.com*). Has single, doubles and triples with cooking facilities, and can be booked through the Panda Hostel as it's owned by the same people. A 5- to 10-minute walk from the Westbahnhof. Go diagonally left across Europa Platz, down Stollgasse into Kaiserstraße.

PRIVATE ROOMS AND APARTMENTS

Private rooms and apartments are only rarely available through Tourist Offices. Apply instead to:

Mitwohnzentrale, Laudongasse 7 (tel. 402 6061). Open Mon.–Fri. 10am–2pm and 3–6pm. This private accommodation agency finds rooms and apartments for those staying at least three days. Room prices start at €18 (£12) per day, while apartments cost from €50 (£33) per day. On top of the cost of your accommodation the agency levies a commission, which varies according to the length of your stay. Tram 5 from Franz-Josefs Bhf to Laudongasse.

ÖKISTA, Türkenstraße 6 (tel. 401480, *info@statravel.at*). Open Mon.–Fri. 9am–5.30pm. ÖKISTA (the Austrian branch of the STA) find slightly cheaper rooms than Mitwohnzentrale, and charge no commission for doing so. U2: Schottentor. From Maria Theresienstraße a short walk along Wahringerstraße or Liechtensteinstraße takes you into Türkenstraße.

Österreichisches Verkehrsbüro, Friedrichstraße 7 (tel. 588000). Write or phone in advance for information.

HI HOSTELS

Expect to pay €11–15 (£7.50–£10) for B&B

Jugendgästehaus Wien-Brigittenau, Friedrich-Engelsplatz 24 (tel. 332 829 40, *jgh.1200wien@chello.at*). Wheelchair accessible, laundry room on premises, breakfast, lunch and dinner available. Curfew 12.30am. U1, U4 to Schwedenplatz, then tram N to Florisdorfer Brücke Friedrich-Engelsplatz, or bus 10A/35A to Friedrich-Engelsplatz. Family rooms.

Myrthengasse, Myrthengasse 7/Neustiftgasse 85 (tel. 523 631 60; *oejhv-wien-jgh-neustiftg@oejhr.or.at*). Curfew 12.30am. U6 to Burggasse, bus 48A to Neuburg. Walk back a short distance then right. 15 minutes on foot from the centre and the Westbahnhof. Clean and efficient hostel with pleasant courtyard. Breakfast and dinner available; laundry room and common room with MTV. Family rooms. Wheelchair accessible. Acknowledged as the best of Vienna's hostels.

Schloherberge am Wilhelminenberg, Savoyenstraße 2 (tel. 485 850 3700, *shb@verkehrsbuero.at*). Curfew midnight. U6 to Thaliastraße (or tram 5 from the Westbahnhof). Then bus 46B or 146B from here to the hostel. Family rooms. Wheelchair accessible.

Ruthensteiner, Robert Hamerlinggasse 24 (tel. 893 4202, *www.hostelruthensteiner.com*, *info@hostelruthensteiner.com*). Singles, doubles, triples and dorms. 24-hr reception. 5-minute walk from the Westbahnhof: exit the main doors at front of station, turn right, then follow the road down to Mariahilfer-straße, turn right and cross the road immediately. Take the second turning on the left and the hostel is on the right-hand side of Robert Hamerlinggasse.

Türmherberge 'Don Bosco', Lechnerstraße 12 (tel. 713 1494). Bed only €6.50 (£4.30). Open 1 Mar.–30 Nov. 11.30pm curfew. Roman Catholic-run hostel in an old church bell tower. Very cheap. Over the years this hostel has sometimes enforced a men-only policy, sometimes not. Women should ring ahead.

HOSTELS/UNIVERSITY DORMS

Wombat's City Hostel, Grangasse 6 (tel. 897 2326, *www.wombats.at, wombats@chello.at*). Dorms from €15 (£10), doubles €18 (£12) pp. Near the Westbahnhof and very popular.

Kolpingfamilie Wien-Meidling, Bendlgasse 10–12 (tel. 813 5487, *office@wien12.kolping.at*). Bed only €11–14 (£7–9.50). Open all year. Cooking facilities. Breakfast and dinner available. U6: Niederhof-Straße.

Haus Erasmus, Kenyongasse 25 (tel. 52187, *erasmus@oejab.at*). Open mid-July–mid-Aug. Slightly cheaper than the main HI hostels. Reluctant to take phone reservations. Ring to check. A 5- to 10-minute walk from the Westbahnhof.

Believe-It-or-Not, Myrthengasse 10 (tel. 526 4658). €12 (£8). See directions for the HI Hostel in Myrthengasse.

Gästehaus Pfeilgasse, Pfeilgasse 4–6 (tel. 40174, *acahot@academia-hotels.co.at*). Singles €21 (£14), doubles €38 (£25). Open July–Sept. From the Westbahnhof and Franz-Josefs Bhf tram 5 to Thaliastraße/Lerchenfelderstraße.

Gästehaus Rudolfinum, Mayerhofgasse 3 (tel. 505 5384). Singles €18 (£12), doubles €35 (£23). Open July–Sept. U1: Taubstummengasse. Mayerhofgasse is off Favoritenstraße on the right as you walk towards the Südbahnhof. A 10-minute walk from the Südbahnhof.

Porzellaneum der Wiener Universität, Porzellangasse 30 (tel. 317 7282, *office@porzellaneum.sth.ac.at*). Singles €18 (£12) and doubles €38 (£25). About 10% extra for one-night stays.

A 5-minute walk from Franz-Josefs Bhf. Porzellangasse begins at J.-Tandler-Platz on Alserbachstraße by the station.

Katholisches Studentenhaus, Peter-Jordan-Straße 29 (tel. 347 47312). Singles and doubles around €18 (£12) per person. Tram 38 from the Westbahnhof to Hardtgasse. From the Südbahnhof tram D to Schottentor (U2: Schottentor) to join tram 38.

CAMPING

Aktiv Camping Neue Donau, Am Kleehaufel (tel. 202 4010, *camping.neuedonau@verkehrsbuero.at*). Open late Apr.–Sept. Near the Praterbrücke, 6km from the centre. U1: Kaisermühlen, then bus 91A to the site, or S-Bahn: Lobau (from the Süd-bahnhof), followed by a 500m walk.

Wien-Süd, Breitenfurterstraße 269 (tel. 867 3649, *camping.sued @verkehrsbuero.at*). Open July–Aug. 6 km from the centre. U6: Philadelphiabrücke, then bus 62A, or S-Bahn: Atzgersdorf Mauer, then an easy walk or bus 66A to the site.

Wien-West, Hüttelbergstraße 80 (tel 914 2314, *camping.west @verkehrsbuero.at*). Open Apr.–Oct. 6 km from the centre. S-Bahn (from Westbahnhof) or U4 to Hütteldorf, then bus 152 to the site.

SLEEPING OUT

Although not really recommended, the Prater Park is the most obvious. S-Bahn/U1: Praterstern (Wien-Nord), or S-Bahn: Stadtlauer Brücke Lusthaus at the other end of the park.

THE BALTIC REPUBLICS

Visiting the Baltic states of Estonia, Latvia and Lithuania is to encounter a fascinating period of great change as they set about catching up with their Western neighbours. As new members of the European Union, they're trying even harder. As a consequence of this, accommodation details can alter, as can phone numbers, prices and services. Nevertheless, visitors are now able to move freely and enjoy a fascinating area of the world that has been out of bounds for too long. The three states played a very significant part in the eventual collapse of Communism in 1991. They were the first of the Soviet Republics to organise effective national protest against Soviet rule, and of the three, Estonia was the fastest to develop in the post-Soviet world, becoming the first to draw up a new constitution, ending a history that consisted largely of domination by other nations.

ESTONIA

Having been occupied in the 16th and 17th centuries by the Swedes, Estonia was ceded to Russia in 1721. After a brief period of independence granted by Lenin in 1918, Estonia was ceded again, this time to the Soviets under Stalin in 1940. All this was with the formal approval of Hitler's Nazi government. However, the following year, Germany invaded the USSR and occupied Estonia until 1944, when Soviet rule was restored.

Despite being the smallest of the Baltic nations, Estonia is still a diverse country that is developing rapidly as a capitalist nation. Hotel prices are already approaching Western standards, but the country as a whole is remarkably affordable. Despite the language barrier, the Estonians are a friendly bunch and it is they who make the country a hidden jewel in Europe's crown.

LATVIA

Due to its position Latvia has had a history of domination virtually identical to Estonia – the indigenous Balt people having been almost wiped out in the attempt to Christianise them. However, despite having been out of power for nearly a millennium, the Latvians are beginning to assert their independence.

The economy is slowly improving and traditional Latvian art and culture are being rediscovered. Unlike its neighbour Estonia, the country boasts many forests, as well as a fine unspoilt coastline.

LITHUANIA

Lithuania has always been the grandest of the three Baltic states, being something of a world power during the period from the 14th to the 16th centuries. Indeed, at this time, Lithuania was one of the largest states in medieval Europe.

However, the 18th century proved to be Lithuania's downfall. Despite uniting with Poland, it fell to Russia after losing the war of 1721. From 1918 onwards, Lithuania was again independent until the arrival of invading German forces during the Second World War. It was during these years of occupation that Lithuania suffered the tragic elimination of the Jewish section of its population. Following this, Lithuania was occupied by the Soviets under Stalin.

Now, after the relaxation of Soviet rule during the 1980s and the eventual collapse of Communism, Lithuania is once again an independent nation and, thanks to the mix of modern cosmopolitan society with the reminders of the country's magnificent past, its former glory has been at least partially restored.

The capital, Vilnius, has maintained its charm and mystique as the country's centre of Catholicism. Although it is the second city, Kaunas, which is regarded by most as the heart of the country, is becoming the hub of sophistication in Lithuania.

ACCOMMODATION DETAILS

The combination of the rich and diverse cultures and histories of the three Baltic states and the tangible atmosphere of their newly won independence makes this a fascinating time to visit the region. And it's become progressively easier to visit. The only potential visa complication is that the principal overnight train service from Poland to Lithuania crosses Belarussian territory, and it is necessary to purchase a transit visa in hard currency (£20; $34) on the way, although this is not always possible and it may be easier to avoid this route. A rail link exists (via Suwalki in Poland

and Šeštokai in Lithuania) which avoids Belarus, but this is far less convenient and requires at least two changes of train.

All three countries now have their own currencies: the Estonian kroon (kr), the Latvian lat (ls), and the Lithuanian lita (lt). You may still find payment preferred in US dollars in some parts of Latvia and Lithuania, so carry a comfortable supply of dollars just in case.

Overnight trains between Tallinn, Riga, Vilnius and Warsaw offer four-berth couchettes, and the price of rail travel is so low that couchette accommodation for the night is a cost-cutting alternative to staying in a hotel or hostel, though the advantages are slightly offset by the limited number of services. You should reserve your place in advance wherever possible. Prices of just a few dollars (paid in the local currency) are typical for an overnight trip: Vilnius to Riga costs approximately $2 (£1.25); Riga to Tallinn about $5 (£3), though prices are more expensive if you are *arriving* in Vilnius *from* Warsaw, for example. A small supplementary charge for bedding is normally payable on the train (in the currency of the country that you are leaving), so keep this in mind when changing currency back into dollars or euros prior to leaving a country.

Many of the **hotels** previously made available to foreign visitors by Intourist are now adapting (in various ways) to the challenges of the free market. Some have gone out of business altogether, others have been converted to hostel-type accommodation (as described below), thereby entering the list of possibilities available to the budget traveller. Those bought out by foreign management have generally moved upmarket, and thus out of the range of those seeking a cheap sleep. Those that have not attempted to adapt to Western tastes should be relatively affordable.

Travellers who have spent time in Eastern Europe will be familiar with the concept of local people congregating in train stations to offer **private rooms** to recently arrived backpackers. This phenomenon has begun to emerge in the Baltic republics, with more locals opening their doors as visitors from the West begin to arrive in greater numbers. Agencies offering this kind of accommodation are springing up in the principal cities.

Only Estonia has a network of **hostels** on familiar HI lines (see Estonia section). Some of the hostels listed in the sections for the individual countries display the familiar HI tree-and-hut symbol, even though they have no affiliation with the HI. This subtle deception doesn't necessarily mean that the accommodation offered is below the standard you would normally expect from this symbol; indeed, the independently managed hostels have some of the most comfortable accommodation available.

Camping is not as widespread as elsewhere in Europe and organised networks do not yet exist. Published information on the authorised sites is scarce, contact the sites listed directly.

Tourist information centres in the form familiar to Western travellers are springing up all over the Baltic republics; Tallinn leads the way with its impressive information office right in the heart of the Old Town. More sources of information are appearing as demand increases. Travellers using the more expensive hotels will have access to lobby service desks which supply local information. You may also care to contact the respective embassies in your own country (addresses below) for general information, and there are also a few decent websites to help you plan your trip. The accommodation agencies and tour organisers listed in the sections for each town will provide information, and you should also make use of travel companies with specialist expertise in the region. Information on trains and buses (both within individual countries and for international journeys) is available at the stations themselves, but long queues are almost inevitable and you should be prepared to negotiate the language barrier (Russian, or sometimes German, is likely to be of more use than English). The *Thomas Cook European Timetable* can be an invaluable asset, particularly for the planning of overnight journeys, but even the most up-to-date edition won't necessarily correspond to the times displayed in the stations.

One of the best sources of current information on the Baltic republics in English is the *Baltic Times*, published weekly and distributed throughout the region. It provides a comprehensive overview of news from all three republics, ranging from general interest articles to in-depth economic and political analysis. You can read it online at *www.baltictimes.com*, where you can take out an online subscription. Once you've arrived it may be useful to look out for the 'In Your Pocket' publications available in all three capital cities, and these can be purchased at tourist information points. You can also visit *www.inyourpocket.com* for the lowdown on what there is to do and where you should look for accommodation.

ADDRESSES

(See also addresses for individual countries)

FAMILY HOTEL SERVICE NETWORK

Mere pst. 6, Tallinn (tel. (00) 372 441187). Offers rooms throughout the Baltic countries.

BED AND BREAKFAST

Mere pst. 4, Tallinn (tel. (00)372 6616 291, *www.bedbreakfast.ee,*
rasastra@online.ee). Offers rooms in all the Baltic States. Open every day 9.30am–6pm.

USEFUL WEBSITES

www.inyourpocket.com, www.balticsww.com, www.baltichostels.net.

Estonia (Eesti) (00)372

USEFUL ADDRESSES

Estonian Tourist Board, Roosikrantsi 11, Tallinn (tel. 627 9770, *www.visitestonia.com, tourism@eas.ee*). The National Tourist Board will provide you with details on all aspects of your stay in Estonia from booking accommodation to things to do.

Eesti Puhkemajade Organisatsioon (Estonian Youth Hostels Association: HI-affiliated), Natva Mnt., Tallinn (tel. 646 1455, *www.baltichostels.net/eyha.html, eyha@online.ee*). The Estonian network of youth hostels is unique in the Baltic region, and as well as their hostels in Tallinn and Tartu there are several others throughout the country, located in varying types of accommodation. Room sizes vary from single rooms to more familiar dormitory accommodation. There are no age limits. Advance reservations are advisable. HI members receive a discount (supposedly 25%, according to the above office, although it is only 15% in Tartu, for example). Full details are given in the booklet available from the above address, which can be obtained on request.

Estonian Embassy: 16 Hyde Park Gate, London SW7 5DG (tel. 020 7589 3428).

Tallinn (2)

TOURIST OFFICE

Tallinn City Tourist Office, Raekoja plats 10, (tel. 645 7777, *www.tourism.tallinn.ee*, *turismiinfo@tallinnlv.ee*). Conveniently located on the main town square. Open summer Mon.–Fri. 9am–8pm, weekends 10am–5pm; winter Mon.–Fri. 9am–5pm, Sat. 10am–3pm. Some English spoken. Make use of their knowledge of the local accommodation situation, particularly with respect to current prices.

ACCOMMODATION AGENCIES

Concordia, Sakala Street 14 (tel. 6442 991). Organises English-speaking guided tours for foreign tourists and also offers an accommodation-finding service in Tallinn. Prices (per person, per night): camping, 100–150 kr (£3–5; $5–8.50); motel, 150–180 kr (£5–7; $8–12); hotel, 150–200 kr (£5–6; $8–10.50); private flats in the centre (breakfast included), 170–200 kr (£6–£7; $8.50–10.50); private flats in a new suburb, 150–180 kr (£5–8; $8.50–10).

BASIC DIRECTIONS

The heart of Tallinn is the Old Town, which consists of Toompea (the Castle Hill) and the area to the east of this, which is still largely contained within the Old Town walls and has Raekoja plats (Town Hall Square) at its centre. The area south and south-east of the Old Town forms the focus of the 'New' Town. The train station is north-west of Toompea, just outside the Old Town; the local bus station is just next to the train station, and the long-distance station is at Lastekodu 46, about 1.5 km south-east of the Old Town. The majority of the accommodation and eating possibilities in Tallinn are concentrated in the Old Town or immediately around it, or in the area immediately south of this, centred on Pärnu maantee.

HOTELS

Pirita, Regati psi. 1 (tel. 639 8600, *hotell@piritatop.ee*). Singles 800 kr (£30; $51), doubles 1,100 kr (£42; $71). Located by the seaside in the north-east of the city.

Mihkli, Endla 23 (tel. 666 4800, *www.mihkli.ee*, *mihkli@anet.ee*). Singles 700 kr (£28; $48), doubles 900 kr (£36; $61). South-west of the Old Town near the national library.

Susi, Peterburi tee 48 (tel. 630 3300, *www.susi.cma.ee*, *susi@susi.ee*). Singles 600 kr (£23; $39), doubles 800 kr (£30; $51). Last stop on tram 2 or 4 towards Lasnamäe.

Stroomi, Randla 11 (tel. 630 4200, *www.stroomi.ee*, *stroomi@stroomi.ee*). Singles 400 kr (£15.50; $26), doubles 700 kr (£28.50; $45). West of city centre.

Kristiine, Luha 16 (tel. 646 4600, *www.kristiine.ee*, *info@kristiine.ee*). Doubles 650 kr (£27.50; $48.50) with own bathroom. Breakfast included. Bus 3, 5, 18 or 36 from city centre.

Pääsu, Sõpruse pst. 182 (tel. 252 0034). Doubles 470 kr (£18; $30).

Dorell, Karu 39-110 (tel. 626 1200, *www.dorell.ee*, *info@dorell.ee*). Comfortable rooms. 10 minutes' walk from the Old Town. Doubles 470 kr (£18; $30).

Tahetorni Hotell, Tahetorni 16 (tel. 677 9100, *www.thotell.ee*). Just out of the town centre. Singles 500 kr (£21; $36) doubles 590 kr (£25.50; $43).

Wam Maria, Asunduse 15 (tel. 611 9500, *www.wammaria.ee*, *wammaria@hot.ee*). Doubles 480 kr (£16.50; $28) Situated in a dreary suburb, but has 120 modernised rooms, many with baths.

PENSIONS

UUS 22, Uus Str. 22 (tel. 641 1464, *www.oldhouse.ee*, *info@oldhouse.ee*) In the old town. Doubles at 650 kr (£27; $46).

Tihase, Tihase 6a (tel. 655 2171, *www.hot.ee/tihase*, *tihase@delfi.ee*). Doubles and singles. Bus 17 from the station.

PRIVATE ROOMS/FURNISHED FLATS

Contact the Tallinn City Tourist Office (see above) or CDS Reisiid, Raekoja plats 17 (tel. 627 6797) for information on rooms and English-speaking hosts.

HOSTELS

Academic Hostel, Akadeemia tee 11 (tel. 620 2275, *www.aca demichostel.com*, *info@academichostel.com*). Brand new hostel next to Tallinn Technical University, 5 miles out of town. Doubles 465 kr (£20; $34). Some rooms with free internet access.

Mereraik, Sopruse 182 (tel. 252 9604, book through *www.baltic hostels.net*). In the same building as Paasu Hotel. Dorm beds 118 kr (£5; $8.50). Take trolleybus 4 from the train station to Linnu Tee.

Mahtra Hostel, Mahtra 44 (tel. 621 8828, *www.mahtra.ee*, *hostel@mahtra.ee*). HI hostel. Doubles, dorms and a sauna.

Hostel Vana Tom (previously The Barn), Väike-Karja 1 (tel. 631 3252). Beds in single-sex dorms for around 170 kr (£6.50; $11). Excellent central location.

CABINS

Kalev, Kloostrimetsa tee 56A (tel. 238686). Open June–Oct. Cottage for two persons: 80 kr (£3; $5).

Leevike, Tallinn (tel. 652 6090). Cabins available May to December. About 5 km from Tallinn by the Pärnu road.

Latvia (Latvija) (00)371

USEFUL ADDRESSES

www.rigalatvia.net, tourist information website giving details of accommodation and sightseeing. Also visit *www.latviatourism .com* and *www.latviatravel.com*.

Latvian Embassy: 45 Nottingham Place, London W1M 3FE (tel. 020 7312 0040).

Latvian Youth Hostels Association, Aldaru 8, Riga (tel 921 8560, *www.hostellinglatvia.com*).

Riga (Rīga) (2)

TOURIST OFFICE

Riga Tourist Information Bureau, Skārņu iela 22 (tel. 722 1731, *tourinfo@lgs.lv*).
Also visit *www.virtualriga.com* for further information.

ACCOMMODATION AGENCIES

Contact these agencies well in advance to obtain up-to-date information on the services they provide:

Latvijas Tūristu Klubs, Skārņu iela 22 (tel. 722 1731). Can provide accommodation in Riga, Kaļķu and Ventspils. Also provides information on the city.

Patricia, Elizabetes iela 22–24 (tel. 925 6731). Provides accommo-dation service.

BASIC DIRECTIONS

Most of the accommodation and eating opportunities are concentrated in the bustling Old Town, located on the east bank of the Daugava. The train and bus stations are immediately to the south-east of the Old Town. To the north-east of the Old Town are a series of gardens and boulevards. The main street is Kaļķu iela, which splits the Old Town in two, and is continuous with October Bridge (which crosses the Daugava) and Brīvības bulvāris, which cuts across the ring of boulevards and parks, leading out to the north-east of the city. The Old Town is a maze of winding streets and lanes, making walking the best way to get around the heart of Riga.

HOTELS

Arena, Palasta 5 (tel. 722 8583). Singles 5 ls (£5; $7.50), doubles 7.50 ls (£8; $13.50). Central and cheap.

Baltija, Raiņa bulvāris 33 (tel. 722 7461). Only Russian spoken. Singles 5 ls (£5; $8.50), doubles 6.75 ls (£7; $12). Near the station. Very cheap and you can pay in lats.

Saulite, Merkela 12 (tel. 722 4546). Singles 7 ls (£7.50; $13), doubles 12 ls (£13; $22). In the centre of town.

Viktorija, Căka iela 55 (tel. 272305). Tram 11 or 18 from stop near train station. Two stops down the line.

Sports, Gogoļa iela 5 (tel. 226780). Doubles from 6.75 ls (£7; $12). Very handy for the train station.

Hotel Laine, Skolas iela 11 (tel. 728 8816). Singles 12.50 ls (£13; $22) doubles 24 ls (£25; $42. Bedlinen included. English spoken. Old Riga is within easy walking distance; approximately 10- to 15-minute walk from the train and bus stations. The same management operates another hostel at Biešu, on the west bank of the Daugava: a bed in 2-bed apartment (including toilet, shower, kitchen) costs around 7.50 ls (£8; $13.50) (whole apartment for one person 8.50 ls (£9; $15). 'Luxury' double/singles 14 ls (£15; $25).

HOSTELS

Latvijas Universitātes Tūristu Klubs (Tourism Club of University of Latvia), Raiņa bulvāris 19 (tel. 223114) run two hostels, also help organise local trips, and will supply general information both for Riga and Latvia. Some English and German spoken. Contact LUTK in advance to book a bed at either hostel.

Studentu Kopmitne, Basteja bulvāris 10 (tel. 721 6221). Doubles £13 ($22). Very popular. Near railway station in Old Town.

Riga Technical Univerisity, Kalku 1 (tel. 708 9395) Very cheap and very popular. 3 ls (£3.20; $5) a bed. Call in advance.

Hostel RPRA, Nicgales 26 (tel. 549 012). Just out of the town centre.

CAMPING

Try asking at LUTK (see Hostels) for details of any sites that are open.

Lithuania (Lietuva) (00)370

USEFUL ADDRESSES

Lithuanian Embassy: 84 Gloucester Place, London W1 6AU (tel. 020 7486 6401).

Lithuanian Youth Hostels Association, Filaretu Street 17, Vilnius (tel. 52 154 624, *www.lithuanianhostels.org*).

Lithuanian Tourist Information, Vilniaus g. 4/35 2600 Vilnius (tel. 52 622 610, *www.tourism.lt*, *info@tourism.lt*).

Vilnius (5)

TOURIST OFFICE

Vilniaus str. 22 (tel. 629 660, *www.vilnius.lt*, *turizm.info@vilnius.lt*). Open Mon.–Fri. 9am–6pm, weekends 10am–4pm.

ACCOMMODATION AGENCIES

Nakvyne Hotel Travel Service, Kauno 8 (tel. 637 732). Offers 'family accommodation' in Vilnius: 'houses with all conveniences'. Contact in advance to find out the prices for their services.

FINDING ACCOMMODATION

A useful publication to have when organising your trip is *Vilnius in your Pocket*, published five times a year and available for 2.5 lt in Vilnius, from the Lithuanian embassy in London, or online at *www.inyourpocket.com*. Includes an accommodation section. Also worth knowing is that Litinterp Bernardinu 7/2 (tel. 212 3850, *vilnius@litinterp.lt*) will book singles for 60 lt and doubles for 100 lt.

BASIC DIRECTIONS

The most prominent feature of central Vilnius is Castle Hill, on the south-west corner of which is Katedros aikštė (Cathedral Square). South from here is the Old Town, the main artery of which is Pilies gatvė/Didžioji gatvė. The train and bus stations are south of the Old Town. Gedimino Prospektas, the main thoroughfare of the New Town, runs west from Castle Hill.

HOTELS

The following should have rooms available for around 52 lt (£10; $17). The security in these hotels may be somewhat suspect and you shouldn't expect service geared towards tourists:

Gintaras, Sodų 14 (tel. 738 003, *www.hotelgintaras.lt, reservation @hotelgintaras.lt*). Gloomy but cheap; close to train station. Singles 50 lt (£8.30; $14), doubles 70 lt (£11.65; $19.50).

Verkiai, Zalių jų ezeru 53 (tel. 729 834). Singles 70 lt (£11.65; $19.50).

Jeruzale, Kalvariju 209 (tel. 271 4040, *www.jeruzale.com, jeruzale @takas.lt*). 3 miles from the centre of town.

Sportas, Bistryčios 13 (tel. 346 953). Singles 50 lt (£8.30; $14), doubles 70 lt (£11.65; $17.50).

Trinapolis, Verkių 66 (tel. 778 913). Singles 50 lt (£8.30; $14). A large hotel on the outskirts.

Electros Tinklai, Sv. Stepono 11 (tel. 260 254). Basic double/triple rooms from around 30 lt (£5; $8.50) per person. Very popular.

PENSIONS

Bernardinu, Bernardinu 5 (tel. 260 8410, *guesthouse@avevita.lt*). In town centre. Doubles and apartments available.

Algis House, Stikliu 4-4 (tel. 212 1112, *algis_rent@yahoo.com*). Town centre. Can also help find other accommodation if they are full.

HOSTELS

Teacher's University Hostel, Vivulskio 36 (tel. 213 0509). From 50 lt (£8; $13.50) per person.

BATS Backpackers Hostel, Geležinio vilko 27 (tel. 661 692). £12 ($18) per person. Take trolleybus 15 or 16 from the bus/train station to the fifth stop ('Kaunas'); then a short walk two blocks north.

Old Town Hostel, Ausros Vartu 20-15 (tel. 625 357, *oldtown hostels@delfi.lt*). Near the train station and very popular. No curfew.

Lithuanian Youth Hostels, Filaretų 17 (tel. 254 627, *www.filaretai.8m.com, filaretai@post.omnitel.com*). Beds from 27 lt (£4; $7). Bus 34 from the train station; seven stops. No curfew.

VUSA, Student Representation of Vilnius University, Universiteto 3 (tel. 617 920). Hostel accommodation available, with kitchen facilities. Contact VUSA directly prior to your arrival to book and confirm prices.

BED AND BREAKFAST

Litinterp, Bernardinu 7-2 (tel. 212 3850, *www.litinterp.lt*, *vilnius @litinterp.lt*). Bed and breakfast accommodation in the Old Town.

Saules Bed and Breakfast, Saules 15/23 (tel. 210 6112, *www.welcome.to/saules*). Doubles from €35 (£23; $39) but you may be able to bargain them down in the quieter months. In the Antakalanis district.

CAMPING

Rytų Kempingas, Mūrininkų gvy., Rukainiai (25 km east of Vilnius, on the main road to Minsk) (tel. 651 195). Small summer lodgings for 3–4 people, or you can pitch your tent.

Camping away from managed sites is prohibited in Vilnius, but permitted in the countryside.

If all else fails, you can sleep in one of the unusual '**train hotels**' at Vilnius train station. Snooze in style in a carriage complete with electric lights, clean linen and a lock on the door. The cost is 15 lt. Enter the departure hall, veer to your right, show your passport and pay at Kasa no. 4.

BELGIUM (België/Belgique) (00)32

Though small, Belgium is increasingly taking centre stage in world affairs as its capital, Brussels, is home and headquarters of both NATO and the European Union. Brussels is also home to some fantastic architecture, food and nightlife, whilst the towns of Antwerp and Bruges are as beautiful as they are friendly.

As well as its luxuriously decadent chocolates, Belgium boasts that it makes the finest beers in the world. While you may have already sampled some of their reassuringly expensive Stella Artois, make sure while you're there that you try out some of their less famous and more esoteric ales. The unfortunate stereotype that Belgium is a boring country could not be further from the truth.

BACKGROUND

Belgium became independent under the crown of Leopold I, then enjoyed a tranquil repose until Germany violated its neutrality in 1914 and, as a consequence, brought Great Britain into the First World War. The military cemeteries around Flanders provide a timely reminder of the tragedy of trench warfare during that period.

It is a unique and individual nation made up of two peoples – the Flemish and the Walloons. The Flemish (NW Belgium) are closely related to their Dutch neighbours, the Walloons are far more like the French. Each is fiercely proud of its distinct culture.

ACCOMMODATION DETAILS

On the whole, Belgium poses no serious problems for the budget traveller but, unless you can afford to stay in hotels all the time, you will have to stay in different types of accommodation as you travel around, since some of the main places of interest lack hostels and/or campsites. However, as Belgium is small, with a very efficient rail network, those with railpasses have the option of choosing one or two bases and visiting other places on daytrips; e.g. from Ghent or Bruges you can easily visit all of Flanders.

If you do have to spend a night or two in a cheap hotel you

should have little cause for complaint about the standard of cleanliness or comfort.

Hostelling is a cheap and, usually, convenient way of seeing the country. With the exception of Lier and Leper, all the main towns of interest have a hostel. Problems are only likely to arise around Easter and during the period July–August, when it can be difficult to find a hostel bed in Brussels, Bruges and Ostend.

There are two HI-affiliated hostel associations in Belgium. The Flemish Association operates around 20 hostels; its Walloon counterpart half that number. The normal overnight charge is €11–12.50 (£7.30–8.40), which includes breakfast. The exceptions are the Flemish YHA-operated hostels in Bruges and Ostend, and the hostels of both associations in Brussels, where prices range from €12.50 to €20 (£8.40–13.30). Where space is available, most hostels admit non-members on the payment of a €5.50 (£3.70) supplement. Curfews are normally 11pm but the hostels in the cities tend to stay open later.

As well as HI hostels, Antwerp, Bruges and Brussels offer a number of independent hostels. Generally free of the organised groups who head for the main HI hostels, the prices and standards of the independent hostels tend to be on a par with those of the official establishments, while curfews are normally more relaxed. In the larger cities you may also find 'Sleep-Ins' with dormitory accommodation as cheap as €10 (£6.70). Wallonia is littered with *gîtes d'étapes* which can provide very cheap lodgings in places not served by hostels. An organisation called Friends of Nature (Natuurvrienden/Amis de la Nature) also operates a network of hostels throughout the country. Ask the local Tourist Office for details.

Despite there being over 500 **campsites** in this small country, camping is not an ideal way to see Belgium unless you have a railpass or a car. Sites are heavily concentrated in the rural parts of Wallonia and along the Flemish coast, and the rest of the country is more sparsely served. Major tourist attractions such as Leper, Kortrijk, Mechelen, Leuven, Lier and Diest all lack campsites, though a short rail trip will invariably find you one in a neighbouring town. Visitors to Liège should head for the site at Tilff, just outside the city. Sites range in quality and are priced accordingly. Compared to other Western European countries, camping in Belgium is very cheap. Prices for a solo traveller can be as low as €4 (£2.70) per night, but €5.50–6 (£3.70–4) is more normal. However, prices at some coastal sites can be as high as €10 (£6.70) per night.

You should only end up on the street by unforeseen disaster. If you do, vagrancy charges can only be pressed if you are penniless. Late arrivals hoping to sleep in train station waiting-rooms should note that only Ostend station stays open all night. The rest close for anything between two and five hours. If you are desperate, your best chance to avoid being thrown on to the street in the early hours is to try the little waiting-rooms on the platforms (there are none in Antwerpen Centraal, but you can try Antwerpen-Berchem).

ADDRESSES

BELGIAN TOURIST OFFICE
29 Princes Street, London W1R 7RG (tel. 0891 600 255, *www.visitbelgium.be*).

FLEMISH YHA
Vlaamse Jeugdherbergcentrale, Van Stralenstraat 40, Antwerpen (tel. 03 232 7218, *www.vjh.be*).

WALLOON YHA
Centrale Wallone des Auberges de la Jeunesse, rue de la Sablonnière 28, Bruxelles (tel. (0)2 219 5676, *www.laj.be*).

GÎTES D'ÉTAPES
Gîte d'Étape du CBTJ, rue Montoyer 31/8, Bruxelles (tel. (0)2 512 5417, *www.cbtj.be, info@cbtj.be*).

CAMPING
Visit *www.campings.be*, or write to Rue du Monument 49, Hotton, Belgium (tel. 86 322 332). Maps are also available from the Belgian Tourist Office.

Bruges (Brugge) (0)50

TOURIST OFFICES
Dienst voor Toerisme, Burg 11 (tel. 44 86 86, *www.brugge.be*). Apr.–Sept. open Mon.–Fri. 9.30am–6.30pm, weekends

10am–12pm and 2–6.30pm; Oct.–Mar. open Mon.–Fri. 9.30am–12.45pm and 2–5.45pm, Sat. 10am–12.45pm and 2–5.45pm. Accommodation service. Excellent map of the city with the sights and suggested walking tours.

The branch office in the train station has a restricted range of information but also offers an accommodation service. Mar.–Oct. open 2.45–9pm; Nov.–Feb. open 1.45–8pm.

BASIC DIRECTIONS

Bruges train station is a 15- to 20-minute walk from the city centre. After crossing Stationsplein in front of the station, the main road leading away to the left passes the equestrian statue of King Albert I, before arriving at the wide expanse of 't Zand. From the right-hand side of the square, Zuidzandstraat runs past Sint-Salvators Kerk into Steenstraat, which leads in turn to the Markt. From the far left corner of the Markt, Philipstockstraat leads into Burg. As you enter this square the Town Hall is on your right-hand side. Across the square is the former palace of the 'Brugse Vrije', now the Tourist Office.

Going across the road from the left-hand side of Stationsplein takes you into Oostmeers. Heading right from Stationsplein round the main road takes you up past the coach park to the junction with the road to Lille (Rijsel) and Kortrijk. Going right from this junction is Baron Ruzettelaan. Heading left along Katelijnestraat and continuing straight ahead takes you past the end of Heilige-Geeststraat into Simon Stevinplein. Crossing the square and turning right takes you down Steenstraat into the Markt.

HOTELS

CHEAPEST DOUBLES FROM €35 (£23)

't Keizerhof, Oostmeers 126 (tel. 33 87 28). Breakfast included. Shared bathrooms.

Speelmanshuys, 't Zand 3 (tel. 33 95 52). Breakfast extra.

De Gulden Kogge, Damse Vaart Zuid 12, Damme (tel. 35 42 17). Damme is a picturesque and historic village about 6 km from Bruges. Buses run to Damme from the train station in Bruges.

Lybeer, Korte Vulderstraat 31 (tel. 33 43 55, *www.hotellybeer.com*, *info@hotellybeer.com*). Town centre.

Hotel Cavalier, Kuiperstraat 25 (tel. 33 02 07). Breakfast included. Town centre.

CHEAPEST DOUBLES FROM €55 (£36.50)

Rembrandt-Rubens, Walplein 38 (tel. 33 64 39). From Oostmeers turn right along Zonnekemeers into Walplein or turn left off Katelijnestraat down Walstraat into the square.

Het Geestelijk Hof, Heilige Geeststraat 2 (tel. 34 25 94). From Zuidzandstraat go right around Sint-Salvators Kerk to the start of Heilige Geeststraat. Next to the cathedral.

Breughelhof, Oostmeers 128 (tel. 34 34 28). By the station.

Hotel Lucca, Naaldenstraat 30 (tel. 34 20 67, *www.hotellucca.be*, *lucca@hotellucca.be*). Town centre.

CHEAPEST DOUBLES FROM €70 (£46)

Singe d'Or, 't Zand 18 (tel. 34 48 48). Breakfast included.

De Pauw, St Gilliskerkhof 8 (tel. 33 71 18). By St Giles church. A 10-minute walk from the Markt.

Gasthof de Krakele, St Pieterskaai 63 (tel. 31 56 43). 2-star hotel.

Jacobs, Baliestraat 1 (tel. 33 98 31, *www.hotelbel.com/jacobs.htm*). A 10-minute walk from the Markt, by St Giles church (Sint-Gillis Kerk).

Imperial, Dweerstraat 24 (tel. 33 90 14, *hotel.imperial.nv@ pandora.be*). Dweerstraat runs left off Zuidzandstraat.

Graaf Van Vlaanderen, 't Zand 19 (tel. 33 31 50, *www.graafvanv laanderen.be*).

't Koffieboontje, Hallestraat 4 (tel. 33 80 27, *hotel_koffieboontje@ unicall.be*). Good central location.

Hotel t'Voermanshuys, Oude Burg 14 (tel. 34 13 96, *voermanshuys@pophost.eunet.be*). Breakfast included. Located in the old town.

BED AND BREAKFAST

CHEAPEST DOUBLES AROUND €50 (£33)

K. & A. Dieltiens-Debruyne, St Walburgastraat 40 (tel. 33 42 94, *koen.dieltiens@skynet.be*). Well located, about 5 minutes' walk from the Markt.

Catherine Nyssen, Moerstraat 50 (tel. 34 31 71, *catherine.nyssen @pandora.be*).

Robert Van Nevel, Carmersstraat 13 (tel. 34 68 60, *robert .vannevel@advalvas.be*). Sixteenth-century loft in a peaceful old quarter less than 10 minutes from the Markt.

Marian Degraeve, Kazernevest 32 (tel. 34 57 11).

Ardewolf, Oost-Proostse 9 (tel. 33 83 66, *www.ardewolf.be*, *ardewolf@pi.be*).

HI HOSTELS

Europa Jeugdberg, Baron Ruzettelaan 143 (tel. 35 26 79, *brugge@vjh.be*). B&B in dorms from €13 (£8.70). Non-members pay a supplement of around €4 (£2.70) if space is available. All meals available. Family rooms available. Excellent for an HI hostel. The bar serves cheap beer from 6pm to midnight. Reserve in advance. A 20-minute walk from the train station or the centre, or bus 2 to Steenbrugge.

Brugge (Dudzele), L. Coiseaukaai 46 (tel. 59 93 21, *brugge .dudzele@vjh.be*). €13.50 (£9) for B&B in dorms. Family rooms available.

HOSTELS

All the hostels advertise in the train station. Some will pick you up if you give them a call. See the adverts for details. Prices for dorms at all the hostels are roughly the same as at the HI hostels. All the hostels include breakfast in the overnight price.

Bauhaus, Langestraat 135 (tel. 34 10 93, *www.bauhaus.be*). Dorm beds from €11 (£7.30). Very popular, and in the town centre.

Bruno's Passage, Dweersstraat 26 (tel. 34 02 32). Dorms from around €11.20 (£7.50) depending on the size of the dorm. Dweersstraat runs left off Zuidzandstraat. We can't work the name out either ...

Snuffel Travellers' Inn, Ezelstraat 49 (tel. 33 31 33, *www.snuffel.be, info@snuffel.be*). Doubles available (although not in busy summer months). Beds in tiny dorm from €11 (£7.30). Highly recommended – very friendly, independently run hostel with one of the cheapest bars in town. From the Markt follow Sint-Jakobsstraat, which runs into Ezelstraat. Bus 3, 8, 9 or 13 from the train station.

Charlie Rockets, Hoogstraat 19 (tel. 33 06 60 33, *www.charlie*

rockets.com). Doubles at €43 (£29) and dorm beds at €13 (£8.70).

CAMPING

St Michiel, Tillegemstraat 55 (tel. 38 08 19). Around €5.50 (£3.70) per tent, €5.50 (£3.70) per person. Open all year. In the Sint-Michiels area of the city. Bus 7 from the train station. Get off at junction St Michielslaan/Rijelstraat.

Memling, Veltemweg 109 (tel. 35 58 45). Around €5.50 (£3.70) per tent, €4 (£2.70) per person. Open all year round. The smaller of the two sites, in the Sint-Kruis area of the city. There is a large supermarket nearby.

Brussels (Brussel/Bruxelles) (0)2

TOURIST OFFICES

TIB, Hôtel de Ville, Grand Place (tel. 513 8940, *www.brussels discovery.com*). Open 9am–6pm daily, but closed Sundays in winter. Sells the useful *Brussels Guide & Map* €2 (£1.30). Free hotel reservations and information on public transport.

National Tourist Office, rue du Marché-aux-Herbes 63 (tel. 504 0390). June–Sept. open daily 9am–6pm; Apr.–May and Oct. 9am–6pm daily; Nov.–Mar. open Mon.–Sat. 9am–6pm, Sun. 1–5 pm. Information on the whole of the country. The office makes hotel reservations in Brussels.

Bed & Brussels, rue Kindermans 9 (tel. 646 0737, *www.bnb-brussels.be*, *info@bnb-brussels.be*). Books rooms in B&Bs.

Tourist Information, Zaventem International Airport. Accommodation service and information on public transport.

BTR, blvd Anspach 111 (tel. 513 7484). For advance reservation of hotels.

STREET SIGNS

Historically, Brussels is a Flemish city, but around 70% are French speakers. It is only in comparatively recent times that the city was declared bilingual, and street names given in their Flemish as well as French forms. The section below uses a mixture of Flemish and

French street names. Do not worry about approaching someone if you get lost. The people of Brussels are generally friendly and few Flemish speakers will object to you using the French version of a street name (or vice versa).

ARRIVING IN BRUSSELS

There are three main train stations of interest to tourists: Gare du Nord, Gare du Midi and Gare Centrale. The latter is most convenient for the sights and for the Tourist Offices, but not all through trains stop at this station. There are frequent connections from Gare du Nord and Gare du Midi to Gare Centrale, though, so this is no problem. There is a half-hourly train service between Zaventem International Airport and Gare Centrale and Gare du Nord until 11.45pm (a 20-minute trip, free with railpasses).

Running along the front of Gare Centrale is the busy Keizerinlaan. Towards the left-hand end of this road, rue de l'Infante Isabella runs away from the station. Follow this street down past the Chapel of Mary Magdalene and continue straight ahead, passing the restaurants to arrive at the start of rue Marché-aux-Herbes, just beyond the entrance to the Galeries Royales St Hubert on your right. Continuing down this street takes you to the National Tourist Office. Turning left takes you into Grand Place. The TIB is located in the Town Hall on the opposite side of the square.

The two main coach companies operating from the UK both drop passengers a short distance from the Grand Place. Hover-speed coaches stop at pl. de la Bourse, from which Boterstraat leads into Grand Place. Eurolines stop a little further away at pl. de Brouckère. From here follow Anspachlaan to pl. de la Bourse, then turn left along Beurstraat down by the Stock Exchange to the start of Boterstraat.

HOTELS

CHEAPEST DOUBLES FROM €40 (£27)

Pacific, rue Antoine Dansaert 57 (tel. 511 8459). Breakfast included. Métro: Bourse.

Osborne, rue Bosquet 67 (tel. 537 9251). A 10- to 15-minute walk from Gare du Midi. From the pl. Louise métro go down av. Louise then turn right along rue Jourdan into rue Bosquet.

Les Bluets, Berckmannstraat 124 (tel. 534 3983, *bluets@swing.be*). Berckmannstraat is right off Jasparlaan coming from Gare du Midi, the second street on the left after rue Bosquet walking from pl. Louise.

La Potiniere, Fr. Jos. Navezstraat 165 (tel. 242 7873, *hotel_lapotiniere@hotmail.com*). A 10- to 15-minute walk from Gare du Nord.

Lloyd George, av. Lloyd George 12 (tel. 648 3072). Town centre.

CHEAPEST DOUBLES FROM €50 (£33)

Brussels Royotel, rue Royale 312 (tel. 21 83 034, *brussels royotel@hotmail.com*). Near town centre.

Residences Europa, rue Berckmans 102 (tel. 538 7297, *hotel europa@wol.be*). Métro: Hotel des Monnaies.

Madou, rue du Congrès 45 (tel. 217 1890, *www.hotelmadou.com*, *hotel.congres@busmail.net*). Near the Madou métro stop. From pl. Madou cross pl. Surlet de Chokier and walk down rue du Congrès.

De Boeck's, rue Veydt 40 (tel. 537 4033, *deboecks@euronet.be*). Métro: Louise.

Barry, pl. Anneessens 25 (tel. 511 2795, *hotelbarry@skynet.be*).

Frederiksborg, avenue Broustin 118 (tel. 425 1422).

CHEAPEST DOUBLES FROM €65 (£44)

Windsor, pl. Rouppe 13 (tel. 511 2014, *www.hotel-windsor.com*, *info@hotel-windsor.com*). Métro: Anneessens.

Albert, rue Royale Sainte-Marie 27–29 (tel. 217 9391, *hotelalbert @hotmail.com*).

Plasky, E. Plaskylaan 212 (tel. 733 7530). Bus 63 from the Madou métro station.

La Grande-Clôche, pl. Rouppe 10–12 (tel. 512 6140, *www.hotel grandecloche.com*, *info@hotelgrandecloche.com*). A short walk from the Anneessens métro; about 750m from Gare du Midi.

Sabina, rue du Nord 78 (tel. 218 2637). About 200m from the Madou métro station.

CHEAPEST DOUBLES FROM €75 (£50)

Opera, rue Grétry 53 (tel. 219 4343, *opera@skynet.be*). Town centre.

Duke of Windsor, Capouilletstraat 4 (tel. 539 1819). Breakfast included.

HI HOSTELS

'Bruegel' (Flemish YHA), Heilige Geeststraat 2 (tel. 511 0436, *brussel@vjh.be*). B&B in dorms around €13 (£8.50). Singles and doubles €23 (£15), triples, quads €15 (£10) per person. Open 7–10am, 2pm–12am. A 5-minute walk from Gare Centrale. Family rooms.

Centre Jacques Brel, rue de la Sablonnière 30 (tel. 218 0187, *brussels.brel@laj.be*). B&B in dorms around €13 (£8.70). Singles €19 (£12.70), doubles €15 (£10) per person, triples and quads €13 (£8.70) per person. Curfew 1am. A 10-minute walk from Gare du Nord; about 400m from the Botanique métro station. Family rooms.

Generation Europe, rue de l'Eléphant 4 (tel. 410 3858, *brussels .europe@laj.be*). Singles €18 (£12), doubles €15 (£10), triples and quads €13 (£9). Métro: Zwarte Vijvers (slightly closer) or Graaf Van Vlaanderen. Under 10 minutes' walk from both.

HOSTELS

Vincent Van Gogh CHAB, rue Traversière 8 (tel. 217 0158, *www.ping.be/chab*, *chab@ping.be*). No curfew. Large co-ed rooms with mattresses on floor around €9.50 (£6.40). Beds in small dorms around €13.50 (£9). Singles €22 (£14.50), doubles €16 (£10.50) p.p. Overnight price includes continental breakfast. Bus 61 from the Gare du Nord to rue Traversière, or a 10-minute walk. Laundry room.

Sleepwell, rue du Dammier 23 (tel. 218 5050, *www.sleepwell.be*, *info@sleepwell.be*). Dorms from €13.50 (£9). Singles €25 (£16.50), doubles €20 (£13.30) p.p. Curfew 1am. Overnight prices include breakfast. Those whose passport includes the number 27 may get a 25% discount on the overnight price – peculiar tradition, but handy if your number fits. Métro: Rogier. Wheelchair access. Very popular.

CAMPING

Beersel, Steenweg op Ukkel 75, Beersel (tel. 331 0561, *camping beersel@pandora.be*). Around €5.50 (£3.70) for a solo traveller.

Open all year. Basic, but very cheap. From Nord-Bourse tram 55, then bus UH. The most convenient site if you are arriving from Paris, Mons and Charleroi on the E10/A7.

Paul Rosmant, Warandeberg 52, Wezembeek-Oppem (tel. 782 1009). Around €4 (£2.70) per tent and per person, plus a municipality tax of €1.70 (£1.10). Open Apr.–Sept. Metro to Kraainem, then change to bus 30 to pl. St Pierre. Just off the Brussels ring road. The most convenient site if you are arriving by road from Leuven, Liège or Germany.

Grimbergen Camping, Veldkantstraat 64, Grimbergen (tel. 269 2597). €5 (£3.30) per tent, €4 (£2.70) per person. Open Jan.–Oct. Bus G from Gare du Nord to the end of the line, then a 10-minute walk. The easiest site to get to if arriving by road from Antwerp.

BULGARIA (00)359

Bulgaria is a country that's easy on the eye, with much natural beauty and unspoilt charm. The long sandy beaches of its Black Sea coast form a magnet for hordes of Eastern and Western visitors each year. Tourism is centred here and many pleasant inland areas and handsome towns lie waiting to be discovered. It is a country far removed in character from its neighbours Greece and Romania. A densely forested interior makes Sofia, the capital, reputedly 'the greenest city in Europe', and it has retained a fair number of its eclectic mosques and churches.

BACKGROUND

The first Bulgars were an Asiatic tribe who invaded in the seventh century and despite their defeat at the hands of the Ottomans, they retained their national identity and eventually gained independence in 1908.

From 1947 to 1989, Bulgaria was known as the Communist People's Republic of Bulgaria. The country soon became one of the most industrial and successful Eastern European nations. The upheavals of 1989 led to the ousting and arrest of Communist hardliner Todor Zhivkov and a new future for Bulgaria. However, its new democratic reforms have yet to bring lasting stability.

Bulgaria has a reputation for being an inexpensive country to visit. While this is true and the largely unspoilt Black Sea coast every year thrives on package deals, prices are rising as in other Eastern European countries. So travel sooner rather than later. Whenever you do, you will be made to feel at home. The extraordinary success of the tourist industry here means that visitors are readily welcomed.

ACCOMMODATION DETAILS

When travelling in Bulgaria the reception you receive from people working in the tourist industry will vary dramatically. In some cases, you will find people willing to do their utmost to help you to find suitably priced accommodation and provide you with advice to help you enjoy your stay. Sadly, there is currently a dearth of tourist information (particularly town plans showing the places of interest) and lists of cheap accommodation, so it is often the case that staff in the tourist industry simply cannot help you, no matter how much they might like to.

The local currency is the lev and £1 is approximately 3 lev ($1 is roughly 2 lev).

Although you no longer need a visa to enter Bulgaria, you are still required to register your passport with the local authorities. If you are staying in a hotel, hostel or campsite, this can usually be done for you. If, however, you take up an offer of private accommodation, you will need to register yourself, as not doing so may result in a large fine for your hosts. If there is no Tourist Office nearby to enquire at, go along to a local hotel and ask there.

Budget travellers will probably be interested in only the one- and two-star **hotel** categories (the only difference is that rooms in one-star hotels do not have a private bath). Prices in one-star hotels are usually around 40 lev (£14; $24) for a single, 50 lev (£18; $30) for a double. Comparable rooms in a two-star hotel cost around 60 lev (£22; $37) and 80 lev (£29; $49) respectively. Hotel accommodation is now more difficult to find than it was during the days of state control because of the increased number of visitors and finding a hotel room on arrival can pose problems throughout much of the year. One-star hotels in popular towns still tend to be filled with groups of East European holidaymakers, so you have a better chance of finding a room in a two-star hotel. Because of language difficulties, it is always better to approach hotels in person if you arrive after the Tourist Office has closed, rather than contacting them by telephone. If you are told upfront that there are no rooms available this is likely to be true and not, as is often the case in neighbouring Romania, a ploy to get you to offer a bribe.

Arranging lodgings in the home of a Bulgarian family is both a cheaper and a more interesting option than staying in a hotel. **Private rooms** can be booked through Balkantourist and, in some cases, through other organisations such as ORBITA (the student travel organisation). In Sofia, doubles cost about 40 lev (£14; $24) per person, with the cheaper rooms generally being located out in the suburbs. As the public transport system in Sofia is cheap and reasonably efficient, it is practical to stay in the suburbs if you cannot find a room in the centre. Outside the capital, doubles in popular destinations such as Plovdiv and Veliko Târnovo rarely cost more than 40 lev (£14; $24) per person. In the countryside, rooms can cost as little as 27 lev (£10; $17) per person, though it can be very difficult to find rooms in rural areas. One occasional drawback to booking rooms through an agency in the past has been the existence of a minimum stay requirement, particularly along the Black Sea coast, where a minimum stay of three to five days was required in some towns. In more popular towns, it is not unusual to be approached by touts at railway and bus stations offering private rooms during the peak season. The rooms on offer are often of lower quality than those offered by accommodation agencies, but they may be your only hope of getting a cheap bed.

During the university summer vacations, mid-July to mid-September, independent travellers do have a very slim chance of finding a place in student accommodation. If you are lucky enough to do so, you can expect to pay around 40 lev (£14; $24) for a bed.

The Bulgarian Tourist Union, which is affiliated to the HI, also operates a chain of hostels. Facilities are little more than basic, and the hostels are often located far from the centre of town, but at around 36 lev (£13; $22) for a bed the price is average. Once again, these should be booked well in advance as they are popular with visiting groups. However, as the staff at these hostels were traditionally more accommodating to Western visitors stuck for a bed than their counterparts in hotels, or ORBITA hostels, it might be worthwhile making a personal enquiry.

Camping is both a cheap way to see the country and an ideal way to meet young East European travellers. Charges are around 15 lev (£5; $8.50) per tent; with a similar fee per occupant. Taking a tent normally provides insurance against having to pay out for a hotel room as virtually all the main tourist destinations have a campsite in or around town (city sites are often located on the outskirts). With the exception of sites along the Black Sea coast, which become very crowded in summer, finding a place to pitch your tent is generally straightforward. The Bulgarian National Tourist Office in London or your country's capital may be able to provide you with a map of campsites. This should cover all the places you are likely to visit, and contains details of site facilities and opening periods (normally May–mid-Oct. inclusive). At most of these sites comfortable chalet accommodation is available to let. A chalet sleeping two normally costs in the region of 30 lev (£11; $19) per night. **Freelance camping** and **sleeping rough** are both illegal and steep fines are usually imposed on those apprehended. However, in recent years the police have been turning a blind eye to people sleeping rough in some of the Black Sea resorts during the peak season, possibly because they are well aware of the dire shortage of accommodation.

Hikers and climbers should contact the Bulgarian Tourist Union for permission to use the network of **mountain chalets** (*hizha*) they operate, and to make the necessary reservations. The standard of accommodation in *hizha* varies tremendously, from those with only the bare essentials to those which seem like hotels.

TOURIST INFORMATION

As the quality of tourist information available locally to visitors is poor, it is advisable to purchase a good guidebook before setting off on holiday.

ADDRESSES

BULGARIAN NATIONAL TOURIST OFFICE
186–188 Queens Gate, London SW7 5HL (tel. 020 7584 9400, *www.travel-bulgaria.com*).

HOTELS
Balkantourist, bul. Vitosha 1, Sofia (tel. (0)2 980 2324, *www.balkan tourist.bg*, *sofia.agency@balkantourist.bg*). They also have offices in Varna at the Grand Hotel Varna (tel. (0)52 361 904).

PRIVATE ROOMS
See Balkantourist, above.

HOSTELS
ORBITA (Student Travel Office), bul. Hristo Botev 48, Sofia (tel. (0)2 80 01 02, *www.orbita.bgcatalog.com*).
Also see *www.hostels.com/bg*.

MOUNTAIN HUTS
Bulgarian Tourist Union, bul. Vassil Levski 75 (tel. (0)287 3409).

Sofia (0)2

TOURIST OFFICES

For information, currency exchange, and to book private rooms, contact one of the several Balkantourist offices in the city or the small branch at Sofia airport.

Bul. Alexander Stamboliiski 37 (tel. 87 06 87). Open summer 7am–10pm; out of season 8am–9pm.

Bul. Vitosha 1 (tel. 43331). Open daily 8am–8pm.

Pirin Tourist, Poszitano 12 (tel. 87 33 80) acts as agent for HI hostels. Their helpful staff can also give information about the city.

HOTELS

In recent years the amount of hotel accommodation available to Western visitors has been increased as non-Balkantourist hotels which were previously debarred from admitting Westerners now admit anyone. Nevertheless, there are still no real bargains to be found in the centrally located hotels. Singles in the hotels below normally cost around 70 lev (£25; $42), doubles around 85 lev (£30; $51). Book hotel rooms through Balkantourist. You can book many of these hotels online at *www.sofiahotels.net*.

Baldjieva, bul. Tsar Asen 23 (tel. 87 29 14). From Sv. Nedelya to the NDK, Tsar Asen is on the right, parallel to bul. Vitosha.

Zdravec, Knyaginya Mariya Luiza (tel. 83 39 49). Tram 1, 7 or 15 from the train station along Knyaginya Mariya Luiza.

Edelvais, Knyaginya Mariya Luiza (tel. 83 54 31). Recently renovated.

Tsar Asen, Tsar Asen 68 (tel. 54 78 01). English speaking. Cable TV.

Beseda, Slavianska 3 (tel. 88 04 41). Near the post office.

Serdika, bul. Yanko Sakâzor 2 (tel. 44 34 11). Bus 13, 213 or 285 from the train station to the junction of Slivnica and Volgograd. Walk down Volgograd (or take trolleybus 1) until you see bul. Yanko Sakâzor, the second major road on the left.

Slaviya, ul. Sofiiski Geroi 2 (tel. 44 34 41). Just outside the centre.

Tram 13 from the train station runs down bul. Hristo Botev before turning right along General Totleben into 9 Septemvri. Sofiiski is to the left near the start of 9 Septemvri.

Sevastopol, bul. Rakovski 116 (tel. 87 59 41). One of the cheaper hotels. Prices at the bottom of the ranges quoted above. Centrally located. To the right of Knyaz Dondukov is Tsar Osvoboditel, which crosses Rakovski.

Hemus, bul. Cherni Vrâh 31 (tel. 91943). Prices at the top of the ranges quoted but a very clean, pleasant hotel. Breakfast is included. Take tram 9 from the train station – this runs along Cherni Vrâh.

As an alternative to the city centre, the suburbs of Dragalevtsi (tram 9 to last stop then bus 64 to the main square) and Simeonovo (bus 67) have a pool of clean, cheap hotels and B&Bs. **Hotel Orhideya**, Angel Bukoreshtliev 9 (tel. 67 27 39) is one such example in Dragalevtsi.

PRIVATE ROOMS

Private rooms arranged through an official agency are the best accommodation option open to travellers in Sofia.

Balkantourist at Stamboliiski 37 will arrange centrally located doubles for around 40 lev (£14; $24).

The rooms offered by touts at the train station are frequently of poor quality and/or far from the centre. It's best to go and take a look at the room before you commit to anything.

The **Markella bureau**, bul. Knyaginya Mariya Luiza 17, has rooms for around 25 lev (£9; $15) a night, as does the Sport Tourist on bul. Marija Luiza 79 (tel. 981 6421).

HOSTELS

There are six hostels in the vicinity of Sofia, and all can be conveniently booked from the Pirin Travel Agency, bul. Alexander Stamboliiski 30 (tel. 87 06 87). Turn left off Vitosha close to pl. Sveta Nedelya and it is opposite the Orbita offices.

Tourist, Komplex 'Krasma polyana' (tel. 88 10 79). Situated 8 km from the railway station; take tram 4 or 11.

Aleko (tel. 88 10 79), in the Vitosha Mountain National Park, about 20 km from central Sofia. Take bus 66.

Usually We Spend Our Time in the Garden, Angel Kanchev 21A (tel. 987 0545, *www.art-hostel.com*, *art-hostel@art-hostel.com*). A more unusual hostel, which you'll reach by taking tram 12 from the station to Slaveikov.

Sofia Hostel, Pozitano 16 (tel. 989 8583, *hostelsofia@yahoo.com*).

Hotel Orbita, bul. James Baucher 76 (tel. 657 447). ISIC card required. Tram 9 from the train station to the junction of Georgi Trajkov and Anton Ivanov (also tram 2 from the city centre). Do not expect to find a place here during the peak season. The ORBITA head office is at Hristo Botev 48 (tel. 80 15 03). Student singles 40 lev (£14; $24). Standard singles from 70 lev (£25; $44).

CAMPING

The two most convenient sites are both about 9.5 km out from the centre. Both offer bungalows for hire:

Cherniya Kos (tel. 57 11 29). Open May–Oct. Twin-bedded bungalows 40 lev (£14; $24). Off the road to Pernik, by the foot of Mount Vitosha. From the train station take tram 6, 9 or 13 along Hristo Botev to pl. Dimitar Blagoev, then take tram 5 to its terminus, then bus 58 or 59.

Vrana (tel. 78 12 13). Open all year round. Off the E80 to Plovdiv. Bus 213 from the train station, then change to bus 5.

There is another site about 16 km out from the city centre:

Lebed (tel. 77 30 45). Open May–Oct. Chalets only. 40 lev (£14; $24) for two-bed chalets. Off the road to Samokov.

Varna (0)52

TOURIST OFFICES

Balkantourist has three offices in the city and can book private rooms for you:

Opposite the train station (tel. 22 56 30). Open daily 8am–6pm.

Ul. Musala 3 (tel. 22 55 24). Near Hotel Musala. Open daily 8am–6pm.

Bul. Knjaz Boris 173 (tel. 22 55 09). Open weekdays 9am–5pm.

Pirin Travel, near Hotel Musala, can also give information and advice, as well as booking tickets and tours: Kabakciev 13 (tel. 22 27 10).

Also take a look at *www.varnacityguide.net*.

HOTELS

You will be able to find and book more hotels at *www.varna hotels.com*.

Musala, ul. Musala 3 (tel. 22 39 25). The cheapest hotel in the town. Singles around 40 lev (£14; $24), doubles around 50 lev (£18; $30). Beside the Tourist Office.

Orbita, bul. Tsar Osroboditel 25 (tel. 22 51 62). Doubles around 70 lev (£25; $42). Rooms with cable TV.

Odessa, bul. Slivnitsa 1 (tel. 22 53 12). Doubles around 110 lev (£40; $68).

Cherno More Hotel, Slivnitsa 35. (tel. 23 21 15). Doubles around 100 lev (£36; $61).

Hotel Orel, bul. Primorski 131 (tel. 22 42 30). Near the beach by the Seaside Gardens. 40 lev (£14; $24) per person.

PRIVATE ROOMS

Available from Balkantourist. Around 25 lev (£9; $15). Located in or around the town centre. **Terziiski**, at ul. Sheinova 8, also has rooms, as does **Varnensky Brzag**, on Musala 3 (tel. 22 55 24).

CAMPING

Galata. Open mid-June–mid-Sept., during which time it is frequently filled to capacity. There are bungalows, but you will have to be very fortunate to get one of them. Bus 17 from bul. Botev to Galata.

SLEEPING ROUGH

Given the vastly increased numbers visiting Varna in recent years there is simply not enough accommodation to go round during the summer. Perhaps it is in recognition of this fact that the local police have been tolerant of people sleeping rough, despite its being illegal. The park by the railway station has become a popular place for sleeping out. For safety's sake, you can deposit your pack at the left-luggage (*garderob*) opposite the station (open 5.30am–10.30pm).

CROATIA (Hrvatska) (00)385

Croatia is a stunning country that is finally getting itself properly back on its feet after years of war. From its mountain ranges, down to the shimmering Dalmatian Coast, it offers more than enough beauty and culture to the average traveller, whilst the tourist infrastructure continues to improve in leaps and bounds.

BACKGROUND

Having been occupied by the Axis powers during the Second World War, Croatia underwent a brief spell of 'independence' under the fascist puppet Ante Pavelic, before rejoining Yugoslavia in 1946.

After the war, Yugoslavia fell under the control of Marshal Tito (a Croat), whose Communist government in Belgrade ensured that the separate nationalities of Serbs, Croats and Muslims lived relatively peaceful, if somewhat suppressed, lives. Tito ruled with a firm grip until his death in 1980, when it was expected that Yugoslavia would finally break up. This didn't happen until over a decade later when, in 1991, nationalistic desires for independent states erupted into full-scale war. Fortunately for the Croats, their country was left relatively unscathed by war, being recognised almost immediately by the EC. Unfortunately the same cannot be said for Bosnia-Hercegovina, which now bears the scars of a nation divided. After much political chicanery, ceasefire agreements have been reached; but if recent history has taught us anything, it is that such agreements are prone to abuse.

ACCOMMODATION DETAILS

After a difficult time in recent years, Croatia's tourist industry is rapidly recovering. The restoration of buildings and monuments in the ancient city of Dubrovnik has been nothing short of remarkable, and tour operators are now reinvesting in the country in a major way. The exchange rate for the national currency, the Croatian kuna (Hkn) is around 11 kunas (kn) for £1 (6 kunas for $1).

Hotels are likely to prove an expensive option for the independent traveller in the summer months but can fall to bargain levels in off-peak periods. A C-class hotel can cost as little as £20 ($34) for a double room, but will double in price In July and August. **Private rooms** tend to be cheaper. These are classified by the Tourist Offices as Category I (doubles from around £15, $25), Category II (£12, $20) and Category III (£10, $17.). Prices will vary between different towns and are often higher in July and August.

There are a few **HI hostels** in Croatia which offer dormitory beds from around £12 ($20), but these tend to fill up quickly. There's also a more informal network of **independent hostels** and **student residences** (summer only) which cost roughly the same. The situation with Croatia's **campsites** is rather different: they are prone to closure. So, before setting off for one of the sites listed below, be sure to ring ahead and check that it is indeed still open.

Lastly, **sleeping rough** is not really an option. Police tour the beaches in the resorts and at best you are liable to be fined.

ADDRESSES

CROATIAN NATIONAL TOURIST OFFICE
2 The Lanchesters, 162–164 Fulham Palace Road, London W6 9ER (tel. 020 8563 7979, *info@cnto.freeserve.com*). Or visit *www.croatia.hr*, the national tourist board website.

ATLAS TRAVEL AGENCY
Pile 1, 20000 Dubrovnik (tel. 38544 22 22).

YOUTH HOSTELS
Visit *www.hfhs.hr* for details of HI hostels, and for booking services.

Dubrovnik (0)20

TOURIST OFFICE
Dubrovnik Tourist Office, C. Zuzorć 1/2 (tel. 324222, *www.dubrovnik.laus.hr*, *tzzdu-ner@du.tel.hr*).

HOTELS
In the peak season (July–Sept.) what hotels are left will be expensive. Even C-class hotels such as the Stadion and the Dubravka

charge around £19 ($32) per person at this time. Prices are lower in May and June, but only if you are travelling in April or October are there more than a handful of hotels with affordable rooms.

Zagreb, Sestaliste Kralja Zvonimira 57 (tel. 436146, *htp.sumratin @du.hinet.hr*). Half-board £20 ($30) per person.

Hotel Petka, obala Stjepana Radica (tel. 418008). Rooms from £22 ($37).

Hotel Lapad, Lapadska obala 37 (tel. 432922, *hotel-lapad@ du.tel.hr*).

Begović Boarding House, Primorska 17 (tel. 435191). Small and friendly, call first to reserve.

Neptun, Kardinala Stepinca 31 (B class) (tel. 440100, *hotel-neptun@du.tel.hr*).

Sumratin (B), Set Kralja Zvonimira 24 (tel. 436333, *htp.sumratin @du.hinet.hr*).

Bellevue (B), P. Čingrije 7 (tel. 413095, *hotel-bellevue@du.tel.hr*).

Adriatic (B), Masarykov put 7 (tel. 437302, *hoteli-maestral @du.tel.hr*).

PRIVATE ROOMS

Private rooms abound and can be booked at various offices in town. In July and August prices per person in doubles are: Category I £13–17 ($22–29); Category II £10–13 ($17–22); Category III £8–10 ($13.50–17). At other times prices can drop by between £2–4 ($3.50–7). *www.dubrovnik-online.com* have an excellent selection of private rooms complete with contact details. Failing that, try these offices for further options;

Bilicic, Privezna 2 (tel. 417152, *apartmentsbilicic@hotmail.com*).

Dalmacijaturist, M. Pracata 7 (tel. 29367/24077/24078).

Dubrovnik Turist, Put Republike 7 (tel. 356959).

Globotur, Placa (tel. 428144).

Gruz OK, Obala Stjepana Radica 32.

HI HOSTEL

YH Dubrovnik, Vinka Sagrestana (tel. 423241, *dubrovnik@ hfhs.hr*). Bed and breakfast from around £13 ($22) a night. Open all year round. 1am curfew. Kitchen facilities available. A 10-minute walk from the bus station. Newly renovated with family rooms.

HOSTELS

Vila Micika, Mata Vodopica 10 (tel. 437332, *vila-micika@ du.tel.hr*). Dorm beds from £12 ($20).
Dubrovnik Youth Hostel, Ulica Bana Jelacia 15 (tel. 23241, *hfhs-du@du.hinet.hr*).

CAMPING

Solitude (tel. 448166). Around £5 ($8.50) per tent, £7 ($12) p.p. Open all year. Roughly 3 km west of the bus station. Bus 6 from the Old Town, or from near the bus station.

There is another site in **Kupari**, about 8 km out of Dubrovnik, accessible by bus 10 (tel. 486020). £4 ($7) per tent, £4 ($7) p.p. Open 15 Apr.–15 Oct.

SLEEPING ROUGH

There is virtually no chance of you getting away with sleeping on the beach as the police make regular patrols. You can take a chance and bed down in the terraced park overlooking the sea below Marsala Tita, but if you are caught you can expect a steep fine. If you really are stuck, head for the campsites: even if you have to pay the price for one person and a tent, it is far better than being fined.

Zagreb (0) |

TOURIST OFFICE

Tourist Information Centre, Trg bana Josipa Jelačića 11 (tel. 481 4051, *www.zagreb-touristinfo.hr*, *info@zagreb-touristinfo.hr*). Open Mon.–Fri. 8.30am–8pm, Sat 9am–5pm, Sun. 10am–2pm.

There's also an office at Trg. Zrinskog 14 (tel. 492 1645). Open through the week 9am–5pm (to 6pm on Tuesday and Thursday).

Take a look at *www.inyourpocket.com* for more ideas on accommodation and things to do.

HOTELS
CHEAPEST DOUBLES AROUND £52 ($88).
Jadran, Vlaska 50 (tel. 455 3777, *www.hup-zagreb.hr*, *jadran@ hup-zagreb.hr*).
Tomislavov Dom, Sljemenska Cesta BB (tel. 455 5833, *sljeme-medvednica@zg.hinet.hr*).
Central, Branmimirova 3 (tel. 484 1422, *www.hotel-central.hr*, *info@hotel-central.hr*).
Panorama, Trg Sportova 9 (tel. 365 8333, *www.hup-zagreb.hr*, *panorama@hup-zagreb.hr*).

PRIVATE ROOMS
Expect to pay £32–40 ($54–68) for doubles.
Evistas, Senonina 28 (tel. 483 9445, *evistas@zg.hinet.hr*).
Di-Prom, Trnsko 25A (tel. 605 0039).
ADP Glorija, Britanski trg 5 (tel. 482 3571, *www.adp-glorija.com*, *lada@adp-glorija.com*).

HI HOSTEL
Omladinski Hotel, Petrijnska 77 (tel. 484 1261, *zagreb@hfhs.hr*). Dorms around £8 ($13.50), doubles and triples around £18 ($30) p.p. Turn right on leaving the station, walk one block and you will see Petrijnska on your left. Fills quickly. Wheelchair access.

INDEPENDENT HOSTELS
Ravnice Youth Hostel, Ravnice 38d (tel. 233 2325, *www.ravnice-youth-hostel.hr*, *ravnice-youth-hostel@zg.hinet.hr*). A brand new hostel just out of the town centre. Beds cost from £9 ($15).
Student Hotel Cvjetno, Odranska 8 (tel. 619 1245, *turizam@ sczg.hr*). Open 15 July–1 Oct. Doubles only £30 ($51). Take tram 4 from the station to Vjesnik.

CAMPING
Plitvice, Zagreb/Lučko (tel. 653 0444, *www.motel-plitvice.hr*, *motel@motel-plitvice.hr*). About 10 km from town, on the road to Maribor.

CZECH REPUBLIC (Cěska Republika) (00)420

The Nineties were a decade of astonishing change for the Czech people, who now face the onslaught of a new type of invaders – tourists. Blessed with some of Europe's finest architecture and arguably the best beers, it is easy to see why. With EU membership, the country is set to become even more popular.

Since 1989, Prague, in particular, has been besieged by visitors, and the numbers, even despite flooding in 2002, are growing all the time. The city is already one of Europe's top tourist destinations, with visitors coming to drink the world's finest Pilsner beer, sit in cafés once frequented by Kafka and soak up the atmosphere of an ever-changing city. But turn away from this delightful tourist trap, and you will encounter some equally fantastic countryside, and friendly locals.

BACKGROUND

On 1 January 1993 came the peaceful split of the Czech and Slovak peoples after almost 75 years as a unified nation. This had considerable economic repercussions, leaving the exchange rate and other facilities in a permanent state of flux, and surprised many observers, seeing as it came hot on the heels of the tumultuous events of 1989. It was during this 'Velvet Revolution' that change swept through Czechoslovakia, toppling the Communist dictatorship, and establishing the dissident playwright Vaclav Havel as president.

Unified in 1918 under the leadership of Tomas Masaryk and Eduard Benes, it did not take the Czechs long to realise that their central position in Europe was somewhat risky. The furious biting of fingernails was justified in 1939 when Hitler was the first to challenge the young republic, and with no help from Britain or France, the country was occupied by the Nazis. They stayed for the duration of the Second World War. After the war the hardline Communist regime was established. Things went from bad to worse in 1968, when Dubček's attempt to reform the system was met with Soviet disapproval and occupation. The crushing of the 'Prague Spring', as it was known, led to an even more oppressive regime, lasting for 21 years under Gustav Husak until the fateful year of 1989. Since then, the Czech Republic has been growing both economically and politcally, and is now home to one of the most visited cities in the world, Prague.

ACCOMMODATION DETAILS

There is a general shortage of cheap accommodation possibilities in the peak season of July and August (late May to early September in Prague), though the situation is improving. Happily, more visitors are finding their way out from the usual tourist destinations to the exquisite small towns. However, a growth in accommodation possibilities tends to follow an influx, so if the town has become reasonably well visited, tourists can toil to find accommodation in peak season. On the other hand, there are many smaller towns (particularly in north Bohemia) where you will have no trouble at all finding cheap accommodation at any time of year.

The local currency is the Czech koruna and £1 is approximately 48 kčs ($1 is 25 kčs).

Hotels are divided into five categories from five-star luxury hotels to budget 'no frills' one-star accommodation. In most towns, the lower three grades are now within the reach of the budget traveller. Even in some popular tourist destinations there are doubles available for as little as 630 kčs (£13; $22). As might be expected, prices are higher in Prague, where it is difficult to find a double room for under 900 kčs (£18.50; $31). More probably, you will have to pay 1,000–1,400 kčs (£22–30; $37–51) if you want a double room in the capital.

Throughout the Czech Republic, it is possible to stay in the homes of local people. Prices for **private rooms** booked through agencies are no longer officially fixed, with the result that they have risen, and rooms are not the bargain they were a few years ago. Now you can expect to pay around 720 kčs (£15; $25) for a single in Prague, around 480 kčs (£10; $15) elsewhere. However, private rooms are the most widely available budget option. With the obvious potential for new agencies in this field, there are now alternatives to dealing with Čedok or Pragotur, the only organisations that let private rooms when the industry was state-controlled. Nevertheless, because of the number of rooms they control, Pragotur are still the best to deal with in the capital, with

Čedok predominant in the country as a whole (České Budějovice is one notable exception). Some rooms in the cities can be far from the centre, but the public transport systems are cheap and efficient.

The asking price for private rooms offered by individuals will not be too dissimilar to those you will pay at one of the local agencies (although breakfast is usually included in private offers). However, whereas the standard of rooms booked through an agency is reasonably uniform, the quality of privately offered rooms varies dramatically. You might be lucky and get a perfectly acceptable room with a decent location but, especially in Prague, many are situated in the vast housing schemes on the outskirts of town and can be difficult to reach by public transport. In peak season, your room for manoeuvre as regards price and location can be severely constrained by the sheer numbers of those looking for accommodation. If you are stuck, you can always stay one night and then get into town early next morning to look for something better. If you do take up a private offer, take care of your valuables.

Hostelling probably offers the best value for money out of all the accommodation possibilities, but finding a hostel bed is not easy. There are roughly 30 hostels listed in the HI handbook. These are operated by CKM (the student travel organisation). Prices range from 390 kčs to 580 kčs (£8-12; $13.50–22) – usually towards the lower end of the scale. The few permanent hostels are a great bargain. Standards are excellent as these are in fact CKM hotels which offer discounts of 70–80% to HI members and students. However, not only do they have to be booked several months in advance if you plan to arrive during the peak season, but a quick comparison of the hostel list with a guidebook will tell you that apart from Prague, the spa towns of Mariánské Lázně and Karlovy Vary, and Banská Bystricá, the places of major interest lack permanent hostels. Many of the temporary hostels listed in the HI handbook (including the four hostels in Brno) are converted student dormitories, which open only during July and August. If you are travelling at that time of year it is always worth contacting the local CKM office, as they control the letting of rooms in student dormitories in many towns not mentioned in the HI handbook. Rooms in student dorms generally cost around 290–380 kčs (£6–8, $10–13.50).

In recent years, there has been a growth in the number of independent hostels, particularly in Prague. Again, the vast majority of these are in converted student dormitories, opening only in July and August. The established tourist agencies (Čedok, CKM, Pragotur) may not be a fruitful source of information on independent hostels, either because they are genuinely unaware of new hostels, or because they are intent on selling you accommodation they control. Ask other travellers about hostelling possibilities, and keep your eyes open for hostels advertised at bus and train stations.

Most small towns have very basic dormitory hostels known as *turistická ubytovna*, where a bunk bed costs around 190 kčs (£4; $7). Facilities seldom extend to anything more than toilets and cold showers. These hostels are meant primarily for workers living away from home or for groups of workers on holiday, but it is most unlikely you will be turned away if there is room at the hostel. Unfortunately, many such hostels open only when they have a group booking. Nevertheless, it is worth enquiring about *turistická ubytovna* at the local Čedok or CKM offices, as they sometimes offer the only hostel accommodation available in town.

If you are travelling between May and September–mid-October, **camping** is a great way to see the country very cheaply (few sites remain open outside these months). Ask at the tourist information centres for details. Prices for a solo traveller are about 240 kčs (£5; $8.50) per night, but, as Čedok warns, 'don't expect luxury'. Sites are usually clean, but at the B-class sites outside showers are the norm. Very occasionally, in peak season, you might have a little trouble finding a space, but even then only at the sites in Prague (and perhaps at weekends in České Budějovice, Tbor, Mariánské Lázně and Karlovy Vary). At the vast majority of the sites it is possible to rent 2- or 4-bed chalets (*chata*). The standard of chalets varies from site to site: while some are quite cramped, others are spacious and very comfortable. At some sites you may be required to pay for all the beds in the chalet, even if they are not all occupied. Expect to pay 190–240 kčs (£4–5; $7–8.50) per person in a fully occupied chalet.

There are numerous other primitive sites, known in Czech as *tbořiště*. Facilities at these sites are spartan: you may have to wash in the river nearby, and may prefer to use the woods to the site's toilets. On the plus side, these sites are exceptionally cheap at around 145 kčs (£3; $5) per night for a solo traveller. Again, few of these sites remain open outside the months of May to September. In the past, these were aimed at East European holidaymakers and were not advertised to Westerners. Indeed, the official agencies were loath even to admit their existence. Nowadays, local Čedok offices are more likely to be forthcoming about *tbořiště*, though it is always worth asking locals if Čedok officials say there are none. Alternatively, the book *Ubytovani CSR* lists all the hotels, hostels and campsites in the Czech Republic (in Czech, but easy to follow), while the 1:100,000 tourist map of the country shows all the campsites in both the Czech and Slovak Republics.

TOURIST INFORMATION

Few cities have really good tourist offices organised along Western lines. In most towns, the information that is available is distributed by accommodation agencies such as Čedok or CKM. In very few towns can you pick up a small plan showing the main sites of interest. If you are heading for the Czech Republic or Slovakia, it is best to buy a good guidebook before setting off on holiday as information can sometimes be limited, and English is not widely spoken.

ADDRESSES

CZECH CENTRE
30 Kensington Palace Gardens, London N3 1TQ (tel. 020 7243 7942).
Also, take a look at *www.czech.cz* for general country information.

ČEDOK TOURS & HOLIDAYS
5th floor Morley House, 314 Regent Street, London (tel. 020 7580 3778, *www.cedok.co.uk*, *travel@cedok.co.uk*).

YOUTH HOSTELS
Visit *www.iyhf.cz* for full listings of HI hostels in the Czech Republic. CKM Club of Young Travellers, Žitná 12, 121 05 Praha 2 (tel. (0)2 2491 5767).

Brno (0)5

TOURIST INFORMATION

Tourist Information Centre, Radnická 8 (tel. 4221 1090).
Mon.–Fri. 8am–6pm, Sat.–Sun. 9am–5pm.

Čedok, across the street from the main train station, sell maps of
the city for around £0.50 ($0.85).

Also see *www.brno-city.cz* for further information and accommodation links.

ACCOMMODATION AGENCIES

CKM, Česká 11 (tel. 4221 0766). Open Mon.–Fri. 10am–12pm
and 2–5pm, Sat. 10am–12pm. CKM operate hostels in converted student dorms from 1 July to 31 Aug. The office is a
15-minute walk from the main train station. Cross the road
and head down Masarykova into náměstí Svobody. Keep
going straight on along the left-hand side of the square into
Česká.

Čedok, Divadelní 3 (tel. 4221 5227). Open Mon.–Fri. 9am–6pm,
Sat. 9am–12pm. Information and reservations for hotels and
hostels available. A 10-minute walk from the main train station.
Head right until you come to Benešova. Go along the left-hand
side of the street.

ARRIVING IN BRNO

Most trains arrive at Brno Hlavní nádraží (main train station) on
the fringe of the Old Town. Some night trains only stop at Brno
Královo Pole on the outskirts of the city. Unless you arrive here on
a Sunday morning, you rarely have to wait more than 20 minutes
for a connecting train to Hlavní nádraží. The main bus station is
located a few blocks behind the main train station.

HOTELS

Astoria, Novobranska 3 (tel. 4221 5953). Singles 820 kčs (£17,
$25.50), doubles 1,000 kčs (£22; $37). Close to the Čedok
office on Divadelní. A 10-minute walk from the main train
station. Head straight down Masarykova from the station, turn

right along Orli, then left after passing the Menin Gate. Tram 1, 2 or 18 from the station to Malilnovskeho nám.

Hotel Pegas, Jakobska 4 (tel. 4221 0104, *www.hotelpegas.cz*, *hotelpegas@hotelpegas.cz*).

Hotel Amphone, Tr Jarose 29 (tel. 4521 1783, *amphone_br@ motylek.com*). Doubles at 1,390 kčs (£30; $51).

Hotel Avion, Ceska 20 (tel. 4221 5016). Doubles around 780 kčs (£16; $27).

If the hotels above are full, the next three hotels as you move up the price scale are the U Jakuba at Jakubské náměstí 6 (tel. 4221 0795), the Slovan at Lidická 23 (tel. 4132 1207); useful names to mention if Čedok are trying to be unreasonable. Failing that, take a look at *www.motylek.com*.

PRIVATE ROOMS
Contact Čedok on Divadelní. Singles 480 kčs (£10; $17), doubles 710–750 kčs (£15–16, $25–27).

INDEPENDENT HOSTELS
Penzion Palacky, Kolejni 2 (tel. 4164 1111). Open all year round.
Koleje Jana Taufera, Jana Babaka 3 (tel. 4132 1355). Open in the summer months only.

CAMPING
Bobrava, Modrice u Brna (tel. 4721 6056). Grade B site. Open 15 Apr.–15 Oct. Tram 2, 14 or 17 to the Modrice terminus, then a 10-minute walk, or a local train to Popovice, 500m from the site. About 16 km out of town.

Pilsen (Plzeň) (0)19

TOURIST OFFICE
The Tourist Information Centre is at náměstí Republiky 41 (tel. 703 2750, *www.plzen-city.cz*). They will also help book accommodation.

ACCOMMODATION AGENCY

CKM, Dominikanská 1 (tel. 723 6393, *ckm_plzen@volny.cz*). Just off nám. Republiky.

HOTELS AND PENSIONS

Enquire at the Tourist Information Office or visit their website as listed above. It is also worth checking with the CKM office (see above)

Penzion V. Solni, Solnji 8 (tel. 723 6652). Singles 580 kčs (£12; $20), doubles 920 kčs (£20; $34). One block from nám. Republiky's northwest corner.

Hotel Slovan, Smetanovy sady (tel. 722 7256, *hotelslovan@ iol.cz*). Good value.

PRIVATE ROOMS

Enquire at the places listed above about the availability of private rooms.

HI HOSTEL

SOU, Vejprnická 56 (tel. 738 2012). Around 240 kčs (£5; $8.50). Tram 2 to Internáty, walk back 50m and head left into the compound.

HOSTELS

During July and August **CKM** let more beds in converted student dormitories.

CAMPING

Intercamping (tel. 35611). Grade A. Open 20 Apr.–15 Sept. Also lets bungalows. In the suburb of Bílá Hora. Bus 20 or 39.

Ostende (tel. 520194). In Plzeň-Bolevec. Grade A, open 1 May–15 Sept. Bungalows available.

Prague (Praha) (0)2

TOURIST INFORMATION

Pražská Informačni Služba (PIS), Na Přikopě 20 (tel. 12 444, *www.pis.cz*, *tourinfo@pis.cz*). Open Mon.–Sat. 9am–6pm, Sun.

9am–3pm. The best source of general information. No accommodation service. Metro: Náměstí Republiky. Na Příkopě runs out of nám. Republiky.
Other information offices: Old Town Square, open Mon.–Fri. 9am–6pm, weekends until 5pm.

ACCOMMODATION AGENCIES

Agentura B&B, Sticchora 588 (tel. 581 0733 evenings only). Books safe and welcoming accommodation with local families.

Pragotur, Za Porícskou branou 7 (tel. 2171 4130, *pis.pragotur@mbox.vol.cz*). Open Mon.–Fri. 8am–7pm, Sat. 9am–6pm, Sun 9am–3pm. Metro: Náměstí Republiky. Pragotur can book rooms in hotels, pensions and hostels, as well as in private accommodation.

Čedok, Na Příkopě 18 (tel. 2419 7210). Open Mon.–Fri. 9am–10pm, weekends 8.30am–2pm. Metro: Náměstí Republiky. Follow Na Příkopě from nám. Republiky.

CKM, Žitná 12 (tel. 2491 5767). Metro: I.P. Pavlova. Walk down Ječná. Accommodation of all types.

Top Tour, Rybnà 3 (tel. 248 1911, *www.toptour.cz*, *mail@toptour.cz*). Open Mon.–Fri. 9am–8pm, weekends 10am–7pm. Metro: Náměstí Republiky. From nám. Republiky walk a short distance down Celetná, turn right on to Králodvorská, then left.

AVE, Wilsonová 8 (tel. 2422 3521, *avetours@avetours.anet.cz*). AVE have two offices on the upper floor of Praha hlavní nádraží. They also operate an office at Ruzyne Airport (tel. 236 2541).

KONVEX, Ve Smeckach 29 (tel. 2221 0473, *www.konvex.cz*, *konvex@konvex.cz*). Open daily 10am–7pm.

Hello Travel Ltd, nám. Gorkého-Senovážná 3 (tel. 421 2741). Open daily 9am–10pm. Metro: Náměstí Republiky then walk down Hybernská, then turn right along Dlážděbá into the square.

Prague Accommodation Centre, Opatovicka 20 (tel. 233 376638, *www.accommodation-prague-centre.cz*, *slavica@login.cz*).

FINDING ACCOMMODATION

The growth in the number of private rooms and apartments available has gone some way to alleviating the terrible accommodation shortage in Prague. Nevertheless, there are still only around 10,000 beds in registered accommodation for 10 million visitors, the vast majority of whom arrive between May and early September. If you are travelling at that time of year, aim to get to Prague early in the morning and start looking for a bed right away. The accommodation situation worsens dramatically at weekends, as the city is exceptionally popular with Germans and Austrians taking short breaks, so arrive between Monday and Thursday if at all possible.

ARRIVING IN PRAGUE

Of the city's five main train stations your most likely point of arrival is Praha hlavní nádraží, a short walk from the Václavské náměstí and within easy walking distance of the Old Town. Some international trains and overnight internal services drop you at Praha-Holešovice, in the northern suburb of Holešovice. Trains terminating at Praha-Smichov, Masarykovo nádraží (the old Praha-Stred), and Praha-Vysocany are usually local services or slow trains from the provinces. Connections between Praha hlavní, Praha-Smichov and Praha-Holešovice are easy as all are served by the metro (line C: Hlavní nádraží; line B: Smichovské nádraží; line C: Nádraží Holešovice, respectively). The Masarykovo nádraží is a short walk along Wilsonova from Praha hlavní nádraží and, in the opposite direction, the Florenc metro station (lines B and C). From Praha-Vysocany, tram 3 crosses Wilsonova a short distance from the Florenc metro stop. The main bus station, Praha-Florenc, is beside the Florenc metro station. The Masarykovo nádraží and Praha hlavní nádraží are both within easy walking distance of Praha-Florenc, to the left along Wilsonova. Arriving at Ruzyně airport, your cheapest option is to take bus 119 (three an hour) from opposite the main exit to its terminus at the Dejvická metro station (line A). The CSA bus is dearer, but takes you direct to the CSA office on Revolučni, a short walk from náměstí Republiky.

HOTELS AND PENSIONS

Čedok deal in two-star hotels, but often claim not to in an attempt to persuade you to take a room in a more expensive hotel. Pragotur specialise in one-star hotels, and are unlikely to be dishonest about the availability of hotel rooms. Both agencies reallocate late cancellations and forfeited reservations from 5pm onwards.

Hotel prices have fluctuated in the past few years. As a rough guide expect to pay £20–27 ($34–46) for the cheapest doubles in a C/one-star hotel, and £25–45 ($42–76) for their equivalent in a B/two-star hotel. Most hotel bills have to be settled in hard currency.

Kafka, Cimburkova 24 (tel. 224 617458, *info@ckvesta.cz*). A few minutes' walk from the town centre.

Balkán, Svorností 28 (tel. 5732 7180, *balkan@motylek.com*). From the Anděl metro station on Nádražní walk down Na Bělidle or Jindřicha Plachty on to Svorností.

Prague Lion, Na Bolisti 26 (tel. 9618 0018, *www.praguelion.com*, *praguelion@praguelion.com*). Doubles, dorms and apartments available.

Hotel City, Belgicka 10 (tel. 222 521606, *www.hotelcity.cz*). Just off Wenceslas Square.

Unitas Pension, Bartolomejska 9 (tel. 224 221802, *www.unitas.cz*, *unitas@unitas.cz*). Great place right in the middle of town.

Libeň, Zenklova 2/37 (tel. 683 4009, *welcome@bed.cz*). Tram 12 from the Malastranská metro station and tram 10 from Vltavská metro station; both run along the street. After crossing the river the trams follow Libeňský most. At the point at which they turn left you are on Zenklova. The hotel is near the turn.

Pension Museum, Mezibranska 15 (tel. 9632 51867, *www.pension-museum.cz*, *pension-museum@pension-museum.cz*). Doubles and apartments available. Great place near Wenceslas Square.

Metros, Bochovská 11/562 (tel. 55 1981, *metros@motylek.com*). From £15 ($25).

Florian, Ohradní 26 (tel. 6121 0653). From £15 ($25).

Sporthotel, U Klikovky 10 (tel. 5721 0146). From £10 ($17).

PRIVATE ROOMS

With the removal of officially regulated prices, the cost of private rooms has soared so that they no longer offer the good value for money they once did. Nonetheless, they are the most widely available accommodation possibility. New booking agencies are still emerging, so it is always worth asking around among other travellers and keeping your eyes open for adverts in bus and train stations. Whichever office you deal with, try to get a room with a decent location, ideally in the centre, but these are scarce. Realistically, you should expect to be staying a few kilometres out. Provided you're within reach of an easy and frequent public transport service to the centre this is no problem, as public transport is cheap and reliable. When paying for a room you may be requested to do so in hard currency (US dollars are preferred). **Mary's Accommodation Service**, Italska 31 (tel. 2225 3510, *www.marys.cz*) has flats in the Old and New Town from £15 ($25).

HOSTELS

More and more private hostels are opening up in Prague all the time, and many now offer a good range of facilities. By June, as the number of visitors grow, finding a hostel bed becomes increasingly difficult. If you don't like the look of the unofficial hostels, head straight for **CKM**, as they are well informed as to where beds are available, and will make reservations for you, as well as giving you directions to the hostel by public transport. As a rule, you can expect to pay 300–500 kčs (£6–10, $10–17) for a hostel bed booked through CKM or direct through the private hostels. Although at peak periods you should probably be glad to get any hostel bed at all, it can be worth asking CKM if they have beds in small rooms available, as dormitory beds at some hostels cost as much per person as singles and doubles at others.

HI HOSTELS

These hostels can be booked through CKM:

Hotel Beta, Rosthotova 1255/1 (tel. 6126 2158). Breakfast included in overnight price, luggage room available; wheelchair accessible. Family rooms.

Hotel Standart, Vodni Stavby 1700 (tel. 875258). Small restaurant on premises. Family rooms.

CKM Junior Hotel, Zitna 12 (Tel. 292984) near to Hlávní Nádraží station.

Hostel Advantage, Sokolska 11–13 (Tel. 2491 4062, *advantage@ iyhf.cz*).

INDEPENDENT HOSTELS

Sir Toby's Hostel, Delnicka 24 (tel. 283 870635, *www.sirtobys .com*, *info@sirtobys.com*). Dorms from £7.50 ($13). Very popular, book in advance.

TJ Sokol Karlin, Malého 1 (tel. 2481 7474, *sokol.karlin@volny.cz*). Around £4 ($7) per night, either in bunk beds or cots set up in the gym. If the hostel is full they may let you sleep on the floor. Open all year. Close to the bus station. Metro: Florenc. From the station go right along Křižíkova. Turn right at the junction with Prvního pluku, followed by a short walk on to Malého.

Dlouha Hostel, Dlouha 33 (tel. 2482 6662, *www.travellers.cz*, *hostel@travellers.cz*). Dorms from £8 ($13.50). Very popular, and very good, so book in advance.

Golden Sickle, Vodickova 12 (tel. 222 230773, *hostelprague .info*, *stay@hostelprague.info*). Central, brand new and a good deal.

Clown and Bard, Borijova 102 (tel. *www.clownandbard.com*, *clownandbard@clownandbard.com*). Very cheap and clean. 15 minutes' walk from the town centre in the Zizkov area.

Arena Hostel, U. Vystaviste 1 (tel. 2087 0252, *www.arena hostel.com*, *contact@arenahostel.com*). New and clean. Internet access and kitchen.

Hostel Elf, Husitska 11 (tel. 222 540964, *www.hostelelf.com*, *info@hostelelf.com*). Friendly and popular. Next to the bus station.

Purple House, Krasova 25 (tel. 0603 413108, *purple_house@ motylek.com*). Clean and central. Rooms £8–£12 ($13.50–20) per night depending on number of people sharing. 5 minutes from station.

CAMPING

Pragotur distribute the brochure *Praha Camping* listing all the sites. It is worth picking up a copy in case any of the telephone numbers have changed from those given below. Pragotur may simply say they have none left. If so, ask them to confirm the information given here. They may also tell you all the sites are full. Don't believe them. Call the sites yourself (all the better if you can speak German; if not, English should let you gather basic info). All sites let bungalows except where indicated otherwise. Expect to pay around 300 kčs (£7; $12) per tent and per person; 600 kčs (£13, $22) per person in a full bungalow.

Sokol Trója, Trojská 171 (tel. 233 542903, *www.camp-sokol-troja.cz*, *info@camp-sokol-troja.cz*). Grade A site, open all year. Bus 112 from the Nádraží Holešovice metro station passes the site. Take the bus to Na Kazance. Often full, so best to reserve. If it is, the house at Trojská 157 (a few minutes' walk away) has a small site to the rear.

Caravancamp TJ Vysoké Školy, Plzeňská 279 (tel. 257 210140, fax 257 215084). Grade A, open 15 May–15 Sept. No bungalows. Trams 4, 7 and 9 run past the site. Walk right from the exit of Hlavní nádraží to catch tram 9 heading left along the street. From the Anděl metro station walk a short distance left on to Plzeňská to catch tram 4, 7 or 9.

Intercamp Kotva Braník, U ledáren 55 (tel. 244 461712). Grade A, open 1 Apr.–30 Sept. Close to the Braník terminus of trams 3, 17 and 21. Shortly after passing the Zápotockého Bridge (first after the islands), you can see the campsite down by the river. From Hlavní nádraží head across the gardens in front of the station and down Jeruzalémská on to Jindřišská. Head left along the street to the tram stop and take tram 3 in the direction you were walking.

Motol Sportcamp, Nad Hlinícken (tel. 257 213080). Grade A, open 1 Apr.–31 Oct. Same directions as for the Caravancamp above. Take trams 4, 7 or 9 to their Motol terminus, from which the site is a 5-minute walk uphill, on the left.

Triocamp Praha, Ústecka ulice (tel. 283 850793). Public camping site. No bungalows.

Autocamp Hájek, Trojská 337/149, Praha 7 (tel. 233 541352).

Autocamp Sokol, Národních hrdinu 290, Praha 9 (tel. 281 931 112).

Autocamp Trojská, Trojská 157/375, Praha 7 (tel. 283 850487, fax 233 542945).

Karavan Park, Císařská louka 599, Praha 5 (tel. 54 50646).

Sky Club Brumlovká, Vyskočilova 2, Praha 4 (tel. 4148 5006). No bungalows.

DENMARK (Danmark) (00)45

Despite its small size, Denmark has a lot to offer. It consists of the mainland (Jutland), and the two larger islands of Funen and Zealand, and about 100 other tiny inhabited isles, which used to be home to the notorious Vikings. As well as its Vikings, Denmark is famous for Lego, Carlsberg lager and Hans Christian Andersen, but once you visit, you may feel that its charming cities and free-spirited people should be added to that list.

BACKGROUND

Denmark prospered during the Middle Ages, and by 1397 both Sweden and Norway were under Danish rule. The union with Norway and Sweden eventually petered out, but Denmark remained relatively strong under an absolute monarchy which was not replaced by a liberal-style government until 1849.

In the 20th century, Denmark remained prosperous and today enjoys one of Europe's highest standards of living. It is a British preconception that Denmark is therefore an expensive country. But while a pint of beer can cost £5 ($8.50) after 8pm, neither food nor accommodation are expensive here if you shop around. Denmark is certainly not in the same league (price-wise) as its Scandinavian neighbours Norway and Sweden. The Danes, an extraordinarily sociable people (many of whom have English as a second language), have organised their tourist industry into a very helpful and accommodating service. This is especially evident in the facilities for young travellers, who are really well catered for.

ACCOMMODATION DETAILS

Few countries have responded as imaginatively and constructively to the growth in budget tourism as Denmark. Tourist Offices will take the time to explain the various cheap accommodation possibilities. Accommodation prices are noticeably lower than in the rest of Scandinavia, increasing the range of your options.

The local currency is the Danish krone (Dkr) and £1 is approximately 11 krone ($1 is roughly 6 krone).

Hotels, however, are still likely to be outside your budget. The cheapest doubles in Copenhagen cost around 500 Dkr (£45; $76); elsewhere around 350–500 Dkr (£31-45, $53-76). The concept of **bed and breakfast** is fast catching on in Denmark. A catalogue of those available is published by Dansk Bed and Breakfast and can be obtained by visiting their website *www.bedandbreakfast.dk*, or writing to them at Postbox 53, DK 2900, Hellerup. They are also available from any Danish Tourist Office both inside and outside Denmark and on ferries to and from Denmark. Rooms in **private homes** are more affordable, with singles costing around 160–220 Dkr (£14–20; $19.50–27.75), doubles 280–350 Dkr (£25–32; $34.50–43.50). Breakfast is optional: usually 35–45 Dkr (£3–4; $5–7). Private rooms are becoming more widely available each year, but are still in short supply in some areas. Where rooms are available, Tourist Offices outside Copenhagen will accept requests for reservations by email or phone. A fee of around 20 Dkr (£1.75; $3) is charged for making a reservation, the same fee paid by personal callers at the office.

Rooms do not have to be booked through the Tourist Office. If you see a house or farmhouse advertising rooms (invariably advertised in several languages), simply approach the owner. Another option, if there are a few of you, is to rent a **holiday home** for a week. In high season, a simple house sleeping four costs 1,300–2,500 Dkr (£118–227, $200–380) per week. If this appeals to you, it may be wise to contact the local Tourist Office for advice.

You will seldom be far from one of the 100 or so **HI hostels** spread throughout this small country. There is a hostel in all the main towns. In many hostels, you have the chance to stay in small rooms as well as in dormitories. While you might baulk at the thought of paying £12–16 ($20–27) in some Norwegian hostels, prices here vary from 90–110 Dkr (£8–10; $13.50–17) in 4-bed rooms to dormitory accommodation costing around 100 Dkr (£9; $17). Prices are very reasonable considering the standard of Danish hostels. As a result of a drive by the hostel association to attract families, high standards of comfort exist. Outside the large towns and ports, hostels are rarely full but, as they may be a couple of kilometres out, phoning or emailing ahead is advisable to get directions, as well as book a bed. Reservations are held until

5pm, unless you state that you will arrive later. Receptions close at 9pm and, outside Copenhagen, an 11pm curfew is normal. If advance warning is given, it is possible to arrive later, but you may be charged 40 Dkr (£3.50; $6) for this. Bring your own bedlinen as it costs around 45 Dkr (£4; $7) per night to hire. It is also advisable to have an HI card. Otherwise you will have to pay around 40 Dkr (£3.50; $6) for an overnight card or 120 Dkr (£11; $19) for a membership card.

In the main towns, there are often **independent hostels** and local authority-run Sleep-Ins. The latter frequently operate only for a period of a few weeks in summer (usually early August), and may be as basic as a mattress on the floor to put your sleeping bag on. Sleep-Ins differ considerably in price, from the 100 Dkr (£9; $15) for B&B in Copenhagen to the free Sleep-In in Odense run by DSB, the state railway. In theory, age restrictions and one-night maximum stays exist, but are seldom stringently enforced.

Sleep-Ins apart, **Town Mission Hostels** can often provide the cheapest lodgings in town. Generally clean and well equipped, there is, however, a strict ban on alcohol. The local Tourist Office will inform you on whether a Sleep-In or Town Mission Hostel is in operation.

There is hardly a town of any size that does not have a **campsite**. Graded from one to three stars, the best are the three-star sites, at which one person will pay around 60 Dkr (£5.50; $9) per night. All sites are open during the summer months; a fair number from April to September; and a few all year round. Unless you have an International Camping Carnet you need to buy either a Danish Camping Pass (valid all year, 40 Dkr (£3.50; $6), or a one-night pass for 10 Dkr (£1; $1.70). Many sites let cabins or caravans for up to four people, which cost 1,400–3,200 Dkr (£127–290; $216–490) per week.

Camping outside official sites is perfectly acceptable, provided you first obtain the permission of the landowner. Do not camp on the beaches, as this is against the law and frequently results in an on-the-spot fine. It is also illegal to sleep rough, so it is asking for trouble to try sleeping in stations, parks or on the streets.

ADDRESSES

THE DANISH TOURIST BOARD

55 Sloane Street, London SW1X 9SY (tel. 020 7259 5959, *www.dtb.dt.dk*).

BED AND BREAKFAST DENMARK

PO Box 53, Hellerup, Denmark (tel. 3961 0405, *www.bedand breakfast.dk, info@bedandbreakfast.dk*). Provides accommodation in private homes from 440 Dkr (£40; $68) for singles and 550 Dkr (£50; $85) for doubles.

DANISH YHA

Landsforeningen Danmarks Vandrerhjem, Vesterbrogade 39, DK-1620 København V (tel. 3131 3612, *www.danhostel.dk, ldv@danhostel.dk*).

CAMPING

Camping Club Denmark, Horsens Turistforening, Søndergade 26, DK-8700 Horsens (tel. 7562 3822).

Also see *www.dk-camp.dk* for an excellent site covering the whole of Denmark.

Danish Camping Union, DCU-Huset, Gl. Kongevej 74D, Frederiksberg (tel. 33 21 06 00, *www.dcu.dk, info@dcu.dk*).

HOLIDAY HOMES

Visit *www.holiday.dk*, or *www.feriehusguide.dk*, for hundreds of listings and contact details.

Århus

TOURIST OFFICE

Århus Turistbureauet, Rådhuset, Park Alle 1 (tel. 89 40 67 00, *www.visitaarhus.com*). Open 14 June–20 June, Mon.–Sat. 9am–5pm; 21 June–8 Aug., daily 9am–8pm; 9 Aug.–12 Sept., daily 9am–7pm; 13 Sept.–31 Dec., Mon.–Fri. 9.30am–4.30pm, Sat. 10am–1pm; 1 Jan.–13 June, Mon.–Fri. 9am–4.30pm, Sat. 10am–1pm. From the train station head left from Banegardspladsen then right along Park Alle.

HOTELS AND PENSIONS

Cab Inn, Kannikegade 14 (tel. 7021 6200, *www.cabinn.dk*, *aarhus@cabinn.dk*). Doubles 630 Dkr (£57; $98) with breakfast.

Get-In, Jens Baggesensvej 43 (tel. 8610 8514, *www.get-in.dk*, *get-in@get-in.dk*). Doubles and singles with own kitchen. Best value in town with doubles at 350 Dkr (£32; $54).

Sports Hotellet, Stadion Alle 70 (tel. 8614 3000, *www.aarhus-idraetspark.dk*, *info@aarhus-idraetspark.dk*). B&B from 350 Dkr (£32; $54).

PRIVATE ROOMS

Available from the Tourist Office. Around 140 Dkr (£12.50; $17.25).

HI HOSTEL

Pavillonen, Marienluindsvej 10, Risskov (tel. 8616 7298, *www.hostel-aarhus.dk*, *danhostel.aarhus@get2net.dk*). 100 Dkr (£9; $15). Open 16 Jan.–15 Dec. Dinner available. Laundry room provided. Wheelchair accessible. 1.5 km from the town centre, in the Risskov forest, about 500m from the beach. Bus 1 or 6. Signposted from the Marienlund terminus.

SLEEP-IN

Århus City Sleep-In, Havnegade 20 (tel. 8619 2055, *www.citysleep-in.dk*, *sleep-in@citysleep-in.dk*). 100 Dkr (£9; $15) p.p.; doubles 320 Dkr (£29; $47). Breakfast is available at 40 Dkr (£3.50; $6). Extra charge of 40DKr (£3.50; $6) for blanket hire.

CAMPING

Blommehaven, Ørneredevej 35, Højbjerg (tel. 8627 0207). Open mid-Apr.–mid-Sept. In the Marselisborg forest, close to the Århus bay beach. In summer take bus 19 straight to the site, otherwise take bus 6 to Horhavevej. Chalets are also available.

Århus Nord, Randersvej 400, Lisbjerg (tel. 8623 1133). A beautiful site, open all year round. Chalets available, heated swimming pool. Buses 117 and 118 run straight to the site.

Copenhagen (København)

TOURIST OFFICES

Danmarks Turistråd (Wonderful Copenhagen), Bernstorffsgade 1
(tel. 33 25 74 00, *www.woco.dk*, *woco@woco.dk*). Open
June–mid-Sept., daily 9am–8pm; mid-Sept.–Apr., Mon.–Fri.
9am–5pm, Sat. 9am–2pm; May, open daily 9am–6pm. The
office hands out a reasonable free map of the city and the
informative *Copenhagen This Week*, as well as being an excellent
source of information on the city and the country as a whole.
On the first corner of the Tivoli amusement park from the main
train station. Go left along the side of the park from the station.
USE-IT, Rådhusstrœde 13 (tel. 3373 0620, *www.useit.dk*). Open
15 June–15 Sept., daily 9am–7pm; at other times, Mon.–Fri.
11am–4pm. An office orientated towards the budget traveller,
it will find rooms in and around Copenhagen. Their free map is
superior to that of the Tourist Office. The organisation also
publishes useful guides to seeing the city on foot, by bike or by
bus, as well as an entertainment guide.

FINDING ACCOMMODATION

During the summer, hostel beds can disappear at an alarming
rate, so try to reserve ahead. If not, USE-IT (see Tourist Offices) are
your best bet. Otherwise, unless you have a tent, you will either
have to sleep rough or pay for a hotel room, neither of which is a
good option. Rest hotels are located outside the inner centre,
around Istegade on the far side of the station.

HOTELS

Ibsens, Vendersgade 23 (tel. 3313 1913, *www.ibsenshotel.dk*,
hotel@ibsenshotel.dk). B&B doubles 900 Dkr (£82; $139).

Amager, Amagerbrogade 29 (tel. 3254 4008, *www.hotel
amager.dk*). B&B in doubles starts around 790 Dkr (£72; $122).
Bus 30, 33 or 34 along Amager Boulevard to Amagerbrogade
from Rådhuspladsen.

Absalon, Helgolandsgade 15 (tel. 3324 2211). Doubles from 875
Dkr (£79; $134), including breakfast.

Cab Inn, Vodroffsvej 55 (tel. 3536 1111, *www.cabinn.dk*, *cab-inn@cab-inn.dk*). Doubles 640 Dkr (£58; $98). Bus 2.

Saga, Colbjørnsensgade 18–20 (tel. 33 84 60 33, *www.saga hotel.dk*, *booking@sagahotel.dk*). Doubles from 460 Dkr (£42; $71), including breakfast.

Sct. Thomas, Frederiksberg Allé 7 (tel. 3121 6464, *www.hotel sctthomas.dk*, *hotel@hotelsctthomas.dk*). Doubles from 500 Dkr (£45; $76), including breakfast.

Jørgensen, Rømersgade 11 (tel. 3313 8186). Doubles from around 500 Dkr (£45; $76). See the entry in the Hostels section below for directions. Popular with gay travellers.

Hotel Windsor, Frederiksborggade 30 (tel. 3311 0830, *www.hotelwindsor.dk*, *hotelwindsor@inet.uni2.dk*). Near Israel Plads, a few minutes from Nørreport S-train station. Hotel aimed at gay clientele.

Hotel du Nord, Colbjørnsensgade 14, Vesterbro (tel. 33 22 44 33, *www.hoteldunord.dk*, *reservations@hoteldunord.dk*). Doubles from 1,080 Dkr (£98; $167).

Euroglobe, Niels Ebbesens Vej 20, Frederiksberg (tel. 3379 7954, *www.euroglobe.aok.dk*, *discount@hoteleuroglobe.dk*). Doubles from 500 Dkr (£45; $76).

Bethel, Nyhavn 22, (tel. 3313 0370). Doubles from 510 Dkr (£46; $78).

PRIVATE ROOMS

Tourist Information, Bernstorffsgade 1 (tel. 33 24 75 00). Rooms found for a 40 Dkr (£3.50; $6) commission. Prices start around 210 Dkr (£19; $32). Personal callers only.

USE-IT (see Tourist Offices). No commission, and often capable of undercutting the prices of rooms from the tourist office. Highly recommended.

Also see *www.bedandbreakfast.dk* for further listings and booking facilities.

HI HOSTELS

Bellahøj, Herbergvejen 8 (tel. 3828 9715, *bellahoej@dan hostel.dk*). 100 Dkr (£9; $15) in 4- to 6-bed dorms. Breakfast available at 40 Dkr (£3.50; $6). Wheelchair accessible. 5 km from the town centre. From the station or from Rådhusplein take bus 2 or nightbus 902. Get off at Fuglsang Allé. Family rooms.

Amager, Vejlands Allé 200 (tel. 3252 2908, *www.copenhagen youthhostel.dk*, *copenhagen@danhostel.dk*). Double rooms or 5-bed dorms. Sheets hire 40 Dkr (£3.50; $6). Breakfast available at 40 Dkr (£3.50; $6). Laundry and storage rooms provided. Wheelchair accessible. Mon.–Fri. bus 46 from Central station (9am–5pm), or bus 37 from Holmens Bro. S-train B, C, H, or L to Valby station (S-trains free with railpasses) to join bus 37 saves a bit of time and money. Family rooms.

Lyngby Vandrerhjem, Rådvad 1 (tel. 4580 3074, *lyngby@ danhostel.dk*). 100 Dkr (£9; $15). Far out, and not easy to get to. Fine if you are stuck for a first night. S-train A, B or L to Lyngby. From there, bus 182 or 183 to Lundtoftvej and Hjorte-kœrsvej. The 3 km walk to Rådvad is marked. Bus 187 provides a direct link between the central station and the hostel, but only runs four times a day. The only HI hostel with a curfew, 11pm.

HOSTELS

City Public Hostel, Absalonsgade 8 (tel. 3131 2070, *www.city-public-hostel.dk*, *info@city-public-hostel.dk*). 130 Dkr (£12; $20) a bed, 150 Dkr (£13; $21) with breakfast, where you can eat as much as you like. Open 5 May–31 Aug. No curfew and round-the-clock reception. More expensive than the HI hostels but central location. In the Vesterbro Ungdomsgård. From the train station walk left along Vesterbrogade to Vesterbros Torv. Absalonsgade is off Svendsgade on the left of the square.

KFUM/KFUK (YMCA/YWCA) Interpoint, Valdermarsgade 15 (tel. 3131 1574). Open 28 June–9 Aug. Dorm beds from around 70 DKr (£6.50; $11). Outside the centre.

Hostel Jørgensen, Rømersgade 11 (tel. 3313 8186). 120 Dkr (£11; $19). June–Aug. the hotel operates a mixed dorm in its basement. From the Nørreport S-train station Vendersgade and Frederiksborggade lead into Rømersgade.

SLEEP-INS

Sleep-in Heaven, Struenseegade 7 (tel. 3535 4648, *www.sleepin heaven.com*, *morefun@sleepinheaven.com*). Open all year for

16–35 year olds. 110 Dkr (£10; $17). Includes shower and breakfast.

Sleep-in Green, Ravnsborggade 18 (tel. 3537 7777, *www.sleep-in-green.dk*). Dorms 95 Dkr (£8.50; $14.50). Open all year.

Copenhagen Sleep-In, Blegdamsvej 132 (tel. 3526 5059, *www.sleep-in.dk, copenhagen@sleep-in.dk*). Open 1 July–31 Aug. 90 Dkr (£8; $13.50).

CAMPING

There is a total of seven sites around Copenhagen. Expect to pay around 70 Dkr (£6.50; $11) per person, tent included, at the following sites:

Strandmøllen, Strandmøllevej 2 (tel. 4550 5510). Open mid-May–Sept. About 14.5 km out, but only 20 minutes on S-train C dir. Klampenborg.

Absalon, Korsdalsvej 132 (tel. 3641 0600, *www.camping-absalon.dk, absalon@dcu.dk*). Open year round. About 8 km out of town. S-train B or L to Brøndbyøster, then a kilometre's walk. Ask locals for directions.

Bellahøj, Hvidkildevej 66 (tel. 3810 1150). Open 1 June–31 Aug. Same buses as for the Bellahøj HI hostel, but get off at the stop after Hulgårdsvej.

Naerum Camping, Ravensbakken (tel. 4580 1957, *www.camping naerum.dk, naerum@dcu.dk*). Train to Jœgersborg then train to Naerum.

FINLAND (Suomi) (00)358

At 338,000 sq. kilometres, Finland is big. It's the seventh largest European country in area and has an amazing 187,888 lakes and 179,584 islands. A third of the country is north of the Arctic Circle. But despite its proximity to Santa Claus territory (a Finnish football club goes by the name of Santa Claus FC), the country is surprisingly green, with over 70% of the total land area being forested. The vast aquatic network of lakes, rivers and canals makes it a very beautiful place to visit.

Finland is notorious for its darkness – anything up to 22 hours a day during the winter. But during the perpetual daylight of summer, the Finns are in their element. Their mood perks up and they may even take pity on visitors struggling with the language – a descendant of Hungarian which has obviously been influenced by the Scandinavian tendency of creating more tenses than one could ever understand, let alone use.

ACCOMMODATION DETAILS

Finland is cheaper than its Scandinavian counterparts, but you will still have to shop around for cheap food and lodgings. You can start by taking note of my suggested accommodation below.

Unless you are desperate you will want to avoid staying in hotels in Finland, as even the cheapest ones charge around €30 (£20) for singles, €40 (£27) for doubles. In the main tourist destinations, you can expect to pay closer to €50 (£33) for the cheapest doubles in town.

B&B accommodation is a cheaper option than hotels, with overnight prices generally in the €25–35 (£16.50–23) range. A substantial breakfast and use of a sauna are usually included. Unfortunately B&B accommodation is nowhere near as widespread as hotel accommodation and is available mainly in the north of the country, particularly on farms.

Hostelling is an excellent way to see Finland, especially if you are travelling outside the peak season of mid-July to mid-August. There are **HI hostels** scattered around the country, with at least one operating in all the main tourist destinations during the summer. Finnish hostels are classified from one up to four stars. Prices in two-star hostels are around €15 (£10), depending on whether you stay in a dorm or a small room. Most common in the larger towns are three-star hostels, which charge around €17 (£11.50) per night in 2- to 8-bed rooms. Prices in the four-star hostels (known as *Finnhostels*) start at €18 (£12), rising to around €30 (£20). The largest rooms in four-star hostels are quads.

Only in the most expensive hostels are HI cards obligatory, but they do entitle you to a €3 (£2) discount. Hiring sheets and towels will cost about an extra €3 (£2), so come well prepared and save your money. Only from June to August, and particularly from mid-July to mid-August, will you experience any difficulty in getting a hostel bed. At this time, hostels in the large cities and in areas popular with hikers are often full, making it imperative to reserve ahead, by email or by telephone. Reservations are held until 6pm, unless you make it clear that you will be arriving later.

In contrast to other Scandinavian countries, Finland has seen little growth in the number of **independent hostels**. Converted student dorms, known as *Summerhotels,* are generally clean and modern. Accommodation is in singles or doubles: around €30 (£20) is the normal price for singles; around €20 (£13.30) per person the usual price for doubles.

There are over 350 well-equipped official **campsites**, graded from one to three stars, covering all the main tourist areas. Prices vary from €4 (£2.70) upwards, according to the classification of the site. If you are not in possession of an International Camping Carnet, you will have to buy a Finnish camping pass at the first site you visit. Few sites remain open all year round. Most open for the period May–June to August–September only. Many of the sites in and around the larger towns are very big, with a tent capacity of 2,000. During July and August, these sites become very busy at weekends. Some sites let cottages (usually without bedding) for two to five people – well worth enquiring about if there are several people prepared to share. Cottages are available for anything from €30 (£20) per day.

It is possible to **sleep rough** in Finland and stay within the law. More advisably, you can take advantage of an old law which allows you to camp anywhere as long as you have the landowner's permission. It is normal practice to camp out of sight of private homes.

ADDRESSES

FINNISH TOURIST BOARD
30/35 Pall Mall, London SW1V 5LP (tel. 020 7839 4048, *www.finland-tourism.com*). Lists of hotels, hostels and campsites.

FINNISH YHA
Suomen Retkeilymajajärjestö-SRM ry, Yrjönkatu 38 B 15, 00100 Helsinki (tel. (0)9 565 7150, *www.srmnet.org*, *info@srm.inet.fi*).

CAMPING
See *www.camping.fi* for full listings and searchable database.

Helsinki (Helsingfors) (0)9

TOURIST OFFICES

Kaupungin Matkailutoimisto, Pohjoisesplanadi 19 (tel. 169 3757, *www.hel.fi/tourism*, *tourist.info@hel.fi*). Open mid-May–mid-Sept., Mon.–Fri. 9am–7pm, Sat. 9am–3pm; at other times, Mon.–Fri. 9am–5pm, Sat. 9am–3pm. A 10-minute walk from the train station left down Mannerheimintie, then left again along Pohjoisesplanadi.

Hotellikeskus, train station (tel. 171133). Open in summer, Mon–Fri. 9am–9pm, Sat. 9am–7pm, Sun. 10am–6pm; at other times, Mon.–Fri. 9am–6pm. Dispenses city maps and hotel/hostel lists, but first and foremost the office is an excellent accommodation service with prices sometimes lower than going direct. A few minutes' walk from the train station in the direction of the post office.

HOTELS

CHEAPEST DOUBLES AROUND €40–60 (£27–40)
Kongressikoti, Snellmaninkatu 15A (tel. 135 6839). Doubles around €50 (£33).

Arthur, Vuorikatu 19B (tel. 173441, *www.hotelarthur.fi*, *reception @hotelarthur.fi*). Rooms from €71 (£47).

Magarita, Itäinen Teatterikuja 3 (tel. 622 4261). Doubles from €50 (£33). Close to the train station.

Omapohja, Itäinen Teatterikuja 3 (tel. 666211). Doubles from €60 (£40). Downstairs from Clairet.

Lönnrot, Lönnrotinkatu 16 (tel. 693 2590). Close to the city's Old Church.

Hotel Finn, Kalevankatu 3B (tel. 684 4360, *www.hotellifinn.fi*, *hotellifinn@kolumbus.fi*). Doubles from €58 (£39) at the weekends.

Ava, Karstulantie 6 (tel. 774751, *www.hotelli-ava.fi*, *varaukset@ hotelli-ava.fi*). Doubles from €40 (£27) at the weekend.

Fenno, Franzeninkatu 26 (tel. 774 980, *www.hotelfenno.fi*). Doubles from €75 (£50).

HI HOSTELS

Stadion Hostel, Pohjoinen Stadiontie 3B (tel. 477 8480, *www.stadionhostel.com*, *stadion@hostel.inet.fi*). Prices start at €14.50 (£9.50) in small dorms, rising to €19.50 (£13) per person in doubles. Curfew 2am. Tram 3T or 7A to the Olympic Stadium, or a 25-minute walk. Open all year.

Satakunta Hostel, Lapinrinne 1A (tel. 695 85231, *ravintola. satakunta@sodexho.fi*). €20 (£13.30) for singles, €40 (£27) for doubles, €15 (£10) for dorms. Ask about student discounts (20–50%). Student accommodation converted into a temporary four-star hostel. Open 1 June–31 Aug. A 10-minute walk from the train station. Tram 4 stops nearby.

Eurohostel, Linnankatu 9 (tel. 622 0470, *www.eurohostel.fi*, *eurohostel@eurohostel.fi*). Singles €36.50 (£24.50), doubles €22 (£14.50) p.p., €22 (£14.50) for dorms, all with sauna included. Close to the harbour and a 20-minute walk from the train station. Tram 4 stops nearby. Open all year.

Finnhostel Academica, Hietaniemenkatu 14 (tel. 1311 4334, *www. hostelacademica.fi*, *hostel.academica@hyy.fi*). Doubles from €59 (£39.50), dorm beds from €16 (£10.50), all with sauna access. Ask about student reductions. Student accommodation converted into a temporary hostel. Open 1 June–1 Sept. Bus 18 or tram 3T run to the hostel. A 10-minute walk from the train station.

Erottajanpuisto, Uudenmaankatu 9 (tel. 642169, *www.erotta janpuisto.com*, *info@errotajanpuisto.com*). Singles €44 (£29), doubles €58 (£39), dorms €22 (£14.50). Open 24 hours. Breakfast available, family rooms and self-catering facilities. Take tram 10 from city centre. Open all year.

HOSTEL
YMCA Interpoint, Vuorikato 17 (tel. 173441). Open 12 July–20 Aug. Ring ahead to check that the hostel is open.

CAMPING
Rastila (tel. 316551, in winter 314428). Open mid-May–mid-Sept. Prices at this municipal site start at €12 (£8) p.p. (tent included). Also lets cabins. About 6.5 km from the city centre. Take the metro to Itäkeskus, then bus 90, 90A or 96.

Rovaniemi (0)16

TOURIST OFFICE
Rovakatu 21 (tel. 346270, *www.rovaniemi.fi*, *travel.info@ rovaniemi.fi*). Open June–Aug., Mon.–Fri. 8am–7pm, weekends, 9am–6pm; rest of the year, Mon.–Fri. 8am–4pm. A short walk from the bus and train stations. Turn left from the bus station, right from the train station, on to Ratakatu, which leads into Hallituskatu. Turn left along Valtakatu and continue until you see the Tourist Office. There is also a tourist counter at the station.

HOTELS
Matka Borealis, Asemieskatu 1 (tel. 342 0130, *matkaborealis. rovaniemi@co.inet.fi*). Doubles from €52 (£35). Near the station, 0.5 km from town centre.

Outa, Ukkoherrantie 16 (tel. 312474). A small guest house in the centre of town.

Aakenus, Koskikatu 47 (tel. 342 2051, *aakenus@co.inet.fi*). Doubles from €50 (£33).

Sky Hotel, Ounasvaarantie (tel. 335 3311, skyhotel@lapland hotels.com). Doubles from €70 (£47).

Hotelli Oppipioka, Korkalonkatu 33 (tel. 338 8111, hotel.oppi poika@ramk.fi). Doubles from €80 (£54) (cheaper at weekends).

HI HOSTELS

Retkeilymaja Tervashonka, Hallituskatu 16 (tel. 344644). Dorms for €17 (£11), doubles for €30 (£20). Three-star hostel. For directions, see Tourist Office.

CAMPING

Ounasjoki, Jäämerentie 1 (tel. 345304). Open 1 June–31 Aug. The site is just over the river from the centre of town.

FRANCE (00)33

The largest country in Western Europe is France, a nation rich in culture, cuisine, fine wines, architecture and history so absorbing and so diverse it is virtually impossible to experience it all in just one visit. The advent of the Channel Tunnel and the country's superb road and rail networks make travelling long distances easy and fast. Generally, if time is limited it is better to concentrate on just one or two regions and experience these in depth. However, even the briefest visit will be rewarding – it is an easy country to fall in love with.

BACKGROUND

The revolution of 1789 and the advent of Robespierre and Madame La Guillotine ended the French nation's zenith as dictator on all matters stylish and cultural.

After the revolution, a series of unsuccessful attempts to establish a lasting republic failed – the first ended up as a dictatorship, as did the second. The third attempt was quelled by the Germans in 1940, which in turn led to the establishment of the fourth after the liberation. This one was dogged by imperial strife in Indochina and Algeria, however, and it was left to de Gaulle to get the fifth off the ground in 1958. The Fifth Republic remains to this day.

ACCOMMODATION DETAILS

Budget travellers should have little difficulty in finding a cheap place to stay in France. There is probably a wider range of good options here than anywhere else in Europe. Even in Paris there are plenty of cheap places to stay. For most of the year, you should be able to find a cheap bed on arrival anywhere outside the capital, unless there is a special event on in the town (such as the Festival d'Avignon). However, it is best to try to reserve hotels ahead in July and August when the French themselves are on holiday. In Paris, hotel reservations are a good idea at any time of year, but especially from Easter to late September, when the city is buzzing with visitors. Youth hostels in Paris should be reserved in advance where possible (around 3–4 months ahead if you are planning a visit in summer), while the two youth hostel associations advise advance reservations of hostels in popular tourist destinations between May and September.

In contrast to other countries, two people can easily stay every night in a hotel without worrying unduly about their budgets as hotel prices are very low (Parisian hotels are ridiculously cheap when compared to London). French custom is to set a price for a room, which means that the charge is the same whether it is occupied by one or two people. In practice, some hoteliers will let rooms to solo travellers at a reduced rate (typically 70–75% of the cost), but often only outside the peak season when trade is beginning to tail off. A third bed normally adds about 30% to the cost of a room.

One-star hotels will be of primary interest to budget travellers, though it is worth noting that many unclassified hotels, particularly in rural areas, offer perfectly adequate standards of accommodation. One-star hotels seldom offer more than the basic comforts, but they represent good value for what you pay. The cheaper two-star establishments are also within the range of the budget traveller. Despite the fact that these are described by the Ministry of Tourism as merely 'comfortable', you will probably find them a bit luxurious when compared to similarly priced accommodation in other West European countries. The cheapest one-star hotels charge around €20–30 (£13.30–20), except in Paris where you will do well to find a room for under €30 (£20). Prices for two-star hotels start at around €30 (£20) outside Paris, around €35 (£23) in the capital.

Although hotel rooms are cheap and good value for money, on the whole hotel breakfasts are not. You can expect to pay €6–8 (£4–5.30) for a basic continental breakfast: very poor value for money when you consider what that amount might buy at the supermarket or baker's, or even in a local café. Legally, hoteliers have no right to insist that you take breakfast (or any other meal), but in practice there are always a few who will try at the height of the season. While you have the right to refuse breakfast, they have the right to refuse your custom. Another charge may be for taking a shower or a bath. You will normally be asked to pay €2–3 (£1.30–2) to use the bath or shower when these are not included in the overnight price. Another budget option (although only really worth it if travelling by car) are the motels run by the Formule 1 chain. These are rather impersonal establishments usually found on the outskirts of towns and operate as a do-it-yourself check-in. Using a credit card you let yourself into a room, night or day, and from as little as €25 (£16.50).

Throughout the provincial towns there are over 5,000 family-run hotels and inns belonging to an organisation known as Logis de France, easily identifiable by their distinctive green-and-yellow emblem. These establishments have generally taken advantage of government grants and now provide guaranteed standards of service, mainly in one- or two-star accommodation, though a number of unclassified *auberges* are also included. See their website (listed below) for further details.

Bed and Breakfast accommodation is found mainly in the countryside, though there are some B&B possibilities in a few of the larger cities. Rural *chambres d'hôtes* (B&B in private homes) are generally similar in price to cheap hotels, but probably offer even better value for money. Another alternative to hotel accommodation open to the budget traveller is to rent self-catering accommodation. Again, this is an option far more prevalent in rural France, most conspicuously in the form of Gîtes de France: self-catering accommodation let by an association of French families. Sleeping between four and six people, they can usually be rented for €200–300 (£134–200) per week. The *gîtes* are normally located in and around small villages, and may be village houses, rural or farm cottages, or flats in private homes. Over 2,500 *gîtes* can be booked through the offices of Gîtes de France Ltd in London. For a small annual membership fee you receive an illustrated guide to all the properties, free use of the reservation service and discounts on ferry routes across the Channel if you are travelling by car or motorbike. Another form of accommodation available to the budget traveller are *cafés couettes* – literally 'coffee and quilts'. Essentially these are bed and breakfast establishments found in and around towns, as well as remote countryside areas and seaside resorts. A list of these can be obtained from the Tourist Office, or through the offical French Tourist Office website (see below).

There are two **youth hostel** associations in France: the

HI-affiliated Fédération Unie des Auberges de la Jeunesse (FUAJ), and the Ligue Française pour les Auberges de la Jeunesse (LFAJ). Relations between the two are strained, to say the least. The HI handbook lists the FUAJ hostels, but only a few of the LFAJ establishments. It is worthwhile finding out about the LFAJ hostels, as they fill in many of the gaps in the FUAJ network, so that there are not many places of major interest that lack a hostel (contact the associations' head offices, or see their websites for up-to-date hostel lists).

Most hostels stay open all year round, except perhaps for a few weeks in winter. Hostelling can certainly be a cheap way to see the country at virtually any time of year, provided you take the trouble to reserve well ahead for hostels in the more popular tourist towns. The drawbacks are the poor quality of some of the hostels, and the curfews. Even the top-rated hostels vary enormously in quality. While some are well maintained and efficiently run, at the other extreme are those in dilapidated buildings, where the warden only appears at certain times and is not on the premises at night. In the very worst of this latter type, you may well have reason to worry about your personal safety. Curfews are normally 11pm at the latest.

Generally, hostel prices vary according to the grade of establishment. Prices can be as low as €7.35 (£4.90), but are normally around €8.85–12.70 (£5.90–8.50). However, in popular tourist destinations such as Paris, Strasbourg, Avignon and Bayeux even low-grade hostels may charge well above the normal hostel price. In these towns, expect to pay around €15 (£10) in the hostels of either association. The HI card permits entry to both FUAJ and LFAJ hostels. Technically, the HI card is obligatory at FUAJ hostels, but non-members are normally allowed to stay on the payment of a €2.50 (£1.70) supplement per night, or are restricted to a one-night stay.

In some of the larger towns, a further possibility available to HI members and students are the Foyers des Jeunes Travailleurs/Travailleuses. These are residential hostels, which provide cheap living accommodation for young workers and students. As such, they tend to offer a higher standard of accommodation than hostels (mainly singles and doubles). Prices are usually on a par with local hostels, but you get better value for money. It is worth enquiring about *foyers* at any time of year, but your chances of finding a place are obviously better during the student vacations.

Gîtes d'étapes (not to be confused with Gîtes de France) are widespread in rural areas, particularly those popular with hikers and cyclists. They provide basic, cheap accommodation; normally bunk-beds in dorms, and simple cooking and washing facilities. The LFAJ maintains 11 *gîtes d'étapes* in the Aveyron-Le Lot region, and another 27 in Corsica (details are included in the LFAJ hostel list). These are ideal for cycling or walking tours in two of the most beautiful areas of the country. Overnight fees range from about €10–15 (£6.70–10). If you are heading into the mountains, there is a plentiful supply of mountain huts, the majority of which are operated by the Club Alpin Français (CAF). Huts are open to non-members, but members of the CAF and its associated clubs receive a reduction on the usual overnight charge of €8 (£5.30).

Camping is very popular in France. Practically every town of any size has a campsite. There are over 7,000 in all, rated from one to four stars. The overnight fee varies from €3 to €6 (£2–4) per person, depending on the classification. Usually, the cheapest will be a site run by the local authority (*camping municipal*). Charges are normally around €5 (£3.30) per night. Outside the main season there may not even be an attendant to collect the fees. These sites are clean and well maintained, and lack only the shopping and leisure facilities of higher-graded sites.

With a few exceptions, camping is a cheap, convenient and pleasant way to see France. There is no centrally located site in Lyon, so you will have to travel to one of the sites on the outskirts. The only site in Nice is pitifully small and far from the centre. Along the Mediterranean, many sites become ridiculously over-crowded during the summer months; so much so that 11 regional information posts, 21 telephone information centres and 59 local reception centres have been established to deal with the problem. See listings below for contacts, or visit the tourist information websites. Try to reserve coastal sites in advance.

In rural areas, many farms are part of a scheme which allows you to camp on the farm (*camping à la ferme*). Facilities are very basic, yet prices are similar to those of other campsites. Many farmers will allow you to camp on their land free of charge, provided you ask their permission first. If you pitch your tent without their consent, expect a hostile confrontation.

Sleeping rough is legal and the weather will seldom cause you any problems, except in the north outside the summer months. However, sleeping rough is not advisable, especially in the cities, or along the beaches of the Mediterranean. Petty criminals realised the easy pickings to be had from those sleeping in and around stations a long time ago (Paris and Marseilles are particularly unsafe). The beaches are 'worked' by gangs who steal for a living. If you are stuck for a place to stay, some stations have emergency lodgings. Ask for the Accueil en Gare. Failing this, you would be better to take an overnight train.

If you are going to sleep rough, leave your pack at the station, and try to bed down beside other travellers. If you are attacked, hand over your money. Thieves have been known to become violent if their victims try to resist. If you have been sensible and have taken out travel insurance you will incur only a small loss, which is preferable to risking serious injury.

ADDRESSES

FRENCH GOVERNMENT TOURIST OFFICE
178 Piccadilly, London W1V 0AL (tel. 09068 244 123 for premium-rate enquiries, or visit *www.franceguide.com*, *info@mdlf.co.uk*).

HOTELS
Visit *www.logis-de-france.fr*. The website also allows you to search their database and book either online or by calling (0033) (0)1 4584 8384.

GÎTES DE FRANCE
Gîtes de France Ltd, 178 Piccadilly, London W1V 9DB (*www.gites-de-france.fr*). Use their website to book accommodation throughout the country, and you can also purchase their publications online.

YOUTH HOSTELS
Fédération Unie des Auberges de la Jeunesse, rue Pajol 27, 75018 Paris (tel. 0(1) 44 89 87 27, *www.fuaj.org*, *centre-national@fuaj.org*).

Ligue Française pour les Auberges de la Jeunesse, 67 Rue Vergniaud, bat. K, 75013 Paris (tel. (0)1 44 16 78 78, *www.auberges-de-jeunesse.com*, *info@auberges-de-jeunesse.com*).

STUDENT ACCOMMODATION

CROUS, 39 av. G-Bernadou, Paris (tel. (0)1 40 51 05 55, *www.crous-paris.fr*, *dad@crous-paris.fr*).

CAMPING

www.campingfrance.com allows you to search its database of over 1,000 campsites by both criteria and region.

OTHER ACCOMMODATION

You can look for and book private rooms all over France at *www.hotes-en-france.com*, or *www.bed-breakfast-france.com*. For *camping à la ferme* you should visit *www.bienvenue-a-la-ferme.com* (French only) to find a room on a farm. Failing that, write to l'APCA, 9 Avenue George V, 75008 Paris.

Bordeaux (0)5

TOURIST OFFICES

Office du Tourisme Bordeaux Centre, cours du XXX Juillet 12 (tel. 56 00 66 00, *www.bordeaux-tourisme.com*, *otb@bordeaux-tourisme.com*). Open June–Sept., Mon.–Sat. 9am–9pm, Sun. 9am–7pm; at other times, Mon.–Sun. 9am–7pm. Accueil de France service. Next to the Opéra.

Office du Tourisme Bordeaux Gare St Jean (tel. 56 91 64 70). Open June–Sept., daily 9am–7pm; at other times, Mon.–Sat. 9am–7pm, Sun. 10am–7pm.

BASIC DIRECTIONS

Bordeaux St-Jean is about 5 km from the town centre. CGFTE buses link the station to various points in the city centre. Maps of the network are available from the Tourist Office. If you want to walk, the simplest route (not the shortest, but the safest) is to follow cours de la Marne from the station to pl. de la Victoire. Then you can walk right along rue Sainte-Catherine into the heart of the city, across cours Victor Hugo, cours d'Alsace et Lorraine and rue de la Porte Dijeaux/rue St-Rémi. Then continue on to the Opéra and the beginning of cours du XXX Juillet. Going along cours du XXX Juillet you will arrive at the Girondins monument on Esplanade des Quinconces.

HOTELS

ROOMS AROUND €23–40 (£15.50–27).

Many of these can be booked through the tourist information website listed above.

De la Boëtie, rue de la Boëtie 4 (tel. 56 81 76 68). Go left from the Forte Dijeaux at the end of rue de la Forte Dijeaux.

D'Amboise, rue de la Vieille Tour 22 (tel. 56 81 62 67). Unclassified hotel, slightly cheaper than the other hotels listed.

Studio, Huguerie 26 (tel. 56 48 00 14, *studio@hotel-bordeaux. com*). Rooms have shower and TV.

Touring, rue Huguerie 16 (tel. 56 81 56 73).

Le Blayais, rue Mautrec 17 (tel. 56 48 17 87). Near Notre-Dame. From the Opéra, take allées de Tourny, then left.

Dauphin, rue du Palais-Gallien 82 (tel. 56 52 24 62). From the Opéra follow allées de Tourny into pl. Tourny, then take rue Huguerie.

De Famille, cours Georges-Clemenceau 76 (tel. 56 52 11 28). From the Opéra, walk along allées de Tourny, then go left from pl. Tourny.

Du Parc, rue de la Verrerie 10 (tel. 56 52 78 20). By the Jardin Public, on the fringe of the town centre. From the Girondins monument follow cours de Maréchal Foch, turn right at cours de Verdun, right again at cours Xavier Arnozan, then left.

Saint-François, rue de Mirail 22 (tel. 56 91 56 41). Rue de Mirail faces the beautiful Grosse Cloche, on cours Victor Hugo heading down towards the river.

Lafaurie, rue Lafaurie-de-Monbadon 35 (tel. 56 48 16 33). The street crosses rue Huguerie (see the Dauphin, above, for directions).

HOSTELS

Cours Barbey 22 (FUAJ) (tel. 56 91 59 51). €16 (£10.50) p.p. Breakfast available at €3 (£2) p.p. Turn right on leaving the station, left up cours de la Marne, then fourth on the left. 11pm curfew.

CAMPING

There is no really convenient site. Two sites within reach of town are:

Les Gravières, Pont-de-la-Maye, Villeneuve d'Ornon, Courrejean (tel. 56 87 00 36). Open all year round. From the bus station on quai Richelieu by the river take bus B to the end of the line (30-minute trip), then a couple of minutes' walk (800m). €4 (£2.70) per person; €5 (£3.30) per tent.

Beausoleil, cours Général-de-Gaulle 371 (tel. 56 89 17 66). From the bus station on quai Richelieu take bus G to the end of the line (45-minute trip). €10 (£6.70) for two people with tent.

Chamonix Mont-Blanc (0)4

TOURIST OFFICE

Office du Tourisme, pl. du Triangle de l'Amitié (tel. 50 53 00 24, *www.chamonix.com*, *info@chamonix.com*). Open daily July–Aug., 8.30am–7.30pm; Sept.–June, 8.30am–12.30pm and 2–7pm. Reserves rooms free of charge (tel. 50 53 23 33) or send them an email. Accueil de France service not available. About 500m from the train station. Down av. Michel Croz, then round to the left of the town hall.

ACCOMMODATION IN CHAMONIX

As it can be very difficult to find accommodation on arrival, try to reserve ahead. If you have not done so you may have to stay outside Chamonix in one of the towns nearby. Those with a railpass will have no problem getting to accommodation outside Chamonix as most of the towns along the valley are served by SNCF (this includes all those mentioned below, unless stated otherwise).

HOTELS

CHEAPEST DOUBLES €40–60 (£27–40)

Valaisanne, av. Ravanel le Rouge 454 (tel. 50 53 17 98).

Chaumière, route de Gaillands 322 (tel. 50 53 13 25, *chaumiere@ chamonix.com*).

Carrier, rue Charlet Straton 242 (tel. 50 54 02 16). In Argentière.

Hotel des Randonneurs, route du Plagnolet 39, Argentière (tel. 50 54 02 80, *les.randonneurs@libertysurf.fr*).

Gorges de la Diosaz (tel. 50 47 20 97, *www.hoteldesgorges.com*). In Servoz.

Cîmes Blanches (tel. 50 47 20 05). In Servoz.

CHEAPEST DOUBLES €60–80 (£40–54)

Aiguille Verte, rue Joseph Vallot 683 (tel. 50 53 01 73).

Stade, rue Whymper 19 (tel. 50 53 05 44).

Etoile des Neiges, Les Houches 74310 (tel. 5054 4059, *www. etoile-des-neiges.fr*, *etoiledesneiges@wanadoo.fr*). About 5km from Chamonix.

Arve, impasse des Anémones 60 (tel. 50 53 02 31).

Boule de Neige, rue Joseph Vallot 362 (tel. 50 53 04 48, *postmaster@hotel-labouledeneige.fr*).

Lion d'Or, rue du Docteur Paccard 255 (tel. 50 53 15 09).

La Prairie, chemin du Lavoussé (tel. 50 53 19 96). In Les Praz. No SNCF station in Les Praz, but the Les Bois station is a 10- to 15-minute walk away.

El Paso, impasse des Rhododendrons 37 (tel. 50 53 64 20, *www.cantina.fr*, *cantina@cantina.fr*).

La Valaisanne, 454 avenue Ravanel-le-Rouge (tel. 50 53 17 98).

HI HOSTEL

Montée J. Balmat 127 (FUAJ), Les Pèlerins (tel. 50 53 14 52, *chamonix@fuaj.org*). Dorms from €12.70 (£8.50). Laundry room on premises. A 30-minute walk from Chamonix. Nearest train station Les Pèlerins. The hostel is about 1km uphill from the station. Alternatively, take the bus dir. Les Houches from pl. de l'Église in Chamonix to the school (*école*) in Les Pèlerins. Wheelchair accessible. Family rooms. Open 1 Dec.–15 Oct.

DORMITORY ACCOMMODATION

Cheap accommodation is provided in several refuges, *gîtes d'étapes* and chalets in and around Chamonix:

Ski Station, route des Moussoux 6 (tel. 50 53 20 25). Bed only around €10 (£6.70). Up the hill from the Tourist Office. Closed from May to June and Sept. to Dec.

Gîte la Tapia, route de la Frasse 152 (tel. 50 53 18 19, *contact@latapia.com*). €14 (£9.50) p.p. Breakfast available. Closed September to 1 December.

Gîtes le Vagabond, av. Ravenel le Rouge 365 (tel. 30 53 15 43, *www.gitevagabond.com*, *gitevagabond@hotmail.com*). €12.50 (£8.40) p.p., breakfast available. Bar and restaurant facilities.

Chalet Glacier du Mont-Blanc, 224 Route des Tissieres, Les Bossons (tel. 50 53 35 84, *glaciermtblanc@imedserv.com*). Beds €19 (£12.50), doubles €45 (£30). Breakfast €5 (£3.30).

Le Chamoniard Volant, route de la Frasse 45 (tel. 50 53 14 09, *www.chamoniard.com*, *mail@chamoniard.com*). Beds €12 (£8), breakfast €4.30 (£2.90), half-board €16.30 (£10.90).

Le Belvedère, route du Plagnolet 501, Argentière (tel. 50 54 02 59, *www.gitebelvedere.com*). Beds around €12 (£8), breakfast €4.60 (£3), half-board around €27 (£18).

CAMPING

Three sites are located about 10 to 15 minutes' walk from the centre of town, just off the road to Les Pèlerins (a full list of the 18 sites in the area is available from the Tourist Office):

Les Arolles, chemin du Cry-Chamonix 281 (tel. 50 53 14 30). Open 25 June–30 Sept. 100 places. 15 minutes' walk from the station.

L'Île des Barrats (tel. 50 53 51 44). Open 1 June–30 Sept., 150 places.

Les Moliasses (tel. 50 53 16 81). Open 1 June–15 Sept. A 15-minute walk from the town centre.

Lyon (0)4

TOURIST OFFICES

Office du Tourisme/Bureau des Congrès de Lyon/Communauté, pl. Bellecour (tel. 72 77 69 69, *www.lyon-france.com*). The Tourist Board operates several tourist information offices throughout the city: Pavilion du Tourisme, pl. Bellecour. Open mid-June–mid-Sept., Mon.–Fri. 9am–7pm, Sat. 9am–6pm, Sun. 10am–6pm; at other times of year, the office closes one hour earlier each day. Accueil de France service available. Métro: Bellecour, or 10 minutes' walk along rue Victor Hugo from Lyon-Perrache train station.

Bureau d'Information Perrache. In the Centre d'Écharges de Perrache, in front of Lyon-Perrache. Open Mon.–Fri. 9am–12.30pm and 2–6pm, Sat. 9am–5pm.

Fourvière. Open, in peak season, daily 9am–12.30pm and 2–6pm.

FINDING ACCOMMODATION

Finding suitable accommodation in Lyon should be relatively easy. Many of the cheapest hotels are in the area around Lyon-Perrache train station. In contrast, the hotels around the Part-Dieu train station are relatively expensive. If you arrive at Part-Dieu, there are frequent connections to Lyon-Perrache by mainline train, while the two stations are also linked by the city's métro. If for any reason you cannot find a bed, head for the Accueil en Gare, located in the covered walkway linking Lyon-Perrache train station to the Centre Perrache.

HOTELS

CHEAPEST ROOMS AROUND €30–35 (£20–23)

Vichy, rue de la Charité 60 bis (tel. 78 37 42 58). Perrache district.

Vaubecour, rue Vaubecour 28 (tel. 78 37 44 91). Perrache.

Le Beaujolais, rue d'Enghien 22 (tel. 78 37 39 15). Perrache district.

Des Facultés, rue Sébastien-Gryphe 104 (tel. 78 72 22 65). Préfecture-Guillotière.

Avy, 6 rue d'Auvergne (tel. 78 92 80 63, *djipezed@aol.com*).

CHEAPEST ROOMS AROUND €35–45 (£23–30)

D'Ainay, rue des Remparts d'Ainay 14 (tel. 78 42 43 42, *hotel.ainay@online.france*). Perrache. Closed 1–15 August.

Alexandra, rue Victor-Hugo 49 (tel. 78 37 75 79). Perrache.

Victoria, rue Delandine 3 (tel. 7837 5761, *www.hotelvictoria lyon.com, contact@hotelvictorialyon.com*). Perrache.

Villages Hotel Espace, 93 Cours Gambetta (78 62 77 72, *www.villages-hotel.com*).

Le Terme, rue Sainte-Cathérine 7 (tel. 78 28 30 45). Terreaux.

Hotel de Bretagne, 10 rue Dubois (tel. 78 37 79 33).

La Loire, cours de Verdun 19 (tel. 78 37 44 29). Perrache. Closed 1–15 Aug.

Touring, cours de Verdun 37 (tel. 78 37 39 03). Perrache.

Hotel le Lys Bleu, 60 rue de la Charite (tel. 78 37 42 58). Closed in August.

BED AND BREAKFAST
You should contact the tourist information office for details of bed and breakfasts available in Lyon, or visit *www.bed-breakfast-france.com*.

HI HOSTELS
Lyon-Venissieux (FUAJ), rue Roger Salengro 51 (tel. 78 76 39 23, *lyonsud@fuaj.org*). €10 (£6.70) for HI members, €2.50 (£1.70) supplement for non-members. Kitchen facilities and laundry room on premises. About 4 km from the centre. From Perrache, before 9pm, take the métro to Bellecour then bus 53 to av. Georges Levy. After 9pm, take bus 53 from Perrache to av. Viviani/blvd des États-Unis. From Part-Dieu, leave the station by the Vivier Merle exit and take bus 36 dir. Minguette to av. Viviani/blvd Joliot Curie. Family rooms. Flexible 12am curfew.

Auberge de Jeunesse du Vieux Lyon (FUAJ), 1–45 Montée du Chemin Neuf (tel. 78 15 05 50, *lyon@fuaj.org*). From place Bellecour head west, crossing the Saône at pont Bonaparte. Go right, through place St Jean and left along rue de la Bombarde, then left again on to Montée du Chemin Neuf and up the hill to the hostel on the right. €12.70 (£8.50) per person.

HOSTELS
CISL, 108 blvd des États-Unis (tel. 37 90 42 42, *www.cis-lyon.com*, *cis-lyon@wanadoo.fr*). Beds from €14 (£9.50). Open all year.

STUDENT ACCOMMODATION
CROUS, rue de la Madeleine 59 (tel. 78 80 13 13). Will find accommodation in student lodgings. Métro: Jean-Maché.

CAMPING
All the sites are about 9.5 km out of the city:
Dardilly. Camping International 'Porte de Lyon' (tel. 78 35 64 55, *camping.lyon@marie-lyon.fr*). Four-star site, well recommended €10 (£6.70) per tent, €5 (£3.30) pp. Open all year. 40-minute ride on Bus 3 from the Town Hall (métro: Hotel de

Ville) to the Parc d'Affaires stop. Showers, games room, TV
room, swimming pool, bar and restaurant.

'Les Barolles', Saint Denis Laval (tel. 78 56 05 56). One-star site
to the south-west of the city. Open 1 Mar.–31 Dec.

There are another three sites at the **Parc de Loisirs de Miribel
Jonage**, north-east of the city.

Nice (0)4

TOURIST OFFICES

Nice Office du Tourisme, 5 Promenade des Anglais (tel. 92 70 74 07,
www.nicetourism.com, *info@nicetourism.com*). Open June–Sept.
8am–8pm, Sunday 9am–6pm. Rest of the year 9am–6pm, closed
Sunday. Other offices in the city are at Bureau d'Accueil Gare
SNCF, av. Thiers (tel. 92 70 74 07). Open 8am–7pm every day.
Free plan of the city. Reserves local hotels for a €1.50 (£1) fee,
but not before 10am. Accueil de France service available. The
office is next to the train station.

Bureau d'Accueil Nice-Ferber. Close to the airport. Open
Mon.–Sat. 7.30am–6.30pm.

FINDING ACCOMMODATION

Beds are difficult to find in Nice at any time in summer, but
especially so during the Jazz Parade in July. If you arrive early in
the morning at this time, try phoning a few hotels or searching for
a room in the area around the train station. If no success, get
along to the Tourist Office for about 9.30am and start queuing to
get the best rooms they have to offer. You can also book hotels
before your arrival at the tourist information website listed above.

HOTELS

All the hotels listed below are close to the station or the town
centre. Some hotels offer reductions of up to 30% for single
occupancy; others offer no reduction at all.

CHEAPEST DOUBLES AROUND €25 (£16.50)
De la Gare, pl. A. Blanqui 4 (tel. 93 55 09 15). Good value.

Lyonnais, rue de Russie 20 (tel. 93 88 70 74). Central.

Interlaken, av. Durante 26 (tel. 93 88 30 15). Next to the train station.

Hotel au Picardie, blvd Jean-Jaures (tel. 93 85 75 51). By the bus station.

Hotel du Piemont, rue d'Alsace Lorraine 19 (tel. 93 88 25 15). Breakfast not included.

Hotel Santa Lucia, blvd Gambetta 74 (tel. 93 88 63 88). Small and friendly. Near the station.

CHEAPEST DOUBLES AROUND €30 (£20)

Hotel Mon Reve, rue Rene Sainson 3 (tel. 93 88 34 23). Central. Rooms come with own kitchens.

Darcy, rue d'Angleterre 28 (tel. 9388 6706, *hoteldarcy@ hotmail.com*). Near the station.

Star Hotel, 14 rue Biscarra (tel. 93 85 19 03, *star-hotel@wanadoo.fr*). A good value, friendly hotel.

Les Orangers, 10 avenue Durante (tel. 93 87 51 41). Good views.

CHEAPEST DOUBLES AROUND €40 (£27)

Bristol, rue Paganini 22 (tel. 93 88 60 72). Good value three-star hotel.

Notre-Dame, rue de Russie 22 (tel. 93 88 70 44). Central, clean and excellent value.

Les Alizès, rue de Suisse 10 (tel. 93 88 85 08). Near the train station.

Alp'Azur, 15 rue Michel Ange (tel. 93 84 57 61). Has its own pool.

CHEAPEST DOUBLES AROUND €45–60 (£30–40)

Fontaine, 49 rue France (tel. 93 88 30 38, *hotel-fontaine@ webstore.fr*). Peaceful.

La Belle Meunière, av. Durante 21 (tel. 93 88 66 15). Dorms also available. Great place with its own garden.

Châteauneuf, rue Châteauneuf 3 (tel. 93 96 82 74). Decent two stars.

Petit Louvre, rue Emma Tiranty 10 (tel. 93 80 15 54). Breakfast not included.

Les Cigales, rue Dalpozzo 16 (tel. 92 70 74 75, *www.hotel-lescigales.com, info@hotel-lescigales.com*). 3 star hotel.

Carlyna, rue Sacha-Guitry 8 (tel. 93 80 77 21). Pleasant.

Baccarat, rue d'Angleterre 39 (tel. 93 88 35 73, *www.hotel-baccarat.com, hotel_baccarat@yahoo.fr*). 2 stars.

Nouvel Hotel, blvd Victor Hugo 19 (tel. 93 87 15 00, *www.nouvel-hotel.com, info@nouvel-hotel.com*). Large breakfast included.

UNIVERSITY ACCOMMODATION

Rooms in vacant student dorms are often let during the summer. Details available from **CROUS**, av. des Fleurs 18 (tel. 92 15 50 50). At any time of year, women can try calling **Cité Universitaire**, Residence 'Les Collinettes', av. Robert Schumann 3 (tel. 93 97 06 64), where singles cost around €18 (£12).

HI HOSTELS

Route Forestière du Mont Alban (FUAJ) (tel. 93 89 23 64, fax 92 04 03 10). Dorms around €8.40 (£5.60). Midnight curfew. Kitchen facilities and laundry room on premises. On top of a hill, about 5 km from the train station. Bus 5 from the train station to pl. Masséna, then bus 14 to Alban Fort.

HOSTELS/FOYERS

Backpackers' Hostel Chez Patrick, rue Pértinax 32 (tel. 93 80 30 72, *chezpatrick@voila.fr*). €10 (£6.70) including shower. In the centre of the city, two minutes from the station.

Espace Magnan, rue Louis de Coppet 31 (tel. 93 86 28 75). €10 (£6.70). Luggage room, €1. Open June–Sept. Close to the beach and the Promenade des Anglais. Swimming pool and supermarket in the vicinity. From the train station, take bus 23.

Relais International de la Jeunesse 'Clairvallon', av. Scudéri 26 (tel. 93 81 27 63). B&B €20 (£13.50). Midnight curfew. Set in an old house in Cimiez, about 9.5 km out of Nice. Easily reached by bus 15 from pl. Masséna.

Auberge de Jeunesse, Route Forestiere du Mont Alban (tel. 93 89 23 64, *www.fuaj.org*). Dorms around €14 (£9.50). Open all year. A way out of town in the hills. Bus 14 from the station.

Baie des Anges, chemin de St-Antoine 55 (tel. 92 15 81 00).

Jean Médecin, ancien chemin de Lanterne 82 (tel. 93 83 34 61).

Forum Nice-Nord, blvd Comte Falicon 10 (tel. 93 84 24 37).
Montebello, av. Valrose 96 (tel. 93 84 19 81).
Saint-Antoine, chemin de St-Antoine 69 (tel. 93 86 37 19).

CAMPING

L'Orée de Vaugrenier, blvd des Groules (tel. 93 33 57 30). Open 15 Mar.–31 Oct.
La Vieille Ferme, blvd des Groules (tel. 93 33 41 44). Two sites: four star and one star.
De l'Hippodrome, av. des Rives 2 (tel. 93 20 02 00).
L'Ensoleillado, av. de l'Église Christophe 49 (tel. 93 20 90 04). Open 15 Feb.–15 Oct.
Neptune, av. des Baumettes (tel. 93 73 93 81). Open 15 Mar.–15 Oct.
La Tour de la Madone, Route de Grasse (tel. 93 20 96 11). Open 15 Mar.–31 Oct.

CANNES AND MONACO

For those fancying a side trip to Cannes or Monaco, there are excellent (and inexpensive) youth hostels in both cities.
Cannes: **Centre International de Séjours**, av. de Vallauris 35 (tel. 93 99 26 79). €12.20 (£8.20). Breakfast included. Open all year. English speaking. Five minutes from centre.
Monaco: **Centre de la Jeunesse**, av. Prince Pierre 24 (tel. 93 50 83 20, *info@youthhostel.asso.mc*). €13 (£8.70). Breakfast included. Open all year. No membership card required, but you must be under 31. Open 7am–1am.

Paris (0)1

Unless you have booked accommodation in advance, the first thing you should do on arrival is head for a room-finding service as this will probably save you time, frustration and money; except perhaps in winter, when the number of visitors has fallen off. The best rooms go early in the day, so the quicker you get there the better. If you arrive by train, there is at least one room-finding organisation at all the stations, with the exception of St-Lazare (which is unfortunate if you are arriving from Dieppe, or from anywhere in Normandy).

ARRIVING BY BUS OR PLANE

The Gare Routière International at pl. Stalingrad 8 is the terminus for most international services arriving in Paris. Access to the city centre is easy from the Stalingrad métro station. Most international flights touch down at the Roissy-Charles de Gaulle airport. A free bus connects the airport to the Roissy train station, from which RER lines B and D run to Gare du Nord and Châtelet-Les Halles. Catch the bus from Aérogare 1 arrival gate 28, Aérogare 2A gate 5, Aérogare 2B gate 6 or Aérogare 2D gate 6. From Orly airport, a free bus service operates between Orly Sud gate H or Orly Ouest gate F and the Orly train station, from which the RER runs into the city.

TROUBLE SPOTS

The areas around Pigalle and Montmartre (the Moulin Rouge and Sacré Coeur are the main attractions) are a favourite haunt of petty thieves and pickpockets during the day, so take care of your valuables. Some of the cheaper hotels in these districts (9ème and 18ème *arrondissements*) are used by prostitutes. In the evening, young women walking in these parts without a male companion may be harassed, or verbally abused. These areas can be dangerous for anyone after dark, but particularly if you are alone and noticeably foreign. Day and night you should avoid the Pigalle, Anvers and Barbés-Rochechouart métro stations.

TOURIST OFFICES

The Office du Tourisme et des Congrès de Paris operates three offices in the city during the peak season. A fee of around €3 (£2) per person is charged for finding a room in a one-star hotel (if this seems high to you, consider the fact that the same service in London costs over three times as much), while for beds in hostels/foyers the fee is €1 (67 pence) per person.

Bureau d'Accueil Central, av. des Champs-Élysées 127 (tel. (0)8 92 68 31 13 – call centre covering all of Paris, *www.paris-touristoffice.com*, *info@paris-touristoffice.com*). The head office. Open daily 9am–8pm. The Accueil de France service is available at this office. Métro: Charles de Gaulle-Etoile.

Bureau Gare du Nord, rue de Dunkerque 18. Open, in peak season, Mon.–Sat. 8am–9pm, Sun. 1–8pm; at other times, Mon.–Sat. 8am–8pm. Métro: Gare du Nord.

Bureau Gare de l'Est. In the station arrivals hall. Open, in peak season, Mon.–Sat. 8am–9pm; at other times, Mon.–Sat. 8am–8pm. Métro: Gare de l'Est.

Bureau Gare de Lyon. By the exit from the main lines. Same hours as Gare de l'Est. Métro: Gare de Lyon.

Bureau Gare d'Austerlitz. In the mainline arrivals hall. Open, in peak season, Mon.–Sat. 8am–9pm; at other times, Mon.–Sat. 8am–3pm. Métro: Gare d'Austerlitz.

Bureau Gare Montparnasse, blvd de Vaugirard 15. Same hours as Gare de l'Est. Métro: Montparnasse-Bienvenue.

Bureau Tour Eiffel, Champ de Mars. Open May–Sept., daily 11am–6pm. Métro: Champ de Mars Tour Eiffel.

ACCUEIL DES JEUNES EN FRANCE

Accueil des Jeunes en France (AJF) is a tourist agency especially for young travellers. AJF is run on a non-profit-making basis, which helps keep charges low. The commission for finding a room in a hotel or hostel/foyer is €1.50 (£1) per person, except for beds in AJF hostels/foyers, which are located free of charge. Payment on booking with AJF is the norm. AJF operate four offices in the city, all of which will help with general tourist information as well as booking beds.

Beaubourg, rue Saint-Martin 119 (tel. 42 77 87 80). The head office of AJF, opposite the Pompidou Centre. Open all year round, Mon.–Sat. 9.30am–7pm. The office also runs a poste restante service. Métro: Rambuteau or Les Halles; RER: Châtelet-Les Halles.

Gare du Nord (tel. 42 85 86 19). Inside the new suburban station. Open June–Oct., daily 8am–10pm. Métro: Gare du Nord.

Hôtel de Ville, rue du Pont Louis-Philippe 16 (tel. 42 78 04 82). Open all year round, Mon.–Fri. 9.30am–6.30pm. Métro: Hôtel de Ville or Pont Marie. From Hôtel de Ville, walk a short distance along the street and turn right. From Pont Marie, face the Seine and then follow the river along to your left.

ACCOMMODATION AGENCIES

La Centrale de Réservations (FUAJ-HI), blvd Jules Ferry 4, 4e (tel. 43 57 02 60), Métro: République. The best agency for hostels and all budget accommodation, can also book beds for the rest of France and even Europe. A €1.50 (£1) deposit is deducted from your bill. Open daily 8am–10pm.

CISP, 6 Avenue Maurice Ravel (tel. 44 75 60 00, *www.cisp.asso.fr*, *cisp@csi.com*). Will reserve rooms in their hostels for young people.

You may also book online at the tourist information website listed above.

HOTELS

The number after the street name (e.g. 7e) refers to the *arrondissement* (district) of the city. Hotels in the 10e *arrondissement* are within easy walking distance of Gare du Nord and Gare de l'Est (the two stations are virtually side by side).

CHEAPEST DOUBLES FROM €25 (£16.50)

Hôtel Bonséjour, rue Burq 11, 18e (tel. 42 54 22 53). 5 minutes' walk from Sacré Coeur.

De Lille, rue Montholon 2, 9e (tel. 47 70 38 76). Off rue Lafayette between the Poissonière and Cadet métro stations.

De l'Industrie, rue Gustave Goublier 2, 10e (tel. 42 08 51 79). Off blvd de Strasbourg between the Château d'Eau and Strasbourg St-Denis métro stations. You can walk straight down blvd de Strasbourg from Gare de l'Est.

Pacific, rue du Château d'Eau 70, 10e (tel. 47 70 07 91). Along rue du Château d'Eau from the Château d'Eau métro station. From the Jacques Bonsergent métro station, walk down rue de Lancry from blvd de Magenta on to rue du Château d'Eau. From the République métro station, walk up blvd de Magenta, then head left along rue du Château d'Eau.

Jarry, rue Jarry 4, 10e (tel. 47 70 70 38). A short walk from Gare de l'Est.

Mary's Hotel, rue de Malte 53, 11e (tel. 47 00 81 70, *www.marys hotel.com*, *hotelmarys@magic.fr*). Métro: Oberkampf.

CHEAPEST DOUBLES FROM €30 (£20)

Hotel Henri IV, place Dauphine 25, 1e (tel. 43 54 44 53). Métro: Pont-Neuf.

Du Marché, rue de Faubourg Saint Martin 62, 10e (tel. 42 06 44 53). Métro: Château d'Eau.

De Medicis, rue Saint Jacques 214, 5e (tel. 43 54 14 66). Métro: Luxembourg.

De Chevreuse, rue de Chevreuse 3, 6e (tel. 43 20 93 16). Off blvd du Montparnasse close to the Vavin métro station (follow ascending street numbers on blvd du Montparnasse).

Sainte-Marie, rue de la Ville Neuve 6, 2e (tel. 42 33 21 61, *sainte mariehotel@yahoo.fr*). Off blvd de Bonne Nouvelle between the Bonne Nouvelle (closest) or Strasbourg–St-Denis métro stations.

De l'Aveyron, rue d'Austerlitz 5, 12e (tel. 43 07 86 86). Métro: Gare de Lyon (closest) or Bastille. Rue d'Austerlitz is off rue de Lyon, between the two métro stations.

Lafayette, rue Lafayette 198, 10e (tel. 40 35 76 07). Métro: Gare du Nord or Louis-Blanc. From Gare du Nord, walk left along pl. Roubaix, then turn left up rue Lafayette. Louis-Blanc is on rue Lafayette.

Luna Park, rue Jacquard 1, 11e (tel. 48 05 65 50). Left off rue Oberkampf, a short walk from the Parmentier métro station (follow descending street numbers along rue Oberkampf).

Tiquetonne, rue Tiquetonne 6 (tel. 42 36 94 58). Métro: Étienne Marcel.

CHEAPEST DOUBLES FROM €45 (£30)

Arian-Hôtel, av. de Choisy 102, 13e (tel. 45 70 76 00). Métro: Tolbiac or pl. d'Italie. Rue Tolbiac crosses av. de Choisy one block from the métro station. From pl. d'Italie, walk along av. de Choisy.

Home Fleuri, rue Daguerre 75, 14e (tel. 43 20 02 37). Métro: Denfert-Rochereau. From pl. Denfert-Rochereau follow av. du Général Leclerc until you see rue Daguerre on the right.

Atlas, rue de l'Atlas 12, 19e (tel. 42 08 50 12). Métro: Belleville. The street runs right off blvd de la Villette.

Wattignies, rue de Wattignies 6, 12e (tel. 46 28 43 78). Métro: Dugommier. From blvd de Reuilly turn down rue de Charenton, then left at rue de Wattignies.

Ouest Hotel, rue de Gergovie 27, 14e (tel. 45 42 64 99). Métro: Pernéty.

Brabant, rue des Petits Hôtels 18, 10e (tel. 47 70 12 32, *hotel.brabant@lemel.fr*). Métro: Poissonière. The street runs between rue Lafayette (at pl. Liszt) and blvd de Magenta.

Studia, blvd Saint-Germain 51, 5e (tel. 43 26 81 00). Between the Odéon and Maubert-Mutualité métro stations.

D'Alsace, blvd de Strasbourg 85, 10e (tel. 40 37 75 41). Between the Gare de l'Est and Château d'Eau métro stations.

CHEAPEST DOUBLES FROM €55 (£37)

Du Printemps, blvd Picpus 80, 12e (tel. 43 43 62 31, *www.hotelduprintempssarl.fr*, *contact@hotelduprintempssarl.fr*). Métro: Picpus.

Cambrai, blvd de Magenta 129 bis, 10e (tel. 48 78 32 13, *www.hotel-cambrai.com*, *hotelcambrai@wanadoo.fr*). Métro: Gare de l'Est. From the station head right along rue du 8 Mai 1945 on to blvd de Magenta. From Gare du Nord follow blvd de Denain away from the station, then head left down blvd de Magenta.

Grand Hôtel des Arts-et-Métiers, rue Borda 4, 3e (tel. 48 87 73 89). Off rue Turbigo at the junction with rue Volta, a short walk from the Arts-et-Métiers métro station.

De Chabrol, rue de Chabrol 46, 10e (tel. 45 23 93 10, *www.hotelchabrol.com*, *office@hotelchabrol.com*). Métro: Gare de l'Est or Poissonière. From Gare de l'Est, head right along rue du 8 Mai 1945.

Des Beaux Arts, rue Toussaint-Féron 2, 13e (tel. 44 24 22 60). Métro: Tolbiac. The street runs off av. d'Italie one block from the junction of rue Tolbiac and av. d'Italie.

Le Brun, rue Lebrun 33, 13e (tel. 47 07 97 02). Métro: Gobelins. Rue Lebrun runs between av. des Gobelins and blvd St-Marcel.

Camelia, av. Philippe Auguste 6, 11e (tel. 43 73 67 50). Métro: Nation.

Port-Royal, blvd du Port Royal 8, 5e (tel. 43 31 70 06, *www.portroyalhotel.fr.st*). Métro: Gobelins. Blvd du Port Royal runs from the end of av. des Gobelins.

Baudin, av. Ledru Rollin 113, 11e (tel. 47 00 18 91). Métro: Richard Lenoir.

De Blois, rue des Plantes 5, 14e (tel. 45 40 99 48). Métro: Alésia.

Walk up av. du Maine, then head left along rue de la Sablière into rue des Plantes.

De la Vallée, rue Saint-Denis 84–86, 1e (tel. 42 36 46 99). The street crosses rue Étienne Marcel close to the Étienne Marcel métro station.

Novex, rue Caillaux 8, 13e (tel. 44 24 22 00, *hotelnovex@ wanadoo.fr*). Off av. d'Italie close to the Maison Blanche métro station.

CHEAPEST DOUBLES FROM €60 (£40)

Hôtel de Parme, rue de Clichy 61 (tel. 48 74 40 41). Métro: Place-Clichy.

Du Loiret, rue des Mauvais Garçons, 4e (tel. 48 87 77 00). Métro: Hôtel de Ville.

Eiffel Rive Gauche, rue du Gros Caillou 6, 7e (tel. 45 51 24 56, *www.hotel-eiffel.com*, *eiffel@easynet.fr*). From the Ecole Militaire métro station head along av. Bosquet, turn left at rue de Grenelle, then left at rue du Gros Caillou.

CHEAPEST DOUBLES FROM €70 (£47)

Andrea, rue Saint-Bon 3, 4e (tel. 42 78 43 93, *hotelandrea rivoli.com*, *hotelandrea@wanadoo.fr*). Métro: Hôtel de Ville. Rue Saint-Bon is off rue de Rivoli as you head in the direction of blvd de Sebastopol and the Palais de Louvre.

Milan, rue de St-Quentin 17, 10e (tel. 40 37 88 50). Métro: Gare du Nord. Off pl. de Roubaix, left of the train station exit.

Terminus Nation, cours de Vincennes 96, 12e (tel. 43 43 97 93, *terminus.nation@lesrelaisdeparis.fr*). Métro: Porte de Vincennes.

Floridor, pl. Denfert Rochereau 28, 14e (tel. 43 21 35 53). Métro: Denfert Rochereau.

Hôtel Beaunier, rue Beaunier 31 (tel. 45 39 36 45, *www.hotelbeaunier.com*, *contact@hotelbeaunier.com*). Métro: Porte d'Orléans.

Celtic, rue d'Odessa 15, 14e (tel. 43 20 93 53). Métro: Montparnasse-Bienvenue or Edgar-Quinet. Rue d'Odessa runs between blvd Edgar-Quinet and rue du Départ in front of Gare Montparnasse.

Le Royal, rue Raymond Losserand 49, 14e (tel. 43 22 14 04). Métro: Pernéty on rue Raymond Losserand.

BED AND BREAKFAST

Mondialoca, avenue Charles de Gaulle 11 (tel. (0)3 23 71 61 40, *www.mondialoca.net*, *info@mondialoca.net*). Book bed and breakfasts online or by telephone. Prices start at €30 (£20).

Bed and Breakfast 1, rue Campagne Première 7, 14e (tel. 43 35 11 26). Singles start around €30 (£20), doubles around €45 (£30). Métro: Notre-Dame-des-Champs.

UNIVERSITY ACCOMMODATION

Cité Universitaire de Paris, blvd Jourdan 19, 14e (tel. 44 16 64 00). Singles around €25 (£16.50), doubles around €20 (£13.30) per person. In summer, there is a 7- to 10-night minimum stay. Full payment in advance is usually required. For further details and reservations contact: Général de Cité Universitaire de Paris, blvd Jourdan 19, 75690 Paris cedex 14. RER: Cité Universitaire. The closest métro stop is Porte d'Orléans Général Leclerc, a 10-minute walk away along blvd Jourdan.

CROUS, Académie de Paris, av. Georges-Bernadou 39, 5e (tel. 40 51 36 00). Rooms in student residences during the vacations.

HOSTELS/FOYERS

FUAJ (Fédération Unie des Auberges de Jeunesse) run four hostels in the city. B&B starts around €11.70 (£7.80):

Auberge Jules Ferry, blvd Jules Ferry 8, 11e (tel. 43 57 55 60, *paris.julesferry@fuaj.org*). Métro: République. 2am curfew. Reception open 8am–9pm. Four-night maximum stay. 2, 4 and 6-bed rooms. Laundry facilities. Handles reservations for the temporary FUAJ hostel set up in the university during the summer vacation (July–mid-Sept.).

Auberge Le d'Artagnan, rue Vitruve 80, 20e (tel. 40 32 34 56, *paris.le-dartagnan@fuaj.org*). Métro: Porte de Bagnolet. No curfew. Round-the-clock reception. 2, 3, 4 and 8-bed rooms. Laundry room provided. Will not accept reservations for individuals. Bar, disco and cinema; wheelchair accessible; family rooms.

Auberge Cités des Sciences, rue des Sept Arpents 24, 19e (tel. 48 43 24 11, *paris.cite-des-sciences@fuaj.org*). Métro: Hoche. 2, 4 and 6-bed rooms. Kitchen facilities, luggage room and laundry room provided; wheelchair accessible; family rooms.

Auberge Leo Lagrange, rue Martre 107 (tel. 41 27 26 90, *paris.clichy@fuaj.org*). Métro: Mairie de Clichy. 2-, 3- and 4- bed rooms. Family rooms.

MIJE (Maison Internationale de la Jeunesse et des Étudiants, *www.mije.com*) operates four hostels in the city. Accommodation is usually in 2- or 4-bed rooms with B&B costing €24 (£16). Reservations are only accepted from 7 days in advance, and the accommodation is for 18-30 year olds only. Only the first three hostels listed may be booked in advance. There is also a €2.50 (£1.70) membership fee. Reserve online or by calling 42 74 23 45.

Le Fauconnier (MIJE), rue de Fauconnier 11, 4e (tel. 42 74 23 45). The largest of the five foyers. Métro: Pont Marie or St-Paul. From Pont Marie follow the Seine downstream about 700m, then turn left up rue de Fauconnier. From St-Paul turn left down rue Prévôt from rue François Miron, then left along rue Charlemagne until you see rue du Fauconnier on the right.

Le Fourcy (MIJE), rue de Fourcy 6, 4e (tel. 42 74 23 45). Off rue de Rivoli and rue François Miron, a short walk from the St-Paul métro.

Maubisson (MIJE), rue des Barres 12, 4e (tel. 42 74 23 45). The smallest of the five foyers. Turn right off rue de l'Hôtel de Ville, then a short walk from the Pont Marie métro station.

Résidence Bastille (MIJE), av. Ledru-Rollin 151, 1e (tel. 43 79 53 86, *bastille@cybercable.fr*). Singles available. Between the Voltaire (closest) and Ledru-Rollin métro stations.

BVJ (Bureau de Voyages de la Jeunesse) run four foyers. Accommodation is mainly in multi-bedded rooms, though there are a few singles. No reservations are accepted, so arrive early, preferably before 9am. Three-night maximum stay:

Paris Quartier Latin, rue des Bernardins 44, 5e (tel. 43 29 34 80). Métro: Maubert-Mutualité. Rue des Bernardins crosses blvd St-Germain about 150m from pl. Maubert.

Paris Louvre, rue Jean-Jacques Rousseau 20, 1er (tel. 42 36 88 18). From the Louvre Rivoli métro station head up rue du Louvre from rue de Rivoli, turn left along rue St-Honoré, then right.

Paris Les Halles, rue du Pélican 5, 1er (tel. 40 26 92 45). From the Louvre Rivoli métro station, follow the directions for the foyer above until you see rue du Pélican, going left off rue Jean-

Jacques Rousseau. From the Palais Royal/Musée du Louvre métro station, follow rue St-Honoré, turn left up rue Croix-des Petits-Champs, then right.

Paris Opéra, rue Thérèse 11, 1er (tel. 42 60 77 23). Off av. de l'Opéra near the Pyramides métro station. An easy walk from the Opéra or Palais Royal/Musée de Louvre métro stations.

CISP (Centre International de Séjour de Paris, tel. 44 75 60 06, *www.cisp.asso.fr*) run two foyers. Around €28 (£19) for singles, €18 (£12) in 2- to 5-bed rooms, €14 (£9.50) in 12-bed dorms. Reception 6.30am–1.30am. The foyers are frequently full by 12pm:

CISP Ravel, av. Maurice Ravel 6, 12e (tel. 44 75 60 00). Métro: Porte de Vincennes.

CISP Kellerman, blvd Kellerman 17, 13e (tel. 44 16 37 38). Blvd Kellerman runs off av. d'Italie by the Porte d'Italie métro station.

Other independent hostels include:

Auberge International des Jeunes, rue Trousseau 10, 11e (tel. 47 00 62 00, *www.aijparis.com*, *aij@aijparis.com*). €13 (£8.70) p.p., free use of luggage room and safe. Good position – in Bastille area, near to a very cheap supermarket. Double rooms, or 4–6-bed dorms. Breakfast and bedlinen included. Open all night. Take métro to Ledru Rollin, turn left, and rue Trousseau is on the left.

Auberge Arpajon, rue Marcel Duhamel 3 (tel. 64 90 28 55). Around 400m from the RER station in Arpajon (line C4 dir. Dourdan from Paris Austerlitz). Camping spaces.

Maison International des Jeunes, rue Titon 4, 11e (tel. 43 71 99 21, *mij.cp@wanadoo.fr*). €19 (£12.50). Three-night maximum stay. Age 18–30, but this rule is not rigorously enforced. Métro: Faidherbe-Chaligny.

Foyer International des Étudiantes, blvd St-Michel 93, 6e (tel. 43 54 49 63). Singles €25 (£16.50), doubles €19 (£12.50) p.p. July–Sept., open to both sexes; Oct.–June, women only. Best reserved in writing two months in advance. A short walk along blvd St-Michel from the Luxembourg RER station.

Peace and Love Hostel, rue Lafayette 245, 10e (tel. 46 07 65 11, *pl@paris-hostels.com*). A lively hostel with its own bar and a reputation for partying. It's 10 minutes from Gare du Nord and Gare de l'Est – take Métro Jaures (line 2–5–7).

The five hostels below are run by the same owner and, as well as being the cheapest in Paris, are extremely welcoming. They all have self-catering facilities, storage rooms, safety deposit boxes and provide free maps/information. Beds €17 (£11.50) in dorms. Doubles €22 (£14.50) more. Curfew 2am in all hostels.

Aloha Hostel, rue Borromée 1, 15e (tel. 42 73 03 03, *www.aloha.fr*, *friends@aloha.fr*). 70 beds in 35 rooms. Reservations accepted with the first night's payment. Métro: Volontaires. Turn down rue Borromée at rue Vaugirard 243.

Young & Happy Hostel, rue Mouffetard 80, 5e (tel. 45 35 09 53, *www.youngandhappy.fr*, *smile@youngandhappy.fr*). 60 beds in 24 rooms. Reserve in advance online, or get to the hostel early. Métro: Place Monge. From pl. Monge follow rue Ortolaun until it is crossed by rue Mouffetard.

3 Ducks Hostel, pl. Étienne Pernet 6, 15e (tel. 48 42 04 05, *www.3ducks.fr*). 70 beds in 26 rooms. Reservations accepted with one night's payment. By the Jean Baptiste de Grenelle church. Métro: Felix Fauré or Commerce. From Commerce, follow the ascending street numbers on rue du Commerce. Has recently installed a bar.

Woodstock Hostel, rue Rodier 48, 9e (tel. 48 78 87 76, *www.woodstock.fr*). 65 beds in 19 rooms. Reservations accepted but not for doubles. Métro: Anvers. Hostel has a bar. Home of Lily the 'mad cow'.

Le Village Hostel, rue d'Orsel 20, 18e (tel. 42 64 22 02, *www.villagehostel.fr*). 60 beds in 24 rooms. The most recent addition to the five hostels, located next to the Sacré Coeur. Métro: Anvers.

CAMPING

Camping du Bois de Boulogne, allée du Bord de l'Eau (tel. 45 24 30 81). Solo travellers pay around €11.50 (£7.70). Open all year. In summer, the site fills fast and becomes very crowded. Métro: Porte Maillot. Then bus 244, followed by a short walk. Bungalows to let.

Toulouse (0)5

TOURIST OFFICES

Office du Tourisme/Syndicat d'Initiative de Toulouse, Donjon du Capitole, place du Capitole (tel. 61 11 02 22, *www.ot-toulouse.fr*, *infos@ot-toulouse.fr*). Open daily May–Sept., 9am–7pm; Oct.–Apr., Mon.–Sat. 9am–6pm. A branch office operates in the train station.

BASIC DIRECTIONS

Trains arrive at Toulouse Matabiau, about 1.5 km from the city centre. Almost directly across the canal from the station is rue de Bayard, which leads down to blvd de Strasbourg. Slightly to the right across blvd de Strasbourg is rue de Remusat, which takes you right into pl. du Capitole, site of the Tourist Office.

HOTELS

CHEAPEST DOUBLES FROM €20 (£13.30)

Beauséjour, rue Caffarelli 4 (tel. 61 62 77 59). Right off allée Jean-Jaurès.

Antoine, rue Arnaud Vidal 21 (tel. 61 62 70 27). Left off allée Jean-Jaurès.

Hotel de l'Université, rue Emile Cartailhas 26 (tel. 61 21 35 69). Small and central. Book through the tourist information website.

Des Arts, rue Cantegril 1 bis (tel. 61 23 36 21). Off rue des Arts. From pl. Wilson follow rue St-Antoine-du-T. into pl. St-Georges, across which is rue des Arts.

Splendid, rue Caffarelli 13 (tel. 61 62 43 02). See Beauséjour, above.

Excelsior, rue Riquet 82 (tel. 61 62 71 25). Left off allée Jean-Jaurès, close to the canal.

Les Jardins, 9 rue Laganne (tel. 61 42 09 04). Book through the tourist information website.

CHEAPEST DOUBLES AROUND €25 (£16.50)

Anatole France, pl. Anatole France 46 (tel. 61 23 19 96). Book through the tourist office website.

Héliot, rue Héliot 3 (tel. 34 41 39 41, *hotel-heliot.com*, *hotelheliot @aol.com*). From rue de Bayard turn left down rue Maynard into pl. de Belfort. Rue Héliot is directly across the square.

Le Lutetia, rue Maynard 33 (tel. 61 62 51 57). Left off rue de Bayard.

Bourse, rue Clémence Isaure 11 (tel. 61 21 55 86). Follow rue Gambetta from pl. du Capitole, turn left along rue Ste-Ursule. Rue Clémence Isaure is off to the right near the junction with rue de Cujas.

Nouvel Hôtel, rue du Taur 13 (tel. 61 21 13 93). The street runs from pl. du Capitole.

Formule 1, rue Jaques Babinet (tel. (0)8 91 70 54 14, *www.hotelformule1.com*). Part of the cheap Formule 1 chain.

CHEAPEST DOUBLES AROUND €30 (£20)

Au Père Leon, pl. Esquirol 2 (tel. 61 21 70 39). From pl. Wilson walk down rue Lapeyrousse on to rue d'Alsace-Lorraine. Turn left, and then right down rue de Metz to reach pl. Esquirol.

François 1er, rue d'Austerlitz 4 (tel. 61 21 54 52). Off pl. Wilson.

Grand Balcon, rue Romiguières 8 (tel. 61 21 48 08). Off pl. du Capitole.

Nuit d'Hotel, 98 boulevard de la Marquette (tel. 62 27 02 03). Central.

Hotel du Grand Balcon, 8 rue Romiguières (tel. 61 21 48 08). Central. Book through the tourist office website.

CHEAPEST DOUBLES FROM €40 (£27)

Hotel Albion, 28 rue Bachelier (tel. 61 63 60 36, *hotel.albion@ gofornet.com*). Two-star hotel near the station.

Croix Baragnon, rue Croix Baragnon 17 (tel. 61 52 60 10). From pl. Wilson follow rue St-Antoine-de-T. into pl. St-Georges, then take rue des Arts, which is crossed by rue Croix Baragnon.

Guillaume Tell, blvd Lazare-Carnol 42 (tel. 61 62 44 02).

Riquet, rue Riquet 92 (tel. 61 62 55 96, *hotelriquet@free.fr*).

Hotel Etap, 27 boulevard des Minimes (tel. 61 13 27 27). Near the train station.

Hotel du Taur, 2 rue du Taur (tel. 61 21 17 54, *www.hotel-du-taur.com*, *contact@hotel-du-taur.com*). Central and very good.

HOSTELS

At the time of writing there were no youth hostels in Toulouse. Check with the tourist information office when you arrive to confirm that this is still the case.

CAMPING

Camping Municipal du Pont de Rupé, av. des États-Unis, chemin du Pont de Rupé (tel. 61 70 07 35). On the northern fringe of the city. Take bus P from the train station.

La Bouriette, ch. de Tournefeville 201 (tel. 61 49 64 46), €6 (£4) per person, €6 (£4) per tent.

GERMANY (Deutschland) (00)49

Regional characteristics are a strong feature of German life and stem from when the country was divided into independent states. As a result, the country is incredibly varied and many of the regional capitals, such as Cologne and Munich, feel like national capitals. Some of the cities are rather ugly as they were rebuilt quickly and cheaply after the Second World War, but the smaller towns are attractive and the countryside is rich and varied.

Germans know how to enjoy themselves – their beer festivals are the envy of the world, and they are genuinely friendly and happy to welcome tourists to their country. Accommodation and food are reasonable on the pocket, so make sure you try some of their famous *Wurst* (sausages) and sample their cheap and tasty beer.

BACKGROUND

Otto von Bismarck's imperialistic ambitions were to fail, adding to the feelings of discontent throughout Europe during the early 20th century and tragically providing the catalyst for what was to become the First World War.

Germany's defeat led to the Weimar Republic and its inevitable collapse, which in turn led to the rise of Hitler, who used the Germans' anger and discontent after the hyper-inflation of the 1920s and the depression of the 1930s to secure his own place in power. Hitler's aggressive invasion of neighbouring countries led to the outbreak of the Second World War, when atrocities were committed on all sides. Germany's eventual defeat led to a partition between east and west, a situation epitomised by Berlin and its famous wall. Since being torn down in 1989, Germany has tried hard to heal the rift between East and West, and progress is finally being made.

ACCOMMODATION DETAILS

Cheap hotels, *Pensionen* and *Gasthäuser* are widely available. Prices in the main tourist destinations generally start around

€20–30 (£14–20) per person in singles and doubles, elsewhere around €20 (£14).

You'll also find a good supply of **farmhouse accommodation** (available mainly in summer) and **private rooms** (found mainly in the smaller towns). Prices for farmhouse accommodation and private rooms start around €18–25 (£12–16.50) per person. The standards of comfort and cleanliness in all the forms of accommodation mentioned above are invariably high, so you are virtually assured excellent value for money, particularly if you make comparisons with similarly priced accommodation in Italy or the UK. Tourist Office accommodation services throughout Germany are usually more than willing to help you find a room in any type of accommodation. In smaller towns, it is feasible to look for rooms on your own. Simply make enquiries at hotels, or wherever you see a *Gasthof* or *Zimmer frei* sign.

The association recommends that **hostels** should be reserved in advance at all times, but particularly between 15 June and 15 September (good advice, but not always possible to adhere to). Unless your reservation is for a longer period, you will be limited to a three-night stay, except where there is plenty of space at a hostel. If you have a reservation, be sure to arrive before 6pm unless you have notified the hostel that you will arrive later, otherwise your reservation will not be held and your bed may be given to someone else. If you turn up without a reservation, priority is given to visitors aged up to 27 until 6pm where beds are available. In theory, this means anyone older is not assigned a bed until after 6pm in case younger guests arrive. In practice, this rule is often ignored. The Association Handbook states that no beds are let after 10pm, even in the city hostels which are open late. Again this is a rule that many wardens choose to ignore, so if you are stuck there is nothing to be lost by approaching city hostels after 10pm.

There are six types of hostel and prices vary according to the standard of comfort, facilities available, location and the time of the curfew. Prices at the different types of hostel also vary according to the age of the user, with those aged 27 and over paying a surcharge of around €4 (£2.70) at all hostels. The main price divide amongst the various grades of hostel is between *Jugendherbergen* (youth hostels) and *Jugendgasthäuser* (youth guest houses). Juniors (age 26 and under) pay between €10–13 (£6.70–8.70) for B&B in dormitories at a *Jugendherberge*. Unless you have your own sheet sleeping bag, you will also have to pay for sheet hire: the charge varies between the 15 regional associations, but you can expect to pay at least €6 (£4) for the duration of your stay. In a *Jugendgasthäus*, prices for juniors range from €15–18 (£10–12). Accommodation is mainly in 2- or 4-bed rooms, with breakfast and the hire of bedlinen included in the overnight price.

Jugendgasthäuser are more expensive partly because they have been modernised in an effort to attract groups. This means that individual travellers are obliged to pay extra for leisure and recreation facilities that will rarely be available for their use. Groups can be a great source of annoyance to individual travellers. Hostels are frequently full of school and youth groups. This is especially true of hostels in the cities, along the Rhine and in the Black Forest, and in the more picturesque small towns; in short, all the places you are most likely to visit. The worst times are weekdays during the summer months and weekends throughout the rest of the year. Space for individual travellers in hostels is often at a premium, and even by 9.30am you may be turned away. Even if you do squeeze into a hostel packed with groups it may not be too pleasant. As groups bring in a lot of money, wardens tend to turn a blind eye to poorly controlled or noisy groups, no matter what the rules say. While the various problems discussed above are by no means peculiar to Germany, the sheer number of groups causes greater irritation than in most other countries. The best advice is neither avoid the hostels, nor stay in them all of the time.

As well as the normal HI hostels, Germany has a network of hostels called **Naturfreundehäuser** (Friends of Nature Hostels) which are also run by the HI. Most are located in the countryside just outside the towns. Accommodation is in singles, doubles or small dorms, and prices are on a par with those of *Jugend-gasthäuser*. Again, you may have problems finding a bed because of groups this time of middle-aged guests, with whom the hostels are very popular.

Camping is an excellent way to see Germany cheaply and without worrying about the likelihood of finding a cheap bed. The chances of you being turned away from a site because it is full are virtually nil (Munich's campsites manage to cope with the huge influx at the time of the Oktoberfest). There are over 3,000 sites, covering all the main places of interest, and most towns and villages with even a minimal tourist trade. The two main operators are local authorities and the Deutscher Camping-Club (DCC). Municipal sites are usually cheaper than those run by the DCC, but the standards of amenities and cleanliness are normally very high, irrespective of who operates the site. Some DCC sites are quite exceptional. Around €5 (£3.30) per tent, €4 (£2.70) per person, which, considering the standards of the sites, represents excellent value for money.

Not all campsites will be close to a town, but in any large city where there is a choice of sites with similar prices, railpass holders may save on transportation costs if there is a site located near a local train station or an S-Bahn stop (railpasses are often valid on city S-Bahn systems). Even if you are not primarily interested in camping, anyone travelling extensively in Germany would be well advised to take a tent, as this will stand you in good stead if you happen to arrive in town during one of the many trade fairs or local festivals that take place in German cities throughout the year. At these times all the cheaper beds fill rapidly, so unless you can camp you will most likely have to either pay for an expensive hotel room, sleep rough or leave town.

In an effort to safeguard the environment **camping outside official sites** has been made illegal, but it is still possible to **sleep rough**, providing you obtain the permission of the landowner and/or the police. There is little point trying to sleep out in parks or town centres. Apart from this being dangerous in some cities, the police will send you on your way if they find you. Police attitudes to **sleeping in stations** vary from place to place. In some of the smaller towns and cities they will wake you to check if you have a valid rail ticket, and if you have they will then let you lie until around 6am, but when they come back at that time be prepared to move sharpish. If you do not have a ticket you will be ejected from the station and arrested if you return later. In Munich, tolerance is shown (especially during the Oktoberfest), but do not expect a peaceful night before you are asked to move on in the morning. The stations of the northern ports and the central cities around Frankfurt are rough, and potentially dangerous at night.

Railpass holders can always take a **night train** if they are stuck for somewhere to sleep. Trains leave the main stations for a multitude of destinations, internal and international. In the central area around Mainz–Heidelberg–Mannheim–Würzburg–Nuremberg there are trains leaving at all hours through the night. Alternatively, there is the Bahnhofsmission, a church-run organisation which operates in the stations of all reasonably sized towns. They are meant for travellers who have no place to stay, or who are leaving early in the morning. If you approach the Bahnhofsmission during the day it is likely that you will be told to return before 8pm. This highly restrictive curfew helps prevent abuses of the system by those who are simply looking to fix themselves up with a cheap bed. You cannot stay more than one night in the shelter. B&B and use of the showers usually costs around €15 (£10).

ADDRESSES

GERMAN NATIONAL TOURIST OFFICE
PO Box 2695, London W1A 3TN (tel. 020 7317 0908 or 09001 600 100 to order one of their brochures). Alternatively visit *www.germany-tourism.de*.

GERMAN YHA
Deutsches Jugendherbergswerk (DJH), Hauptverband fur Jugendwandern, und Jugendherbergen e.V., im GILDE Zentrum, Bad Meinberger Str.1, D-32760 Detmold (tel. 05231 74010, *www.djh.de*).

FRIENDS OF NATURE
Naturfreundejugend, Haus Humboldtstein, Remagen D53424 (tel. (0)2228 94150, *www.naturfreundejugend.de*).

BED AND BREAKFAST
Visit *www.bed-and-breakfast.de* for an excellent website enabling you to choose and book bed and breakfast accommodation by region and price-bracket. (The option for choosing English is at the foot of the homepage.)

CAMPING
Deutscher Camping-Club (DCC), Mandelstraße 28, 80802 München (tel. (0)89 380 14 20, *www.camping-club.de* – German only, *info@camping-club.de*). The DCC sells the official,

comprehensive guide to Germany's campsites. A considerably abridged list is available from the German National Tourist Office.

Berlin (0)30

TOURIST OFFICES

For information before you arrive, contact Berlin Tourismus Marketing GmbH, am Karlsbad 11 (tel. (0)190 754040, *www.berlin-tourism.de*, *information@btm.de*). Each listing below includes the Berlin district in which it is situated, for instance Spandau or Charlottenburg.

Berlin Tourist Information, Europa Center, Budapesterstraße 45 (tel. 25 00 25) (Charlottenburg). Open Mon.–Sat. 10am–7pm, Sun. 10am–6pm. Basic plan of the city. Rooms found in local hotels either on their website, or by calling (0)1805 754040. From the Zoologischer Garten train station (mainline, S-Bahn and U-Bahn) head along Budapesterstraße past the ruins of the Kaiser-Wilhelm-Gedächtniskirche. The Europa Center is on the right after about 500m. There are other branches at the Brandenburg Gate, on Alexanderplatz, and in the department store KaDeWe on Tauentzienstraße 21.

HOTELS, PENSIONS AND GUEST HOUSES

CHEAPEST DOUBLES FROM €20 (£13.30)

Hotel Hamburger Hof, Kinkelstraße 4 (tel. 333 4602) (Spandau).
Pension Rotdorn, Heerstraße 36 (tel. 3009 9292) (Charlottenburg).
Hotel-Pension Insel Rügen, Pariser Straße 39/40 (tel. 884 3940, *www.insel-ruegen-hotel.de*, *ir-hotel@t-online.de*) (Wilmersdorf).

CHEAPEST DOUBLES FROM €30 (£20)

Pension Fischer, Nürnberger Straße 24A (tel. 218 6808) (Charlottenburg). Breakfast not included.
Pension Adamshof, Emanuelstraße 3 (tel. 5010 700) (Lichtenburg). Without breakfast.
Pension Ulrich, Krontaler Straße 17 (tel. 942 0910, *info@hotel-pension-ulrich-berlin.de*) (Weißensee).

Hotel-Pension Conti, Potsdamer Straße 67 (tel. 261 2999) (Tiergarten). Without breakfast.

Hotel Adler, Friedrichstraße 124 (tel. 2829 352). Central. S-Bahn: Orienburger Strasse.

CHEAPEST DOUBLES FROM €40 (£27)

Hotel-Pension Majesty, Mommsenstraße 55 (tel. 323 2061) (Charlottenburg).

Hotel Charlottenburger Hof, Stuttgarter Platz 14 (tel. 329 070, *charlottenburgberlin@inthotels.com*) (Charlottenburg). Without breakfast.

Hotel Crystal, Kantstraße 144 (tel. 312 9047) (Charlottenburg).

Pension Silvia, Knesebeckstraße 29 (tel. 881 2129) (Charlottenburg). Breakfast not included.

Pension Messe, Neue Kantstraße 5 (tel. 326 5619). Breakfast included. S-Bahn: Charlottenburg.

Die Etage, Katharinenstraße 14 (tel. 8909 0820, *dieetage@ aol.com*). Doubles and dorm beds available. Special weekend rates available.

CHEAPEST DOUBLES €50 (£33)

Haus Wichern, Waldenserstraße 31 (tel. 395 4072) (Tiergarten).

Pension Schultze, Friedrichrodär Straße 13 (tel. 779 9070, *www.pension-schulze.de*, *mail@pension-schulze.de*) (Steglitz). Breakfast not included.

Gribnitz, Kaiserdamm 82 (tel. 308 20716) (Charlottenburg).

CHEAPEST DOUBLES FROM €60 (£40)

Hotel Charlottenburger Hof, Stuttgarter Platz 14 (tel. 329 070, *charlottenburgberlin@inthotels.com*) (Charlottenburg). Without breakfast.

Hotel-Pension Bellevue, Emser Straße 19/20 (tel. 881 5429) (Wilmersdorf).

Artist Hotel-Pension, Friedrichstraße 115 (tel. 2807 513). Central.

Aletto Jugendhotel, Grunewald Straße 33 (tel. 21003 680, *www.aletto.de*, *info@aletto.de*). Singles, doubles and dorms (€14, £9.50) available.

Sickinger Hof, Beusselstraße 44 (tel. 345 3738). Breakfast included.

PRIVATE ROOMS AND APARTMENTS

Berlin Tourist Information, Europa Center, Budapesterstraße 45 (tel. 262 6031) (Charlottenburg). Around €25 (£16.50) p.p., with breakfast for private rooms. Two-night minimum stay. For opening hours and directions, see **Tourist Office** section above.

Home Company Mitwohnzentrale, Joachimstalerstraße 17 (tel. 19445, *www.homecompany.de*, *berlin@homecompany.de*) (Kurfürstendamm). Biggest of the Mitwohnzentralen. Prices for apartments start around €25 (£16.50) per person for one night, falling with the length of your stay. A percentage fee is also charged. Open Mon.–Fri. 9am–6pm, Sat. 11am–2pm.

Freiraum, Wiener Straße 14 (tel. 820 08, *www.freiraum-berlin.com*, *info@freiraum-berlin.com*).

www.berlin-economy-hotels.com. For a fee of €2 (£1.30) payable online, you can access a large database of private rooms, budget hotels from €13 (£8.70) a night and accommodation agencies.

Fine and Mine, Neue Schoenhauser Straße 20 (tel. 235 5120, *www.fineandmine.de*). Will find both long and short term accommodation throughout Berlin.

Enjoy Bed and Breakfast, Nollendorfplatz 5, Haus B (tel. 236 23610, *www.ebab.de*, *info@ebab.de*). Finds private accommodation for gay and lesbian travellers from €20 (£13.30) a night. Open every day from 4.30pm–9.30pm.

HI HOSTELS

Advance reservation is advisable, particularly if you are travelling in summer, or will be arriving in Berlin at the weekend. You should reserve online at the relevant website (see above). The hostels are open to HI members only. Cards can be purchased online, or will be given for free once you have stayed in any HI hostel for 6 nights.

Jugendherberge 'Ernst Reuter', Hermsdorfer Damm 48–50 (tel. 404 1610, *jh-ernst-reuter@jugendherberge.de*) (Hermsdorf). Juniors €15 (£10); over 26 €18.60 (£12.50) for B&B. Midnight curfew. U-Bahn: Tegel (line 6), then bus 125 dir. Frohnau to the fourth stop. Laundry room provided.

Jugendgasthaus Berlin, Kluckstraße 3 (tel. 261 1097, *jh-berlin@jugendherberge.de*) (Tiergarten). Juniors around €19 (£12.70); over 26 €23 (£15.50) for B&B. Midnight curfew. Bus 129 from Kurfürstendamm towards Oranienplatz or Hermannplatz. Laundry room provided.

Jugendgasthaus Wannsee, Badeweg 1 (tel. 803 2035, *jh-wannsee@jugendherberge.de*) (Wannsee). Juniors around €18.50 (£12.50); over 26 €22.60 (£15) for B&B. Midnight curfew. S-Bahn: Nikolassee (line 3) then a 10-minute walk towards the beach. The hostel is at the junction of Badeweg and Kronprinzessinnenweg. Wheelchair access.

HOSTELS

A+O Backpackers Am Zoo, Joachimstraße 1–3 (tel. 2922 810, *www.aobackpackers.de*, *hostel@web.de*). Doubles €34 (£23) p.p., dorm beds from €15 (£10).

Meininger 10, Meininger Straße 10 (tel. 7871 7474, *www. studentenhotel.de*, *welcome@meininger-hostels.de*) (Schöneberg). Dorm beds from €13 (£8.70). U-Bahn: Rathaus Schöneberg, or bus 146 from Zoologischer Garten train station to the same stop. They have another hostel at Hallesche Ufer 30 which can be contacted at the same web and email address.

Jugendgasthaus Central, Nikolsburger Straße 2–4 (tel. 873 0188, *www.jugendgaestehaus-central.de*, *berlin@jugendgaestehaus.de*) (Wilmersdorf). €21 (£14) for B&B. 1am curfew. 2- to 6-bed rooms. U-Bahn: Güntzelstraße.

Jugendgasthaus Feurigstraße, Feurigstraße 63 (tel. 781 5211, *www.jgh.de*) (Schöneberg). Dorm beds from €19 (£12.70) (sheets €2 (£1.30) unless staying more than 3 nights, then free). U-Bahn: Kleistpark.

Sunflower Hostel, Helsingforser Straße 17 (tel. 440 44250, *www.sunflower-berlin.de*, *hostel@sunflower-hostel.de*). Doubles €45 (£30), dorms start at €13 (£8.70). 7th night is free. S-Bahn: Warschauer Straße.

Odysee Hostel, Grunberger Straße 23 (tel. 2329 000081, *www.globetrotterhostel.de*, *odysee@globetrotterhostel.de*). Doubles €52 (£35), dorms from €13 (£8.70) with discounts offered online. Take the S-Bahn to Ostbahnhof.

Jugendgasthaus Tegel, Ziekowstraße 161 (tel. 433 3046, *info@jugendgaestehaus-tegel.de*) (Tegel). Quads €13 (£8.70) p.p. Breakfast, evening meal and bedlinen included. U-Bahn: Tegel. Bus: 222.

Jugendhotel Berlin, Kaiserdamm 3 (tel. 322 1011, *info@jugend-hotel.de*) (Charlottenburg). Dorms from €19.50 (£13), doubles €60 (£40) per room. Breakfast included. U-Bahn: Sophie-Charlotte-Platz.

CVJM-Haus, Einemstraße 10 (tel. 264 9100, *info@cvjm-berlin.de*) (Schöneberg) (YMCA). €25 (£16.50) p.p., including breakfast. No curfew. Book ahead.

Alcatraz Backpacker Hostel, Schönhauser Allee 133A (tel. 484 96815, *www.alcatraz-backpacker.de*). Beds from €13 (£8.70). U-Bahn: Parkplatze.

Lette'm Sleep, Lette Straße 7 (tel. 44733 623, *www.back packers.de*, *info@backpackers.de*). Doubles €44 (£29), dorm beds from €13 (£8.70). U-Bahn: Eberswalderstraße.

Die Fabrik, Schlesische Straße 18 (tel. 611 7116, *www.die fabrik.com*, *info@diefabrik.com*). Doubles €49 (£33), dorms from €18 (£12).

Circus (tel. 2839 1433, *www.circus-berlin.de*, *info@circus-berlin.de*). Have two hostels in the city; one at Rosa-Luxemburg-Straße 39 and another at Weinbergsweg 1A. Both can be contacted as above. Doubles around €22 (£14.50) p.p., dorms around €14 (£9.50). No curfew. Internet access (cheap) and washing machines. Cheap bike hire.

Mittel's Backpacker Hostel, Chausseestraße 102 (tel. 2839 0965, *www.backpacker.de*). The hostel currently has two floors and can accommodate approximately 60 guests. Prices vary according to room size.

Bax Pax Hostel, Skalitzer Straße. 104 (tel. 6951 8322, *www.baxpax.de*). Bax Pax offers 59 beds and provides wheel-chair access. Prices vary according to room size.

INTERNATIONAL TENT

Übernachtung im Zelt, or Backpacker's Paradise, Waidmann-sluster/Ziekowstraße 161 (tel. 433 8640, *backpackersparadise @web.de*). A large covered area, with mattresses and sheets provided, or space for your own tent. Open 1 July–4 Sept. Age limit 27. €8 (£5.30) per night. Bus 222 from the Tegel U-Bahn station, direction Alt-Lübars.

CAMPING

The campsites below are open all year round (unless stated otherwise). €6 (£4) per person and €4 (£2.70) for a small tent site is the standard charge at all four sites. Advance reservations can be made by contacting the Deutscher Camping-Club, at Mandelstraße 28, 80802 München (tel. (0)89 380 14 20, info@camping-club.de).

Kohlhasenbruck, Neue Kreiss Straße 36 (tel. 805 1737). Most convenient site for the centre, but be warned, still 15 km away. Take bus 118 in the direction of Drewitz. Restaurant, showers and laundry room. Open April to Sept.

Kladow, Krampnitzer Weg 111/117 (tel. 365 2797) (Spandau). From the Rathaus Spandau U-Bahn station take bus 135 to its terminus, then continue along Krampnitzerweg about 500m.

Dreilinden, Kremnitz Ufer (Albrechts-Teerofen) (tel. 805 1201) (Wannsee). Bus 118 from the Oskar-Helene-Heim U-Bahn station, then a 20-minute walk along Kremnitz Ufer to Albrechts-Teerofen.

SLEEPING ROUGH

The Grünewald is the most obvious, but there are lots of places at the end of the S-Bahn lines, or along the shores of the Krossinsee.

If you are stuck for a bed, but do not want to sleep out, go to the Bahnhofsmission in Zoologischer Garten station, where you will be given a bed for around €12 (£8). One night only.

Cologne (Köln) (0)221

TOURIST OFFICE

Verkehrsamt der Stadt Köln, Unter Fettenhennen 19 (tel. 221 3345, www.stadt-koeln.de, koelntourismus@stadt-koeln.de). Open Mon.–Sat. 9am–9pm, Sun. 10am–6pm. You can book accommodation online, or by emailing the Tourist Office. They also sell the Cologne Welcome Card.

BASIC DIRECTIONS

Leaving Köln Hbf by the main exit on to Bahnhofvorplatz, the vast bulk of the cathedral is to your left. Going right along the front of the train station as far as you can and then following the street which runs away to your left, you arrive at the junction with Marzellenstraße. Across Bahnhofvorplatz from the train station, almost opposite the main entrance to the cathedral, is the Tourist Office on Unter Fettenhennen. Running away from the cathedral near the Tourist Office is Hohe Straße. To the left of Hohe Straße is the old market (Alter Markt) and the Town Hall, beyond which is the Rhine. The Hohenzollern Brücke crosses the Rhine by the cathedral. The next bridge downstream is the Deutzer Brücke. Along the Rhine between the two are the Frankenwerft and the Rheingarten. Buses 32 and 33 from Köln Hbf wind their way through the area around the Town Hall before running the whole length of Severinstraße and on beyond the Severinstor.

HOTELS, PENSIONS AND GUEST HOUSES

CHEAPEST DOUBLES AROUND €45 (£30)

Hubertushof, Mülenbach 30 (tel. 217 388). Gay-friendly hotel complete with sauna and breakfast included in the price.

Flintsch, Moselstraße 16–20 (tel. 921 232 142). Take a local train to Köln Südbahnhof. Moselstraße is the street running along the front of the station.

Pension Otto and **Pension Jansen**, Richard-Wagner Straße 18 (tel. 252977 or 251875). No breakfast.

Hotel Thielen, Brandenburger Straße 1 (tel. 123333). Welcoming and good value.

CHEAPEST DOUBLES AROUND €60 (£40)

Berg, Brandenburger Straße 6 (tel. 121124). Breakfast available.

Haus Trost, Vogelsanger Straße 60–62 (tel. 516647, *info@hotel-trost.de*). Bed and breakfast just out of the town centre.

Lint Hotel, Lintgasse 7 (tel. 920 550, *www.lint-hotel.de*, *contact@lint-hotel.de*). From Hohe Straße turn left down Große Budengasse and continue on along Kleine Budengasse and Mühlengasse. Turn right down Unter Kaster and then right again. Buses 132 and 133 from Köln Hbf pass the end of the street, but it takes just over five minutes to walk.

Das Kleine Stapelshauschen, Fischmarkt 1–3 (tel. 257 7862). One of the most beautiful hotels in town.

HOSTELS

Station Hostel for Backpackers, Marzellenstrasse 44–48 (tel. 912 5303, *www.hostel-cologne.de*, *station@hostel-cologne.de*). Right in the town centre, dorm beds €15 (£10), doubles €40 (£27).

Station Hostel 2, Rheingasse 34–36 (tel. 230 247, *station2@hostel-cologne.de*). Sister hostel to the Station Hostel above, can also be booked at the same website.

HI HOSTELS

Jugendgasthaus Deutz, Siegestraße 5A (tel. 814711, *jh-koeln-deutz@djh-rheinland.de*). Curfew 12.30am. Dorm beds from €19 (£12.70). Fills quickly. Reception opens 12.30pm. 150m from Köln-Deutz station. Well signposted. Laundry room on premises. Take S-Bahn 6, 11 or 12.

Jugendgasthaus Köln-Riehl, An der Schanze 14 (tel. 767081, *jh-koeln-riehl@dkh-rheinland.de*). B&B from €20 (£13.30). Reception 24hrs. About 3 km from the main train station. Laundry room on premises. No curfew. Wheelchair accessible. From Breslauer Platz, walk right down to the river, turn left, on under the Zoobrücke, along Niederlander Ufer into An der Schanze. From Köln Hbf take U-Bahn lines 5, 16 or 18 to Boltensternstraße.

CAMPING

All the sites are quite a distance from the centre. If you take tram 16 to Marienburg there are two sites on the opposite side of the Rhine, about 15 minutes' walk over the Rodenkirchener Brücke in Köln-Poll.

Campingplatz der Stadt Köln, Weidenweg (tel. 831966). Open 1 May–10 Oct. Intended mainly for families, but you will not be turned away. Reception 8am–12pm and 3–10pm. Around €4 (£2.70) per person; €3 (£2) per tent and €3 (£2) per car.

Campingplatz Waldbad, Peter-Baum-Weg, is in Köln-Dünnwald (tel. 603315). Open all year round.

Hamburg (0)40

TOURIST OFFICES

For information and reservations before you arrive, call the Hamburg Hotline on 3005 1300; open daily 8am–8pm. The staff all speak English. Alternatively visit *www.hamburg-tourism.de* or email *info@hamburg-tourism.de*.

Tourist Information im Hauptbahnhof. By the main exit on to Kirchenallee. Open daily 7am–11pm.

Tourist Information am Hafen, St Pauli Landungsbrücken. Between landing stages 4 and 5 of the port. Open daily 9am–7pm.

Tourist Information im Flughafen. In the airport at Terminal 3 (Arrivals). Open daily 8am–11pm.

BASIC DIRECTIONS

The area around Hamburg Hbf contains some of the city's least expensive hotels. Leaving the train station by the main exit on to Kirchenallee and heading left you arrive at Hachmannplatz. At this point, Kirchenallee runs into St Georgstraße, while Lange Reihe runs away to your right. Turning around so that Lange Reihe is on your left, then walking along Kirchenallee, you come to Ellmenreichstraße on the left. This street leads into Hansaplatz, as does the next street on the left, Bremer Reihe. Continuing along Kirchenallee, you reach Steintorplatz, from which three streets run off to the left: sharp left is Steintorweg, leading into Bremer Reihe, then Steindamm, then, almost at a right angle to Kirchenallee is Adenauerallee. While there are relatively inexpensive hotels in all of these streets, Bremer Reihe and Steindamm offer the most possibilities. Unfortunately, the cheapest hotels in these streets are often used by prostitutes, which, even though the hotels are invariably safe for you and your belongings, hardly makes for a peaceful night.

HOTELS

CHEAPEST DOUBLES AROUND €50 (£33)
Hotel Figaro, Neuer Kamp 21 (tel. 430 4270). Breakfast included.

Inter-Rast, Reeperbahn 154–156 (tel. 312 420). S-Bahn: Reeperbahn. In the red light district. Street noise is a problem, unless you are a sound sleeper.

Annenhof, Lange Reihe 23 (tel. 243426). Town centre. Book ahead.

Hotel Terminus Garni, Steindamm 5 (tel. 280 3144, *www. hotel-terminus-hamburg.de*, *hotelterminushh@aol.com*). Breakfast included. Can usually get a place.

Alt Nürnberg, Steintorweg 15 (tel. 246023). Close to the city centre. Can be booked through the tourist information website.

St Georg, Kirchenallee 23 (tel. 241141, *www.hotel-stgeorg.de*). Town centre, rooms with or without bathrooms.

Schanzenstern, Bartelsstraße 13 (tel. 439 8441, *www.schanzen stern.de*, *info@schanzenstern.de*). S-Bahn: Sternschanze. Bartelsstraße runs between Schanzenstraße and Susannenstraße. Managed by a politically and ecologically progressive cooperative. Book in advance.

Kieler Hof, Bremer Reihe 15 (tel. 243024). Breakfast included. Book online at the tourist information website.

Pension Hildebrand, Schifferstraße 9 (tel. 7001 720). Charming friendly pension.

CHEAPEST DOUBLES FROM €60 (£40)

Nord, Bremer Reihe 22 (tel. 2805 1733). Close to the main railway station. Can be booked online at the tourist information centre.

Wernecke, Hartungstraße 7A (tel. 455357). U-Bahn: Hallerstraße, then a few minutes' walk down Rothenbaumchaussee, passing Hermann-Behn-Weg to Hartungstraße on the right. A 10-minute walk from mainline S-Bahn station Dammtor. Follow Rothenbaumchaussee from Theodor-Heuss-Platz to Hartungstraße on the left.

Sarah Petersen, Lange Reihe 50 (tel. 249826, *www.galerie-hotel-sarah-petersen.de*, *galerie-hotel-petersen@hamburg.de*).

Wilkinger Hof, Steindamm 53 (tel. 243 834 34). Centre of town. Breakfast available.

HI HOSTELS

'Auf dem Stintfang', Alfred-Wegener-Weg 5 (tel. 313488, *jh-stint fange@t-online.de*). B&B from €20 (£13.30). Curfew 1am. From the Hauptbahnhof, take S1, S2, S3 (S-Bahn free with railpasses) or the U3 to Landungsbrücke. The hostel is on top of the hill.

Jugendgasthaus 'Horner-Rennbahn', Rennbahnstraße 100 (tel. 651 1671, *jgh-hamburg@t-online.de*). €18 (£12); over 26 €20 (£13.30). Open Mar.–Dec. Curfew 1am. Quite far out. U3 to Horner-Rennbahn, then a 10-minute walk. Alternatively take the Wandsbek bus from the centre.

HOSTELS

Backpacker Hostel Instant Sleep, Max. Brauer Straße 277 (tel. 4318 2310, *www.instantsleep.de,, backpackerhostel@instant sleep.de*). Dorms from €15 (£10), doubles at €42 (£28). €2 (£1.30) for bed linen.

CAMPING

Buchholz, Kielerstraße 374 (tel. 540 4532, *www.camping-buchholz.de, info@camping-buchholz.de*). Near the Hamburger SV football stadium. 53 dir. Pinneberg, or 521 dir. Elbgaustraße to the Stellingren (Volksparkstadion) stop. €4 (£2.70) per person, €7 (£4.70) per tent.

Heidelberg (0)6221

TOURIST OFFICES

Tourist-Information am Hauptbahnhof (tel. 19433, *www.cvb-heidelberg.de, info@cvb-heidelberg.de*). On the square outside the main train station. General information and a room-finding service, both online and at the office. Open Mon.–Sat. 9am–7pm, Sun. 10am–6pm. Closed Sun. in winter (mid-Nov.–mid-Feb.). When closed, details of hotels with rooms available at closing time are posted outside.

Tourist-Information am Schloß, Neue Schloßstraße 54 (tel. 21144). Open 9am–5pm. At the top of the Bergbahn funicular railway, a short walk from the castle.

Tourist-Information Neckarmänzplatz. Open 9am–6.30pm (closed in winter). Follow the River Neckar upstream from the Karl-Theodor-Brücke (Alter Brücke) along Am Hackteufel to the coach park.

BASIC DIRECTIONS

The main train station (Heidelberg Hbf) is about 20 minutes' walk from the town centre. Buses 10 and 11 link Heidelberg Hbf with Universitätsplatz. Bus 33 runs from the station to the Kornmarkt just beyond Marktplatz, while bus 11 continues from Universitäts-platz to the Bergbahn stop, close to the Kornmarkt at the foot of the funicular railway leading up to the castle and the Königsstühl. Railpass holders can save money by taking a train from Heidelberg Hbf to Heidelberg-Karlstor, about 8 minutes' walk from the Marktplatz.

FINDING ACCOMMODATION

Finding suitable accommodation can be difficult in Heidelberg because the city is popular with older, more affluent tourists, guaranteeing the hotels a steady trade and pushing hotel prices above the norm for Germany. As the city also receives large numbers of young visitors, you cannot always count on getting a bed in the HI hostel, even with its large capacity (451 beds). Even camping is not without its problems: the two sites are about 8 km out of town, and although there is a train station nearby, the service is so infrequent that you will almost certainly have to travel by bus, adding to the cost of an overnight stay at either of the sites.

HOTELS

CHEAPEST DOUBLES AROUND €30 (£20)

Jeske, Mittelbadgasse 2 (tel. 23733). 2- to 5-bed rooms. All the same price p.p. Right in the centre of the Old Town. Understandably popular, but only takes reservations an hour ahead. Mittelbadgasse runs off the Marktplatz.

CHEAPEST DOUBLES FROM €60 (£40)

Waldhorn, Peter-Wenzel-Weg 11 (tel. 895 330, *www.zum-waldhorn.de*, *info@zum-waldhorn.de*). Beautifully located, high in the hills above the suburb of Ziegelhausen. Fine if you have your own transport.

Endrich, Friedhofweg 28 (tel. 801086, *www.gaesthaus-endrich.de*, *webmaster@gaesthaus-endrich.de*). In the suburb of Ziegelhausen.

Haus Sedlmayer, Gerhart-Hauptmann-Straße 5 (tel. 412 872). In Neuenheim. A 15-minute walk from Heidelberg Hbf. Cross the Neckar by the Ernst-Walz-Brücke, go straight ahead on Berlinerstraße, then right at Gerhart-Hauptmann-Straße.

Am Kornmarkt, Kornmarkt 7 (tel. 24325). Very popular. Central.

Sean Og, Hauptstraße 93 (tel. 138000). One of the best, and liveliest, places to stay in town.

CHEAPEST DOUBLES FROM €70 (£47)

Hotel Vier Jahreszeiten, Haspelgasse 2 (tel. 24164, *www.4-jahreszeiten.de*, *info@4-jahreszeiten.de*). Town centre, only cheap in the winter months.

Astoria, Rahmengasse 30 (tel. 402929). North of the river.

Elite, Bunsenstraße 15 (tel. 25734, *www.hotel-elite-heidelberg.de*). Turn right off Bahnhofstraße down Landhausstraße, then left along Bunsenstraße.

PRIVATE ROOMS

The staff in the second-hand clothes shop **Flic-Flac** at Untere Straße 12 can help young travellers find lodgings with local people. Untere Straße runs between the Heumarkt and the Fischmarkt.

HI HOSTEL

Tiergartenstraße 5 (tel. 412066, *www.jugendherberge-heidelberg .de*, *info@jugendherberge-heidelberg.de*). From €16 (£10.50) with breakfast. Curfew 11.30pm. About 4 km from Heidelberg Hbf. Bus 33 from the station, or Bismarckplatz. After 8pm, tram 1 to Chirurgische Klinik, then bus 330 to the first stop after the zoo. Book ahead as it's always full.

HI HOSTELS NEARBY

'Lindenhof', Rheinpromenade 21, Mannheim (tel. 621 822718). In many ways the best hostel option for anyone with a railpass. Set on the banks of the Rhine, the Mannheim hostel is both cheaper and more pleasant to stay in than the Heidelberg hostel. Midnight curfew. 10–15 minutes' walk from Mannheim Hbf (main station). Train journey from Heidelberg around 12–20 minutes.

CAMPING

Haide (tel. 06223 2111, *www.camping-haide.de*, *info@camping-haide.de*). Located between Ziegelhausen and Kleingemünd. Bus 35 to the Orthopaedic Clinic in Schlierbach-Ziegelhausen, about 8 km out of town. The site is across the Neckar. Popular with groups on camping holidays. €4.60 (£3.10) per person; from €3 (£2) per tent; cabins €10.50 (£7) per person.

Camping Heidelberg, Schlierbacher Landstraße 151 (tel. 06221 802506, *www.camping-heidelberg.de*, *mail@camping-heidelberg. de*). Same bus as above, but get off at the Im Grund stop. The site is near the clinic. More basic than the site across the river, but perfectly adequate. Tends to be free of groups. Cheaper too. Expect to pay around €5.50 (£3.70) per person and €3 (£2) per tent. Passports held at reception, which means you cannot leave before the office opens at 8am.

Lübeck (0)451

TOURIST OFFICES

Breite Straße 62 (tel. 122 5419, *www.luebeck-tourism.de*, *info@luebeck-tourismus.de*). Book accommodation online. Helpful office. Open Mon.–Fri. 9.30am–6pm, Sat.–Sun. 10am–2pm. Breite Straße runs from the Markt in the Altstadt (Old Town).

Informationsschalter im Hauptbahnhof (tel. 864 675). Operated by the Lübecker Verkehrsverein. Charge a commission for finding accommodation plus 10% of your hotel bill, so avoid. Relatively poor information service.

BASIC DIRECTIONS

From the train station you can follow Beim Retteich or Konrad-Adenauer-Straße down to the Puppenbrücke. After crossing the bridge the road forks, but either way will take you to the Holstentor, the old gate which is the symbol of the city. Crossing the Holstenbrücke, you arrive at the start of Holstenstraße. Going up Holstenstraße, you arrive at the Kohlmarkt, from which you can turn left into the Markt. From Lübeck Hbf to the Markt is about 12 minutes' walk.

HOTELS, PENSIONS AND GUEST HOUSES

CHEAPEST DOUBLES FROM €20 (£13.30)

Pension Scharnweber, Moislinger Allee 163 (tel. 891042, *info@pension-scharnweber.de*). Family-friendly pension.

Pension Fey, Schönbökenerstraße 24 (tel. 478952). Breakfast included.

CHEAPEST DOUBLES FROM €30 (£20)

Hotel Schweizerhaus, Travemunde Allee 51 (tel. 388730). Breakfast €5 (£3.30) extra.

Hotel Stadt Lubeck, Am Bahnhof 21 (tel. 83883, *www.stadt-luebeck-hotel.de*, *info@stadt-luebeck-hotel.de*). Town centre.

Hotel Stadtpark, Röckstraße 9 (tel. 34555). B&B.

Hotel Hanseatic, Hansastraße 19 (tel. 83328). Buffet breakfast. The street runs off Beim Retteich.

Hotel Petersen, Hansastraße 11A (tel. 84519). The street runs off Beim Retteich.

Hotel Zur Alten Stadtmauer, An der Mauer 57 (tel. 73702, *stadtmauer@aol.com*). In the Old Town. Breakfast not included.

CHEAPEST DOUBLES FROM €40–60 (£27–40)

Pension Köglin, Kottwilzstraße 39 (tel. 622432). Breakfast included.

Hotel Victoria, Am Bahnhof 17/19 (tel. 81144). Near the train station.

Hotel Astoria, Fackenburger Allee 68 (tel. 46763). Friendly hotel.

Baltic Hotel Priebe, Hansastraße 11 (tel. 85575). Two minutes from train station and 5 minutes from the Old Town.

Hotel Oymanns, Stormarnstraße 12 (tel. 290240). Pleasant hotel. Book through the tourist information website.

PRIVATE ROOMS AND APARTMENTS

Apartments can be booked online at the tourist information office, and they can likewise organise private rooms. Visit their website or drop them an email.

HI HOSTELS

Jugendherberge Gerd am Gertrudenkirchhof 4 (tel. 33433, *jhluebeck@djh-nordmark.de*). B&B from €20 (£13.30). Curfew 11.30pm. Outside the historic centre, 5 minutes' walk from the Bürgtor. A 25- to 30-minute walk from Lübeck Hbf. From the station, bus 1 or 3 to Am Burgfeld.

Jugendgasthaus Lübeck, Mengstraße 33 (tel. 702 0399, email as above). B&B from €18 (£12). Curfew midnight, but over 18s can get a key. Breakfast included. In the Old Town. Turn right off An der Untertrave.

HOSTELS

Sleep-In (YMCA), Große Petersgrube 11 (tel. 71920, *info@cvjm-luebeck.de*). Dorm beds from €10 (£6.70); doubles €40 (£27). Breakfast €4 (£2.70). Open to men and women. Midnight curfew. Turn left off An der Obertrave.

Rucksackhotel, Kanalstraße 70 (tel. 706892, *rucksack-hotel-luebeck@freeserve.de*). Dorm beds from €24 (£16) (10 in room). About 20 minutes' walk from Lübeck Hbf on the eastern edge of the Old Town.

CAMPING

Steinraderdamm 12, Lübeck-Schönböcken (tel. 893090). Around €5 (£3.30) p.p. Showers, washing machines and cooking facilities. Open 1 Apr.–31 Oct. From the centre of town 10 minutes on bus 7 or 8 dir. Dornbreite. Both stop near the entrance to the site.

Munich (München) (0)89

TOURIST OFFICES

Fremdenverkehrsamt, Sendlinger Straße 1 (tel. 233 96500,

www.muenchen-tourist.de,   *tourismus@muenchen.de*).   Open
Mon.–Sat. 9am–8pm, Sun. 10am–6pm. Queues can be
lengthy in summer, expect to wait 15–30 minutes. If all you
want is a simple city map with the main tourist attractions,
these are normally available from the self-service brochure
stand.

EurAide (tel. 593889) is opposite track 11 in the main train
station, by the Bayerstraße exit. It has masses of useful info in
English and will book rooms for a small fee. Open Mon.–Fri.
7.45am–12pm and 1–4.30pm and on Sat. mornings.

Flughafen München 'Franz Josef Strauss' (tel. 9759 2815). In the
central building of the airport. Open daily 8.30am–10pm,
except Sun. and public holidays 1–9pm.

FINDING ACCOMMODATION

Munich is one of the most popular destinations in Europe, so
reservation of accommodation is advisable at any time of year, as
far in advance as possible. Hotels can be booked in advance online
at the tourist information website listed above. Alternatively you
should call 233 30236 or email *hotelservice@muenchen.de*. The
Fremdenverkehrsamt operates three branches in the city which
will book rooms for you on arrival. The city is exceptionally busy
between June and August, then, in September, just when it is
becoming easier to find accommodation elsewhere, Munich
receives a huge influx of visitors for the start of the Oktoberfest. If
you are arriving without reservations at this time it is highly
unlikely you will find a hostel bed, or even a room in one of the
cheaper hotels listed below. Railpass holders totally stuck for a bed
should refer to the Sleeping Rough section below for details of a
useful train service.

HOTELS, PENSIONS AND GUEST HOUSES

Note: Roman numerals refer to the floor of the building.
Be aware: many hotels increase their rates during the Oktoberfest
(late September, early October).

CHEAPEST DOUBLES FROM €50 (£33)
Pension Margit, Hermann-Lingg Straße (tel. 533340). Near Hbf.
Am Kaiserplatz, Kaiserplatz 12 (tel. 349190). U3, U6: Münchener

Freiheit, then a few minutes' walk along Herzogstraße, first left, then right along Kaiserstraße.

Fleischmann, Bischof-Adalbert-Straße 10 (tel. 3509870). U2, U3: Petuelring. From Petuelring, a short walk down Riesenfeld-straße, right after Keferloherstraße, then left.

Strigl, Elisabethstraße 11/II (tel. 271 3444). U2: Hohenzollern-platz, then a few minutes' walk down Tengstraße and left along Elisabethstraße.

Lugano, Schillerstraße 32 (tel. 591005). A 5-minute walk from Munich Hbf. Leaving the station by the main exit, Schillerstraße begins almost opposite the right hand end of Bahnhofplatz, across Bayerstraße.

Lipp, Herzogstraße 11 (tel. 332951). U3, U6: Münchener Freiheit.

Flora, Karlstraße 49 (tel. 597067, *www.hotel-flora.de*, *info@hotel-flora.de*). Just over 5 minutes' walk from Munich Hbf, left off Dachauer Straße.

Locarno, Bahnhofplatz 5 (tel. 555164). Breakfast included.

Seibel, Reichenbachstraße 8 (tel. 2319180, *pension.seibel@t-online.de*). By Marienplatz.

Hungaria, Brienner Straße 42/II (tel. 521558). A 10-minute walk from Munich Hbf. Exit left on to Arnulfstraße, cross over and take Dachauer Straße, second right, across Karlstraße. Carry on down Augustenstraße into Brienner Straße. The hotel is located roughly 250m from both. U1: Stiglmaierplatz and U2: Königsplatz.

Frank, Schellingstraße 24 (tel. 281451, *pension.frank@gmx.net*). Schellingstraße runs off Ludwigstraße. A 5-minute walk from the U-Bahn station.

Haydn, Haydnstraße 9 (tel. 531119). A 10–15-minute walk from Munich Hbf, left off Herzog-Heinrich-Straße at Kaiser-Ludwig-Platz (see Hotel Herzog-Heinrich, below). U3, U6: Goetheplatz, then a few minutes' walk along Mozartstraße, then right.

CHEAPEST DOUBLES FROM €60 (£40)

Pension Geiger, Steinheilstraße 1 (tel. 521556). Arrive by 6pm or telephone.

Theresia, Luisenstraße 51 (tel. 521250). U2: Theresienstraße. Follow Theresienstraße two blocks in the direction of the Alte Pinakothek, then right on Luisenstraße (about 300m in all).

Helvetia, Schillerstraße 6 (tel. 590 6850, *www.hotel-helvetia.de, info@hotel-helvetia.de*). Near the station. Has dorms.

Würmtalhof, Eversbuschstraße 91 (tel. 892 1520, *www.wuermtalhof.de, wuermtalhof@web.de*). S2: Allach, then a 250m walk along Versaliusstraße into Eversbuschstraße. The hotel is near the junction.

Westfalia, Mozartstraße 23 (tel. 530377, *www.pension-westfalia.de, pension-westfalia@t-online.de*).

Augsburg, Schillerstraße 18 (tel. 597673). About 300m from Munich Hbf, see Lugano, above.

Härtl, Verdistraße 135 (tel. 811 1632). S2: Obermenzing, then a 5-minute walk along Verdistraße or bus 73 or 75.

Isabella, Isabellastraße 35 (tel. 271 2903). U2: Hohenzollernplatz, a 400m walk along Kurfürstenstraße, then right down Isabellastraße.

Am Knie, Strindbergstraße 33 (tel. 886450). Tram 19 from Munich Hbf towards Pasinger Marienplatz. Get off at junction of Landsbergerstraße and G.-Habel-Straße. Walk down the latter, then left.

Central, Bayerstraße 55 (tel. 543 9846, *pension.central@t-online.de*).

Westend, Landsbergerstraße 20 (tel. 508090, *htlwestend@aol.com*). 10 minutes' walk west of station, or catch tram 18 or 19 for three stops.

HI HOSTELS

The HI hostels in Munich are part of the Bavarian section of the Deutsches Jugendherbergswerk, which admits only those aged 27 or under to hostels under its control. Because of the popularity of the hostels in Munich there is virtually no chance of this rule being ignored, although this can sometimes be the case in other cities in the region.

DJH Jugendherberge München, Wendl-Dietrich-Straße 20 (tel. 131156, *jhmuenchen@djh-bayern.de*). This is the most central hostel. B&B in dorms €24.50 (£16.50) p.p. 1am curfew. U1: Rotkreuzplatz, then a short walk along Wendl-Dietrich-Straße. The entrance is on Winthirplatz, second on the right.

DJH Jugendgasthaus München, Miesingstraße 4 (tel. 723 6550, *jghmuenchen@djh-bayern.de*). Dorm bed and breakfast from

€24.50 (£16.50). 1am curfew. Take the underground (U-bahn 3) directly from Marienplatz (direction Fürstenried-West to Thalkirchen, the 200 stop. 15-minute ride. Hostel is then signposted from station (5-minute walk).

HOSTELS

CVJM-Jugendgasthaus, Landwehrstraße 13 (tel. 552 1410, *info@cvjm-muenchen.org*). Singles from around €31 (£21), doubles around €26 (£17.50) p.p. Over 27: 16% surcharge. Overnight price includes breakfast. Prices fall after two nights. YMCA hostel, but open to girls as well. 12.30am curfew. A 5- to 10-minute walk from Munich Hbf. Closed over Easter and the Christmas period.

Euro Youth Hostel, Senegelder Straße 5 (tel. 599 08811, *www.euro-youth-hotel.de*, *info@euro-youth-hotel.de*). Singles €45 (£30), doubles €36 (£24) p.p., dorms from €17 (£11.50). Breakfast for €4.90 (£3.25). Right next to the train station. Open 24 hours.

Haus International, Jugendhotel, Elisabethstraße 87 (tel. 120060, *www.haus-international.de*, *info@haus-international.de*). Singles from €30 (£20), doubles from €26 (£17.50) p.p., triples €24.50 (£16.50) p.p., larger rooms available. Ensuite facilities optional. U2: Hohenzollernplatz, then a 5-minute walk along Hohenzollernplatz, left down Schleiheimer Straße into Elisabethstraße.

4 You, Hirtenstraße 18 (tel. 552 21660, *www.the4you.de*, *info@the4you.de*). Singles €33.50 (£22.50), doubles €24 (£16) p.p., dorms from €16.50 (£11). More for over 27s.

Kolpinghaus St Theresia, Hanebergstraße 8 (tel. 126050, *st.theresia@t-online.de*). Singles €27 (£18), doubles €54 (£36). From Munich Hbf, take tram 20, 25 or 27 heading left from the station to the stop after Dachauerstraße crosses Landshuter Allee. Walk back, then right down Landshuter Allee, then right again at Hanebergstraße (a 5-minute walk).

THE TENT

Jugendlage Kapuzinerhölzl 'Das Zelt', In den Kirschen 30 (tel. 141 4300, *www.the-tent.com*, *see-you@the-tent.com*). Around €7 (£4.70). Actually two circus tents, with mattresses and blankets provided. Open 5pm–9am, late June–early Sept. Three-night maximum stay. Max age 24, not rigorously enforced. Leave your pack at the station. U1 to Rotkreuzplatz, then tram 12 dir. Amalienburgstraße to the Botanischer Garten stop on Miesingerstraße. Along Franz-Schrank-Straße and left at the top on to In den Kirschen. You will see 'The Tent' on the right.

CAMPING

Munich-Thalkirchen, Zentralländstraße 49 (tel. 723 1707, *www.camping-muenchen.de* – German only). Cheap municipal site. Open 15 Mar.–31 Oct. Crowded, especially during the Oktoberfest. From the train station, take S1–S7 to Marienplatz, then U3 dir. Forstenrieder Allee to Thalkirchen (Tierplatz), followed by bus 57 to Thalkirchen (last stop).

Munich Obermenzing, Lochhausener Straße 59 (tel. 811 2235, *www.campingplatz-muenchen.de*, *campingplatz-obermenzing@ t-online.de*). S2: Obermenzing, then bus 75 to the junction of Pippingerstraße and Lochhausener Straße, followed by a 10-minute walk along the latter. Open 15 Mar.–31 Oct.

Langwilder See, Eschenriederstraße. 119 (tel. 864 1566). Open April–mid-Oct. Nearest train station is München-Lochhausen, but that's still about 2 km away.

SLEEPING ROUGH

The police tolerate people sleeping in the main train station during the Oktoberfest, though make sure you move quickly when they wake you in the morning (usually around 6am). For obvious reasons, you cannot expect a peaceful night's sleep. If you have a railpass, you could always hop on the night train to Stuttgart and return to Munich in the morning.

GREECE (Hellas) (00)30

Holidaymakers flock to Greece every year either to savour the culture of the capital city, Athens, or to soak up the sun on one of the 166 inhabited islands. While Athens has earned a reputation as Europe's most polluted city, the islands are still a magnet for those seeking escapism. There are islands to suit all tastes, from the small and peaceful, where there is only a weekly boat which brings supplies, to those which rival Ibiza – built-up resorts with a nonstop party atmosphere.

BACKGROUND

Conquered by the Ottomans in the 15th century, the Greeks did not regain their independence until 1829, when they defeated their perennial adversaries, the Turks, in a bloody war. The poor relations between the Greeks and the Turks were intensified in 1974 by Turkey's invasion of Cyprus – the island that is, ironically, the supposed birthplace of the goddess of love, Aphrodite. Even as recently as 1998, the Cyprus problem was threatening the present peace between Greece and Turkey.

ACCOMMODATION DETAILS

Although accommodation prices have risen relatively sharply over the past few years, by European standards accommodation in Greece is still a bargain. At most times of the year, there is an ample supply of cheap beds and, except in the peak months of July and August, you are unlikely to encounter any trouble in finding a place to stay, even if you arrive late in the day. However, finding a cheap bed in Athens during the peak season becomes a bit of a problem (which unfortunately wasn't improved by the Olympics held here in 2004), while the supply of reasonably priced accommodation on most of the islands fails miserably to satisfy the huge demand.

Hotels are graded into six categories: deluxe, and then downwards from A to E. D- and E-class hotels are well within the range of the budget traveller, with singles from €20 (£13.30) and doubles from €30 (£20) (prices are for rooms without a shower/bath). Prices in C-class hotels generally start around €25 (£16.50) for singles and €35 (£23) for doubles, though some C-class hotels offer much cheaper rooms. Beds in triples or quads invariably work out much cheaper per person than those in singles or doubles. During the peak season, hotels may levy a 10% surcharge if you stay for fewer than three nights. Off-season, hotels cut their rates by up to 40% and are often prepared to negotiate, as they know you can easily take your custom elsewhere.

Pensions are cheaper than hotels. Though you may not notice much of a difference between the prices of pensions and those of cheap hotels in Athens, the difference is readily apparent else-where: even in such popular destinations as Rhodes, where pensions are often cheaper than private rooms, but especially so in rural areas, where prices can be as low as €10 (£6.70) per person.

Private rooms (*dhomatia*) are normally a fair amount cheaper than hotels. These are also officially classified, from A down to C. C-class rooms start around €8 (£5.30) for singles, €15 (£10) for doubles and €20 (£13.30) for triples. Comparable A-class rooms start around €10 (£6.70), €18 (£12) and €25 (£16.50) respec-tively. Private rooms are most common on the islands and in the coastal resorts. In most towns with a considerable supply of rooms, they can be booked through the local Tourist Office or Tourist Police. In some places, these offices operate an annoying policy of only booking rooms when the local hotels are filled to capacity. It is possible to look for rooms on your own: they are frequently advertised in several languages in an effort to attract tourists' attention (typically Greek, German, English, French and Italian). At the height of the tourist season, travellers arriving by bus or ferry in popular destinations are almost certain to encounter locals touting rooms in their homes at train and bus stations or ferry terminals. Given the severe accommodation shortage on most of the islands, it makes sense to accept any offer where the price and the location are reasonable. Few private rooms remain open during the period from November to April. For any small group looking to stay put for a week or so, renting a house or a flat can be an excellent option, particularly on the islands. Unfortunately, you will have to make enquiries locally on arrival to see what possibilities exist.

The **youth hostel** network is not extensive, numbering around 30 hostels in total. Generally, they are a bit ramshackle, but the atmosphere is usually quite relaxed. Currently, the only hostel affiliated with Hostelling International (HI) is the excellent one in Athens. Contact the Athens International Hostel (16 Victor Hugo Street, tel. 523 4170, *athenshostel@interland.gr*) for up-to-date news. The hostels in Greece charge from €5–10 (£3.30–6.70) per night. Between June and September, curfews are usually 1am; at other times of the year, midnight. However, there are some hostels which close as early as 10pm. With the warden's agreement, you can stay longer than the normal three-day maximum.

In Athens, there are several **student houses**. These are non-official hostels which offer cheap dormitory accommodation (and not just for students). As international trains approach Athens, young people from various student houses often board the train to hand out leaflets advertising their establishment. The leaflets are always flattering, of course, but some of these places are fine. Others, however, are of very poor quality. By and large, the cheapest are also the least secure for your belongings. The average price for dorms is €8 (£5.30).

Student houses frequently offer sleeping accommodation on their roof, as do some hotels and HI hostels. In the countryside, and on the islands, the best bet for renting **roof space** are the local *tavernas*. To find out about availability you will have to ask in person, question the hostel touts or rely on word of mouth. The Tourist Office is unlikely to be very expansive regarding the availability of roof space, as the practice was made illegal in 1987, ostensibly because the government was concerned about hoteliers overcharging. At present, the law is flouted on a wide scale, and renting a spot on a roof to throw down a mat and a sleeping bag remains a cheap and pleasant way to spend the summer nights. In Athens, you can expect to pay about €8 (£5.30), but elsewhere you will rarely pay more than €5 (£3.30).

There are around 90 official **campsites**, of which 13 are run by the Greek National Tourist Organisation (GNTO); the rest are privately operated. The GNTO sites are usually large, regimented establishments. The standard of the private sites varies widely. While some are very pleasant, others, especially those on the islands, are often little more than fenced-off patches of land (or sand). Typical prices are around €5 (£3.30) for a small tent, €5 (£3.30) per occupant, though some of the GNTO campsites charge up to €7 (£4.70). At the larger sites it is possible for two people and a tent to add up to the price of a basic room. While private sites may be prepared to drop their prices a little, there is no chance of this at state-run sites. If you are travelling between late June and early September, it is advisable to pack a tent as it guarantees you a cheap night's sleep. Travelling without a tent in the peak season, you are going to have to be incredibly fortunate to find a cheap bed every night of your trip.

Freelance camping and **sleeping rough** were made illegal as long ago as 1977, although many travellers are completely unaware of this. In part this is because many people still camp and sleep rough without encountering any difficulties with the authorities. Certainly, the law is not always stringently enforced. In the rural parts of the mainland there is virtually no chance of you having any problems, provided you ask permission before you pitch a tent and do not litter the area. Even on the islands, the police are tolerant of transgressions of the law, within certain limits. You will usually be all right if you show some discretion in your choice of site. This is important because in July and August your chances of finding a room or hostel bed are slim, so at some point you are likely to have to camp or sleep rough. *Avoid the main tourist beaches as the local police patrol them regularly.* Raids are also likely if the police hear that large numbers are beginning to congregate in one spot. The police are increasingly prone to using force to clear people away.

In most of the mountainous regions of the country, the Hellenic Alpine Club (HAC) maintains **refuge huts** for the use of climbers and hikers. Some of these are unmanned, so you have to visit the local HAC office in advance to pick up a set of keys. Unless you are a member of the HAC, or one of its foreign associates, you will have to pay a surcharge on the normal overnight fee.

Most **monasteries and convents** will put people up of the appropriate sex – it is still common practice on the mainland but less so on the islands. Always ask locally before heading to the building and dress respectfully – no shorts or short skirts. Also make sure that you arrive early in the evening, no later than 8pm or sunset (whichever is earlier).

ADDRESSES

GNTO

National Tourist Organisation of Greece, 4 Conduit Street, London WIR ODJ (tel. 020 7496 9300, *www.gnto.gr*, *info@gnto.co.uk*).

HOTELS

Advance reservations. Greek Chamber of Hotels, Stadiou Street 24, Athens 105–64 (tel. (0)1 210 33 10022, *grhotels@otenet.gr*, or visit the above website).

GREEK YHA

Greek Youth Hostel Association, Dragatsaniou Street 4, Fl.7, Athens 105–59 (tel. 210 323 4107).

CAMPING

Greek Camping Association, Solanos Street 76, Athens 106–80 (tel. 210 362 1560). Failing that there's an excellent search facility at the GNTO website listed above.

MOUNTAIN REFUGES

Hellenic Alpine Club (HAC), Karageorgi Street 7, Athens (tel. 210 323 4555).

Athens (Athina) (0)10

TOURIST OFFICES

Greek National Tourist Organisation (GNTO), Amerikis 2 (tel. 3310 565, *eotda01@mail.otenet.gr*). GNTO head office. Contact this office for information on the city or the country before you set off, or visit the GNTO website as listed above. On arrival, you can obtain information at any of the counters they operate in the city, but most will not give help with finding accommodation. Open Mon.–Fri. 9am–7pm, Sat. 10am–2pm.

Karageorgi Servias 2 (tel. 322 2545). The office is located in the National Bank on Syntagma Square. Open Mon.–Fri. 8am–6.30pm, Sat. 9am–2pm, Sun. 9am–1pm.

Ermou 1 (tel. 323 41 30). In the General Bank of Greece on Syntagma Square. Open Mon.–Fri. 8am–8.30pm, Sat. 8am–2pm.

Airport (tel. 353 0445). Open every day 8am–10pm in the arrivals hall.

Piraeus, Zea Marina (tel. 4284 100). Information and help with accommodation is available.

Hellenic Chamber of Hotels. Room-finding service. Stadiou Street 24. A–C-class hotels only. In the National Bank on Syntagma Square. Open Mon.–Fri. 8.30am–2pm, Sat. 9am–12.30pm (tel. 33 10022).

FINDING ACCOMMODATION

Unless you arrive late in the day during July or August you should find a reasonably cheap place quite easily. Expect to pay from €20 (£13.30) for a single, €30 (£20) for a double, €10 (£6.70) for a dormitory bed, and around €8 (£5.30) for a mattress on a hostel roof. Do not sleep in the city parks; camping anywhere in Athens is illegal and dangerous. A word of warning: men arriving from the airport by bus should avoid 'friendly bar keepers' who may send you to brothels rather than hotels.

PENSIONS/HOSTELS

There's plenty of cheap accommodation close to the railway station and around Omonia Square, which is handy if you're passing through Athens but rather inconvenient for the main sights and night life. For Omonia Square, turn right outside the station along Theodorou Diligiani to Karaiskaki Square, then turn left along Agiou Konstandinou. Be wary of pickpockets in the subway and around the Omonia Sq. area.

Aphrodite, Einardou 12 (tel. 881 0589, *www.hostelaphrodite. com*, *info@hostelaphrodite.com*). Walk left from the station, past the end of Peonious, then turn right up Karditsas on to Liossion. Cross the street, head left, and then almost immediately right at Einavdou. Dorms start at €16 (£10.50).

Exarchion, Themistokleous 55 (tel. 380 0731). Beds in rooms from €25 (£16.50) per person. Close to Omonia Square.

Hotel Museum, Bouboulinas 16 (tel. 380 5611). Doubles from €50 (£33). Behind the Archaeological Museum.

Appia, Menandrou 21 (tel. 524 5155). Singles €13 (£8.70), doubles €20 (£13.30). Cafeteria and 24-hour. Free luggage storage. Left off Agiou Konstandinou. Book ahead.

Feron, Feron 43 (tel. 823 2083). Doubles around €20 (£13.30).

Orpheus, Halkokondili 58 (tel. 522 4996). Singles around €20 (£13.30). Near Omonia Square.

Zorbas, Glyfordou 10 (tel. 8234 239, *www.zorbashotel.com*, *info@zorbashotel.com*). Singles €30 (£20), doubles €22 (£14.50) p.p., dorms from €14 (£9.50). Just off Victoria Square.

Arta, Nikitara 12 (tel. 382 7753). €25 (£16.50). Rooms with A/C and baths available.

Accommodation around Syntagma Square is slightly more expensive than on average, but is conveniently located near the centre and the places of interest. As you look across Syntagma with the Parliament to your rear, Ermou is the road leading out of the centre of the square. Kar. Servias (which becomes Perikleous) runs from the far right-hand corner, Mitropoleos from the far left. Filellinon runs from the left-hand side of the square.

Hotel Tempi, 29 Eolou Street (tel. 321 3175, *hoteltempi@travelling.gr*). Doubles €42 (£28). At Ermou. Bus route 91.

Festos, Filellinon 18 (tel. 323 2455). Great arrangement – stay and work. The hotel employs travellers to staff the desk and work in the lounge. Doubles €50 (£33), dorm beds from €18 (£12). Baggage storage available.

John's Place, Patrou 5 (tel. 322 9719). Off Mitropoleos, four blocks from Syntagma. Doubles from €35 (£23).

Thisseus, Thisseos 10 (tel. 324 5960). Curfew 1am. Dorms from €11 (£7.30). Right off Perikleous.

Imperial Hotel, Mitropoleos 46 (tel. 322 7617). Singles from €8 (£5.30) without bath. Close to Athens cathedral.

Pella Inn, Ermou 104 (tel. 325 0598, *www.pella-inn.gr*, *pella@pella-inn.gr*). Singles €20 (£13.30), doubles €30 (£20). Free baggage storage. The entrance is on Karaisaki. A 10-minute walk from Syntagma, close to the Monastariki underground station.

Athenian Inn, Haritos 22 (tel. 723 8097). From Syntagma walk past the left-hand side of the Parliament. At the Benaki Museum turn left away from the National Garden up Koumbari into Filikis Eterias Square. Cross the square and head right along Patriarhi Iokm, turn left up Irodotou, then right into Haritos.

Cecil, Athinas 39 (tel. 3217 079, *cecil@netsmart.gr*). Doubles around €30 (£20). Excellent pension.

The Plaka, beneath the Acropolis, is both centrally located and a cheap area to stay in:

Dioskouros House, Pitakou 6 (tel. 324 8165). Doubles €40 (£27). Outdoor bar and breakfast served in the courtyard.

Kimon, Apollonos 27 (tel. 3314 658). Very cheap but no frills.

Student Inn, Kidathineon 16 (tel. 324 4808, *www.student travellersinn.com, info@studenttravellersinn.com*). Internet access. 1.30am curfew. Singles, doubles, triples and quads. 10% discount with student ID. Luggage storage. Turn right off Filellinon as you walk from Syntagma Square (see above). Highly recommended.

Byron, Vironis 19 (tel. 3253 554). Doubles around €45 (£30). Clean and with good views.

Kouros, Kodrou 11 (tel. 322 7431). Doubles €30 (£20). Walking from Syntagma Square along Mitropoleos, turn left down Voulis and continue straight on across Nikodimou into Kodrou.

Acropolis House, Kodrou 6–8 (tel. 322 2344). Doubles around €35 (£23). Adding an extra bed to a room increases the original price by 20%. Luggage storage. See Kouros, above.

Adonis, Kodrou 3 (tel. 324 9737). Great views of the Acropolis from the rooftop bar. See Kouros (above) for directions.

Veikou, Koukaki, Arditos and Pangrati districts: on the other side of the Acropolis from the Plaka, these are quieter residential areas.

Art Gallery, Erehthiou 5 (tel. 923 8376). Family-run pension. Luggage storage.

Marble House, An. Zini 35 (tel. 923 4058). Singles around €20 (£13.30), doubles €30 (£20). Free luggage storage. Take tram 1 or 5 to the Zini stop. Bookings essential.

Tony's, Zaharitsa 26 (tel. 923 0561). Close to Marble House (see above) but slightly more expensive.

Elli, Heidhen 29 (tel. 8815 876). Welcoming and excellent value.

HI HOSTEL

Athens International, Victor Hugo Street 16 (tel. 523 4170, *athenshostel@interland.gr*). B&B from €7 (£4.70). This is the only IYHF-affiliated hostel in the whole of Greece. From Omonia Square, take Third September Street then left at Veranzerou. Recently moved from Kypselis. Book ahead.

HOSTELS

Youth Hostel No. 5, Damareos 75 (tel. 751 9530). Dorms €5.30 (£3.60). Take trolleybus 2, 11 or 12 to Pangratiou Square, then walk down Frinis until it is crossed by Damareos. A little bit out of town, but clean and friendly.

XEN (YWCA), Amerikis 11 (tel. 362 4291). Women only. Cheapest doubles €25 (£16.50).

CAMPING

Athens Camping, Leoforos Athinon 198, Peresteri (tel. 581 4114). Bus 822 or 823 from Eleftherias Square (Underground: Thission). Open all year, 7 km from the centre.

Dionissioti Camping (tel. 800 1496). 18 km north of the city on the national road at Nea Kiffissia.

Voula, Alkyonidon 2 (tel. 895 2712). Bus 118, 122 or 153 from Vass. Olgas Avenue.

Dhafni Camping. About 13 km out in Dafni (tel. 581 1562). Bus 862 or 853 from Platia Eleftherias.

SLEEPING ROUGH

Definitely not advised. It is illegal and the police make regular checks on the city's parks, especially those located close to the train station. The police, however, are likely to be the least of your worries given the considerable numbers of travellers who are robbed or assaulted while sleeping rough.

THE ISLANDS

Probably *the* favourite Greek destination for holidaymakers; there are hundreds of islands to choose from. There is room here only to list a few of the most popular places.

Santorini (Thira) – Fira (0)2860

The Tourist Police office (tel. 22649) is close to the main square on 25th Martiou, the road leading to Oia. Alternatively you can visit *www.santonet.gr*.

FINDING ACCOMMODATION

Fira has a large number of pensions and cheap hotels, but in summer these are frequently full by midday. You might be well advised to take up the first reasonable offer you receive from the locals with rooms to let, who are on hand every time a boat docks in the harbour. If you are having no luck finding a room in Fira, there are good supplies of pensions and private rooms in many of the small towns nearby, such as Karteradhos (20 minutes away), Messaria, Pirgos and Emborio.

HOTELS/PENSIONS

Pension Petros, on road to Camping Santorini (tel. 22573, book online at *www.santonet.gr/hotels/petros*). Run by friendly family. All rooms have bath and most have fridges. The owner supplies free transport to and from the port. Doubles €20 (£13.30). Triples available.

Anemone (tel. 22615, book at *www.santonet.gr/hotels/anemone*). Villa run by Petros, the owner of Pension Petros (see above).

Fregata (tel. 71276, *www.fregata.gr*). Doubles from €40 (£27)

Leta, on way to Oia (tel. 22540). Cheap doubles and triples.

HOSTELS

Anna Youth Hostel, Perisa Beach (tel. 82182). Take their minibus from the port to this hostel. Dorms from €7 (£4.70).

Thira Youth Hostel, approx 300m north of the square (tel. 22387). Open Apr.–Oct. Dorms and private rooms available. Quiet after 11pm. Dorms €7 (£4.70); doubles around €25 (£16.50). Great views, cheap restaurant.

CAMPING

Perissa (tel. 81604). On the beach, a minibus will pick you up from the port.

Camping Santorini (tel. 22944, *www.santorinicamping.gr*, *santocam@otenet.gr*). Open Apr.–Oct. €30 (£20) to rent a tent, €5 (£3.30) p.p. 400m east of Plateia Theotocopoulou. Free use of swimming pool. Cafe, bar and minimarket on site.

THE IONIAN ISLANDS

These are the islands off the north-west coast. Corfu is the main tourist centre.

Corfu Town (Kerkira) (0)6610

TOURIST OFFICES

GNTO (tel. 37520) is at the corner of Rizospaston Voulefton and Iak. Folila. Open May–Sept., Mon.–Fri. 7.30am–2.30pm. The office distributes a list of local hotels and has information on the availability of private rooms.

The Tourist Police (tel. 30265) is in the direction of Sanrocco Square. Turn right on I. Theotaki and take the first right. It's on the fourth floor. Open daily 7.30am–2.30pm.

Alternatively visit *www.corfu-greece.biz*.

FINDING ACCOMMODATION

At most times of year you should find yourself an E-class hotel without too much trouble, either from the list given out by the EOT office or simply by looking round on your own (the streets between the Igoumentsa Dock and N. Theotki are your best bet, especially if it is singles you are after). In summer, you are more likely to have to ask the Tourist Office about a private room, but it is worth noting that many of the tourist agencies lining Arseniou (between the Old Port and the Old Fortress) and Stratigou (beside the New Port) book rooms in pensions, frequently without commission.

HOTELS

Europa, Yitsaiali 10 (tel. 39304). Not far from the New Port ferry terminal. Well located and well priced. Doubles €20 (£13.30).

Ionion, Xen. Stratigou 46 (tel. 39915). Doubles from €24 (£16).

Konstantinoupolis, Zavitsanou 1 (tel. 48716, *www.konstantin oupolis.com.gr*, *info@konstantinoupolis.com.gr*). At the end of N. Theotki. On the waterfront. Doubles from around €70 (£47).

Astron, Donzelot 15 (tel. 39505). Near the New Port on the waterfront. Doubles €55 (£37).

Atlantis, Xen. Stratigou 48 (tel. 35560). Many rooms have A/C. At the New Port. Doubles from €50 (£33).

The Pink Palace, Agios Gordios Beach (tel. 53024, *www.thepink palace.com*). Mention Corfu to any backpacker and they will ask: 'Did you stay at the Pink Palace?' Famed for its all-night Ouzo-fuelled parties, the Palace more than likely lives up to its reputation. If this puts you off, don't even consider it. If you want to party all night with an international crowd, then the Palace is the place for you.

CAMPING

Kontokali Beach International (tel. 91170). Same bus as the hostel.

Camping Dionysus, Dafnilas Bay (tel. 91417, *www.dionysus camping.gr*). About 9 km north of the town, connected by a morning bus service.

THE CYCLADES

Of all the Greek islands these are the most popular with tourists, and the prices (and summer crowds) reflect this. Ios, Mykonos, Naxos and Paros all offer stunning scenery and are well served by the ferry operators.

Ios Town (0)2860

TOURIST OFFICE

The Tourist Office (tel. 91028) is by the bus stop in Ios Town. Open daily 9am–3pm and 4.30–10.30pm. Local information and ferry schedules. Ios Town is easily reached from the ferry port in Yialos by bus, or by a 20-minute walk up the hill.

Alternatively visit *www.iosgreece.com*.

FINDING ACCOMMODATION

Accommodation on Ios is noticeably cheaper than on most of the Cyclades, with the exception of the ferry port of Yialos. That said, singles are in short supply at any time of year, while rooms of any type become difficult to find during the peak season of July/Aug.

HOTELS

Francesco's (tel. 91223). Dorm beds, doubles and triples. Up the hill from the bank. Great views. Book ahead.

Markos Pension (tel. 91059, *marcovlg@otenet.gr*). From the bus stop, take the right just before the supermarket. It's well signposted (just to the left of The Wind). All rooms have bath. Doubles from €23 (£15.50). Reserve in good time.

Far Out Hotel (tel. 91446, *www.thefaroutclub.com*, *info@thefar outclub.com*). Located above Mylopotas beach. Doubles from €50 (£33).

Petros Place (tel. 91421). Just up the street which faces you as you get off the ferry. Great hotel with swimming pool and tennis courts. A bargain with doubles for only €35 (£23).

CAMPING

Far Out Camping (tel. 92301, *www.thefaroutclub.com*, *info@far outclub.com*), from €5 (£3.30) p.p. This site is at the far end of Mylopotas beach and is a fantastic, fun place to stay. There's lots of organised sport and party nights.

Stars (tel. 91612, *www.purplepigstars.com*, *info@purplepig stars.com*). On Mylopotas beach. Nice site but quieter than Far Out. Swimming pool and other amenities. About €6 (£4) per person. This company also runs the nearby Purple Pig campsite.

SLEEPING ROUGH

Sleeping on the beach is no longer to be recommended, despite its past popularity. Not only is there a considerable risk of theft but police patrols are becoming increasingly regular, as is their readiness to clear the beach forcibly. Although it is still illegal, you should have little trouble with the authorities if you stick to quieter beaches such as Koumbara or Manganari.

Paros (Parikia) (0)2840

TOURIST OFFICE

In the old windmill by the port (tel. 22079). Open 8am–10pm daily. Local maps and transport schedules, but no accommodation service.

Alternatively, *visit www.parosweb.com.*

FINDING ACCOMMODATION

Paros is not only one of the most popular of the Cyclades in its own right, but it is also an island many people pass through due to its importance as a ferry hub. Consequently, finding hotels in the peak season can be a frustrating experience (many are block-booked by tour operators). The Room Association (tel. 24528) by the docks will help in your search. In the summer months, locals touting private rooms await the arrival of every ferry. Provided the price is not extravagant, you should take the first offer you receive.

HOTELS

Hotel Dina (tel. 21325). Open May–Oct. Advanced reservation advised, preferably in writing. Just off the main street, at the foot of Market Square, past the National Bank.

Festos Hotel, close to the Dina (see above) (tel. 21635). Reserve ahead.

Rooms Mimikos (tel. 21437). Close to the National Bank, just off Agorakitau (signposted).

Hotel Kypreou, 18 Borbona (tel. 21383). Not far from the Tourist Office, by the Olympic Airways office.

Hotel Parko (tel. 22213). Along the street from Olympic Airways.

Sophia Rooms, behind Cinema Paros (tel. 22085).

Pelagos Studios (tel. 22725, fax 22708). Good clean accommodation but at the end of a dark dirt track. Arrive during the hours of daylight. Doubles from €20 (£13.30), rising to €45 (£30) in high season.

Rena Rooms (tel. 22220). Go left from the docks and take the right which leads to Top laundromat, first right then follow the signs. All rooms have bath and balcony. Doubles from €20 (£13.30). Book ahead.

Argonaftis (tel. 21440). Next to the National Bank. A/C rooms. Doubles from €30 (£20). Reserve.

CAMPING

Koula (tel. 22081, *koula@otenet.gr*). €3 (£2) per tent, €4 (£2.70) per person. At the northern end of the town's beach, only 400m from the centre.

Parasporas (tel. 21394). About 2 km out of town, but less crowded than Koula. Buses run from the port.

THE DODECANESE

The most easterly of the Greek islands, the Dodecanese are actually closer to Turkey than they are to Greece. Ferries can take up to 20 hours to make the crossing, so you may want to consider flying across. Kos and Rhodes are the two main islands.

Kos Town (0)2420

TOURIST OFFICE

Municipal Tourist Information, Akti Miaouli (tel. 29200). Open daily 7.30am–9.30pm from 15 Apr.–31 Oct.; Mon.–Fri. 7.30am–3pm at other times. Information on accommodation, local maps and transport schedules. On the shore, at the junction of Akti Miaouli with Vas. Pavlou.

Tourist Police, Akti Miaouli (tel. 22444). In the large yellow building next to the castle.

FINDING ACCOMMODATION

Looking towards town from the harbour, the majority of the cheaper establishments are located over to your right. In July and August, you will struggle to find a bed in a pension or private room if you look on your own, unless you begin your search early in the day. At this time of year, it is better to accept any reasonable offer you receive from locals touting at the ferry port.

HOTELS AND PENSIONS

Pension Alexis, Irodotou 9 (tel. 28798). Doubles from €20 (£13.30). The owners will often accommodate those stuck for a room in beds on the patio for €6 (£4). Off Megalos Alexandrou Street.

Hotel Afentoulis, Evripilou 1 (tel. 25321). Run by the same crowd as the Alexis, but on the other side of town. Doubles €27 (£18).

Hotel Dodecanissos, Alex. Ipsilantou 2 (tel. 28460). From the Tourist Office head away from the shore, then first right.

Rooms to Let Nitsa, Averof 47 (tel. 25810). North of town, near the beach.

CAMPING

Kos Camping (tel. 23275). Open Apr.–Oct. In the village of Psaldi, 2.5 km from Kos.

Rhodes Town (0)2410

TOURIST OFFICES

EOT, Archbishop Makariou/Papagou Street 5 (tel. 23655). Open all year, Mon.–Fri. 7.30am–3pm.

City of Rhodes Tourist Office, Rimini Square (tel. 35945). Open Mon.–Sat. 8am–8pm, Sun. 9am–12pm. Closed during the winter. Accommodation service. Free town plan and bus and ferry information.

Alternatively you can visit *www.rodos.com*, or *www.rhodesinfo.com*.

FINDING ACCOMMODATION

You should not have much trouble finding suitably priced accommodation in Rhodes Town. There are plenty of cheap pensions, virtually all of which are conveniently situated within the Old Town, in the area roughly bounded by Sokratous on the north, Perikléos on the east, Omirou on the south, and Ippodhamou on the west. In the winter, many pension owners close their doors; those that remain open will often drop their rates if you haggle.

HOTELS

Hotel Andreas, Omirou 28 (tel. 34156, *www.hotelandreas.com, andreasch@otenet.gr*). Doubles from €50 (£33). In the Old Town.

Pink Elephant, Irodhotou 42 (tel. 22469). Fun, cheap pension.

Billy's Pension, Perikléos Street 32 (tel. 35691). In the Old Town.

New Village Inn, Konstantopedos 10 (tel. 34937). Doubles from €25 (£16.50).

Niki's, Sofokleous 39 (tel. 25115). Doubles from €35 (£23).

Spot, Perikleous 21 (tel. 34737). Open March–end November. Doubles from €40 (£27).

Hotel Faliron, Faliraki (tel. 85483). Open Apr.–Oct.

Hotel Via-Via, Pythagora 45 (tel. 27895). Doubles from €20 (£13.30).

La Luna, Ierokleous 21 (tel. 25856). Doubles around €45 (£30).

HOSTEL

Youth hostel, Ergiou 12 (tel. 30491). Dorm beds from €8 (£5.30). Near Sokratous.

CAMPING

Faliraki Camping (tel. 85358), 2 km north of Faliraki beach. Swimming pool, minimarket. Take a bus from the east side of Plateia Rimini. Expect to pay around €5 (£3.30) per person and €3 (£2) per tent.

CRETE (Kriti)

In summer it can be exceptionally difficult to find rooms. Your best bet is probably to head straight for the nearest Tourist Office.

Agios Nikolaos (0)8410

TOURIST OFFICE
S. Koundourou 21A (tel. 22357). By the bridge near the port. Room-finding service. The office is open Apr.–Oct. 8.30am–9.30pm daily.

Tourist Police, Kontoghianni 34 (tel. 26900). Gives out general tourist information. Open 24hrs.

Alternatively, visit *www.crete-greece.biz*.

FINDING ACCOMMODATION
The best places to look for rooms are the streets up the hill from the hostel or the side streets leading off the roads heading out of town.

HOTELS
Argyro Pension, Solonos 1 (tel. 28707). Doubles from €15 (£10). From the Tourist Office head up 25th Martirou, turn left along Manousogianaki, then right at Solonos.

Hotel Rea, Marathonos 1 (tel. 82023). Doubles from €35 (£23). Excellent views.

The Green House, Modatsou 15 (tel. 22025). Doubles from €18 (£12). From the Tourist Office follow Koundourou to the left, go left again at Iroon Polytechniou, then right at Modatsou.

Rooms Mary, Evans 13 (tel. 24384). Rooms and apartments from €25 (£16.50).

Pension Perla, Salaminos 4 (tel. 23379). Doubles €20 (£13.30).

Victoria (tel. 22731). On Akti Koundourou, near Amoudi Beach. About 1 km from the harbour. Doubles from €15 (£10).

HOSTEL

Odos Stratigou Koraka 3 (tel. 22823). Walk up the concrete steps from the bridge at the harbour.

CAMPING

Although some people camp on the beach in front of the bus station, this is not to be recommended. It is better to head out of town to some of the beaches along the coast. The cove at Kalo Horio, about 13 km out, is one of the best places to pitch a tent.

HUNGARY (00)36

Hungary has always been very different from its East European neighbours. The people identify strongly with the West while displaying a strong pride in themselves as Magyars.

Hungary's popularity as a tourist destination is growing by the year, and is only likely to increase with membership of the European Union. This is understandable as Budapest becomes known as one of the world's most beautiful cities – as sophisticated and fashionable as any in Western Europe.

BACKGROUND

The attempted revolution from the Communists in 1956 is ingrained in most people's memories, as are the images of Soviet tanks trundling into Budapest to suppress rebellion. It was a more peaceful revolution in 1989 that established Hungary once more as an independent republic.

The majority of Hungarians are descended from the Magyars – an Asiatic tribe that reached the Danube in the 9th century, and settled there to establish the Arpad dynasty. They enjoyed a good 600 years of independence before the Ottomans moved in and occupied the area now known as Hungary. In the 17th century, the Hungarians succumbed to the charms of the Austrian Habsburgs who, in 1867, agreed to grant them an equal status under the joint Austro-Hungarian Empire. This partnership proved fruitful enough until war broke out in 1914. The Hungarians were then independent again until 1944 and the German occupation of their country. Following the horror of the Second World War, Hungary dabbled with republicanism before falling to the Communists in 1949 – a subjugation that was to last just over 40 years.

ACCOMMODATION DETAILS

Neither the local offices of the national tourist agency IBUSZ nor the regional or local tourist agencies will attempt to pressure you into staying in expensive hotels. On the contrary, they will generally do their best to arrange the type of accommodation you want, or at the very least direct you to organisations that will help you out. IBUSZ can be an especially useful organisation for travellers, as its nationwide presence allows it to operate an advance reservation system so that you can book hotels or private rooms ahead for a fee of around £1.50 ($2.50). This service is well worth using if you are heading for Budapest in peak season, when queues at accommodation agencies can be horrendous, or if you know you will arrive late in the evening or on a Saturday afternoon or a Sunday (when many accommodation agencies outside Budapest are closed).

Hotels (*szálló* or *szálloda*) are rated from one up to five stars. There is a shortage of singles throughout the country in all the various grades of hotels. Unless you are looking for a private bathroom, rooms in one-star hotels are normally perfectly acceptable, assuming you can find them: in recent years the number of one- and two-star hotels has dwindled considerably. Outside Budapest and the Lake Balaton area, where prices are normally about 30% higher, the remaining one-star hotels charge on average around £18–25 ($30–42) for doubles. The Hungarian National Tourist Office or local offices will provide details on any three-star hotels offering substantially reduced rates. Beware: the 10% tax on hotel bills which was introduced in 1993 should be included in the quoted price, not added on afterwards.

Rooms in a **pension** (*penzio* or *panzio*) or inn (*fogado*) are normally slightly cheaper than at a one-star hotel, with singles (more widely available than in hotels) costing around £12–15 ($20–25), doubles £15–20 ($25–40). Breakfast is included in the overnight price at all hotels, pensions and inns. This may be only an uninspiring continental breakfast, but on other occasions you may be treated to a substantial buffet of cold meats.

In the countryside it is possible to stay in **farm cottages** and **B&Bs**. Details of these establishments are contained in the brochure *Holidays in the Countryside* available from IBUSZ, although in the vast majority of cases it is the regional tourist agencies with whom you must make reservations.

The local currency is the forint and £1 is approximately 370 ft ($1 is 200 ft).

Probably the best accommodation bargains in Hungary are **private rooms** (*fizeto vendégszoba* or *Fiz* for short). Doubles range from around 1,500 ft (£4, $7) in provincial towns to around 4,500 ft (£12, $20) in Budapest. A surcharge may be added to the price of the room if you stay for fewer than four days (common in Budapest); for example, another 30% for one-night stays. It is standard practice to pay the agency rather than the householder. Although there's a general shortage of singles, the low prices mean even doubles are usually within reach for the solo traveller. The vast majority of private rooms are controlled by the old state tourist organisations IBUSZ or EXPRESS (the student travel organisation), or by more specialised local agencies such as Szegedtourist or Egertourist (in the towns of those names), or Balatontourist (around Lake Balaton). Some new agencies have been established, and, with such a potentially lucrative market to be tapped, further growth cannot be ruled out. However, in the more popular towns, long queues can be a deterrent to finding out what various agencies are charging. As a rough guide, IBUSZ offers the best service in Budapest as it controls the major share of the market and has a good supply of very cheap rooms. If you arrive in Budapest from another Hungarian town, it is well worth getting the local IBUSZ to reserve one of the cheaper rooms for you. Outside the capital, IBUSZ generally cannot compete with local agencies. However, if you are arriving late at your next destination it is probably worth paying a little extra to reserve a room through IBUSZ.

In peak season, it is still quite common to be approached by locals offering rooms, most probably in and around the train stations and outside IBUSZ offices. Outside Budapest these rooms are likely to be fine, but you should be wary of offers made in Budapest. The rooms on offer in the capital are generally of an inferior standard to rooms booked through an agency and are likely to be poorly located as well, although the asking price will be similar. However, solo travellers arriving late in the afternoon might want to consider such offers for the first night. If you do accept a private offer, keep an eye on your valuables or, better still, leave them at the station.

In the smaller towns, it is feasible to look for rooms on your own. Watch out for houses displaying a *szoba kiado* or *Zimmer frei* sign, then simply approach the owner to view the rooms on offer.

EXPRESS operates a chain of 30 **youth hostels** and **youth**

hotels, a number of which are listed in the HI handbook. They also control the letting of some of the non-EXPRESS hostels listed in the HI handbook, and many of the temporary hostels set up in college dormitories during the summer vacation (late June to the end of August). You can expect to pay around £3–4 ($5–7) per person in a dormitory (except in Budapest, where it costs twice as much). There are no curfews in EXPRESS accommodation, but you are expected to remain quiet after midnight.

As well as youth hostels, there are also numerous local hostels, which are known by different names according to their location. In provincial towns, enquiries should be made regarding the availability of beds in *turistaszálló* but in highland areas they are referred to as *turistahaz*. Local and regional accommodation agencies are generally the best source of information on these hotels. Standards vary much more than simple A or B grading implies. While some are spartan, others can be very comfortable. As a rule the overnight price of £2–10 ($3.50–17) reflects this.

Camping is popular with Hungarians, and the Magyar Camping and Caravanning Club (MCCC) is very active. Both the MCCC and an organisation called Tourinform produce excellent, easy-to-follow lists of the sites, complete with opening times, facilities available and a map showing their locations. The comprehensive guide *Camping Hungary* is generally available from IBUSZ or from local tourist agencies. There are about 140 sites in total, the heaviest concentration of which are along the shores of Lake Balaton, though there are sites in all the places you are likely to visit. The season runs from May to October inclusive, but many sites only open for the peak months of July and August. Outside July and August, there is usually no need to make reservations or to check about the availability of space before heading out to the site, and even at peak times this should only be necessary in Budapest and the Lake Balaton area. Sites are graded from one up to three stars. The three-star sites usually have a supermarket and leisure facilities, whereas the one-star sites seldom offer more than the basic necessities. A solo traveller can expect to pay £4–7 ($7–12) for an overnight stay at a two- or three-star site, though discounts are available to members of the International Camping and Caravanning Club (FICC). Prices in a one-star site can be as little as £1.50 ($2.50) per tent, plus a similar charge per person. Either side of the high season, most sites reduce their prices by 25–30%. At the larger sites it is possible to rent bungalows (*faház*). To hire a typical bungalow sleeping 2–4 persons generally costs between £5–12 ($8.50–20). You pay for the bungalow, so there is no discount for unoccupied bed space. Details of sites letting bungalows are contained in the various camping lists mentioned above. Freelance camping is illegal but is practised by many young people, Hungarians especially; most likely because offenders are rarely heavily punished. Favourite locations are the forests of the Danube Bend and the highland regions of the country, where rain shelters (*esöház*) are common.

ADDRESSES

HUNGARIAN NATIONAL TOURIST BOARD
P.O. Box 4336, London SW18 4XE (tel. 0891 171200, *www.hungarytourism.hu*).

IBUSZ
Ferenciek tere 10, Budapest (tel. (0)1 485 2700, *www.ibusz.hu*, *ut.irodak@ibusz.hu*).

DANUBE TRAVEL AGENCY
45 Great Cumberland Place, London W1H 7LH (tel. 020 7724 7577).

YOUTH HOSTEL ASSOCIATION
Magyarországi Ifjúsági Szállások, Almassy ter 6, 1077 Budapest (tel. (0)1 343 5167, *www.youthhostels.hu*, *info@youthhostels.hu*).

Another very good site for budget travel all over Hungary is *www.backpackers.hu*.

CAMPING
Magyar Camping & Caravanning Club (MCCC), Ülbi útca 6, 1085 Budapest (tel. (0)1 317 1711). Also see *www.camping.hu* for full campsite listings.

Tourinform, Süto útca 2, 1052 Budapest (tel. 117 9800, *tourinfo@mail.hungarytourism.hu*).

Lists of camping sites are available from the Hungarian National Tourist Office, or at their website as listed above.

Budapest (0)1

TOURIST OFFICE

Tourinform, Süto útca 2 (tel. 117 9800, *www.budapestinfo.hu*, *tourinfo@mail.hungarytourism.hu*). Open Mon.–Fri. 9am–7pm, Sat. and Sun. 9am–4pm. Not only a good source of general information on the city, but the multilingual staff do their best to answer more unusual enquiries. The staff can advise you on accommodation possibilities, but the office does not make bookings. About 50m from the Károly körút exit of the Deák tér metro station.

ACCOMMODATION AGENCIES

IBUSZ has the best supply of private rooms. They have offices at Ferenciek tér 10 (tel. 485 2700), on the corner of Petöfi Sándor útca (opening times: Mon.–Fri. 8.15am–5pm), another at Bartok Bela 15B (tel. 209 0320) and a third at Dob útca 1 (tel. 322 7214) open Mon.–Fri. 8am–6pm, Sat. and Sun. 8am–4pm.

Budapest Tourist (*www.budapestinfo.hu*) book private rooms, and 2- and 4-bed bungalows at the city's campsites. There are five offices, one at Roosevelt tér 5 (tel. 317 3555), open Mon.–Thur. 9am–4.30pm, Fri. 9am–4pm. About 10 minutes' walk from the Deák tér metro station. From the Károly körút exit, head left along Bajcsy-Zsilinszky útca, then left down József Attila útca. into Roosevelt tér. The others are at Nyugati Station (tel. 302 8580) (downstairs in the underpass in front of the station); Liszt Feren Square (332 4098); Szentharomsag 1(488 0475) at the castle.

EXPRESS book beds in hostels and converted student dorms. The EXPRESS head office is at Semmelweis útca 4 (tel. 317 8045, *www.expresstravel.hu*, *expresstravel@mailbox.hu*). From the Deák tér metro station, exit on to Károly körút, walk along the street then turn right down Gerlóczy útca, and then first left. There is an EXPRESS branch office which operates at the Keleti train station (tel. 342 1772). As well as hostel beds, this office also books private rooms.

Coopturist books private rooms. Their office is at Bajcsy-Zsilinszky útca 17 (tel. 311 7034). From the Deák tér metro station, exit on to Kártoly körút and head left along Bajcsy-Zsilinszky útca. Mon.–Fri. 9am–5pm.

HAWKERS

Upon arriving in Budapest (particularly at Keleti station), expect to be met by eager hostel hawkers and guest house proprietors touting their hostels/rooms. Although this can be quite an alarming experience for the first-time visitor, don't be put off, as there are good deals to be had. More than likely your first encounter will be with a representative from the hostel company Travellers which is no bad thing as they operate many hostels in the city (see **Hostels** below). As regards private rooms these will, in all likelihood, be of lower quality than the rooms you can book through an agency, and possibly poorly located as well. If you can agree on a suitable price, the main thing to find out is how easy it is to get to the room, particularly the metro links. Do not hand over any money until you have seen the room and are happy with it, and be firm with pushy hawkers.

HOTELS

The prices of hotels and pensions have risen sharply over the last few years, with the result that few remain within the budget category. The exception is if you are travelling in winter, when hotels often drop their rates. Enquire about current prices at the accommodation agencies or the Tourist Office.

CHEAPEST DOUBLES GENERALLY AROUND £20–40 ($42-68)

Citadella Hotel, Gellérthegy (tel. 166 5794). Recommended – breathtaking views of the city. Advance reservation advised. From the Deák tér or Kálvin tér metro stations, take tram 49 to Móricz Zsigmond körtér, then change to bus 27, which runs up to the Citadel. Also dorm rooms – see under **Hostels**.

Hotel Flandria, Szegedi útca 27 (tel. 350 3181, *hotelflandria@ axelero.hu*). Close to Arpád Bridge, take tram 12 from Keleti underground station.

Medosz, Jókai tér 9 (tel. 374 3000). Ugly building but close to the Opera House. The hotel takes cash only.

Hotel Express, Beethoven útca 7–9 (tel. 375 3082). In the centre of Buda, near Déli pályudvar station.

Jäger-Trió Panzió, Ördögorom útca 20 (tel. 246 4558). From Marcius 15 tér near the Ferenciek tér metro station, take bus 8 to its terminus in the Buda hills. The pension is a 10-minute walk from the bus stop.

ELTE Peregrinus Vendégház, Szerb útca 3 (tel. 266 4911). Located in a quiet backstreet in central Pest.

San Marcó Panzió, San Marcó útca 6 (tel. 188 9997). In northern Buda.

Csillaghegy Strand Hotel, Pusztakúti útca 3 (tel. 368 6624). In northern suburbs, only 10 minutes by HEV train to centre. Thermal pools. Price includes breakfast and entry to the pools.

Central Hotel, Munkácsy Mihály útca 5–7 (tel. 321 2000). Dirt cheap hotel with large rooms but overlooks a busy road.

PRIVATE ROOMS

IBUSZ have the best supply of rooms and the largest stock of well-located rooms. Prices start around £10 ($17) for doubles. During the summer, you will have to get to one of their offices early to be sure of getting one of the cheaper rooms. Otherwise you may find that only the more expensive doubles are left – around £16 ($27). On the whole, the rooms on offer at Coopturist, Budapest Tourist, and the EXPRESS office at the Keleti train station are slightly more expensive than those controlled by IBUSZ.

HOSTELS

Visitors are spoilt for choice for hostel accommodation in Budapest, especially in summer. Besides the 20 or so hostels currently listed in the HI handbook, there are more independent hostels springing up every year. In summer many of the city's college and university dorms become temporary hostels. Only a few of the HI hostels require a membership card, and these can be bought for around £2 ($3.50) at any EXPRESS office. It's often easier to make bookings through a hostel's group headquarters:

EXPRESS is the largest chain, with offices at Semmelweis útca 4 (tel. 317 8045) and Baross tér (Keleti station) (tel. 342 1772).

Travellers (tel. 0660 322719, *info@reservations.hu*). Office at Keleti station. Open daily 7am–11pm.

Travellers Hostels: Hostels 1–4 below are run by Travellers. All are open 24 hours with no curfew. The company operates a 'never full' policy which effectively means that you will be guaranteed somewhere (if only a mattress) to sleep should everywhere be full. They also provide tours in and around Budapest and organise a music festival at the end of July. Reservations can be made through the central office (tel. 413 2062, *www.backpackers.hu*, *travellers@hostels.hu*).

Marco Polo Hostel, Nyar útca 6 (tel. 413 2555, *info@marcopolo hostel.com*). Doubles from £20 ($34), dorms from £11 ($19). Take bus number 7 from Keleti train station to the Kazinczy útca stop. Open all year.

Hostel Fortuna, Gyali útca 3b (tel. 215 0660, *fortuna@ reservation.hu*). Singles, doubles and dorms available. Take the metro to the Nagyvarad stop.

Hostel Donáti, Donáti útca 46 (tel. 329 8644). Open 5 July–28 Aug. Free baggage storage. Great location. From the Batthyány tér metro station, follow Batthyány u. until you see Donáti u. on your left. Keep your eyes open for the painted footprints showing the way to the hostel.

Hostel Bánki, Podmaniczky útca 8 (tel. 340 8585). Open 10 July–20 Aug. Excellent downtown location. Metro 2 from Keleti to Deák tér then metro 3 to Nyugati Pu.

Landler, Bartók Béla útca 17 (tel. 463 3621). Open 1 July–5 Sept. 2-, 3- and 4-bed rooms. Free luggage storage. Well located. Tram 49 from the Deák tér or Kálvin tér metro stations runs along the street.

Citadella Hostel, Citadella sétány (tel. 166 5794). See **Hotels** above for directions. Dramatic setting, with dorm beds for around £5 ($8.50).

Backpack Guesthouse, XI Takács Menyhért útca 33 (tel. 385 8946, *www.backpackbudapest.hu*). Information, bike rental, no curfew. Beds around £4 ($7) in 5- and 8-bed dorms (breakfast included), doubles and quads also available. Bus 1, 7 or 7A or Tram 49 from the city centre, alight at Tetenyi útca. Reservations accepted by telephone.

Sirály Hostel, Margitsziget 1138 (tel. 153 0501). £4.50 ($7.50) per night. Take bus 26 from the bus station to Margitsziget (an island on the Danube).

Strawberry Youth Hostel, Kinizsi 2–6 (tel. 217 3033, *www.straw berryhostel.com*, *strawberryhostels@hotmail.com*). Near Kálvin tér. Rooms with 2–6 beds and dorms. Internet access. Discount for HI members. Open July and Aug.

Yellow Submarine, Teréz Körút 56 (tel. 327 283, *www.yellow submarinehostel.com*). Near Nyugati station. Dorm beds from £5 ($8.50). Friendly and they give out info.

Museum Hostel, Mikszáth Kálman tér 4 (tel. 318 9508, *museum@budapesthostel.com*). Beds from £4 ($7). Small, friendly place. Nearest metro station is Kálvin tér.

CAMPING

Budapest Tourist is the best organisation to approach with any enquiries regarding camping. They can also book 2- and 4-bed bungalows at the city's campsites. Solo travellers should expect to pay £3–5 ($5–8.50) to camp. By the time you add on the cost of leaving your pack at the station, camping becomes a poor option in comparison to a hostel bed.

Haller Camping (tel. 215 5741). On the corner of Haller útca and Öbester útca. About 2.5 km out of the city centre. Tram 24 stops outside. Close to Nagyvárad metro station. Open June–mid-Sept.

Római, Szentendrei útca 189 (tel. 388 7167). Open all year round. Bungalows available. From Batthyány tér take the HÉV to Rómaifürdo. The site is just over the road from the HÉV station.

Zugligeti 'NICHE', Zugligeti útca 101 (tel. 200 8346). Open mid-Mar–mid-Oct. Bungalows available. From the Moszkva tér metro station take bus 158. Occupies a disused tram cutting in the hills.

Csillebérci Camping, Konkoly Thege M. 21 (tel. 395 6537). Large, well-equipped site. Bungalows available. Take bus 21 from Moszkva tér and get out at last stop. Open all year.

FREE CAMPSITE

In the Budapest X district, close to the **Jászberényi útca bridge**. From the Örs vezér tere metro station, take bus 61 to the Jászberényi útca bridge. Do not leave anything at the site during the day. Check with Tourinform or Budapest Tourist as to whether the site is operating when you're here.

Eger (0)36

TOURIST INFORMATION

Tourinform-Eger, Bajcsy-Zsilinszky útca 9 (tel. 517 715, *www.eger.hu*, *eger@tourinfo.hu*). Open Mon.–Sat., 9am–6pm. Will find accommodation also.

The accommodation agencies below hand out a small photo-copied map of the town which will be quite sufficient if you have a good guidebook to help you locate the sights. If you want a more detailed plan with a street index it will cost around £0.60 ($1).

ACCOMMODATION AGENCIES

IBUSZ, Széchenyi útca 9 (tel. 311 451).

EXPRESS, Széchenyi István útca 28 (tel. 427 757). Open Mon.–Fri. 8am–4pm. Hostel beds, as well as student dorm accom-modation in summer.

For information on accommodation in student halls phone 411 686 or email *davidi@gemini.ektf.hu*. (Available in July and August only.)

HOTELS

Tourist, Mekcsey útca 2 (tel. 429 014). Just along from the castle. Doubles from £8 ($13.50).

Minaret, Knezich útca 4 (tel. 410 020). Doubles £20 ($34). Comfy hotel with swimming pool, faces a minaret.

Hotel Park-Eger, Szálloda útca 1–3 (tel. 413 233). Swimming pool, bowling alley and sauna.

Flóra Hotel, Fürdo útca 5 (tel. 320211). Near thermal baths. All rooms have TV and many have balconies.

PENSIONS

Sas, Sas útca 34 (tel. 269 7320, *tfejlbf@axelero.hu*). Friendly guesthouse in the centre of town.

Fortuna, Kapas útca 35a (tel. 316 480, *net570@axelero.hu*). Doubles and triples with bath.

Welcome Panzió, Szaloki útca. 8 (tel. 322604). Near the town centre.

Ferienhaus Zalanki, Joo Janos útca 11 (tel. 515 360, *www.eger online.com/zalanki, zalanki@agria.hu*). Self-catering apartments in the town centre.

Bacchus Panzió, Szépasszonyvolgy (tel. 428950, *www.bacchus panzio.hu, bacchuspanzio@axelero.hu*). Doubles in the centre of town.

HOSTELS

Junior Hotel es Ifjhsagi Szallo, Pozsonyi útca 4–6 (tel. 512 641, *www.youthhostels.hu*). Open all year.

CAMPING

Autós Caravan Camping, Rákóczi útca 79 (tel. 410 558). Open mid-April–mid-Oct. Bungalows available. Book in advance at Egertourist, or at the site. A 10-minute walk from the town centre. Bus 5, 10, 11 or 12.

Tulipán Camping (tel. 410 580, *tulipan-freddy@freemail.hu*). Small site at the entrance to the Szépasszony Valley. Open July and Aug.

Sopron (0)99

TOURIST INFORMATION

Tourinform, Liszt Ferenc útca 1, beside the casino (tel. 338 592, *www.sopron.hu, sopron@tourinform.hu*).

ACCOMMODATION AGENCIES

IBUSZ, Füredi sétány 9 (tel. 315 903, *i350@ibusz.hu*). Open Mon.–Fri. 8am–4pm, Sat. 8am–12pm.

Ciklámen Tourist, Ogabona tér 8 (tel. 312 040). Open Mon.–Fri. 8.00am–4.30pm, Sat. 8.00am–1pm.

Express, Mátyás király útca 7 (tel. 312 024).

Lokomotiv Tourist, Uj útca 1 (tel. 311 111). Open Mon.–Fri. 9am–5pm.

HOTELS AND PENSIONS

Sopron, Fövényverem útca 7 (tel. 512 261, *www.hotelsopron.hu*, *sopron@ohb.hu*).

Palatinus Hotel, Uj útca 23 (tel. 311 395). Doubles around £40 ($68).

Sas Fogadó, Lövér körút 69 (tel. 316 183). Has a solarium.

Bástya, Patak útca 40 (tel. 325 325). A 10-minute walk north of the old town. Book through Ciklámen Tourist.

PRIVATE ROOMS

IBUSZ: Singles and doubles are both around £10 ($17).

Ciklámen Tourist: Singles around £6 ($10), doubles around £10 ($17).

HOSTEL

Tájékoztató Hostel, Brennbergi útca (tel. 313 116). £3 ($5). Open 15 April–15 Oct. Bus 3 or 10 from the bus station. There's also a pension section where beds are slightly more expensive.

CAMPING

Lövér, Kòszegi útca (tel. 311 715). 2- and 4-bed bungalows available. Bus 12 runs hourly from Várkerület until 9.50pm and stops in front of the site. The site is about 25 minutes' walk from the train station. Open 15 April–15 Oct. Book through Ciklámen Tourist.

Ozon Camping, Erdei Malom kös (tel. 331 144). 5 km out of town. Open 15 April–15 Oct.

REPUBLIC OF IRELAND (00)343

Ireland is widely regarded as one of the friendliest and most relaxing countries in Europe to visit. The geniality and amiability of the Irish in general is really quite surprising, considering their highly turbulent history.

Like neighbouring Scotland, Ireland was never conquered by the Romans. The climate was probably too much for the Italians, who called Ireland 'Hibernia' (literally 'winter quarters'). Instead, it was invaded by the Celts in the fourth century BC, who developed their own civilisation steeped in folk culture and legend.

Eire is a peaceful country, where visitors are readily welcomed and the hospitality is legendary. Only here can one enjoy the traditional Irish pub, an institution far removed from the pseudo-Irish pubs in mainland Britain and Western Europe. This is a land where pints are meant to be savoured, and where even strong brews like Guinness, Murphy's and Beamish play second fiddle to the real lure of the pub: cosy conviviality and a good old-fashioned yarn or two.

BACKGROUND

By 1801 and the Act of Union, Ireland had become a part of the United Kingdom; however, it was not a peaceful or lasting transition. A series of disasters followed, culminating in the Great Potato Famine of 1845. Feelings of Irish nationalism grew. The British had no trouble in suppressing the minor insurrections, but by the time of the Easter Rising in 1916, it became clear that the 'Irish Problem' was getting out of hand. The execution of the leaders of the 1916 uprising led to a fully fledged War of Independence in 1919 and by 1921 the British had withdrawn from all but the six counties that presently make up Northern Ireland. These six counties have been a source of argument and violence up to the present day.

ACCOMMODATION DETAILS

Hostelling is probably the best way to see the Irish Republic. There are 32 **HI hostels** throughout the country, operated by the

Irish YHA, An Óige. Many of these are set out in the country, ideally spaced for a day's walking or cycling, and most (but not all) of the main towns have a hostel. Impeccable levels of cleanliness are virtually guaranteed at An Óige hostels. Prices are normally €10–15 (£6.70–10) for dormitory accommodation between October and May, rising to €12–18 (£8–12) in the peak season of June to September. A few hostels are more expensive. Peak season prices for the hostels in Dublin and Galway are around €18 (£12), with the price of the main Dublin hostel falling to €12 (£8) off season (the Galway hostel and the other Dublin hostels operate in summer only). There are no daytime lockouts, and the midnight curfew at all hostels is late by HI standards. Booking other hostels ahead is easy as wardens will do this for you free of charge. Although you are expected to do any domestic duties required by the warden, An Óige hostels are more friendly and easygoing than is the norm. Indeed, the high esteem in which they are held by hostellers is reflected by their consistently high rating in surveys of European HI members.

Few countries have seen such a growth in **independent hostels** as the Irish Republic. Around 50 of these hostels have joined together to form the Independent Hostel Owners (IHO) Association, while another 21 are united under the name Irish Budget Hostels (marketed as Irish Approved Independent Hostels). Both organisations issue lists of their establishments. Like the An Óige hostels, a number of these independent hostels have been officially approved by the Irish Tourist Board. Such hostels are referred to as 'holiday hostels' (all the Irish Budget Hostels are officially approved). Independent hostels frequently fill in the gaps in the An Óige network, as well as offering an alternative to An Óige hostels in some towns. Unlike An Óige hostels, where HI membership is obligatory, these hostels have no such requirements and they are almost always free of curfews. Most independent hostels charge from around €12 (£8) for dormitory accommodation, although several in Dublin cost €15–20 (£10–13.30). A feature of some independent hostels is also the availability of more expensive singles and doubles.

Unless you are planning on getting right out into the countryside, carrying a tent may not be particularly worthwhile, other than as insurance in case you cannot find suitably priced accommodation. Some of the official **campsites** serving the main towns are located well outside town. With prices generally in the range of €4–8 (£2.70–5.30), a solo traveller can spend almost as much as the cost of a hostel bed once the cost of getting to the site is taken into account. Where there is no convenient site, one possibility can be camping in the grounds of an independent hostel. For around €4 (£2.70) you can camp outside some of the independent hostels and make use of their facilities. In rural areas, farmers seldom object to you pitching a tent on their land if you ask their permission. The only place you definitely can't camp is in state forests. However, it is quite legal to **sleep rough**, though this leaves you open to a soaking at any time of year.

ADDRESSES

IRISH TOURIST BOARD

150–151 New Bond Street, London W1Y 0AQ (tel. 0800 039 7000, *www.ireland.travel.ie*, *info@irishtouristboard.co.uk*). The office sells a guide to all the officially approved hostels and official campsites. You will also find all this information, along with online booking, at their website.

B&B

Town and Country Homes Association, Belleek Rd, Ballyshannon, Co. Donegal (tel. (0)7198 222 22, *www.townandcountry.ie*, *admin@townandcountry.ie*).

Irish Farm Holidays, 2 Michael St., Limerick (tel. (0)61 400700).

Irish Guesthouse Owners' Association, Kathleen's Country House, Killarney, Co. Kerry (tel. (0)64 32810).

Irish Cottages and Holiday Homes Association, 4 Whitefriars, Aungier St., Dublin 2 (tel. 01 475 1596, *www.ichh.ie*, *info@irish-cottageholidayhomes.com*).

YOUTH HOSTELS

An Óige, 61 Mountjoy Street, Dublin 7 (tel. 01 830 4555, *www.irelandyha.org*).

Independent Hostel Owners (IHO), Dooey Hostel, Glencolumcille, Co. Donegal (tel. 073 301 30).

Independent Holiday Hostels, 57 Lower Gardiner St., Dublin 1 (tel. (0)1 836 4710, *www.hostels-ireland.com*).

MUSA (Marketing University Summer Accommodation), UCC Castlewhite Apartments, University College, Cork (tel. (0)21

902793, *www.irelandinsummer.com*). For campus accommodation from June–Sept. in the university towns.

CAMPING

Irish Caravan and Camping Council, PO Box 4443, Avenue,
Dublin 2 (fax (0)98 28237, *www.camping-ireland.ie*, *info@
camping-ireland.ie*).

Dublin (Baile Átha Cliath) (0) I

TOURIST OFFICES

Tourist Information, Suffolk Street, off Dame St. (tel. 850 230330
or 0800 0397 000, *www.visitdublin.com*). Open July–Aug.,
Mon.–Sat. 9am–8.30pm, Sun. 11am–5.30pm; rest of year
Mon.–Fri. 9am–5.30pm. Books rooms locally both online and
in person.

There are Dublin Tourism Offices at the airport, at Baggot Street
Bridge, 14 Upper O'Connell Street and on the waterfront at
Dun Laoghaire.

FINDING ACCOMMODATION

On the whole, you should have little trouble finding a bed in a
hostel or in one of the cheaper B&Bs. The one time of year when
it can become tricky to find cheap accommodation are the days
leading up to and after one of Ireland's home games in the Six
Nations rugby championship, when hordes of visiting rugby fans
descend on the city. Games are played in the winter months. You
should also remember that the town will be packed out around
17 March for Saint Patrick's Day.

PUBLIC TRANSPORT

Although most of the cheaper B&Bs are outside the city centre,
you will have no trouble getting to them as the city has an
efficient bus service, while the DART commuter train can be
useful, depending on where you are staying (same price as buses
to similar destinations). Information on the city's bus network is
available from the office at 59 Upper O'Connell Street (tel. 836
6111 during office hours, tel. 873 4222 thereafter). Most city

buses depart from the streets off Upper O'Connell Street (see Tourist Office for directions), especially the Eden Quay, Abbey Street and Talbot Street. B&B proprietors will invariably be able to tell you which bus to get to their establishment, where to catch the bus and where to get off.

TROUBLE SPOTS

The area around the Connolly train station is one of the more depressed parts of the city. Most of the hostels are in this part of town. Although the district is in no way dangerous it is advisable not to leave rucksacks and valuables lying in the hostels. Either make use of hostel storage facilities (where available) or leave your pack at the station.

HOTELS/GUEST HOUSES

Anchor Guest House, 49 Lower Gardiner Street (tel. 878 6913, *www.anchorguesthouse.com*, *gtcoyne@iol.ie*). B&B from €36 (£24). Three-star guest house located in the centre of Dublin.

Carmel House, 16 Upper Gardiner Street (tel. 874 1639). B&B from €30 (£20). Three-star guest house on the north side of the city.

Phoenix Park House, 38–39 Parkgate Street (tel. 677 2870, *www.dublinguesthouse.com*, *info@dublinguesthouse.com*). B&B from €30 (£20) per person. Welcoming family-run guest house.

Clifden House, 32 Gardiner Place (tel. 874 6364, *www.clifden house.com*, *bnb@indigo.ie*). B&B from €36 (£24) per person. Three-star guest house. Five-minute walk from O'Connell Street.

BED AND BREAKFAST

All prices quoted below are for double rooms, based on two people sharing a room without a bath/shower. For more ideas visit *www.dublintourist.com*, who have an excellent selection of B&Bs throughout the city.

Valentia House, 37 Kincora Court (tel. 833 8060). Doubles and garden.

Aaronmor Guest House, 1B Sandymount Avenue (tel. 668 7972). Near the Irish national stadium.

Applewood B&B, 144 Upper Drumcondra Road (tel. 837 8328). From €60 (£40).

Tinode House, 170 Upper Drumcondra Road (tel. 837 2277). Ten minutes from centre of town. From €60 (£40).

Springvale, 69 Kincora Drive, Clontarf (tel. 833 3413). Off Kincora Grove. Bus 28, 29A, 31, 32 or 44A. From €54 (£36).

Bayview, 265 Clontarf Road, Clontarf (tel. 833 3413). Bus 30. From €54 (£36).

St Dunstans, 25A Oakley Road, Ranelagh (tel. 497 2286). Just under 1.5 km from the centre. Bus 11, 11A, 11B or 13.

Blackstone House, 105 Upper Rathminer Road (tel. 496 7232). From €70 (£47).

Harvey's, 11 Upper Gardiner Street (tel. 874 8384, *www.harveys guesthouse.com, info@harveysguesthouse.com*).

Celtic Lodge Guesthouse, 81–82 Talbot Street (tel. 677 9955, *www.celticlodge.com*). From €90 (£60). Complete with own pub.

Aona House, 48 Merrion Road (tel. 668 4349). All rooms with TV.

Aaron House, 152 Merrion Road (tel. 260 1644, *www.aaron-house.com*). All rooms with TV. From €76 (£51).

HI HOSTEL

Dublin International Youth Hostel, 61 Mountjoy Street (tel. 830 1776, *dublininternational@anoige.ie*). B&B from €12 (£8); doubles €36 (£24). Relatively flexible midnight curfew. Reserve in July and Aug. Kitchen free to use. Free luggage lockers. Near the city centre. Wheelchair accessible. From the airport take bus 41A to Dorset Street. A free bus meets incoming ferries.

OTHER HOSTELS

Abbey Court, 29 Bachelor's Walk (tel. 878 0700, *www.abbey-court.com, info@abbey-court.com*). Right in the town centre. En-suite dorms from €18 (£12). Breakfast included.

ISAACS, 2–5 Frenchman's Lane (tel. 855 6215, *www.isaacs.ie, hostel@isaacs.ie*). Basic dorms from €11.75 (£7.80), doubles from €28 (£19). Open all year. No curfew. 24-hour reception. Free baggage storage, lockers available. Close to the Connolly Station, off Lower Gardiner Street. The website will link you to other hostels run by the same company.

Kinlay House, 2–12 Lord Edward Street (tel. 679 6644, *www.kinlayhouse.ie, kinlay.dublin@usitworld.com*). Dorms from

€16 (£10.50), quads from €22 (£14.50) doubles from €25 (£16.50) per person. Dorm prices increase by €4 (£2.70) July–Sept. Breakfast included. Irish Budget Hostel. Open all year. 24-hour reception. Lockers available. Centrally located near Christ Church cathedral. Bus 50/54/65 or 77.

Avalon House, 55 Aungier Street (tel. 475 0001, *www.avalon-house.ie*). Dorms from €15 (£10), quads from €20 (£13.30), doubles from €27 (£18) per person. Supplement in high season. Open all year. No curfew. Laundry facilities. St Stephen's Green 250m, a 15-minute walk from the Connolly station across the Liffey.

Morehampton House, 78 Morehampton Road (tel. 668 8866, *morehamp@indigo.ie*). Dorms from €11 (£7.30), doubles €30 (£20). Open all year. From Dun Laoghaire take DART to Lansdowne station. From the city centre take bus 10 or 46A/B.

Barnacle's Temple Bar House, 19 Temple Lane, Temple Bar (tel. 671 6277, *www.barnacles.ie*, *tbh@barnacles.ie*). Dorms from €13 (£8.70), doubles from €31 (£21).

Marlborough Hostel, 82 Marlborough Street (tel. 874 7629). Dorms from €7.50 (£5), doubles €26 (£17.50). Beside St Mary's Pro-cathedral.

Brewery Hostel, 22–23 Thomas Street (tel. 453 8616, *brewery@irish-hostel.com*). Not far from Temple Bar. Dorms from €11 (£7.30), doubles from €54 (£36).

Globetrotters Tourist Hostel, 46–48 Lower Gardiner Street (tel. 873 5893, *gtrotter@indigo.ie*). Single beds from €12 (£8). Breakfast included. Round the corner from the bus station.

Goin' My Way, Cardijn House, 15 Talbot Street (tel. 878 8484, *goinmyway@esatclear.ie*). B&B from €10 (£6.70). Midnight curfew. Baggage room with a safe. No lockers. Over Tiffany's shoe shop, close to Connolly station.

CAMPING

Shankill Caravan & Camping Park (tel. 282 0011). Open all year round. The closest site to Dublin, 16 km south of the city on the N11 to Wexford. Bus 45, 45A, 84, or the DART to Shankhill.

North Beach Caravan and Camping Park, Rush (tel. 843 7131, *www.northbeach.ie*, *info@northbeach.ie*). Open all year round. The park is about 27 km north of the city.

ITALY (Italia) (00)39

Best known for ice cream, pizza, and effortless style, Italy is one of the most fascinating and romantic countries in the world. Sure, they have appalling drivers, and a love for bureaucracy, but that's all part of the charm.

BACKGROUND

Italy is synonymous with the Romans. The ancient amphitheatre, the Colosseum, is the symbol of Rome. A famous Roman saying goes 'When the Colosseum falls, Rome will fall'. By 275 BC, the Romans – the race founded in legend by Romulus – had made Italy their own, as well as much of the rest of Europe. Their rule ended in the fifth century AD. The Roman Empire's downfall led to chaos, as not even the Pope or the Holy Roman Emperor could decide who ruled what. Ironically, as the power of Rome declined, it became the centre of the Christian Church, the legacy of which can be seen today in the Vatican City – a tiny independent state which attracts tourists and devout Roman Catholics alike, and has its own police force (the Swiss Guards) and postal service.

The Renaissance in the 15th century and the emergence of artistic giants like Da Vinci and Michelangelo breathed new life into the country.

The advent of Mussolini (or *Il Duce* – the chief – as he liked to call himself) and the rise of Fascism in Italy marked the country's darkest days. Having gained his position through his excellent public relations skills, Mussolini then entered into an alliance with Hitler – a man whose respect Mussolini craved but never won. Italy's alliance with Germany was a mistake that cost thousands of lives, including inevitably that of *Il Duce* himself. Since then, Italy has had more than 50 governments. This peculiar statistic is attributed to widespread political corruption, which in the home country of the Mafia, is hardly surprising.

ACCOMMODATION DETAILS

Anyone who thinks of Italy as a place where accommodation prices are low is likely to be disappointed. Compared to Greece,

Portugal and Spain, accommodation is no bargain and, in some ways, this is also true when comparisons are made with northern Europe. In the major Italian cities, hostels are around the same price as those in the Netherlands and Denmark, but rarely approach the same standards. Similarly, cheap Italian hotels cost roughly the same as their German counterparts, but the latter offer much higher standards.

In the main places of interest, accommodation options for solo travellers can be restricted to hostelling or camping, unless they can find someone to share a room with, or can afford to pay upwards of €25–40 (£16.50–27) for one of the limited supply of singles. For two or more people travelling together, hostelling or staying in cheap hotels are the best. Rooms in private homes (*camere libere*) can be much cheaper, but are not easy to find. Ask the Tourist Office for details.

Hotels are rated from one up to five stars. Charges, which are fixed by the Provincial Tourist Board, should be clearly displayed in the room. It should also be stated whether overnight price is inclusive of breakfast, showers and IVA (VAT), as these are often charged separately. If there is no notice in the room, ask the management for written confirmation of the relevant details. At the lower end of the hotel market IVA is charged at 10%. Showers normally cost €2–4 (£1.30–2.70). Breakfast can add anything from €5–10 (£3.30–6.70) to the overnight price per person, but, legally, breakfast is optional for those staying only a few days. Hoteliers can insist, however, that you take half-board if you stay for a lengthy period.

In most of the main towns you should consider yourself fortunate if you find a double in the region of €35 (£23). It is more likely that you will have to pay around €40–60 (£27–40). For triples, you will rarely pay more than another third on top of the price of doubles. Florence, Milan, Bologna and Venice are the places most likely to cause you problems in your search for one of the cheaper rooms, due to a combination of higher than average prices and demand exceeding supply. If you are beginning to despair in Venice, consider staying in nearby Mestre or Padua (regular trains leave right up to midnight; 10- and 30-minute trips respectively). In the off-season, hotels often reduce their prices and you can expect some success if you try to bargain them down.

The **Italian YHA** operates about 70 hostels, split into three grades. Even the top-rated hostels can vary dramatically in quality. Prices start at around €10 (£6.70), but normally you will pay around €15 (£10). Prices are highest in the main cities of Rome, Venice, Florence, Milan and Naples, where prices are rarely under €18 (£12) per night. Breakfast is usually included in the price. Non-members can normally stay for a small surcharge if there are spaces. However, in Venice, non-members are only admitted if they buy a membership card, costing around €18 (£12). In summer, hostel curfews are normally around 11.30pm–midnight. Hostels are seldom in the centre of town and many of the smaller towns have no hostel.

In the cities, there are also some **independent hostels** and some run by local authorities. Prices and curfews are similar to those of HI hostels. In most of the larger cities, women have the option of staying in one of the dormitories run by the various religious orders. These establishments, known as *Protezione della Giovane*, offer high standards of accommodation and security to female travellers. Prices are normally around €18 (£12) in singles, €15 (£10) per person in doubles, but can reach €25 (£16.50) per person in some institutions in Venice. Curfews are usually between 10 and 11.30pm.

During university vacations, it is possible to stay in vacant **student residences**. You should contact the local Tourist Office for full details of these.

There are over 2,000 registered **campsites**. Strictly speaking, you are not supposed to camp outside these sites, but the authorities are unlikely to trouble you if you are camping on privately owned land with the permission of the owner. Unless you are planning to do a considerable amount of touring outside the main cities there is not much to commend taking a tent, other than as an insurance should all else fail. Sites serving the cities are usually large, crowded, noisy and located far from the centre; by and large, they are more suited to those travelling by car than those relying on public transport. Camping is also quite expensive. Normally, charges are around €5 (£3.30) per tent, and €5 (£3.30) per occupant, but can rise well above this at city sites. Some of the sites near Venice charge a ridiculous €15 (£10) per tent, €6 (£4) per person, and above, in peak season. Security is also a problem, so you can add the cost of storing your pack at the station (€3.50 (£2.30) per day, or each time you want access to it).

Anyone who would like to spend some time in the countryside might consider **renting a cottage** or a farmhouse (see Addresses below). Hikers and climbers should contact the Italian Alpine Club for details of the 600 refuge huts in the Italian Alps. The overnight fee is normally around €9 (£6), but this rises by 20% in winter.

ADDRESSES

ITALIAN STATE TOURIST OFFICE
1 Princes Street, London W1R 9AY (tel. 020 7408 1254, *www.enit.it* or *www.italiantourism.com*).

ITALIAN YHA
Associazione Italiana Alberghi per la Gioventù, Via Cavour 44 (terzo piano). 00184 Roma (tel. (0)6 487 1152, *www.ostelli online.org*, *info@ostellionline.org*).

STUDENT ACCOMMODATION
Write to the Italian Ministry of Education, Viale Trastevere 000153 Rome for full listings of student accommodation. If you fancy testing your Italian, visit their website at *www.istruzione.it*.

CAMPING
Federcampeggio, Castella Postale 23, 50041 Calenzalo (Firenze) (*www.federcampeggio.it*, *federcampeggio@tin.it*). Supplies lists and maps, as does the Italian State Tourist Office. If you want to buy a guide while in Italy, the *Euro Camping* guide is easy to pick up and one of the best available.

Another very good website is *www.camping.it*, which provides plenty of information in English.

FARMHOUSES AND COTTAGES
Agriturist, Corso V. Emanuele 101, Roma (tel. (0)6 651 2342). Connection service.

MOUNTAIN REFUGES
Club Alpino Italiano (Rifugi Alpini), Via Ugo Foscolo 3, Milano (tel. 02 720 2255, *www.cai.it* – Italian only). Connection service.

Bari (0)80

TOURIST OFFICE
Piazza Aldo Moro 33 (tel. 524 2244, *www.pugliaturismo.com*). Beside the train station. Open Mon.–Sat. 9am–2pm.

STOP-OVER IN BARI
Between mid-June and mid-Sept., the Stop-Over in Bari organisation operates a site where travellers under 30 can camp or sleep out for free for one night at Pineta San Francesco (tel. 577 2349). The site is on the fringe of the city, but is easily reached by bus 5 from the train station, or by bus 1 from Corso Cavour. Toilet and washing facilities are available on site, as is free luggage storage. Stop-Over in Bari also offers cheap two-night stays in private flats – great value if you want to spend a couple of days looking around Bari. Any of the four Stop-Over offices will give you details of the other offers open to under-30s for one day, such as free bus travel, free bike hire. Stop-Over offices:

The main office at Via Nicolai 47 (tel. 5121 4538) provides masses of information and free luggage store. Open in the summer Mon.–Sat. 8.30am–8.30pm, Sun. 9am–6pm (shorter hours in winter).

Piazza Aldo Moro. By the main train station.

Registration desk at Pineta San Francesco. There is also a summer hotline here: 577 2349.

HOTELS
Accommodation can also be booked online at the tourist information website listed above.

Fiorini, Via Imbriani 69 (tel. 554 0788). Breakfast included.

Albergo Serena, Via Imbriani 69 (tel. 554 0980). Doubles from €55 (£37).

Pensione Universo, Corso Cavour 225 (tel. 524 2496).

Pensione Giulia, Via Crisanzio 12 (tel. 521 6630). Singles from €25 (£16.50). Close to the station.

Pensione Romeo, Via Crisanzio 12 (tel. 523 7253). Good value.

PRIVATE ROOMS

The Tourist Office has a list of private rooms available in the city.

CAMPING

Sea World Italia, via Michelangelo Interese 80, San Giorgio (tel. 491175, *www.seaworlditalia.it, sworld@tin.it*). Open all year round. By the SS16, about 6.5 km south of the centre. From the Teatro Petruzzeli bus 12.

Brindisi (0)831

TOURIST OFFICE

Ente Provincial per il Turismo (EPT), Viale Regina Margherita 5 (tel. 521944, *www.brindisi.toitaly.net/eng*). Open Mon.–Sat. 8am–2pm. Very helpful office.

ARRIVING IN BRINDISI

The train station is on Piazza Crispi, about 20 minutes' walk from the ferry terminal at the Stazione Marittima down Corso Garibaldi to its end, then along Via del Mare. There are plenty of buses which make the journey along the length of Corso Garibaldi.

FINDING ACCOMMODATION

Finding a place to stay in Brindisi is seldom a problem as most of the people who arrive in town depart on one of the overnight ferries. You can also book and search for hotels online at the website listed above.

HOTELS

Venezia, Via Pisanelli 4 (tel. 527511). One-star hotel.
Europa, Piazza Cairoli 5 (tel. 528546). Two stars, in the town centre.
Altair, Via Tunisi 2 (tel. 562289). Two-star hotel.
Hotel Regina, Via Cavour 5 (tel. 562 2001, *www.hotel reginaweb.com, info@hotelreginaweb.com*). Modern and clean. Doubles from €60 (£40).

HOSTEL

Hostel Carpe Diem, Via Brandi 2 (tel. (0)338 323 5545 – mobile, *www.hostelcarpediem.it*, *hostelbrindisi@hotmail.it*). Around €13 (£8.70) per person in dorms (breakfast and sheets included). In Casale, about 1.5 km from the centre, but easily reached by bus 3, 4 or 5 from the train station. If you phone the hostel, the free shuttle bus will come and get you. Open 24hrs in summer.

Florence (Firenze) (0)55

TOURIST OFFICES

Azienda di Promozione Turistica (APT), Via Cavour 7r (tel. 290832, *www.comune.firenze.it*). Open March–Oct., Mon.–Sat. 8am–7pm, Sun. 8am–2pm; Nov.–Feb., Mon.–Sat. 8am–2pm.

Informazione Turistica (tel. 212245) at Piazza della Stazione, outside the train station (take the exit by track 16). Open daily Apr.–Oct. 8.30am–7.30pm, Nov.–Mar. 8.15am–5.30pm. Free map of the city. (Does not book accommodation.)

Borgosanta Croce 29 (tel. 234 0444). Open every day 8.15am–7.15pm.

Consorzio ITA (tel. 294883). In the train station next to platform 16. They will find you accommodation but it may not be the cheapest available or good value. A commission rate is charged.

For more accommodation ideas visit *www.florenceby.com* for an excellent selection of hotels, bed and breakfasts and so forth.

BASIC DIRECTIONS

The vast majority of the accommodation suggestions below are within reasonable walking distance of the Santa Maria Novella train station. The cathedral is 10–15 minutes' walk away from the station. Piazza della Stazione is the square in front of the train station. Via Nazionale leads out of the left-hand side of the square. Within a short distance, Via Nazionale passes one end of Via Fiume and crosses Via Faenza, two streets with a good supply of relatively inexpensive hotels. A few blocks further on, Via Faenza crosses Via Guelfa. There are also a number of cheap hotels in the streets running off Via Guelfa, parallel to the right of Via Nazionale. At the bottom left of Piazza della Stazione is Piazza della Unità Italiana, from which Via de' Panzani runs to Via de' Cerretani, crossing Via del Giglio on the way. Going along Via de' Cerretani you arrive at Piazza S. Giovanni with the baptistry, beyond which is the cathedral. If from Piazza della Unità Italiana you head round the Santa Maria Novella church, you arrive at Piazza Santa Maria Novella.

STREET NUMBERS

The city's streets are not numbered in the conventional manner. Instead, there are two sets of numbers: red indicating business premises and blue or black denoting residential properties. Most hotels have blue or black numbers. In local publications, an *r* is added to the street number of commercial buildings.

HOTELS

Room prices in Florence's one-star hotels are more or less standard. With a few exceptions, you can expect to pay around €35 (£23) for a single with bath/shower and €60 (£40) for a double with bath/shower. The first five hotels in the list below offer slightly cheaper rooms, generally around €30 (£20) for a single with bath/shower and €50 (£33) for a double with bath/shower. All other hotels charge the standard rate.

DOUBLES AROUND €50 (£33)

Ausonia e Rimini, Via Nazionale 24 (tel. 496547). Cosy and cute.

La Mia Casa, Piazza Santa Maria Novella 23 (tel. 213061). Central location. No singles with bath/shower.

Montreal, Via della Scala 43 (tel. 238 2331, *www.hotelmontreal. com*, *info@hotelmontreal.com*). Friendly and very central.

Sampaoli, Via San Gallo 14 (tel. 284834). The street runs off Via Guelfa, three blocks to the right of Via Nazionale.

Armonia, Via Faenza 56 (tel. 211146). Doubles from €55 (£37)

Merlini, Via Faenza 56 (tel. 212848, *www.hotelmerlini.it*, *info@hotelmerlini.it*). Doubles from €45 (£30).

Scaletta, Via Guicciardini 13 (tel. 283028, *www.lascaletta.com*), stunning views over Boboli Gardens. Singles €51 (£34), doubles from €93 (£62), breakfast included.

Sofia, Via Cavour 21 (tel. 283930). Doubles from €50 (£33).

Soggiorno Panerai, Via dei Servi 36 (tel. 264103). Opposite Duomo.

Tina, Via San Gallo 31 (tel. 453519). Singles €30 (£20), doubles €50 (£33).

DOUBLES AROUND €60 (£40)

Pensione Azzi (tel. 213806). Doubles from €65 (£44). Laid back.

Locanda Orchidea, Borgo degli Albizi 11 (tel. 248 0346, *hotelorchidea@yahoo.it*). One of the most beautiful hotels in Florence.

Hotel Tina, Via S. Gallo 31 (tel. 483519, *hoteltina@tin.it*). Very friendly.

Albergo Anna, via Faenza 56 (tel. 239 8322). Breakfast included.

Bavaria, Borgo degli Albizi 26 (tel. 234 0313). From the cathedral, head down Via del Proconsolo, then left.

Brunori, Via del Proconsolo 5 (tel. 289648). Near the cathedral.

Colomba, Via Cavour 21 (tel. 284323). Australian owned.

Concordia, Via dell'Amorino 14 (tel. 213233, *concordia@fol.it*).

Donatello, Via V. Alfieri 9 (tel. 245870). Very welcoming.

Elite, Via della Scala 12 (tel. 215395). Two-star hotel, town centre.

Il Perseo, Via de Cerretani 1 (tel. 212504, *www.hotelperseo.it*, *info@hotelperseo.it*).

Kursaal, Via Nazionale 24 (tel. 496324). Town centre.

La Romagnola, Via della Scala 40 (tel. 211597). Midnight curfew.

Orchidea, Borgo degli Albizi 11 (tel. 248 0346).

Pensione Sorelle Bandini, Piazza San Spirito 9 (tel. 215308), overlooks the Duomo and Boboli Gardens. Ideal for large groups.

Hotel San Marco, Via Cavour 50 (tel. 281851, *san_marco@ inwind.it*).

DOUBLES FROM €70 (£47)

Albergo Brunetta, Borgo Pinti 5 (tel. 247 8134). Central.

Hotel Nazionale, Via Nazionale 22 (tel. 238 2203, *www.nazionale hotel.it*). Doubles from €80 (£54). Near the train station.

Hotel Berkleys, Via Fiume 11 (tel. 521 2302). Old hotel in town centre, near the train station. Doubles around €70 (£47).

Pensione Ottaviani, P. Ottaviani 1 (tel. 23962). Doubles from €50 (£33).

Hotel Bretagna, Corsini 6 (tel. 289618). Central and stunning.

Visconti, Piazza Ottaviani 1 (tel. 213877). Doubles from €80 (£54).

Ausonia & Kursaal, Via Nazionale 22 (tel. 496547, *www.kursonia. com*). Doubles from €80 (£54), but worth it.

Albergo Firenze, Piazza dei Donati 4 (tel. 214203, *www.hotelfirenze-fi.it*, *firenze.albergo@tiscali.it*). Doubles €88 (£59), including breakfast. Caters for wheelchairs.

HI HOSTEL

'Ostello Villa Camerata', Viale Augusto Righi 2–4 (tel. 601451). Members only. Reservations by letter only. B&B from €12 (£8) per night. Breakfast, lunch and dinner available. Laundry room. Wheelchair accessible. Family rooms. About 5.5 km from the town centre. Bus 17B from the station.

HOSTELS

Ostello Archi Rossi, Via Faenza 94 (tel. 0290804, *www.hostel archirossi.com*). Dorm beds from €13 (£8.70) (breakfast extra). Dinner also available. Curfew 12.30am. Wheelchair access. Station 200m.

Ostello Santa Monaca, Via Santa Monaca 6 (tel. 268338, *www.ostello.it*). Dorm beds €16 (£10.50), sheets and showers included. No meals. 1am curfew. Reception 6am–9.30am, 2pm–12.30am. Take bus 36 or 37 from Piazza Santa Maria Novella to the first stop over the river, or 20 minutes on foot. Via Santa Monaca is right off Via dei Serragli, opposite Via S. Agostino.

Istituto Gould, Via dei Serragli 49 (tel. 212576). Singles €25 (£16.50); doubles, triples, quads and quints also available. No curfew. No arrivals or departures on Sat. pm or Sun. Bus 36 or 37 from Piazza Santa Maria Novella to the first stop after the river, or a 20-minute walk.

Suore Oblate dell'Assunzione, Via Borgo Pinti 15 (tel. 214582). Singles €18 (£12), doubles €35 (£23). Open mid-June–July and Sept. Midnight curfew. From the Duomo, follow Via dell'Oriuolo to the start of Via Borgo Pinti. Run by nuns but open to men and women.

Suore Oblate dello Spirito Santo, Via Nazionale 8 (tel. 239 8202). Singles, doubles and triples from around €18 (£12) per person with breakfast. Open mid-June–Oct. Midnight curfew. Women and married couples only.

CAMPING

'Camping Michelangelo', Viale Michelangelo 80 (tel. 681 1977, *michelangelo@camping.it*). €5 (£3.30) per tent, €8 (£5.30) per person, €4.50 (£3) per car. Open all year. Frequently crowded. Tend to say they are full if you phone during peak season, but can usually find space if you turn up. Bus 13 from the station.

Villa Camerata, Viale Augusto Righi 2–4 (next to the youth hostel) (tel. 601451). €4 (£2.70) per small tent, €8 (£5.30) per large tent, €4 (£2.70) per person. Open Apr.–Oct. Bus 17b from the station.

Panoramico, Via Peramonda 1 (tel. 599069). €9 (£6) per person. Bus 7 from the station.

'AREA DE SOSTA'

A covered area where you can put down a mat and a sleeping bag. Run by the city authorities at Via Rocca Tedalda in Villa Favard, about 6.5 km from the town centre. Washing and toilet facilities are available at the site. No charge. Maximum stay one week. Open 7pm–10am (tel. 690022). Bus 14A, 14B or 14C from the station. Leave your pack at the station.

Milan (Milano) (0)2

TOURIST OFFICES

Azienda di Promozione Turistica (APT), Via Marconi (tel. 725 24300, *www.ciaomilano.com*). Open Mon.–Fri. 8.30am–8pm, Sat. 9am–1pm and 2–7pm, Sun 9am–1pm, 2–5pm.

The branch office is at the Milano Centrale train station (tel. 725 24360) (on the first floor). Open Mon.–Fri. 8.30am–7pm, Sat. 9am–1pm, 2–6pm, Sun. 9am–12.30pm, 2–5pm.

Hotels can be booked online at the website listed above.

Alternatively you can pick up hotel listings at the tourist information office at Via Marconi 1.

BASIC DIRECTIONS

In front of the Milano Centrale station is Piazza Duca d'Aosta, to the right running alongside the station is Piazza IV Novembre, to the left also running alongside the station is Piazza L. di Savoia. Along the side of the station, Via Tonale leads out off Piazza IV Novembre. Diagonally right from the main exit of Milano Centrale is the start of Via Galvani. Via Copernico runs right off Via Galvani after one block. The main road leading away from Piazza Duca d'Aosta in the direction of the city centre is Via Pisani. At the start of Via Pisani, Via Vitruvio runs left out of Piazza Duca d'Aosta to Corso Buenos Aires at Piazza Lima (metro MMI: Lima), across which is Via Plinio. Walking down Via Pisani, you pass the ends of Via S. Gregorio and then Viale Tunisia on the left-hand side. The next street on the left after Viale Tunisia leads into Via Castaldi. Continuing on to the end of Via Pisani you arrive in Piazza Repubblica. Heading left at this point brings you into Via V. Veneto, which ends at the Porta Venezia (metro MMI: Porta Venezia). Via Lazzaretto runs parallel to the left of Via Piani between Via Vitruvio and Piazza Repubblica.

HOTELS

DOUBLES FROM €50 (£33)

Pensione Cantore, Corso di Porta Genova 25 (tel. 835 7565). 2am curfew.

San Tomaso, Viale Tunisia 6, 3rd floor (tel. 2951 4747, *hotelsantomaso@tin.it*). Quads available.

Comercio, Via Mercato 1 (tel. 8646 3880). Price for doubles includes bath/shower. Close to the city centre. Metro M2: Lanza is a few minutes' walk from the hotel.

Nettuno, Via Tadino 27 (tel. 2940 4481). Close to the railway station.

DOUBLES FROM €60 (£40)

Albergo Brasil di Ramella Luisa, Via G. Modena 20 (tel. 02 749 2482).

Verona, Via Carlo Tenca 12 (tel. 6698 3091). Air conditioning.

San Marco, Via Piccinni 25 (tel. 02 2951 6414). Metro M2: Loreto.

Ca'Grande, Via Porpora 87 (tel. 2614 5295, *www.hotel cagrande.it, info@hotelcagrande.it*). Metro M2: Loreto.

Arno, Via Lazzaretto 17 (tel. 670 5509). Near the station, gets very busy from March to July. Charges extra for shower, soap and towels.

Eva, Via Lazzaretto 17 (tel. 670 6093). In the same building as the Arno.

Hotel Sara, Via Sacchini 17 (tel. 201773, *www.hotelsara.it*). Internet access.

DOUBLES FROM €70 (£47)

Kennedy, Viale Tunisia 6 (tel. 2940 0934). Rooms with or without bathrooms. Triples available.

Aurora, C. Buenos Aires 18 (tel. 204 7960, *www.hotel aurorasrl.com, info@hotelaurorasrl.com*). Town centre. Metro M1: Lima.

Speronari, Via Speronari 4 (tel. 02 8646 1125). Near the Duomo.

Manzoni, Via Senato 45 (tel. 02 7602 1002). Very central.

Nuovo, Piazza Beccaria 6 (tel. 8646 4444). Near the Duomo.

HI HOSTEL

Ostello Piero Rotta, Via Martino Bassi 2 (tel. 3926 7095, reserve via *www.ostellionline.org*). B&B from €16.50 (£11). Strict lock-out enforced 9am–4pm. Curfew 12.30am. A laundry room is available. Members only, but HI cards are sold at the hostel, around €15 (£10). From Central station, take metro line 2 to Cadorna, then line 1 heading for S. Leonardo to QT8/San Siro. Line 1 splits, so make sure you don't get on a train to Inganni. The hostel is close to AC and Inter Milan's San Siro football stadium.

WOMEN'S HOSTEL

Protezione della Giovane, Corso Garibaldi 121A–123 (tel. 2900 0164). Around €18 (£12) per night. Women under 26 only. Very safe, but a 10.30pm curfew. A 5–10-minute walk from Milano Porta Garibaldi train station. Take a train from Milano Centrale, walk down Corso Como which leads into Corso

Garibaldi. Metro MM2: Moscova is much closer. Bookings are required.

Padua (Padova) (0)49

TOURIST OFFICE

Azienda di Promozione Turismo di Padova (APT), Riviera dei Mugnai 8 (tel. 876 7911, *www.padovanet.it*, *apt@padovanet.it*). Email or write to this office if you want information on the city in advance. The website listed is in Italian only.

APT office, train station (tel. 875 2077). Open Mon.–Sat. 8am–6pm, Sun. 8am–12pm. Hotel listings but no reservations.

FINDING ACCOMMODATION

Except in the period June to early September, when many tourists unable to find suitable accommodation in Venice make their way to Padua (shamefully many never even bother to visit the wonderful attractions of Padua itself), you should have little trouble finding a reasonably priced bed in the city.

HOTELS

Prices for rooms without showers are more or less standard in the city's one- and two-star hotels. In one-star hotels you can expect to pay around €28 (£19) for a single, €40 (£27) for a double. Rates in a two-star hotel are around €40 (£27) and €55 (£37) respectively. Doubles with showers are more common and usually cost in the region of €60 (£40).

ONE-STAR HOTELS

Al Camin, Via Felice Cavallotti 44 (tel. 687835). At the opposite end of the Old Town from the train station. From Prato delle Valle head down Corso Vittorio Emmanuele. Go straight ahead across Piazzale S. Croce into Via Felice Cavallotti.

Al Santo, Via del Santo 147 (tel. 875 2131). Central location. From Piazza Eremitani follow Via degli Zabarelli into Via del Santo.

Da Marco, Via Sorio 73 (tel. 871 7296). Outside the city walls on the way to the airport.

Pavia, Via Papafava 11 (tel. 661558). From Via Roma take the right turning after Solferino and look for Via Papafava running left off Via Marsala.

Riviera, Via Rudena 12 (tel. 665413). From Piazza Eremitani follow Via degli Zabarella and then Via del Santo. Via Rudena runs left off Via del Santo.

Venezia, Via Venezia 30 (tel. 807 0499). Head left from the station exit on to Via Nicoló Tommasseo, which leads into Via Venezia.

Vienna, Via Beato Pellegrino 106 (tel. 871 6331, *piccolo vienna@libero.it*). From P. Stazione take Viale Codalunga and head straight on until you see Via Beato Pellegrino on your right.

TWO-STAR HOTELS

Casa del Pellegrino, Via Cesarotti 21 (tel. 823 9711). From Piazza degli Eremitani follow Via degli Zabarella then Via del Santo into Piazza del Santo, from which Via Cesarotti runs to the left.

Alla Fiera, Via Ugo Bassi 20 (tel. 875 5094). From the train station head left on to Via Nicoló Tommasseo. Continue straight ahead until you see Via Ugo Bassi on the right.

Buenos Aires, Via Luca Belludi 37 (tel. 651844). A little more up-market with rooms for up to €100 (£67).

HI HOSTEL

Centro Ospitalità Città di Padova, Via A. Aleardi 30 (tel. 654210, *www.ctgveneto.it/ostello*, *ostellopadova@ctgveneto.it*). B&B around €13 (£8.70) (cheaper for 3 or more nights, max. 5, breakfast, sheets and shower included). Open 1 Feb.–14 Dec. Curfew 11pm. Family rooms. 2 km outside Padua. Bus 3 or 8 from the train station. Wheelchair accessible. Reserve at least one week in advance.

WOMEN'S HOSTEL

Casa della Famiglia, Via Nino Bixio 4 (tel. 875 1554). Beds from around €15 (£10). Christian hostel. Women under 29 only. Open July–Aug.

HI HOSTEL NEARBY

Rocca degli Alberi, Castello degli Alberi (Porta Legnago), Montagnana (tel. 0429 81076, can be booked through *www.ostellionline.org*). B&B around €13 (£8.70). Open Apr.–mid-Oct. Montagnana is about 40 km from Padua, accessible by local train and bus. The hostel is 500m from the train station.

CAMPING

Montegrotto Terme, Via Roma 123–125, Montegrotto (tel. 049 793400). Open Mar.–early Nov. The closest site to Padua. Bus M runs to Montegrotto Terme, just over 16 km away.

Perugia (0)75

TOURIST OFFICES

The main tourist office is at Piazza IV Novembre 3 (tel. 573 6458, *info@iat.perugia.it*). For general information about the area visit *www.umbria-turismo.it*, or *www.perugiaonline.com*.

HI HOSTEL

Spagnoli, nr station on Via Cortonese (tel. 501 1366, *perugia hostel@tiscalinet.it*). Bed and breakfast from €13 (£8.70).

CAMPING

Both these sites are 5 km out of town in Colle della Trinità. Bus 36 from the station.

Paradise d'Été, Strada Fontana 29/h (tel. 075 517 3121, *jnlagu@tin.it*). Hot shower and use of pool included. Tents from €4.20 (£2.80), €5.20 (£3.50) per person. Open all year.

Il Rocolo, Str. Fontana Trinità 1/N (tel. 075 517 8550, *www.ilrocolo.it*, *ilrocolo@ilrocolo.it*). Open 15 June–15 Sept.

Rome (Roma) (0)6

TOURIST OFFICES

Azienda di Promozione Turistica di Roma (APT), Via Parigi 5 (tel. 488 991, *info@aptroma.com*). APT Head Office, open Mon.–Sat. 9am–7pm. Much shorter queues than at the EPT branch office in the Roma Termini train station. Only 500m from Termini. On leaving the station, head for the far left-hand corner of the square in front of you (Piazza dei Cinquecento), go up Viale L. Einaudi, around Piazza della Repubblica to the right, then along Via G. Romita to the start of Via Parigi on the right.

There are also 3 information kiosks dotted around the city at the following locations: Largo Goldini, Via Nazionale and Largo Corado Ricci (Colosseo). All open every day from 10am–6pm.

APT, Stazione Termini (tel. 360 04399). Platform 3. Open daily 9am–1pm and 3–8pm. Very long queues are the norm in summer. The office claims to have no information on campsites.

APT, Aeroporto Intercontinentale Leonardo da Vinci (tel. 65 951). In the arrivals hall of the airport.

APT, Autostrada del Sole A1 (Salaria services).

APT, Autostrada del Sole A2 (Frascati services).

Ente Nazionale per il Turismo (ENIT), Via Marghera 2/6 (tel. 497 11, *www.enit.com*). Open Mon.–Tues. and Thur.–Fri. 9am–1pm, Wed. 4–5pm. Information on the rest of the country only.

Enjoy Rome Information Centre, Via Marghera 8a (tel. 4451 843, *www.enjoyrome.com*, *info@enjoyrome.com*). Open Mon.–Fri. 8.30am–7pm, Sat. 8.30am–2pm. Excellent information office which books accommodation in hostels, hotels and private rooms (no commission), gives out free maps and offers free luggage storage. Also provides 'emergency aid'. Near to Termini station.

CTS, Via Genova 16 (tel. 462 0431) off Via Nazionale. Free accommodation service.

FINDING ACCOMMODATION

Rome has a vast stock of hotel rooms, so even in July and August when hordes of visitors flock into the city, there are still enough beds to go round. Nevertheless, finding one can still be frustrating. The area around the Termini station has the largest concentration of rooms and is the cheapest area of the city to stay in. Understandably, this is the area most popular with budget travellers. The sheer number of rooms in the area means you can make personal enquiries at a lot of hotels without having to walk very far, but consider leaving your pack at the station as many establishments are on the upper floors. Prices are generally higher in the city centre and over the River Tiber around the Vatican City. Few owners will show you their cheapest rooms if they have others available. Cheaper rooms are usually only offered if you are on the point of leaving. The price set by the Tourist Authority for a room should be displayed in the room. Make sure that what you are being asked to pay tallies with the price shown. It is not really wise to try and haggle an owner down from the official price in summer, as they can send you packing, safe in the knowledge that someone else will be along shortly. Although both the EPT offices in the city centre find rooms, they are not interested in finding rooms at the prices you will want to pay. Usually, however, they can be persuaded to phone any suggestions you give them, but do not expect them to consider such requests during July and August. At these times, the Student Travel Office (CTS) is likely to be more help.

TROUBLE SPOTS

There is no area of the city you are likely to visit that is really violent, although the area around Termini station can get rough late at night. Unless you are stupid enough to sleep rough, there is little chance of you being robbed at knifepoint, but there is a high incidence of non-violent petty theft, particularly among crowds, where wallets can be taken or rucksacks cut open. Obviously, the metro and buses offer a perfect setting for the sneak thief, so pay particular attention to your belongings as you travel about (keep your rucksack in front of you; hold small daysacks to your chest).

BASIC DIRECTIONS

The *Centro Storico* (historical centre) of Rome lies on the east bank of a bend of the River Tiber, which runs north to south through the city. The main railway station, Termini, is to the east of the centre, while the Vatican City lies to the west. The familiar landmarks of the Colosseum and the Roman Forum are just to the south of the centre, while to the north are the plush, expensive suburbs which surround the Spanish Steps.

Emerging from Termini station you face Piazza dei Cinquecento. To the left Via Cavour leads off towards the Forum and Colosseum, a walk of around 12 minutes. From the top left corner of Piazza dei Cinquecento, Viale L. Einaudi leads into Piazza della Repubblica. From here, Via Nazionale runs off to the left. An 8-minute walk brings you to Piazza Venezia and the Vittorio Emanuele II monument on the eastern edge of the Centro Storico. Key locations are the Piazza Navona, to the north of Corso Vittorio Emanuele II, and Campo dei Fiori to the south – both can also be reached on bus 64 (night bus 70) from Termini station.

To the right of Piazza dei Cinquecento, Via Solferino leads into Piazza Indipendenza, from which Via San Martino della Battaglia, Via Magenta, Via dei Mille, Via Varese and Via Castelfidardo all run, scattered with some of the cheapest accommodation in Rome.

Down to the right of Termini station runs Via Marsala, which connects with Via Marghera, Via Milazzo and Via Vicenza. In the opposite direction, up the right-hand side of Piazza dei Cinquecento, Via Marsala becomes Largo Montemartini and then Via Volturno.

HOTELS

CHEAPEST DOUBLES AROUND €40 (£27)

Andreina, Via G. Amendola 77 (tel. 06 481 8657). One-star hotel.

Hotel Hollywood Stella Elsa, Via Principe Amedeo 79/A (tel. 446 0634, *hotelhollywoodstella@libero.it*). Near Termini train station.

California, Via Principe Amedeo 47 (tel. 482 2002). Two-star hotel.

Virginia, Via Montebello 94 (tel. 445 7689, *www.hotelvirginia roma.com*). Near the Colosseum.

Perugia, Via del Colosseo 7 (tel. 679 7200). Near the Colosseum, off Via Cavour. Metro: Colosseo or Cavour.

Hotel Washington, Via G. Amendola 77 (tel. 489 04316). Near Termini train station.

Positano, Via Palestro 49 (tel. 490 360). Dorm beds available.

Il Castello, Via V. Amedeo II 9 (tel. 7720 4036, *www.ilcastello. com, info@ilcastello.com*). Ten minutes' walk from the Colosseum in Manzoni.

CHEAPEST DOUBLES FROM €55 (£37)

Ottaviano, Via Ottaviano 6 (tel. 397 38138, *www.pensione ottaviano.com*). A short walk from St Peter's Square. Dorms available. Metro: Ottaviano.

Katty, Via Palestro 35 (tel. 444 1216). Very popular, near Termini.

Ester, Viale Castro Pretorio 25 (tel. 495 7123). Near Termini.

Giamaica, Via Magenta 13 (tel. 06 490121). One-star hotel.

Papa Germano, Via Calatafimi 14A (tel. 486919, *www.hotelpapa germano.com, info@hotelpapagermano.com*). Dorms available. Discount for cash payments, cheaper in winter.

Castelfidardo, Via Castelfidardo 31 (tel. 446 4638). Accepts credit cards.

Hotel Jonella, Via della Croce 41 (tel. *679 7966, www.lodging italy.com, info@lodgingitaly.com*). No reception, therefore phone ahead, or email to make booking.

CHEAPEST DOUBLES FROM €70 (£47).

Tizi, Via Collina 48 (tel. 482 0128). A 15-minute walk from Termini station.

Baltic, Via XX Settembre 89 (tel. 485509). Two-star hotel near Via Veneto.

Hotel des Artistes, Via Villafranca 20 (tel. 445 4365, *www.hotel desartistes.com, info@hoteldesartistes.com*). Doubles without bathroom from €80 (£54) (cheaper off-season). One floor of the hotel is used as a hostel (tel. 4454 365, *www.hostel rome.com*). Dorms €20 (£13.30), doubles €60 (£40).

Romano, Largo Corrado Ricci 32 (tel. 679 5851). Town centre.

Everest, Via Cavour 47 (tel. 488 1629, *www.everesthotels.it*). Also Everest 2 at Via Nazionale 243 (tel. 488 5727, *hoteleverest2@ yahoo.it*).

HI HOSTELS

Ostello del 'Foro Italico', Viale delle Olimpiadi 61 (tel. 323 6267, *www.ostellionline.org*). B&B €16 (£10.50). 11pm curfew. Well out from the centre, by the Olympic stadium. Metro A to Ottaviano, then bus 32. Luggage store available. Wheelchair accessible.

HOSTELS

The Backpackers group (*www.backpackersgroup.it*) own four hostels in Rome, as well as a few cheap B&Bs. Their website has full details and booking facilities, and the first four hostels below can be contacted by emailing *info@backpackers.it*.

Backpackers, Via Turati 37 (tel. 447 02506). Dorms from €22 (£14.50), €16 (£10.50) in the winter months. From the Termini station, exit the building opposite McDonalds. Cross the road and turn left and carry on walking until Via Goberti. Turn down here, and take first street on the left, which should be Via Turati.

Angel's House, Via Montebello 47 (tel. 4470 2506). Dorms from €18 (£12). Exit Termini on Via Marsala, and turn left. Continue 4 blocks, until the street becomes Via Volturno. The first left after Via Catalfini is Via Montebello.

Asterix Inn Keepers, Via Castelfiardo 78 (tel. 445 4649). Dorms around €22 (£14.50). Take the Via Marsala exit from Termini, and turn along Via Vicenza. Carry on until Via Bachelet on your left. Take this road until it becomes Via Castelfiardo.

Freestyle, Via Principe Amedeo 132 (tel. 4470 3603). Dorms around €18 (£12). Exit Termini opposite McDonalds, turn left along Via Giolitti until Via Rattzazzi on your right. Turn down here until you hit Via Principe Amedeo. The hostel will be on your right.

YWCA, Via Cesare Balbo 4 (tel. 488 0460). Singles around €17 (£11.50). Midnight curfew. Women and married couples only. Near Roma Termini. Follow Via D'Azeglio from Piazza dei Cinquecento, go right at Via Torino, then left along Via Cesare Balbo.

Fawlty Towers, Via Magenta 39 (tel. 445 0374, *www.fawlty towers.org*, *info@fawltytowers.org*). Dorms from €18 (£12), doubles from €62 (£42), singles from €44 (£29.50). No curfew; 24-hour reception. A short walk from Termini train station. Take the exit by platforms 1/2 on to Via Marsala. Cross over on to Via Marghera and Via Magenta bisects Marghera.

Hostel on the right. The website also has links to three other cheap hotels run by the same company.

Sandy, Via Cavour 136 (tel. 488 4585, *www.sandyhostel.com*). Dorms for €18 (£12), cheaper in winter. On the fourth floor next door to Hotel Valle. Metro: Cavour.

Alessandro Palace Hostel, Via Vicenza 42 (tel. 446 1958, *www.hostelsalessandro.com*, *palace@hostelsalessandro.com*). In high season around €20 (£13.30) a dorm bed. It is cheaper in the winter. Breakfast and sheets included.

Alessandro Downtown Hostel, Via Cattaneo 23 (tel. 4434 0147, *downtown@hostelsalessandro.com*). Owned and run by the same people as the Palace Hostel. Prices as listed above.

CAMPING

No central site, but the following are within reach:

Flaminia Village, Via Flaminia Nuova 821 (tel. 333 2604, *www.villageflaminio.com*, *info@villageflaminio.com*). Open Mar.–Dec. From €8.90 (£5.90) per person; €5 (£3.30) per tent. One of the closest to the centre (8 km out). Metro A to Flaminio, then bus 202, 204 or 205.

Roma, Via Aurelia 831 (tel. 662 3018). Open all year. Bus 38 from Termini station to Piazza Fiume, then bus 490 to the last stop. Change to bus 246.

Nomentano, Via Nomentana (corner of Via della Cesarina) (tel. 414 00296). Open Mar.–Oct. Bus 36 from Termini to Piazza Sempione, then bus 336 to Via Nomentana.

Seven Hills, Via Cassia (tel. 3036 2751, *www.sevenhills.it*, *info@sevenhills.it*). 8 km north of Rome. Take bus 907 from P. Risorgimento to Via Cassia or bus 201 from Flaminio. Open late March–late Oct.

SLEEPING ROUGH

Lunacy.

Venice (Venezia) (0)41

TOURIST OFFICES

The main APT office is on Piazza San Marco (tel. 529 8711, *www.turismovenezia.it, info@turismovenezia.it*). Open 10am–6pm every day.

The APT office in Venezia Santa Lucia train station (tel. 529 8727) finds rooms and gives out information. Open 8am–7pm daily. Exceptionally long queues in summer.

The AVA Hotel Information at the train station (to the right of the tourist office), open May–Sept., offers advice on accommodation and books hotel rooms (tel. 715016). There's another office at P. Roma 540d (tel. 522 8640). You can also use this service online before you get here. The Venice Hoteliers association (tel. (00) 390 415 2222 64, *www.veniceinfo.it, info@veniceinfo.it*) will book you rooms in all price brackets though, and the service is free.

ADDRESSES

Streets and buildings in Venice are not numbered in the normal manner. Instead, districts are numbered, so that the number a house bears is its district number rather than a street number. There are six districts in the city: Cannaregio, San Polo, Santa Croce, Dorsoduro, San Marco and Castello.

FINDING ACCOMMODATION

If you arrive in Venice during the summer it is safe to say you will never have seen a city so packed with tourists. Ideally, you should reserve hotels in writing or via email well in advance (Italian or English) stating clearly the type of room you want. Inform the hotelier at what time you expect to arrive, but if you get to Venice early go to the hotel as soon as you arrive just to make sure the room has been held. You can try phoning ahead, but even if you can communicate with owners, they are generally loath to reserve one of their cheaper rooms. If you arrive in Venice early in the morning, start queueing at one of the offices before opening time, as it could make the difference between getting one of the cheaper rooms or not. As inexpensive singles are few and far between, solo travellers might wish to team up in the queue and get a double.

You can search the Tourist Office's database of accommodation online by type of accommodation, and they have a good selection of youth hostels listed. If you want to stay in the HI hostel, reservations are recommended at all times. In the summer, you have to spend about three hours in a queue to have a hope of getting in without a reservation. Reservations for the city-run hostels are best made over the internet or in writing one month in advance.

If you are having trouble finding suitably priced accommodation, consider staying in nearby Venezia-Mestre, where hotel prices are slightly lower, or in Padua. Both are linked to Venice by frequent trains, right up to midnight (Mestre is a 10-minute trip, Padua is only 30 minutes away).

Apart from *www.turismovenezia.it*, other good websites for finding cheap accommodation include *www.1st-venice-hotels. com*, and *www.venicebanana.com*.

HOTELS

DOUBLES FROM €50 (£33)

Bernardi Semenzato, SS Apostoli, Cannaregio 4363/4366 (tel. 522 7257). English-speaking owner. Just off Strada Nuova, near the Church of the Holy Apostles. Walk left from the station along Lista de Spagna and keep going straight on until you reach Strada Nuova, or take a boat to the stop by the Ca d'Oro.

Minerva e Nettuno, Lista da Spagna, Cannaregio 230 (tel. 715968). A short walk from the train station. Head left into Lista da Spagna.

Hotel Giovanna, Via Dante 113, Mestre (tel. 926396). Close to Mestre station. With or without bathroom. Breakfast included.

Hotel Vidale, Via G Parini 2, Mestre (tel. 531 4586). With or without private bathroom.

Hotel Col Di Lana, Via Fagare, Mestre (tel. 926879). Very cheap without private bathroom.

Albergo Santa Lucia, Calle Misericordia, Cannaregio 358 (tel. 715180, *www.hotelslucia.com*, *info@hotelslucia.com*). Head left from the train station into Lista da Spagna, then go left.

Noemi, Calle dei Fabbri 909 (tel. 523 8144, *www.hotelnoemi. com*, *info@hotelnoemi.com*). Five minutes from St Mark's Square.

Ai do Mori, Calle Larga San Marco, San Marco 658 (tel. 520 4817, *www.hotelaidomori.com*, *reception@hotelaidomori.com*). Excellent location, a few minutes' walk from St Mark's Square. Right off Mercerie, just behind the Clock Tower.

Al Gobbo, Campo San Geremia, Cannaregio (tel. 715001). Small but good value.

Sant'Anna, Sant'Anna, Castello 269 (tel. 528 6466). Near the Arsenal. Turn right on Via Garibaldi and follow the street into Sant'Anna.

San Samuele, Salizzada San Samuele, San Marco 3358 (tel. 522 8045). Very clean and excellent value.

Silva, Fondamenta Remedio, Castello 4423 (tel. 522 7643). Popular.

DOUBLES FROM €70 (£47)

Hotel Al Vagon, Cannaregio 5619 (tel. 528 5626, *www.hotel alvagon.com*, *info@hotelalvagon.com*). Located between Rialto Bridge and Ca d'Oro museum.

Art Hotel, Via dei Pensieri 13 (tel. 430062, *www.art-hotel.it*, *info@art-hotel.it*). Situated in the historical town of Mirano, 20-minute train ride from the centre of Venice.

Toscana-Tofanelli, Via Garibaldi, Castello 1650–1653 (tel. 523 5722). Near the Arsenal in Castello. From Pier 18 on the Piazzale Roma-Lido service cross the Rio di S. Giuseppe and walk down Viale Garibaldi into Via Garibaldi.

Corona, Calle Corona 4464, Castello (tel. 522 9174). Triples also available.

Casa Peron, Salizada San Pantalon 84/85 (tel. 710021). Follow the signs to the Rialto until you come to the Rio delle Muneghette. The hotel is over the bridge.

Montin, Fondamenta di Borgo, Dorsoduro 1147 (tel. 522 7151). From Pier 11 of the Piazzale Roma-Lido *vaporino* service, walk down past the S. Barnaba church, then go left over Rio Malpaga after passing through the square.

DOUBLES FROM €85 (£57)

Hotel Abbazia, Calle Priuli 68, Cannaregio (tel. 717 333, *www.abbaziahotel.com*, *info@abbaziahotel.com*). 150m from Santa Lucia station. Former monastery.

Hotel Florida, Calle Priuli 106, Cannaregio (tel. 715 23, *www.hotel-florida.com*, *info@hotel-florida.com*). Backs on to the Canal Grande.

Hotel Locanda Art Deco, Calle delle Botteghe 2966, San Marco (tel. 2770 558, *www.locandaartdeco.com*, *deco@locandaart deco.com*). Five-minute walk from St Mark's Square.

Al Gallo, Calle Amai, Santa Croce 197/G (tel. 523 6761). Cheaper without private bathrooms.

Hotel Ai Due Fanali, Santa Croce 946 (tel. 718 490, *www.aiduefanali.com*, *request@aiduefananli.com*). Facing the Canal Grande. Doubles start at €93 (£62).

Hotel Graspo de Ua, San Marco, Rialto 5094 (tel. 520 5644, *www.graspodeua.com*, *info@graspodeua.com*). Near the Rialto bridge.

Villa Rosa, Calle della Misercordia, Cannaregio 388 (tel. 718976). Two-star hotel.

Doni, San Zaccaria, Castello 4656 (tel. 522 4267). Not far from St Mark's Square. From the square go past the Bridge of Sighs (Ponte dei Sospiri) and Pier 16 of the *vaporino* service, over the Rio del Vin, then first left to San Zaccaria.

Albergo Alla Scala, San Marco 4306 (tel. 521 0629). Closed during August.

HI HOSTEL

'Ostello Venezia', Fondamenta di Zitelle 86, Isola della Giudecca (tel. 523 8211, *vehostel@tin.it*). B&B €16.50 (£11) (sheets included). On Giudecca island. 11.30pm curfew. Members only, but temporary and full membership cards are sold at the hostel. Waterbus 82 from the train station. Hostel open 7–9am and 2–11.30pm. Reserve as far in advance as possible.

HOSTELS

In the past, the city authorities have operated hostels during the summer (mid–July to mid–Sept.). Prices and curfews similar to those of the HI hostel, but the city hostels are more conveniently located. Reservations for the city hostels (first three listed below) are handled by the HI hostel (address above). It is always advisable to write at least one month before your date of arrival.

S. Caboto, Cannaregio 1105F (tel. 716629). By the Canale di Cannaregio, 10 minutes from the station. Head left along Lista da Spagna to the Guglie Bridge and the Canale di Cannaregio. The hostel is signposted from the bridge. Various accommodation options. Cheapest of all is throwing down a mat and a sleeping bag in the grounds; then camping in your tent in the grounds; followed by a night in the tents they hire out; and, lastly, dorm beds.

R. Michiel, Dorsoduro 1184 (tel. 522 7227). Close to the Accademia (waterbus 1, 2 or 34).

Santa Fosca, Cannaregio 2372 (tel. 715775). A short walk from Campo S. Fosca. Dorm beds around €15 (£10).

Instituto Suore Cannosiane, Giudecca, Ponte Piccolo 428, Isola della Giudecca (tel. 522 2157). Dorm beds €13 (£8.70). Reservations taken from 7.30am–12pm and 4–10.30pm. Take number 82 waterbus from S. Lucia to Traghetto-Planaca stop. Curfew 10.30pm. Women only. Run by nuns. Open all year.

Foresteria Valdese, Calle Lunga Formosa 5170, Castello (tel. 528 6797). B&B from €19 (£12.70), doubles also available. No curfew. *Vaporetto* stop: S. Zaccaria. Walk away from the water to the S. Zaccaria church then head left. Go right along S. Provolo, then left over the Rio dell'Osmarin and down Ruga Giuffa into Campo S. Maria Formosa. From the right-hand side of the square follow Calle Lunga to its end. The hostel is by the bridge. Reserve by phone if possible.

Domus Civica, Calle Campazzo, San Polo 3082 (tel. 721103). Near the Frari church. Prices start at €26 (£17.50) per person. Singles and doubles available. 20% off with ISIC card. Open mid-June–Sept. Curfew 11.30pm. Reserve. Wheelchair access.

Domus Cavanis, Rio Terra Foscarini, Dorsoduro 912 (tel. 528 7374). Doubles €30 (£20). Open June–Sept. 11.30pm curfew. Separate rooms for men and women in this church-run hostel.

Alloggi Calderan, Campo San Germia 283 (tel. 715562). Dorms from €18 (£12), doubles from €50 (£33).

Ostello Mira, Via Giare 169, Giare di Mira (tel. 567 9203). Take the bus from Piazzale Roma to Sottomarina, bus stop Giare. B&B €13 (£8.70).

CAMPING
Waterbus 14 will take you to the Littorale del Cavallino, a peninsula with a string of campsites along its beach. Some charge ridiculously high prices.

Camping Marina da Venezia, Via Montello 6 (tel. 302511, *www.marinadivenezia.it*). Open Apr.–Sept. Minimum stay 3 nights.

Camping Fusina, Via Moranzani 79, Fusina (tel. 547 0055, *www.camping-fusina.com*, *info@camping-fusina.com*). In the summer, waterbus 16 goes directly to the site from the Zatteri stop. At other times, take bus 2 to the 'Fusino' stop of S. Marta, a one-hour trip. Mosquito repellent is essential. Open all year. Book ahead.

Camping Serenissima, Via Padana 334, Oriago (tel. 920 286). From Piazzale Roma with ACTV bus Venezia–Padova line, stop at Camping Serenissima.

Camping Miramare, Punto Sabbioni (tel. 966150, *www.camping-miramare.it*, *info@camping-miramare.it*). Take waterbus 14 from Piazza S. Marco to Punta Sabbioni. Bungalows to rent. Open March to end November.

SLEEPING ROUGH
Thieves patrol the beaches of the Lido island looking for easy targets. If you choose to sleep here, bed down beside other travellers. Even then, ants and mosquitoes can make for an unpleasant night. Sleeping on the train station forecourt is illegal and the police occasionally use water hoses to clear people away.

Verona (0)45

TOURIST OFFICES
The main APT office is at Via degli Alpini 11 (tel. 8068 680, *www.tourism.verona.it*, *info@tourism.verona.it*). Open 9am–7pm,

closing at 3pm on Sundays. Visit their website for general information and accommodation listings.

There is also an office at the train station (tel. 800861). If you are arriving by car or motorbike from Milan or Venice, there is a city information office at the turn-off from the motorway (Viale del Lavoro 7).

BASIC DIRECTIONS

The Verona Porta Nuova train station is about 20 minutes' walk from the Piazza delle Erbe in the centre of the Old Town. Going right from the station, you arrive at the Porta Nuova, the old city gate from which the station takes its name. Turning right at this point, you can follow the road under the railway lines and down Viale Piave and Viale delle Lavoro to the Milan–Venice highway. Turning left at the Porta Nuova, you can follow Corso Porta Nuova towards the town centre. Passing through the old city walls, you arrive at Piazza Bra' with the famous Roman Arena. To the left as you enter the square, Via Roma leads off in the direction of the Castelvecchio by the River Adige. Going around the Arena, you can take Via Giuseppe Mazzini from the opposite side of Piazza Bra' into the Piazza delle Erbe. Buses 1, 2 and 8 run from Verona Porta Nuova to the Piazza Bra', if you want to save yourself about two-thirds of the walk.

HOTELS

DOUBLES FROM €30 (£20)

Locanda Catullo, Via V. Catullo 1 (tel. 800 2786, *locanda catullo@tiscali.it*). Left off Via Mazzini between the Piazza Bra' and the Piazza Erbe. Three-night minimum stay for reservations July–Sept. Reserve.

DOUBLES FROM €45 (£30)

Hotel Armando, Via Dietro Pallone 1 (tel. 800 0206). Breakfast extra. 5 minutes' walk from the Arena.

All'Incontro, Via Mantovana 138 (tel. 8622 251). Minimum three night stay.

Ciopeta, Vicolo Teatro Filarmonico 2 (tel. 800 6843, *www.ciopeta.it*, *albergo@ciopeta.it*). Doubles from €60 (£40).

Aurora, Piazzetta XIV Novembre 2 (tel. 594 717). Views over Piazza della Erbe.

HI HOSTEL

'**Villa Francescatti**', Salita Fontana del Ferro 15 (tel. 590 360, *www.ostellionline.org*). Dorm beds for €13.50 (£9) (including breakfast and sheets). Dinner also available. Curfew 11pm, extended for opera-goers. Laundry facilities. Kitchen facilities available. Family rooms. Camping permitted. Behind the Teatro Romano, 3 km from the station, but only 10 minutes' walk from the town centre. Bus 73 or nightbus 90 to P. Isola. HI or student card required. No reservations accepted.

WOMEN'S HOSTEL

Casa della Giovane (ACISJF), Via Pigna 7 (3rd floor) (tel. 596880, *www.casadellagiovane.com*, *info@casadellagiovane.com*). Curfew 10.30pm but, for an extra €2 (£1.30), you can get an extension if you are going to the opera. Dorm beds from €13 (£8.70); singles around €18 (£12); doubles €25 (£16.50). Great views. Bus 2 from the station. Phone or email to see whether there are spaces.

CAMPING

Camping Castel San Pietro, Via Castel San Pietro (tel. 592 037, *www.campingcastelsanpietro.com*, *info@campingcastelsanpietro* *.com*). Pleasant campsite within the city walls. Open mid-May to mid-October. Take bus 1 from the train station to the Marsala stop. Book in advance, this place is popular.

For further ideas, ask at the tourist information office.

LUXEMBOURG (Lëtzebuerg) (00)352

Size doesn't matter when it comes to Luxembourg – 'the green heart of Europe'. It is one of the continent's smallest and richest countries and its plentiful forests make it ideal for camping and hiking.

BACKGROUND

Having become a Duchy in 1354, Luxembourg came under the control of Burgundy in 1443, before being ceded once again in 1482, this time to the Habsburgs. In 1815, Luxembourg became a Grand Duchy under the Dutch crown, but soon joined the Belgian revolt against the Netherlands, eventually gaining independence in 1867. Occupation by the Germans during both world wars left the country surprisingly intact and since then Luxembourg has enjoyed a very high standard of living, its status as a tax haven having courted the interest of many foreign investors.

ACCOMMODATION DETAILS

If you arrive in Luxembourg having previously visited Belgium, you will notice a similarity both in the types of accommodation on offer and in the prices of different accommodation options. On the whole, with the exception of HI hostels, standards in the various types of accommodation are also on a par with those in Belgium. Prices in **hotels** and **pensions** start around €25 (£16.50) in singles, €35 (£23) in doubles.

A less expensive option in the more popular tourist towns such as Echternach, Vianden, Clervaux and Wiltz is the availability of rooms in private homes. Prices for **private rooms** range from €20–25 (£13.30–16.50) per person. These tend to fill quickly, so it is best to make enquiries as early in the day as possible. You can either ask about their availability at the local Tourist Office (i.e. not the National Tourist Office in the city), or approach the owner of any house advertising rooms to let (signs are usually printed in French, German, Dutch and English).

Considering their price, the facilities on offer and the high standards of comfort and cleanliness, the Grand Duchy's small network of **HI hostels** must rank among the best in Europe. All the hostels are open from mid-April to September but, at other times, different hostels are closed for anything between two days to six weeks. Curfews are normally midnight. Non-members can usually stay at the hostels for an additional nightly charge of €2.73 (£1.80). The cost of B&B varies between €13.60 (£9) and €15.50 (£10.20). Duvets (rather than the usual blankets) are supplied, but you must have a linen sheet sleeping bag – either your own, or one hired from the hostel. The maximum stay at any hostel is limited to three days, and only one day at peak periods (July and August). These rules are only enforced when the hostel is full, but it is as well to be aware of them.

Most of the main places of interest have a hostel. One notable exception is Clervaux, but here there is the choice of two of the small network of *gîtes d'étapes*. Most are open all year and prices range from €7–12 (£4.70–8).

Of the 120 or so **campsites**, only around 30 are open for the whole year. However, the vast majority are open March/April to September. The Luxembourg Tourist Office listed below provides a brochure on camping, which can be obtained either online or by telephone.

ADDRESSES

LUXEMBOURG NATIONAL TOURIST OFFICE
122 Regent Street, London W1R 5FE (tel. 020 7434 2800, *www.luxembourg.co.uk, tourism@luxembourg.co.uk*).

LUXEMBOURGEOIS YHA
Centrale des Auberges de Jeunesse Luxembourgeoises, 24–26 Place de la Gare, Luxembourg (tel. 26 293 500, *www.youth hostels.lu, information@youthhostels.lu*).

CAMPING
www.camping.lu is an excellent website that will let you search for campsites by region and criteria. The tourist information website also has a large selection of sites.

GÎTES D'ÉTAPES
Visit *www.gites.lu* for full listings, prices and booking facilities.

Luxembourg City (Lëtzebuerg)

TOURIST OFFICES
Office National du Tourisme, Place de la Gare (tel. 4282 8220). Open daily, July–mid-Sept., 9am–7.30pm; at other times, daily 9am–12pm and 2–6.30pm, except mid-Nov.–mid-Mar. when the office is closed Sundays. By the Luxair terminal to the right of the train station. There is another branch at Luxembourg-Findel airport. Both offices provide information and services covering the whole country.

Syndicat d'Initiative et de Tourisme de la Ville de Luxembourg, place d'Armes (tel. 222809, *www.luxembourg-city.lu*, *tourist info@luxembourg-city.lu*). Open July–mid-Sept., Mon.–Fri. 9am–1pm and 2–8pm, Sat. closes at 7pm, Sun. 10am–12pm and 2–6pm; at other times, open Mon.–Sat. 9am–1pm and 2–6pm. Information and services for the city only. Place d'Armes is right in the heart of the city.

HOTELS
All the hotels listed are about a 5- to 10-minute walk from place de la Gare in front of the train station, unless otherwise stated.

CHEAPEST DOUBLES FROM €45 (£30)
Hotel Carlton, 9 rue Strasbourg (tel. 299660, *carlton@pt.lu*). Breakfast extra. Head right past the Luxair terminal. Rue de Strasbourg is across the road on the left.

Hotel Bristol, 11 rue de Strasbourg (tel. 485829). Directions as Hotel Carlton above.

Zurich, 36 rue Joseph Junck, 1839 Lux. (tel. 491350). The street is at the right end of place de la Gare.

Papillon, 9 rue Origer (tel. 494490). Right from pl. de la Gare. At the fork right down av. de la Gare, then left.

Hotel de l'Avenue, 43 avenue de la Liberte, (tel. 406812, *hotelav@pt.lu*). Near the train station.

New Chemin de Fer, 4 rue Joseph Junck (tel. 493528). Can be booked through *www.luxembourg-city.lu*.

CHEAPEST DOUBLES FROM €70 (£47)

Bella Napoli, 4 rue de Strasbourg (tel. 484629). Near the station.

Le Parisien, 46 rue Ste-Zithe (tel. 492397). Right from pl. de la Gare. At the fork left down av. de la Liberté. Rue Ste-Zithe is left off pl. de Paris.

Hotel des Ducs, 12 rue d'Anvers (tel. 490161, *msteil@pt.lu*). By the train station.

Paradiso, 23 rue de Strasbourg (tel. 484801). For directions see Hotel Carlton, above.

Hotel Casanova, 10 place Guillaume (tel. 220493, *www.hotel casanova.lu*, *info@hotelcasanova.lu*). Excellent hotel with good weekend rates.

HI HOSTEL

2 rue de Fort Olisy (tel. 226889, *www.youthhostels.lu*, *luxembourg@youthhostels.lu*). B&B €15.50 (£10.40). Doubles also available. Non-members pay €2.73 (£1.80) extra per night. 1am curfew, reasonably flexible. Snack bar and kitchen. About 2.5 km from the station. Wheelchair accessible, family rooms. Bus 9 from the station (or the airport) to the Vallée d'Alzette (last bus goes at 9pm).

CAMPING

Luxembourg-Kockelscheuer, 22 route de Bettembourg (tel. 471815, *www.camp-kockelscheuer.lu*, *mail@kockelscheuer.lu*). Open 1 Apr.–31 Oct. About 4 km from the train station. Bus 2 from the station.

Bon Accueil, 2 rue du Camping (tel. 367069). 5 km south of town in Alzingen. The bus from the train station to Alzingen stops nearby. Open Apr. to Oct.

MOROCCO (Maroc) (00)212

Morocco's proximity to mainland Spain means that it is easily negotiable on a 'European tour'. If you travel by train from Europe, your first port of call will be Tangier, a crowded, frustrating city. If you want to get a true impression of Morocco, you would be advised to head south to the popular but less commercialised cities of Fez and Marrakech. Getting to the south does not pose a problem. The Moroccan government is ultra-keen on encouraging tourism, and as a consequence, the railway system is very good indeed.

BACKGROUND

Formerly a protectorate of the French and Spanish, Morocco became a kingdom in 1957 under Mohammed V – the father of the present ruler, King Hassan II. French and Spanish are still widely spoken, and English is often understood in the more touristy areas, so communication is not a big problem. Morocco is a Muslim country, though, and is governed under the strict guidelines of Islamic law; women travellers should therefore cover up in the more out of the way places, where people may not be as used to Western tourists.

Alcohol isn't illegal, but water should be your prime concern in Morocco. It's unsafe to drink from the tap, so you will have to stock up on mineral water from the local stores – the main brands are *Sidi Ali* and *Sidi Harazem*.

The local currency is the Moroccan dirham (dh). There are around 15.50 dh in £1, and 10 dh in $1.

Morocco is about as different from Europe as it is possible to be, and while not everyone's cup of tea, a trip there will provide some new and memorable experiences.

ACCOMMODATION DETAILS

The price of accommodation in Morocco is so low that a decent hotel room should be well within your budget. **Hotels** are divided into two main categories, *classé* and *non-classé*. The former are regulated by the national tourist authority, which both grades them on a scale rising from one star to five-star luxury, and fixes their prices. The one- to four-star grades are further subdivided A and B. The *classé* hotels are listed in a free hotel guide which you can get from any tourist office. At the lower end of the scale there is only a small variation in price, and in the facilities offered. Even the one-star establishments offer a level of comfort and cleanliness you are unlikely to find in a *non-classé* hotel. As a rule, *classé* hotels are situated in the *villes nouvelles* – the new town or administrative quarters built during the French colonial period. All *classé* hotels are listed online at *www.maroc.net/hotel*.

Non-classé hotels enjoy two advantages over *classé* hotels: location, and, outside peak periods, price. In peak season (August, Christmas and Easter) it is not uncommon for *non-classé* hotels to raise their prices sharply, so that they actually exceed the price of one-star B and one-star A establishments. *Non-classé* hotels, which are neither listed nor regulated by the national tourist authority, are generally located in the *medina*, the old, Arab-built part of the town. Staying here, you will be close to the markets, historic buildings and the bewildering array of street performers. However, the *medina*, with its twisting, narrow streets, can be an intimidating place. The quality of hotels varies greatly: while some offer spotless, whitewashed rooms looking out on to a central patio, there are also many that are filthy and flea-ridden. You are also far more likely to encounter problems with a poor water supply and primitive toilet facilities in the *medina*.

A room in the *medina* should cost in the region of 50–100 dh (£3.25–6.50; $5.50–11). A spacious, more comfortable room in a *classé* hotel in the *ville nouvelle* might cost about 100–150 dh (£6.50–9.50; $11–16), possibly with a small extra charge for showers. At this lower end of the price scale, hot water may only be available at certain times of the day. Only during the peak season and in the main towns are you likely to have any problem finding a room.

For those reaching the end of their funds, even cheaper possibilities exist. Prices at Morocco's **46 campsites** are extremely cheap, at around 16 dh (£1; $1.70) per tent and per person. On no account should you leave any valuables unattended. All the major towns have a campsite, and most also have an **HI hostel**. The 11 hostels differ tremendously in quality. Anyone without a membership card is usually permitted to stay on the payment of a small supplement and some hostels sell cards on the spot for around 160 dh (£10; $15). Call ahead for reservations as beds can be scarce. There are rarely lockouts or curfews. All but one of the hostels are situated in the larger towns. The other, at Asni, is well worth considering as a base for hiking in the Atlas Mountains.

The French Alpine Club (CAF) has a network of **refuge huts** for the use of those hiking.

ADDRESSES

MOROCCAN NATIONAL TOURIST OFFICE
205 Regent Street, London W1R 7DE (tel. 020 7437 0073, *www.tourisme-marocain.com*).

MOROCCAN YHA
Fédération Royale Marocaine des Auberges de Jeunes, Parc de la Ligue Arabe, B.P. 15998, Casa-Principale, Casablanca 21000 (tel. 2 220551, *www.iyhf.org/mediterranean_morocco_gb.html*).

REFUGE HUTS
Club Alpin Français, 24 avenue de la Laumiere, 75019 Paris (tel. 01 53 72 87 00, *www.clubalpin.com*, *editions.com@clubalpin.com*).

Fez (Fès) 055

TOURIST OFFICES

Office National Marocaine du Tourisme (ONMT), pl. de la Résistance (tel. 623 460). Open Mon.–Fri. 8.30am–12pm and 2.30–6.30pm. At the end of av. Hassan II, in the Immeuble Bennani. From the train, follow rue Chenguit, go left at pl. Kennedy, then turn left on to av. Hassan II. From the CTM bus station, follow blvd Mohammed V, then go right at av. Hassan II.

There are Syndicats d'Initiative on pl. Mohammed V (tel. 624 764) by Bab Boujeloud, the main entrance to the *medina*, and outside the more expensive hotels (generally open Mon.–Fri. 8.30am–6.30pm and Sat. 8.30am–12pm).

FINDING ACCOMMODATION

Fez lacks sufficient hotel accommodation of all types, which means that prices are higher than elsewhere in the country. It is best to phone ahead and try to get a reservation. The best of the cheap rooms in the new town are located just to the west of blvd Mohammed V, between av. Hassan II (near the post office) and av. Mohammed es Slaoui (near the CTM bus terminal). Rooms in the *medina* are concentrated around Bab Boujeloud.

UNCLASSIFIED HOTELS

Du Commerce, place des Alaouites, Fes el-Djedid (tel. 622 231). Across from the royal palace. The cleanest and best hotel in the *medina*. Doubles 65–100 dh (£4–6.50; $7–11).

Erraha, place Boujeloud, Fes el Bali (tel 633 226). Excellent value.

Kaskade, Bab Boujeloud, Fes el Bali (tel. 638 442). Popular.

Lamrani, Talâa Seghira, Fes el Bali (tel. 634 411). Opposite an old *hammam*.

The Grand, blvd Abdallah Chefchaouni (tel. 932 026). Near pl. Mohammed V.

Savoy, near blvd Abdallah Chefchaouni (tel. 620 608).

Du Jardin Public, Kasbah Boujeloud 153 (tel. 633 086). Cold showers. Close to Bab Boujeloud down an alleyway by the Boujeloud mosque.

Rex, place de l'Atlas (tel. 642 133). No frills, but cheap and very clean.

Regina, rue Ghassan Kanfani 21 (tel. 622 427). Fine rooms. Prices are raised considerably during the summer.

Moussafir, place de la Gare (tel. 651 902). Near the station.

Renaissance, rue Abdel el-Khattabi 29 (tel. 622 193). Clean, basic rooms.

CLASSIFIED HOTELS

TWO-STAR A

Olympic, blvd Mohammed V (tel. 622 403). Doubles from 200 dh (£13; $22). All have bathrooms and hot water.

TWO-STAR B

Amor, rue Arabic Saoudite 31 (tel. 562 2724). All rooms with bath. Has a restaurant and bar.

Royal, rue du Soudan 36 (tel. 624 656). Doubles with shower.
Lamdaghri, Kabbour el Mangad 10 (tel. 620 310). Popular.

ONE-STAR A
Kairouan, rue du Soudan 84 (tel. 623 590). All rooms with showers.

ONE-STAR B
Central, rue Brahim Roudant 50 (tel. 562 2333). Very popular, so get there early. Off blvd Mohammed V.
CTM, av. Mohammed V (tel. 622 811). Next to the old CTM station.
Excelsior, rue Larbi el-Kaghat (tel. 562 5602). Right off blvd Mohammed V, three blocks up from the main post office. '

HI HOSTEL
Rue Abdesslam Serghini 18 (tel. 624 085). It's supposed to be for members only but they will accommodate non-members for around 50 dh (£3.25; $5.50) a night. Breakfast is available. 10pm curfew. Roof space available when the dormitories are filled. A clean hostel with friendly staff.

CAMPING
Camping International (tel. 731 439). About 3 km south of town on the Sefrou road. Swimming pool, tennis courts, restaurants and bars. 50 dh (£3.25; $5.50). Take bus 38 from place Atlas in the new town.
Camping Diament Vert, off the Ilfrane road, 6 km away (tel. 608 367) Bus 218.

Marrakech 044

TOURIST OFFICES
Office National Marocaine du Tourisme (ONMT), pl. Abdel Moumen ben Ali (tel. 436 239). Open Mon.–Fri. 9am–12pm and 2.30–6.30pm, Sat. 9am–12pm; during Ramadan, 9am–3pm only.

Further down the street in the direction of the *medina* is the GRIT (Groupement Regional d'Interet Touristique) at av. Mohammed V 170 (tel. 431 016). Open Mon.–Fri. 9am–12pm and 2.30–6pm, Sat. 8.30am–12pm. Bus 1 runs along av. Mohammed V from the Koutoubia Minaret near the Djemaâ el Fna.

UNCLASSIFIED HOTELS

Hôtel de France, 197 rue Zitoun el Kadem (tel. 443 067). Excellent value, but popular, so book in advance.

Hôtel Essaouira, Derb Sidi Bouloukate 3 (tel. 443 805). Has a rooftop terrace. On the same street as the Medina hotel (see directions below). Hot showers extra.

Hôtel Afrique (tel. 442 403) is in the same street as the Hôtel Essaouira above.

La Gazelle, 12 rue Bani Marine (tel. 441 112). Showers.

Toulousain, 44 rue Tariq Ben Ziad, Gueliz (tel. 430 033). Popular, book in advance.

Chellah (tel. 442 977). The Chellah is in an alley left off Zitoune el-Kedim. Watch out for the sign pointing to the hotel.

Medina, Derb Sidi Bouloukate 1 (tel. 442 977). A particularly good unclassified hotel, in an alley to the right off Zitoune el-Kedim.

Souria, 17 rue de la Recette (tel. 426 757).

CLASSIFIED HOTELS

TWO-STAR

Koutoubia, 51 blvd Mansour Eddahbi (tel. 430 921). Comfortable.

Islane, 279 av. Mohammed V (tel. 440 081). Facing the Koutoubia minaret. Noisy but comfortable.

Ali, rue Moulay Ismail 10 (rue du Dispensaire/pl. de Foucauld) (tel. 444 979). Doubles with shower, toilet and A/C. You can also sleep on the terrace. Good restaurant. Extremely popular. Near Djemaâ el Fna, behind the post office.

La Palmeraie, rue Souraya (tel. 431 007). In the New Town.

Du Pacha, rue de la Liberté 33 (tel. 431 326). Good value.

El Hamra, av. Abdelkrim Khattabi BP575 (tel. 448 423). Self-catering.

La Menara, av. des Ramparts (tel. 436 478, fax 447 386). Just outside the city walls.

Nouzha, 116 Camp el Ghoul (tel. 435 510). Book in advance.
Redouane, av. Allal el Fassi (tel. 307 676).

ONE-STAR

CTM, Djemaâ el Fna (tel. 442 325). Over the old bus station. Clean and cheap.

Farouk, av. Hassan II 66 (tel. 431 989). Near the train station in Gueliz.

Des Voyageurs, av. Zerktouni 40 (tel. 447 218). ONMT office 100m.

Tazi, Angle av. El Mouahidine (tel. 442 152). In the *medina* at the corner of av. El Mouahidine and Bab Agnaou.

De Foucault, av. El Mouahidine (tel. 445 499). A fine hotel, but particularly good value if three or four people share one of the larger rooms. Bathrooms with hot water, A/C, restaurant. Rooftop terrace.

Des Ambassadeurs, av. Mohammed V 2 (tel. 447 159).

HI HOSTEL

Rue el Jahid, Quartier Industriel (tel 447 713). Technically an HI card is obligatory, but non-members are usually admitted outside the peak season. Very clean. Lock-out between 9am–12pm and from 2–6pm. About 700m from the train station. Turn right after crossing av. Hassan II, then take the first left and keep on going until you see the hostel on the right.

CAMPING

Camping Ferdaous (tel. 02 331 3167). 13 km north on the road to Casablanca. It costs 15 dh (90p; $1.50) per person and 15 dh per tent. Swimming pool, warm showers and supermarket. Call ahead.

THE NETHERLANDS (Nederland) (00)31

Everyone has their own impression of the Netherlands: clogs, windmills, coffee shops, and people who speak better English than even the English themselves. The Netherlands is a highly sophisticated country with a healthy attitude to tourism and a superb public transport system. A trip to the Netherlands is, of course, incomplete without a visit to its capital – Amsterdam – a city stuck in the 1960s, living out a debauched lifestyle of sex, drugs, and rock and roll, yet a city just as famous for its tulips and beautiful canals.

The Netherlands is a flat country, particularly in the north. Much of the land had to be reclaimed from the sea, and a comprehensive collection of dams and dykes was introduced to keep it from being submerged again. The south of the country is slightly different from most people's expectations – the occasional incline masquerading as a hill interrupts the landscape, and the Protestant influence begins to fade. Many here are Catholic, and in that respect are more like the French than the northern Dutch.

Access to the Netherlands from Great Britain and Ireland is both easy and affordable nowadays, with the Channel Tunnel rail-link and the budget airlines. The friendly nature of the Dutch people will make any trip a pleasure. One thing people forget to mention about the Netherlands is the excellence of the Dutch pubs and beers, so make sure you give them a try when you visit.

ACCOMMODATION DETAILS

It is a pleasure to travel in the Netherlands, not least because the Dutch are responding particularly well to the growth in independent, budget tourism. Reserving accommodation before you set off on holiday is easy. Local Tourist Offices (VVV) will book hotel rooms and B&B accommodation over the internet, though if you plan to travel around a fair bit you can save yourself the trouble of contacting individual offices by visiting the general Netherlands tourist board website. Here you can book hotels, youth hostels, bed and breakfasts, farm-stays and even castles

DUTCH YHA

Stichting Nederlandse Jeugdherberg Centrale NJHC, Prof Tulpstraat 2, ND-1018 GX Amsterdam (tel. (0)20 551 3133, or (0)10 264 6064 for information, *www.njhc.org*).

BED AND BREAKFAST HOLLAND

T. de Bockstraat 3, 1058 TV Amsterdam (tel. (0)20 615 7527, fax (0)20 669 1573). You must book a minimum of two nights and there's an admin. fee of €5 (£3.30).

CAMPING

See the tourist information website above for full listings.

Amsterdam (0)20

TOURIST OFFICES

VVV Amsterdam Tourist Office, PO Box 3901, 1001 AS Amsterdam (tel. 0900 400 4040, *www.visitamsterdam.nl*, *info@amsterdamtourist.nl*). Contact this office, or visit their website, for information in advance.

VVV Amsterdam Tourist Office, at the Centraal Station (CS) on platform 2. Open Mon.–Sat. 8am–8pm, Sun. 9am–5pm.

VVV Amsterdam Tourist Office, Stationsplein. Open daily 9am–5pm.

VVV Amsterdam Tourist Office, Leidseplein 1. Open Sun.–Wed. 9am–5pm, Thu.–Sat. 9am–7pm.

Incidentally, do not expect to get anything free from these tourist offices. You will even have to pay for a map.

TROUBLE SPOTS

There are a few wild stories about drug-crazed gangs roaming around the city mugging tourists. Wild stories are all they are! Because of the number of tourists visiting it, the red light area is particularly safe, at least until the early hours of the morning, although, as in the most crowded areas of all cities, pickpockets are to be found operating among the hustle and bustle. Although you are more likely to be offered drugs in Amsterdam than in almost any other city, pushers are rarely aggressive. Amsterdam drug culture has become so integrated that the pushers almost see themselves as a public service! One place you might want to avoid after dark is the Nieuwemarkt (location of the Waag), only a short walk from Oudezijds Achterburgwal in the red light district down Bloedstraat or Barndesteeg. Many of the casualties of the hard drug scene congregate around the square, as do those who supply them.

BASIC DIRECTIONS

From Stationsplein in front of Amsterdam Centraal, head across the bridge (avoiding the trams) before crossing Prins Hendrikkade to the start of Damrak. Walking up Damrak, turning left at the end of the water takes you to Oude Brug Steeg, across Warmoesstraat and down Lange Niezel into the red light district. Continuing up Damrak you arrive at Dam, the large square containing the Royal Palace and the National Monument. To the right, behind the palace, Raadhuisstraat leads off across the ring of canals which encircle the town centre. Directly across Dam from Damrak is Rokin, which leads to Muntplein. The walk from Amsterdam Centraal to Dam takes about 10 minutes, that from Dam to Muntplein slightly less. Trams 4, 5, 9, 16, 24 and 25 run from the station to Muntplein.

FINDING ACCOMMODATION

Of all the cities in Europe, only Rome, Paris and London receive more visitors than Amsterdam, so if you want to be sure of reasonably cheap accommodation, you should reserve as far in advance as possible, particularly in summer. If you have not reserved ahead but are stopping in another Dutch town before visiting Amsterdam, you can ask the local VVV to reserve ahead for you. Otherwise, try to arrive in Amsterdam as early as possible because, for obvious reasons, the cheapest accommodation goes quickly. In the sections below, directions are given for most accommodation options, often from a reference point in the Basic Directions section above.

Useful accommodation websites include: *www.channels.nl*, *www.amsterdam-hotels-guide.com* and *www.amsterdamhotspots.nl*.

HOTELS

CHEAPEST DOUBLES FROM €45 (£30)

Aspen, Raadhuisstraat 31 (tel. 626 6714, *www.hotelaspen.nl*, *info@hotelaspen.nl*). Without breakfast.

Pax, Raadhuisstraat 37 (tel. 624 9735). Without breakfast. A 10- to 15-minute walk from Amsterdam Centraal, or take tram 13 or 17 along the street from the station.

Westertoren, Raadhuisstraat 35B (tel. 624 4639, *www.hotel westertoren.nl*, *info@hotelwestertoren.nl*). Breakfast included.

Galerij, Raadhuisstraat 43 (tel. 624 8851). Without breakfast. See Hotel Pax, above.

Beursstraat, Beursstraat 7 (tel. 626 3701). On one of the main red-light canals.

Impala, Leidsekade 77 (tel. 623 4706). From Amsterdam Centraal take tram 1, 2 or 5 to Leidseplein. Dorms available for €20 (£13.30). Minimum 5-night stay at peak periods. Doubles from €100 (£67).

Casa Cara, Emmastraat 24 (tel. 662 3135). B&B. Good value hotel. Out by the Vondelpark. Trams 2 and 16 from Amsterdam Centraal cross the Emmastraat.

Arena Budget Hotel, 's-Gravesandestraat 51 (tel. 850 2400). Tram 9, Metro Weesperplein, Bus 22. Nightbus 77. Cheaper dormitories also available. Also cultural centre and café-restaurant.

The Crown, Oudezijds Voorburgwal 21 (tel. 626 9664, *www.hotelthecrown.com*, *info@hotelthecrown.com*). Lively bar. €45 (£30) per person. Book 4 weeks in advance.

CHEAPEST DOUBLES FROM €60 (£40)

Apple Inn, Koninginneweg 93 (tel. 662 7894, *www.apple-inn.nl*, *info@apple-inn.nl*). B&B. Two-star hotel near the Vondelpark. Tram 2 from Amsterdam Centraal runs along the street. Excellent value.

Hotel Abba, Overtoom 120 (tel. 618 3058). Tram 1 to Constantijn Huygensstraat. Minimum 5-night stay over the weekend in summer.

Hotel P C Hooft, P C Hooftstraat 63 (tel. 662 7107). Breakfast included.

Schröder, Haarlemerdijk 48B (tel. 626 6272). Without breakfast.

Two-night minimum stay in peak season. Right along Prins Hendrikkade, left at Singel, then right along Haarlemerstraat into Haarlemerdijk. A 5- to 10-minute walk from Amsterdam Centraal.

De Leydsche Hof, Leidsegracht 14 (tel. 623 2148). Breakfast included.

Old Quarter, Warmoesstraat 22 (tel. 626 6429). Lively.

Old Nickel, Nieuwebrugsteeg 11 (tel. 624 1912). B&B. Left along the waterside at the start of Damrak into Nieuwebrugsteeg. A few minutes' walk from Amsterdam Centraal.

Weber, Marnixstraat 397 (tel. 627 0574, *bboog@xs4all.nl*). Without breakfast. Tram 1 or 2 from Amsterdam Centraal to Leidseplein, then a few minutes' walk along Marnixstraat.

Van Rooyen, Tweede Helmersstraat 6 (tel. 618 4577). B&B. Tram 1, 2 or 5 to Leidseplein from Amsterdam Centraal. Walk right along Nassaukade, past the end of 1E Helmersstraat then left on 2E Helmersstraat.

Oosterpark, Oosterpark 72 (tel. 693 0049). B&B. Metro: Weesper plein, then change to tram 6 which runs along Oosterpark. A 5- to 10-minute walk from Amsterdam-Muiderpoort train station. Follow Wijtenbachstraat into Oosterpark.

CHEAPEST DOUBLES FROM €75 (£50)

Clemens, Raadhuisstraat 39 (tel. 624 6089, *www.clemenshotel.nl*, *info@clemenshotel.nl*). B&B. For directions, see Hotel Pax above.

CHEAPEST DOUBLES FROM €90 (£60)

Bema, Concertgebouwplein 19B (tel. 679 1396, *www.bema hotel.com*, *postbus@hotel-bema.demon.nl*). B&B. Tram 16 from Amsterdam Centraal.

La Bohème, Marnixstraat 415 (tel. 624 2828). For directions, see Weber, above.

Amstelzicht, Amstel 104 (tel. 623 6693). Two-star hotel in a good location between Muntplein and the Blauwe Brug (Blue Bridge). B&B. Tram 4 from Amsterdam Centraal runs down part of Amstel before turning off into Rembrandtsplein. From the metro stop on Waterlooplein you can take tram 9 the whole length of Amstel.

HI HOSTELS

City Hostel 'Vondelpark', Zandpad 5 (tel. 589 8996, *www.njhc.org*). Around €20–€22 (£13.30–14.50) p.p. in dorms. Open all year, 24 hours a day. Holland's largest hostel, Vondelpark was renovated during 1997 and offers 2-, 4-, 6- and 8- bed rooms, all with wash facilities. The hostel also has a 'Backpacker's Brasserie', open 10am–1am. From Amsterdam Centraal take tram 1, 2 or 5 to Leidseplein. Zandpad is off Stadhouderskade at the left-hand end of Leidseplein.

'Stadsdoelen', Kloveniersburgwal 97 (tel. 624 6832, can be booked through *www.hostelbooking.com*). B&B €20–€22 (£13.30–14.50). Open all year. Curfew 1.30am. Laundry facilities. Between Muntplein and the Nieuwmarkt. From Muntplein follow Nieuwe Doelen Straat into Kloveniersburgwal. A 15-minute walk from Amsterdam Centraal, through the red light district. From Lange Niezel follow Korte Niezel, then go right at Oudezijds Achterburgwal then left at Dude Hoögstraat into Kloveniersburgwal. Trams 4, 9, 16, 24 and 25 go to Muntplein. Cycles available for hire.

CHRISTIAN HOSTELS

Both are safe, very cheap, and not as rule-bound as you might imagine. 1am curfew Fri. and Sat., midnight the rest of the week. Reservations to be made through the website or by phone only.

The Shelter City, Barndesteeg 21–25 (tel. 625 3230, *www.shelter.nl*, *city@shelter.nl*). A 10-minute walk from Amsterdam Centraal to the hostel in the red light district. From Lange Niezel follow Korte Niezel, go right on Oudezijds Achterburgwal, then left at Barndesteeg.

The Shelter Jordan, Bloemstraat 179 (tel. 624 4717, *www.shelter.nl*, *jordan@shelter.nl*). Tram 13 or 17 from Amsterdam Centraal to the Marnixstraat stop. Walk back to Rozengracht, and Bloemstraat is parallel to the left.

HOSTELS

Durty Nelly's Inn, Warmoesstraat 117 (tel. 638 0125, *nellys@xs4all.nl*). B&B €15 (£10). Conveniently located above Irish pub Durty Nelly's! Open all year, 24 hours. From Centraal station walk up the Damrak and turn left down Beursplein. Left again on to Warmoesstraat.

Flying Pig Palace, Vossiusstraat 46 (tel. 400 4187, *www.flying pig.nl*, *palace@flyingpig.nl*). Dorms from €16.50 (£11) including breakfast, there are also singles and doubles. Bar and kitchen facilities. Tram 1, 2, 5 or 11 to Leidseplein. Go straight on, cross the bridge and the street towards Vondelpark entrance. The website also has details of the nearby beach hostel, open in the summer only.

Flying Pig Downtown, Nieuwendijk 100 (tel. 420 6822, *www.flyingpig.nl*, *downtown@flyingpig.nl*). Dorms from €17.50 (£11.70) including breakfast, also singles and doubles. No curfew. All night bar. From Centraal station, walk towards the Damrak, past the Victoria Hotel. Take first alleyway on right.

Kabul, Warmoesstraat 38–42 (tel. 623 7158). Dorms from €22.50 (£15), doubles from €70 (£47). Open all year, 24 hours. No curfew. Includes breakfast. In the red light district, 5 minutes' walk from Amsterdam Centraal. Right off Oudebrugsteeg.

Hotel My Home, Haarlemmerstraat 82 (tel. 624 2320, *www.amsterdambudgethotel.com*, *info@hotelmyhome.a2000.nl*). Dorms from €25 (£16.50), doubles from €57 (£38). Breakfast included. 5 minutes from Centraal.

Cosmos Hostel, Niewe Nieuwstraat 17-1 (tel. 625 2438, *www.hostelcosmos.com*, *info@hostelcosmos.com*). Dorms from €25 (£16.50). Doubles available. Near Centraal.

Anna Youth Hostel, Spuistraat 6 (tel. 620 1155). Dorms from €16 (£10.50). Near Centraal. Lovely.

International Budget Hostel, Leidsegracht 76 (tel. 624 2784, *www.internationalbudgethostel.com*, *info@internationalbudgethostel.com*). Dorm beds from €23 (£15.50). Breakfast is extra. No curfew. Take tram 1, 2 or 5 from the station to Prinsengracht.

Bob's Youth Hostel, Nieuwezijds Voorburgwal 92 (tel. 623 0063). B&B in dorms works out cheaper if you have a mattress on the floor, expect to pay around €15 (£10). Good location, close to Dam, about 8 minutes' walk from Amsterdam Centraal. Trams 1, 2 and 5 run along the street from Amsterdam Centraal.

Hans Brinker, Kerkstraat 136 (tel. 622 0687). B&B in dorms €20 (£13.30). Doubles available. Tram 16 from Amsterdam Centraal crosses Kerkstraat on its way down Vijzelstraat.

The Bulldog, Oudezijds Voorburgwal 220 (tel. 620 3822, www.bulldog.nl, hotel@bulldog.nl). Dorms from €19 (£12.70). Breakfast included.

Euphemia Budget Hotel, Fokke Simonszstraat 1 (tel. 622 9045, www.euphemiahotel.com, info@euphemiahotel.com). Dorms from €25 (£16.50), doubles €35 (£23) p.p. with breakfast. Tram 16, 24 or 25 from Amsterdam Centraal to Weteringschans. Go back over the canal (Lijnbaansgracht), then turn right.

Adam and Eve, Sarphatistraat 105 (tel. 624 6206). Mixed and single sex dorms. Nearest metro station is Weesperplein. Trams 6, 7 and 10 run here from Leidseplein.

White Tulip Hostel, Warmoesstraat 87 (tel. 625 5974, www.wittetulp.nl, reservations@wittetulp.nl). Dorms from €20 (£13.30). See directions for Kabul above.

CAMPING

Zeeburg, Zuider-Ijdijk 20 (tel. 694 4430, www.camping zeeburg.nl, info@campingzeeburg.nl). Open year round. €4.50 (£3) p.p., €3.50 (£2.30) per tent. Aimed at young travellers. Live music regularly. Take the metro to Waterlooplein (where there is a pleasant open-air market), and ask which bus to take from there, or take bus 37 from Amstel Station which stops at the site, or bus 22 from Centraal station. Camp shop and cycle hire next door.

Gaasper, Loosdrechtdreef 7 (tel. 696 7326, www.gaspercamping-amsterdam.nl). Tent €3.50 (£2.30). Metro to Gaasperplas or night bus 75. Approx. 20-minute trip from Centraal station.

Vliegenbos, Meeuwenlaan 138 (tel. 636 8855, www.vliegenbos .com). Use of hot shower. Also travellers' huts at €53 (£35.50) for four people. From Centraal station tram 1, 2 or 5 to Leidseplein, then bus 172, or take bus 32 or 36 from Centraal Station. Alternatively, take the ferry from behind Centraal station; it's then a 20-minute walk.

De Badhoeve, Uitdammerdijk 10 (tel. 490 4294). North of Amsterdam.

Het Amsterdamse Bos, Kleine Noorddijk 1 (tel. 641 6868, *www.amsterdamsebos.amsterdam.nl*, *camping@dab.amsterdam.nl*). €5 (£3.30) p.p., €3 (£2) per tent. On outskirts of city in Aalsmeer.

SLEEPING ROUGH

Sleeping rough is not to be recommended in Amsterdam as a whole and certainly not in Amsterdam Centraal train station. Even if you are not physically attacked, it is almost guaranteed someone will try to rob you as you sleep. If you do decide to sleep rough, at least try to gain some extra security by bedding down beside other travellers, rather than in some quiet spot on your own. The most popular spots for sleeping out are the Vondelpark, the Julianapark and the Beatrixpark. Those with a railpass who are totally stuck but do not want to sleep rough should put their luggage and all but a little of their money into the left luggage office (or the lockers) and then ride the trains, which keep up a virtually constant service between Amsterdam and Rotterdam through the night. You will not get a lot of sleep, but it is much safer than trying to sleep in Amsterdam Centraal.

NORWAY (Norge) (00)47

In some parts of Norway, there is daylight for 24 hours a day in the summer. Because of this, Norway is known as 'the Land of the Midnight Sun'. It is also known as the land of the very expensive holiday. Norway's standard of living is one of the highest in Europe, and as a result, it is generally not suited to the budget traveller. Even buying food in supermarkets can be a strain on the purse strings, and you'll need to take out a mortgage before imbibing in a Norwegian bar.

Despite the prices, it is well worth a visit. The country is visually stunning, as you may well expect from a mountainous country twice the size of Britain, but with a population half that of London. Thick forests, great lakes, and fjords dominate the landscape.

BACKGROUND

Norway's livelihood comes from the sea – most notably the oil, fishing and cruise liner industries. The sea was also home to a mob of rampaging Norwegians from the 9th to the 11th centuries. The Vikings were keen to leave behind their bitterly cold motherland to conquer Britain, a process which eventually ended with the death of their leader Harold Hardrada at the battle of Stamford Bridge in 1066. The Vikings aside, Norwegian history is unspectacular.

ACCOMMODATION DETAILS

Cheap accommodation options are severely limited in Norway. The currency is the Norwegian krone (kr) and £1 is approximately 12 kr ($1 is roughly 6.5 kr). Even if the prices below seem affordable to you, remember that you are also going to spend a considerable amount of money feeding yourself. Even in summer when **hotels** reduce their prices, it is rare to find prices lower than 300 kr (£25; $42) for singles, 500 kr (£41; $69) for doubles. The only consolations are the excellent standards and the chance of gorging yourself on the buffet breakfast. There are however some nationwide chains, such as Rainbow and Rica, which offer good summer and weekend deals. If you buy a Skanplus Hotel Pass (sold at hotels for 90 kr (£7.50; $12.50), or online at *www.skanplus.no*) you'll get charged the lowest rate at Rainbow hotels and the pass will usually pay for itself on the first night. Each pass is valid for two adults, along with any children. The pass gives up to 50% discounts at 200 hotels in Scandinavia. The Fjordpass (FJO) is also an excellent investment – it costs 100 kr (£8.50; $14.50) and one pass is valid for two adults and children under 15 for an entire year. The pass gives decent discounts at over 200 hotels, guest houses, apartments and holiday cottages in Norway. For more information, *visit www.fjordpass.no.*

A room in a small **boarding house**, known as a *pensjonat* or *hospit* is cheaper, but you can still expect to pay at least 180 kr (£15; $25) for a single, 320–450 kr (£27–37.50; $46–63) for a double, without breakfast. These are usually available in the more popular tourist towns.

More affordable is a **room in a private home**, at 150–180 kr (£13–15; $22–25) for singles and 200–280 kr (£17–23; $29–39) for doubles, without breakfast. These have to be booked through the local Tourist Office, which charges a fee of around 20 kr (£1.50; $2.50). Unfortunately, private rooms may be difficult to find outside the larger towns and they may also have a specified minimum stay.

There are around 90 **HI hostels** around the country, with convenient clusters in the western fjords, the popular hiking areas of the centre, and in the vicinity of Oslo. Standards are unquestionably excellent, but prices are high. Overnight fees start at around 100 kr (£8.50; $14.50), but are normally around 200 kr (£17; $29). However, prices can be as high as 300 kr (£25; $42). One slight consolation is that a substantial buffet breakfast is included at most hostels charging over 150 kr (£13; $22); otherwise most serve breakfast for 40–50 kr (£3.30–4; $5.50–7) or evening meals for around 85 kr (£7; $12). It is advisable to have an HI card, otherwise you will have to pay an extra 25 kr (£2; $3.50), assuming you are admitted. Only a few hostels operate throughout the year. Most open from June to September only; some for even shorter periods.

Groups of three to seven travellers planning to stay in the same area for a while might consider hiring a **chalet**. Chalets (*hytte*) are let by the week only. Prices 80–170 kr (£6.50–14; $11–24) per person per night. In the peak period of late June to mid-August expect to pay 100–120 kr (£8.50–10; $14.50–17) per person per night. At other times prices fall, so that in May, or September to December, chalets are let out for perhaps two-thirds of the peak-season price. Most chalets are in rural areas, ideal for hiking and fishing.

There are some 1,300 **campsites**, rated from one to three stars according to the facilities available. There are no fixed prices, so charges can vary considerably. Most sites cost 80–150 kr (£6.50–13; $11–22). Sites do not accept reservations, but these are not necessary in any case, and while the FICC camping carnet is valid, it is not essential. An increasing number of sites offer self-catering chalets for rent, with one-night stays possible. Sleeping between 4–6 people, these chalets have fully equipped kitchens. Prices range from 260 kr to 360 kr (£21.50–30; $36.50–51) per night. All the sites, complete with addresses, telephone numbers, facilities and opening times, are listed in the brochure *Camping in Norway*, published annually by the Norwegian Tourist Board.

As in neighbouring Sweden and Finland, the right to **sleep rough** is written into the law, with certain restrictions. You are allowed to camp for two days on any uncultivated land or open area without asking permission, provided you pitch your tent at least 150m away from the nearest habitations. Between 15 April and 15 September, avoid lighting fires in open fields or woodland areas. Wherever you may be camping or sleeping rough, it is likely to get very cold at night, even during the summer, so a good sleeping bag and tent with a flysheet is recommended. Nor is there any time of the year that is particularly free of rain (Bergen especially is renowned for its wet weather). It is also advisable to have a good mosquito repellent.

Anyone heading out into the countryside who would prefer a roof over their head should contact the Norwegian Mountain Touring Association for a list of the simple **mountain huts** they operate throughout the country. Open at Easter, and from late June to early September, these huts usually cost between 100–180kr (£8.50–13; $14.50–22) per person per night. Non-member prices tend to be about 100kr (£8.50; $14.50) more. Mountain huts never turn guests away so at times they can be fairly crowded. In the Lofoten Islands, it is possible to rent old **fishermen's cabins** (*rorbuer*), although advance booking is essential.

ADDRESSES

NORWEGIAN TOURIST BOARD

Charles House, 5–11 Lower Regent Street, London SW1Y 4LR (tel. 0906 302 2003, 50 pence per minute, *www.visitnorway.com*, *greatbritain@ntr.no*).

DISCOUNT HOTEL PASSES AND ACCOMMODATION WEBSITES

Skanplus Hotel Pass (*www.skanplus.no*). Search and book hotels. Purchase the Skanplus Pass at this website.

Fjord Tours AS, Stromgaten 4, N-5015 Bergen (tel. 55 55 76 60, *www.fjordpass.no*, *fjordtours@fjordpass.no*). Buy the Fjordpass online, book hotels and tours. You can also order a brochure.

Rainbow Hotels (tel. 23 08 02 00, *www.rainbow-hotels.no*, *service@rainbow-hotels.no*). Search their hotel database and book online or by telephone.

NORWEGIAN YHA

Norske Vandrerhjem, Torggt. 1, N-0181 Oslo (tel. 23 13 93 00, *www.vandrerhjem.no*, *hostels@vandrerhjem.no*).

HYTTE (CHALETS)

Den Norske Hytteformidling, PO Box 3404 Bjolsen, Oslo (tel. 22 35 67 10).

Fjordhytter/Novasol, Lille Markevei 13, N-5001 Bergen (tel. 55 23 20 80).

BED AND BREAKFAST

Bed and Breakfast Norway, Osterdalsgaten 1J, N-0658 Oslo (tel. 99 23 77 99, *www.bbnorway.com*). Provides lists of private rooms available across Norway.

RORBUER (FISHERMEN'S CABINS)

www.visitnorway.com offers a selection of cabins under 'rental accommodation'.

MOUNTAIN HUTS

Den Norske Turistforening, Postboks 7 Sentrum, 0101 Oslo (tel. 22 82 28 00, *www.turistforeningen.no*, *turinfo@dntoslo.no*).

CAMPING

Norwegian Hospitality Association, Essendropsgaten 6, 0305 Oslo (tel. 23 08 86 21, *www.camping.no*) has an excellent website listing all campsites in Norway.

Oslo

TOURIST OFFICES

The main tourist information office is at Fridtjof Nansens Plass 5 (tel. 24 14 77 00, *www.visitoslo.com*, *info@oslopro.no*). Open every day 9am–7pm June–Aug., closed Sundays the rest of the year. Open Sept. 9am–5pm, Oct.–Mar. 9am–4pm, Apr.–May 9am–5pm.

Turistinformasjon Centralstasjon. Open daily 8am–11pm.

USE IT, Møllergata 3 (tel. 22 41 51 32, *www.unginfo.oslo.no/useit/*, *useit@unginfo.oslo.no*). Lists of the cheapest accommodation possibilities in the city. Closed on Sundays.

HOTELS

City Hotel, Skippergaten 19 (tel. 22 41 36 10, *www.cityhotel.no*, *booking@cityhotel.no*). Doubles from 600 kr (£50; $85); singles from 395 kr (£33; $56).

Ritz Hotell, Frederik Stangsgate 3 (tel. 22 44 39 60). Doubles around 850 kr (£71; $121). Discounts with FJO.

Hotel Astoria, Dronningensgate 21 (tel. 22 14 55 50, *astoria@rainbow-hotels.no*). Part of the Rainbow chain. Good weekend and summer rates. (Central reservations tel. 23 08 02 00.)

White House Hotel, President Harbitzgate 18 (tel. 22 44 19 60). Doubles from 720 kr (£60; $102).

Fønix Hotel, Dronningensgate 19 (tel. 22 42 59 57). A few blocks down from the station. Singles from 450 kr (£37.50; $63); doubles 900 kr (£75; $127). Discounts with FJO.

Frogner Hotel, Frederik Stangsgate 33 (tel. 23 27 51 50, *frogner@rainbow-hotels.no*). One of the Tulip Inn Rainbow chain hotels. Doubles from 800 kr (£67; $114). Discounts with Scanplus Hotel Pass.

PENSIONS/GUEST HOUSES

Villa Frogner, Nordraaksgate 26 (tel. 22 56 19 60, *www.bedand breakfast.no, booking@bedandbreakfast.no*). Doubles from 600 kr (£50; $85). Tram 12 or 15 to Vigelandsparken stop (Frogner-Majorstuen direction).

Solveig's Bed and Breakfast, Tasen Terrasse 11 (tel. 22 23 60 41, *www.solveigs.com, raeverso@online.no*). Doubles 500 kr (£42; $71). 3 miles out of Oslo.

Cochs Pensjonat, Parkveien 25 (tel 23 33 24 00, *www.cochs.no, booking@cochs.no*). Doubles start at 520 kr (£43.50; $74), singles at 380 kr (£31.50; $53.50), more for room with bath. Beside the royal park, at the corner of Hegdehaugsveien. The entrance is on Hegdehaugsveien.

Ellingsens Pensjonat, Holtegaten 25 (tel. 22 60 03 59). Singles around 250 kr (£20; $34); doubles around 400 kr (£33; $56). Tram 1 to the Uranienborg Church (Uranienborgveien) from the National Theatre.

Dybwadsgate Pensjonat, Dybwadsgate 8 (tel. 22 55 23 90). Doubles and singles. Excellent value.

St Katarinahjemmet, Majorstuveien 21B (tel. 23 31 53 10). Doubles around 400 kr (£33; $56) per person. Open mid-June–mid-Aug. Run by nuns. Tram 1 from the National Theatre to Valkyrie Plass.

PRIVATE ROOMS

Innkvartering in the central station and the **Tourist Office** book rooms with a two-day minimum stay. Singles are in short supply at around 300 kr (£25; $42); doubles around 500kr (£41; $69). Commission 20 kr (£1.50; $2.50).

USE IT (see details above) book rooms with no minimum stay and no booking fee.

HI HOSTELS

Vandrerhjem Haraldsheim, Haraldsheimveien 4 (tel. 22 22 29 65, *www.haraldsheim.oslo.no, oslo.haraldsheim.hostel@vandrerhjem. no*). Dorms from 175 kr (£14.50; $24.50). There are also singles and doubles. No curfew. The hostel is 4 km out of the centre. Get there on tram 10 or 11, or take a local train to Grefsen. Open all year.

Vandrerhjem Holtekilen, Micheletsveien 55 (tel. 67 51 80 40, *oslo.holtekilen.hostel@vandrerhjem.no*). Open Feb.–Dec. Breakfast included. Take a local train to Stabekk station and then follow the footbridge.

LBM-Ekeberg Hostel, Kongeveien 82 (tel. 22 74 18 90). Open June–mid-Aug. Breakfast included. Take tram 18 or 19 to Holtet.

SLEEP-IN

Sleep in (YMCA), Møllergata (tel. 22 20 83 79). 100 kr (£8.50; $14.50) for a mattress on the floor (sleeping bag required). Open July–Aug. Midnight curfew. About 500m from Oslo Sentral, just past the cathedral (hostel entrance on Grubbegata).

HOSTELS

Anker Hostel, Storgata 55 (tel. 22 99 72 00, *www.ankerhostel.no*, *hostel@anker.oslo.no*). Open all year. Doubles 420 kr (£35; $59.50). Beds in 4-person dorms 165 kr (£14; $24); beds in 6-person dorms 140 kr (£11.50; $19.50).

Oslo Vineyard, Lillogata 5 (tel. 22 15 20 99). Church-run hostel. Take tram 12 or 17 to Grefsenveien.

Marius Meisfjord, Thomas Heftyes Gate 46 (tel. 22 55 38 46). Stay at this guy's house near Vigeland Park for 200 kr (£17; $29) per person. Breakfast (excellent) is extra.

Perminalen, Ovre Slottsgate 2 (tel. 23 09 30 81, *www.perminalen. com*, *206.resepsjon@perminalen.com*). Dorms 275 kr (£23; $39), doubles 650 kr (£54; $92).

CAMPING

Bogstad, Ånkerveien 117 (tel. 22 51 08 00, *www.bogstad camping.no*, *mail@bogstadcamping.no*). Open year round. 125 kr (£10.50; $18) for two people and a tent. Also chalets for rent at around 500 kr (£41; $69) per night. Bus 41 from the National Theatre or bus 32 from Oslo Sentral to Bogstad, about a 35-minute journey.

Ekeberg, Ekebergveien 65 (tel. 22 19 85 68, *www.ekeberg camping.no*, *mail@ekebergcamping.no*). Open June–Aug. 115 kr (£9.50; $16) for two people and a tent. About 3 km from the centre. Bus 24 or 72 from Oslo Sentral, or bus 72 from the National Theatre.

Oslo Fjordcamping, Ljansbrukvn 1 (tel. 22 75 20 55, *fjorcamp@ online.no*).

FREELANCE CAMPING

You can pitch a tent in the woods to the north of Oslo, provided you stay clear of public areas. Take the metro to Sognsvann. Free camping is also allowed on the Oslofjord island of Langøyene.

POLAND (Polska) (00)48

The Polish are proud of their identity and fiercely protective of their independence. The beautiful cities of Cracow and Warsaw, once scarred by war, have been rebuilt in the image of their former glory.

Poland is a joy to the budget traveller. Prices are low, and you will be surprised at how little you spend. You may have to haggle with street vendors, who may see Western tourists as something of a money-making opportunity, but remember, the price you pay here will inevitably be cheaper than at home, so don't think that wherever you go, you are bound to get ripped off.

BACKGROUND

The Nazi invasion was the greatest tragedy in Poland's long history. Poland lost six million of its population during the Occupation. The concentration camp at Auschwitz, a town in southern Poland, bore witness to abomination on an unparalleled scale.

After the war, Poland was established as a Soviet state, and was a people's republic until 1989, when it became the first of the Eastern European nations to open to a tide of change under a democratically elected government. When the elections placed Solidarity Trade Union member Tadeusz Mazowiecki in charge of the nation, Poland was once again free. Accession to the EU in 2004 has completed the process, or so most Poles hope.

The Poles have faced great economic hardship in the face of transition from Communism to capitalism, and the new consumer society is viewed somewhat cynically by those who are worse off now than they ever were before. The arrival of the American fast-food chains and designer labels is not to everyone's taste in Poland, especially in the face of rising unemployment.

ACCOMMODATION DETAILS

Good quality tourist information is available in most of the main towns (more and more privately run tourist offices and travel agencies are springing up all the time) and finding reasonably priced accommodation is relatively straightforward. This said, if you arrive late in a popular town like Cracow or Warsaw you are no longer guaranteed a cheap bed. Prices are also increasing steadily, but remain cheap by Western standards.

Although in Warsaw you will struggle to find doubles in **hotels** for under £45 ($76), elsewhere there are some excellent hotels offering doubles for as little as £20–25 ($34–42). Even in Cracow there are several hotels offering singles for £12–16 ($20–27). These days it is advisable to try and reserve ahead, preferably in writing (use German if you can) a month or so in advance.

The Polish currency is the złoty and £1 is approximately 6.30 zl ($1 is 3.5 zl).

It is the widespread availability of **private rooms** that has helped Poland avoid a dire accommodation shortage. In most well-visited towns, private rooms can be arranged through the Biuro Zakwaterowania (and occasionally by other organisations). Prices are generally very low, with singles available for £7 ($12) in destinations as popular as Danzig and Poznan. Even in Warsaw you can find singles for around £11 ($19), with rooms in Cracow being the most expensive, from £13 ($22) for singles, £18 ($30) for doubles. Payment is to the booking agency rather than to your host. It is not uncommon to be approached by locals offering rooms, particularly in the vicinity of the train stations and Tourist Offices. These rooms are normally clean, and safe for you and your belongings. As a rule, prices are a bit lower than rooms fixed up through the local Biuro. The one problem you might have with such offers is the location of the rooms. If you are not specifically asked to pay in hard currency you can often obtain a reduction by offering to do so (Deutschmarks and US dollars are especially welcome).

The Polish affiliate of the HI, the Polish Federation of **Youth Hostels** (PTSM), runs a network of hostels known as *Schroniske Mlodziezowe*. A comprehensive list of Polish hostels is available at their website (see below). Hostels in the main towns should be reserved in advance, preferably by means of a reservation card. At all hostels priority is given to schoolchildren and students, but there is no maximum age limit. All hostels have a 10pm curfew, but you must arrive before 9pm. Prices are low (but increasing all the time), with dormitory accommodation ranging in price from

£3 to £8 ($5–13.50). A fuel charge is also made for use of self-catering facilities.

The PTTK, the Polish Tourist Association, has its own network of hostels called *Dom Turysty* or *Dom Wycieczkowy*. Accommodation is usually in 3- and 4-bed rooms with shared facilities. Average prices are £3–6 ($5–10) per person per night. Some of the old PTTK hostels, especially in some of the larger cities, are now under private management and these are slightly more expensive.

PTTK also runs a chain of cheap mountain refuges (*Schroniska gorskie*). The refuges are open all year. Some, in more isolated places, operate a 'welcome everyone' policy. As a result, you may find you have to kip on the floor. Ask at the nearest PTTK office for locations of the refuges.

The camping season runs from April/May to September/October. There are **campsites** in all the places you are likely to visit. Polish campsites are certainly cheap, with prices for an overnight stay rarely rising above £5 ($8.50) for a solo traveller. Although facilities at some sites can be very basic, prices are generally set accordingly, so you seldom have cause to grumble about lack of value for money. At many sites it is possible to hire bungalows sleeping 2–4 people. Average prices work out at around £3.50 ($6) per person (if all the beds are taken). The *Campingi w Polsce* map lists details of all the sites. The maps are available from main bookstores, some travel bureaux and from PZMot (the National Automobile Club). If you are willing to attempt a little Polish, then the easy to use *www.infolinia.pl/campingidb* has extensive listings of campsites and contact details throughout the country. ALMATUR also operates a chain of sites in summer. Any of their local offices will supply you with a list. A few of the HI hostels also allow camping in their grounds, but this is not usually permitted. If you're discreet, **camping rough** shouldn't be a problem, but don't set up camp in the national parks.

ADDRESSES

POLISH NATIONAL TOURIST OFFICE
1st floor, 310–312 Regent Street, London W1N 7DE (tel. 020 7580 8811, *www.visitpoland.org*, *info@visitpoland.org*).

PTTK

www.pttk.pl, *poczta@pttk.pl*. Provides general information about Poland, as well as links to Dom Turysty hostels, campsites, climbing organisations and mountain refuges.

HOSTELS

Polskie Towarzystwo Schronisk Mlodziezowych (HI affiliated), ul. Chocimska 28, 00791 Warszawa (tel. 22 849 8354, *www.ptsm. com.pl*, *hostellingpol.ptsm@pro.onet.pl*).

ALMATUR, ul. Kopernika 23, Warszawa (tel. 22 826 2639, *www.almatur.pl* (Polish only), *office@almatur.pl*).

CAMPING

Polska Federacja Campingu i Caravaningu, ul Grochowska Warszawa (tel. 22 331 03 838).

Also see *www.infolinia.pl/campingidb/*.

SCHRONISKA GORSKIE (MOUNTAIN REFUGES)

33-300 Nowy Sacz, Rynek (tel. 18 443 8610, *www.schroniska-pttk.com.pl* (Polish only), *karpaty@schroniska-pttk.com.pl*).

USEFUL ACCOMMODATION WEBSITES

www.polhotels.com, *www.travel-poland.pl*, *www.hotelspoland.com*.

Cracow (Kraków) (0)12

TOURIST OFFICE

KART city tourist office, ul. Pawia 8 (tel. 422 0471). Opposite the train station. Open June–Sept., Mon.–Fri. 8am–6pm, Sat. 9am–1pm; Oct.–May 8am–4pm weekdays only.

ORBIS is at Rynek 41 (tel. 224035, *www.orbis.krakow.pl*, *info@orbis.krakow.pl*).

ALMATUR, ul. Grodzka 2 (tel. 422 4668, *krakow@almatur.pl*).

Jordan Tourist Office, ulica Floriańska 37 (tel. 422 6091, *www.jordan.krakow.pl*, *it@jordan.pl*). Books accommodation and provides tourist information.

Dexter Tourist Office, Rynek (in the cloth hall) (tel. 421 7706). Open Mon.–Fri. 9am–6pm, Sat. 9am–1pm.

BASIC DIRECTIONS

The main bus station is beside the main train station, Kraków Głowny. When you finally make your way through the market stalls in front of the stations, you arrive on ul. Pawia. Crossing the street and heading left, you pass the Tourist Office and the Hotel Warszawski before arriving at the junction of ul. Pawia with ul. Basztowa (right), ul. Westerplatte (more or less straight ahead) and ul. Lubicz (left). Turning right on ul. Basztowa you pass the information booth for the tram network on the left, and then, again on the left, the end of ul. Szpitalna. Next on the left is the Barbican (Barbakan). Turning left through the Barbican and going straight ahead you can follow Floriańska into Rynek Głowny, the market square at the heart of the city. The walk from the train station takes around 10 minutes.

FINDING ACCOMMODATION

Over the past few years, Cracow has (understandably) become exceptionally popular, especially during the period mid-June to August. If you are travelling at this time it makes sense to try to book accommodation as far in advance as possible. Jordan, ul. Floriańska 37, next to the KART tourist information, books hotels in advance, or on arrival. Email or telephone in advance in the summer months. Details above.

HOTELS

Wisła, ul. Reymonta 22 (tel. 633 4922). Near the Wisła Kraków football stadium (one of Poland's best teams over the years). Bus 144 stops nearby. Alternatively, you can take tram 15 along al. 3 Maja to the Cichy Kacik terminus, followed by a short walk along ul. D. Chodowieckiego into wł. Reymonta. Singles and triples only, £15 ($25) per bed.

Korona, ul. Kalwaryiska 9/15 (tel. 656 1780, *www.korona. krakow.pl, korona@korona.krakow.pl*). Doubles from £19 ($32). On the fringe of the wartime Jewish ghetto. Take tram 10.

Hotel Start, ul. Kapelanka 60 (tel. 629 0405, *www.hotelstart. com.pl, hotel.start@krakow.mtl.pl*). Doubles from £19 ($32). Near Tesco's in the town centre.

Dom Kultury Kolejarza, ul. Filipa 6 (tel. 624 3363, *ktk@pkp .krakow.pl*). Very cheap but basic. Singles and doubles. Close to the train station.

Saski, ul. Sławkowska 3 (tel. 421 4222, *www.hotel-saski.com.pl, info@hotel-saski.com.pl*). Close to the Rynek. Singles £30 ($51); doubles £33 ($56). More for rooms with their own bathroom.

Polonia, ul. Basztowa 25 (tel. 422 1233, *www.hotel-polonia .com.pl, polonia@bci.pl*). Doubles £30 ($51).

Hotel KCD, ul. Meiselsa 1 (tel. 424 0554, *www.noclegwkra kowie.pl, biuro@noclegwkrakowie.pl*). Doubles around £30 ($51). Town centre.

Hotel Pokoje Goscinne, ul. Krowoderska 5 (tel. 421 4444, *www.pokojegoscinne.krakow.pl, biuro@pensjonaty.krakow.pl*). Doubles £16 ($27). Very busy, but excellent value.

PRIVATE ROOMS

Jordan (ul. Floriańska 37, see above) can fix you up with private rooms. Check the exact location before you agree to a room as some are a long way out of town. Expect to pay around £12 ($20) for a single and £18 ($30) for a double (although you can pay a lot less for a decent room).

PTTK DOM TURYSTY

Westerplatte 15 (tel. 422 9566). 8-bed dorms £7 ($12) per person. There are also rooms available but these are overpriced. Good location, near the main post office, within easy walking distance of the town centre and the bus and train stations. Friendly, English-speaking staff. Book ahead.

HI HOSTELS

Ul. Grochowa 21, (tel. 653 2423, *www.ptsm.pl/krakow, krakow@ ssm.com.pl*). Dorms £4 ($7). Bus 15 from the train station.

Ul. Oleandry 4 (tel. 633 8822). Open all year. Tram 15 along al. 3 Maja, until you see ul. Oleandry, the first street on the right. The hostel is a 10- to 15-minute walk from the centre. Kitchen facilities and baggage store available. 11pm curfew.

Szablowskiego, ul. Szablowskiego 1C (tel. 637 2441). B&B from around £7 ($12). Kitchen facilities available. Take tram 4 or 12 from the city centre. Open in July and Aug. only.

HOSTELS AND STUDENT HOSTELS

ALMATUR, ul. Grodzka 2 (tel. 482 4668). (Office open Mon.–Fri. 9am–5pm). ALMATUR will inform you of the current locations of student hostels, as some change annually. The Tourist Office will also be able to help.

U Zeweckiego, ul. Librowszczyzna 1 (tel. 429 5596, *www. zewecki.com*, *hostel@zewecki.com*). Open all year. Town centre. Book in advance.

Piast Dom Studencki, ul. Piastowka 47 (tel. 622 3100, *www. piast.bratniak.krakow.pl*, *piast@bratniak.krakow.pl*). Student dorm open summer only. Very busy. Bus 203 from the train station.

Trzy Kafkie, al. Slowackiego 29 (tel. 632 9418, *www. trzykafkie.pl*, *trzykafkie@trzykafkie.pl*). Town centre. Singles, doubles, triples and quads.

Schronisko Turystyczne Ekspres, ul. Wroclawska 91 (tel. 633 8862). 2 km north-west of the city centre. Cross between a hostel and a guest house. Open all day and no curfew. Dorm beds £4 ($7); beds in double rooms £5 ($8.50). Take bus 130 from the train station and get out at the fifth stop. Popular so book ahead.

Student Hotel Zaczek, al. 3 Maja 5 (tel. 633 1915, *www.zazcek.com.pl*, *zazcek@zazcek.com.pl*). 1–6 beds per room. Open summer only. Near the Biblioteka Jagiellońiska on al. Zygmunta Krasińiskiego. (Also close to the main youth hostel.) Take bus 119 or tram 15 from the train station.

CAMPING

Krak, ul. Radzikowskiego 99 (tel. 637 2122, *www.krak.com.pl*). Category 1 site. The largest, best equipped and most expensive site. Open May–Sept. 5 km from town centre on the Katowice road. Tram 8 or 12 to Fizyków, or bus 118, 173, 208, 218 or 223.

Krakowania, ul. Zywiecka Boczna 4 (tel. 266 4191). A good category 2 site, cheaper and quieter than Krak. Open May–Oct. Bungalows to rent. Take tram 19 to the Borek Fałecki terminus along Zakopiańska from ul. Basztowa (or any tram to Łagiewniki, then change to tram 19). From the terminus, head in the direction of the housing estate to the right, then take the path which leads away to the right.

There are also two privately run campsites, both a few kms from the centre:

Ogrodowy, ul. Krolowej Jadwigi 223 (tel. 622 2011 ext. 67). On the road to the Balice airport. Take bus B, 102 or 134.

Smok, ul. Kamedulska 18 (tel. 421 0255). On the Oswiecim road. Take bus 109 or 229. Open all year.

Warsaw (Warszawa) (0)22

TOURIST OFFICES

The city Tourist Office is at pl. Zamkowy 1/13 (tel. 524 9431). Open weekdays 8am–8pm, Sat. 9am–5pm and Sun. 9am–3pm. There are also outlets at the airport and Warszawa Centralna train station (tel. 654 2447)

ORBIS, ul. Bracka 16 (tel. 827 6766, *www.orbis.pl*, *orbissa@orbis.pl*).

ALMATUR, ul. Kopernica 23 (tel. 826 2739, *office@almatur.pl*).

BASIC DIRECTIONS

The main road running past Warszawa Centralna station is al. Jerozolimskie. Opposite the station are the IOT terminal and the multi-storey Hotel Marriott. Facing these buildings al. Jerozolimskie runs right towards pl. Artura Zawiszy, and then on to the Zachodnia train station and the main bus station. Going left, the street crosses Emilii Plater and Marszałkowska before continuing straight on Most Ks. Józefa Poniatowskiego, which crosses the River Wisła. Going left up Emilii Plater from al. Jerozolimskie takes you round the back of the Palac Kultury and on to ul. Świêtokrzyska.

HOTELS

There are not many cheap hotels in central Warsaw and ones that charge under £32 ($54) for a double fill up fast. Reserve in advance and consider staying in one of the suburbs.

Dom Literatury, Krakowskie Przedmieście 87 (tel. 828 3910). At the entrance to the Old Town. Most rooms have superb views over Castle Square.

Hotel Mazowiecki, ul. Mazowiecka 10 (tel. 827 2365, *www.mazo wiecki.com.pl*). Doubles £42 ($71). Town centre.

Hotel Saski, Plac Bankowy 1 (tel. 620 4611). Around £30 ($51) for a double. Nice hotel but try to avoid getting a room which overlooks the tram lines as it can be noisy.

Federacja Melalowcy, ul. Dluga 29 (tel. 831 4021). From pl. Zamkowy, take ul. Gen. Swierczewskiego west to ul. Dluga. One of the cheapest hotels in central Warsaw at around £15 ($25) a double.

Hotel Belfer, Wybrzeze Kosciuszkowskie 33 (tel. 625 5185). This is a former teachers' hotel, but it is now open to all. Doubles from £25 ($42). The hotel is down by the river.

Agra, ul. Falecka 9/11 (tel. 849 3881). In the Mokotow district. Doubles for £25 ($42).

Hera, ul. Belwederska 26/30 (tel. 411308). Also in the Mokotow district. Doubles from £22 ($37).

Hotel Na Wodzie (tel. 628 5883). This hotel is in two boats, the *Anita* and *Aldona*, which are anchored between the railway and Poniatowski bridges. Open Apr.–Nov. Double cabins from £17 ($29).

Hotel Polonia, al. Jerozolimskie 45 (tel. 628 7241). A short walk from the central train station. Doubles from £37.50 ($64).

Harctur, ul. Niemcewicza 17 (tel. 659 0011). The street is off ul. Raszyńska. Within walking distance of Warszawa Centralna. Take bus 136, 175 or 512, or tram 7, 9 or 25. Popular with students.

Dom Chłopa, pl. Postańców (tel. 625 1545). Located between Nowy Świat and the Palac Kultury.

Harenda, Krakowskie Przedmiescie 4/6 (tel. 826 0071, *www.hotelharenda.com.pl*). Near university campus.

PRIVATE ROOMS

Ask at the Tourist Offices. However, your best bet is to contact Syrena's office, ul. Krucza 17 (tel. 629 0537, *biuro@syrena-pl.com*). The office is a 15-minute walk from the station, near the Grand Hotel. Open Mon.–Sat. 9am–7pm, Sun. 9am–5pm. Get there as early as possible as the cheaper beds go quickly.

HI HOSTELS

Ul. Karolkowa 53A (tel. 632 8829, *www.ptsm.com.pl/ssmnr6*, *ssmnr6@ptsm.com.pl*). 11pm curfew. Clean, but not central.

Out in the Wola suburb. From the station or al. Jerozolimskie take tram 22 or 24 to Okopowa. Go left on al. Solidarnoski, then right on to Karolkowa. Open all year.

Ul. Smolna 30 (tel. 827 8952). 11pm curfew. Well located, off Nowy Świat, opposite the National Museum on al. Jerozolimskie. Within walking distance of Warszawa Centralna. More rules than you could possibly imagine, but at least it's clean and safe. Open all year.

Hotel Agrykola, ul. Mysliwiecka 9 (tel. 622 9110, *www.hotel agrykola.pl*, *recepcja@hotelagrykola.pl*). Very popular, book well in advance.

SEASONAL HOSTELS

Ul. Miedzyparkowa 4/6 (tel. 831 1766). Open 1 Apr.–31 Oct. Tram 2, 6 or 18 from ul. Marszałkowska to K.K.S. Polonia. The hostel is across the street as you continue down the road. Or take bus 174 from the train station, bus 175 from the airport. Small, murky hostel.

INTERNATIONAL STUDENT HOSTELS

From late June to mid-Sept. ALMATUR run hostels in the student halls. Contact ALMATUR at ul. Kopernica 23 (tel. 826 2639). Even when the student hostels are not open ALMATUR may help students to find reasonably priced accommodation.

CAMPING

Expect to pay around £5 ($8.50) per person including tent.

Gromada, ul. Zwirki i Wigury 32 (tel. 825 4391). Twin-bedded bungalows £8 ($13.50) per night. Bus 136, 175, 188 or 512 heading along al. Jerozolimskie towards pl. Artura Zawiszy.

Majawa, ul. Bitwy Warszawskiej 1920r 15/17 (tel. 822 9121). In the Ochota suburb, close to the central bus terminal.

PTTK Camping, ul. Połczyńska 6A (tel. 664 6736). In the suburb of Wola. Bus 129, 149 or 506. Tram 10 or 26.

Zakopane (0)18

TOURIST OFFICES

Informacji Turystycznej, ul. Kościuszki 17 (tel. 201 2211). The main information office for Zakopane and its surroundings (in a wooden chalet by the side of the road). Open daily 9am–7pm. Good for maps and guides.

ORBIS, ul. Krupówki 22 (tel. 201 4609, www.orbis.zakopane.pl). Books trains, buses and local excursions, hotels and private rooms. Open Mon.–Fri. 9am–5pm, Sat. 9am–1pm.

PTTK, ul. Krupówki 12 (above the Snake disco) (tel. 201 6848). A good selection of maps and guidebooks, plus information on the mountain refuges operated by PTTK in the area.

ALMATUR, ul. Marusarzowny 15 (tel. 201 5706, zak@almatur.pl). Hotel bookings, mountain refuges and tourist information.

HOTELS

Gladiola, ul. Chramcowki 25 (tel. 206 8623). Close to the train station.

Imperial, ul. Balzera 1 (tel. 201 4021). Central.

Tatry, ul. Wierchowa 4 (tel. 206 6040). Short uphill walk from the bus station. Wonderful views of the mountains.

Giewont, ul. Kosciuszki 1 (tel. 12011, giewont@orbis.pl). Central. Breakfast included.

Helios, ul. Sloneczna 2a (tel. 201 3808, hotelhelios@wp.pl). Near the train station. Good value.

Hotel Api, ul. Kamieniec 13a (tel. 206 2931, api@zakopane. top.pl). Doubles, and some larger rooms available.

Gerlach, ul. Chramcowki 25 (tel. 206 8623). Breakfast included.

PRIVATE ROOMS

Contact any of the Tourist Offices listed above. Some travel agencies which can also help include:

Tatry, ul. Chramcowki 35 (tel. 201 4343). Just off the train station.

Kozica, ul. Jagiellonska 1 (tel. 201 3277, kozica@regle.pl). Behind FIS bar.

In the high season you may find that you have to stay a minimum of three nights.

PTTK DOM TURYSTY

Ul. Zaruskiego 5 (tel. 206 3281, *www.domturysty.z-ne.pl*, *domturysty@z-ne.pl*). A large chalet in the town centre near the post office. Does get flooded with school children. 11pm curfew. Beds in dorms (up to 28 people in some of them), doubles and triples.

HI HOSTEL

'Szarotka', ul. Nowotarska 45 (tel. 201 3618). 11pm curfew. From the train and bus stations, head towards the centre, go right along ul. Sienkiewiza, then straight across. Large hostel (mainly 8- and 12-bed dorms) but always busy. Open all year.

HOSTEL

Schronisko Mlodziezowe Zak, ul. Marusarzowny 15 (tel. 201 5706, *zak@almatur.pl*). Friendly and cheap. Open all year. Run by ALMATUR. May be easier to find a bed here than at the HI hostel.

CAMPING

Pod Krokwia, ul. Zeromskiego (tel. 201 2256). Open May–Aug. Opposite the foot of the ski jump. Tent sites and large heated bungalows. From the bus/train stations take any bus to Kuznice or Jaszczurowka and get off at Rondo.

Za Strugiem, ul. Za Strugiem 39 (tel. 201 4566).

PORTUGAL (00)351

Portugal attracts thousands of visitors every year on the basis of its wonderful sandy beaches and its reputation as one of Europe's cheapest countries. The fact that Portugal is a poor country crippled with high unemployment is inescapable. The 1990s were plagued with recession and a backwardness in education and agriculture. However, the Expo in '98 attracted over eight million visitors and brought Portugal back to the world's attention.

Despite their lack of prosperity, the Portuguese are a fun-loving people who enjoy a good time just as much as their neighbours, the Spanish. As a foreign visitor to their country, you will be made to feel very welcome.

BACKGROUND

A republic since 1910, Portugal's heyday came during the 15th century when explorers such as Vasco Da Gama helped its overseas empire to expand through the discovery of the African coast, India, China and finally, Brazil. Conflict with Spain and other European countries eventually put paid to Portugal's imperialistic ambitions, but she went on to form an alliance with Britain – a special relationship which still remains to this day.

ACCOMMODATION DETAILS

By northern European standards accommodation is cheap and there are plenty of possibilities open to budget travellers. In most places it should be quite easy to find somewhere cheap to stay, but it can be difficult on the Algarve in peak season, where it is advisable to write or telephone ahead as early as possible.

Pensions and cheap hotels are inexpensive and convenient options. They are graded and priced by the municipal authority, albeit in a manner which at times seems quite arbitrary. Location does not affect the price, so you have the bonus of being able to stay in the town centre, or near the train station, without having to pay extra for the privilege. **Hotels** are rated from one star up to five stars, with the less expensive *penses* and *residencias* graded from one up to three stars. In general, three-star pensions and one-star hotels are roughly similar in price. However, it is quite possible to pay more for a very poor one-star hotel than for a comfortable three-star pension, and vice versa. Prices in one-star hotels/three-star pensions range from €15 to €40 (£10–27) for singles and anything from €45 (£30) upwards for doubles. In the lower-rated pensions in high season, singles cost around €15 (£10) and doubles from €25 (£16.50).

In the smaller towns, seaside resorts and areas particularly popular with tourists, **rooms in private homes** (*quartos* or *dormidas*) can be both less expensive and more comfortable than pensions. Private rooms are sometimes offered to travellers at bus and train stations. Such offers may be worth considering as private rooms are generally more difficult to find than pensions. Local Tourist Offices have lists of private rooms available in the locality. Alternatively, simply enquire at any house with a sign in the window advertising private rooms (signs are frequently written in several languages).

Hostelling can be a cheap way to see much of the country, but, during the peak periods, you may not feel it is worth the added effort, considering the restrictions hostelling imposes. However, hostelling can be an attractive option in the off-season, as the hostels offer an excellent opportunity to meet other travellers, especially outside Lisbon. Most of the main places of interest have an HI hostel of some sort, or can be reached on a day-trip from a hostel nearby. Depending on the standard of the hostel, the age of the user and the time of year, the overnight charge for B&B and sheets varies from €6–15 (£4–10). Hostels are open to HI members only, but it is possible to buy a membership card on arrival, though the €15 (£10) fee is roughly twice what under-26s pay to join one of the British associations in advance. Unless the warden agrees to you staying longer, you are limited to three consecutive nights. Curfews (midnight 1 May–30 Sept.; 11.30pm at other times) can be a real nuisance, since bars and clubs stay open late, many football matches kick off at 9pm, and cinemas often show late films in English. The peak periods for the hostels are June to September, around Christmas, and Holy Week. At these times, it is advisable to write or phone ahead to reserve a bed. To have a chance of getting a bed at any time of year you will either have to write in advance, or arrive at the hostel or phone 9–10.30am.

In contrast to Mediterranean countries, **camping** is well worth considering in Portugal. Sites tend to be more conveniently located in and around the main towns than in Greece, Italy or neighbouring Spain. Portuguese sites are seldom more than 5 km out from the town centre, and usually have a direct bus link. Nor will you have problems carrying around your tent, as left-luggage stores are available at all train stations. Camping is a great way to meet the locals as the Portuguese themselves are enthusiastic campers. The relative unpopularity of camping with budget travellers is due to the widespread availability of other cheap accommodation, and nothing to do with the standard of the campsites, which is actually quite high. There are 97 official sites, graded from one star up to four stars, many of which require a Camping Carnet. All the sites have the basic, essential facilities – most even have a café and a supermarket – so bearing in mind the facilities available, prices are very reasonable. Even at some of the more expensive sites around Lisbon and on the Algarve charges are unlikely to exceed €6 (£4), with around €4 (£2.70) for a tent and one person being the norm elsewhere. **Camping outside official sites** is permitted with the consent of the landowner, but is not allowed in towns, at any spot less than 1 km from a beach, or from an official site, or in the vicinity of a reservoir.

ADDRESSES

PORTUGUESE NATIONAL TOURIST OFFICE
22–25A Sackville Street, London W1X 1DE (tel. 020 7494 5723, *www.portugal.org*).

PORTUGUESE YHA
Movijovem-Agencia de Turismo Jovem, Cooperativa de Interesse Publico e Resposabilidade Lda, Av. Duque d'Avila 137, 1050 Lisbon (tel. 707 20 3030, *www.pousadasjuventude.pt*, *reservas@ movijovem.pt*).

CAMPING
Federaçao Portuguesa de Campismo, Av. Colonel Eduardo Galhardo 24D, Lisbon (tel. 21 812 6890, *www.fpcampismo.pt*, *info@fpcampismo.pt*).
Orbitur, Intercambio de Turismo SA, Rua Diogo do Couto 1-8, Lisboa (tel. 21 811 7000, *www.orbitur.pt*, *info@orbitur.pt*).

Orbitur operates over 20 sites which are among the best managed, but also the most expensive, in Portugal.

A free list of the official sites, *Portugal Camping*, is available from the Portuguese National Tourist Office and from local Tourist Offices.

Faro (0)289

TOURIST OFFICE

Turismo, Rua da Misericórdia 8–12 (tel. 803604). By the harbour. Open daily in summer 9.30am–7pm; winter 9.30am–5.30pm.

FINDING ACCOMMODATION

During the summer, cheap accommodation can be difficult to find in Faro unless you look early in the day. Many people only stay one night (before flying out or after flying in) so if you can start your search early you can benefit from this turnover of visitors. The Tourist Office will supply you with a list of pensions, but leave it up to you to phone around or call in person. The best streets for pensions are Filipe Alistão, Alportel, Conselheiro Bivar, Infante Don Henrique and Vasco da Gama. Not only are beds difficult to find in July and August, but, in response to the high demand, hoteliers often increase their prices. At the very height of the season, private rooms may be your best option.

HOTELS

Residencial Adelaide, Rua Cruz dos Mestres 7 (tel. 802383). Doubles around €25 (£16.50). Dorms also available. Very popular, so book in advance.

Residencial Algarve, Rua Infante Don Henrique 52 (tel. 895700, *www.residencialalgarve.com*). Doubles from €40 (£27). Charming old hotel.

Dandy, Rua Filipe Alistão 62 (tel. 824791). Recommended.

São Felipe, Rua Infante Don Henrique 55a (tel. 824182). Doubles around €50 (£33).

Avenida, Av. da República 150 (tel. 823347). Doubles from €45 (£30). Friendly.

Madalena, Rua Conselheiro Bivar 109 (tel. 805807). Doubles from €40 (£27). One of the best.

Ibis Hotel, 125 Pontes de Marchil (tel. 806 771, *www.ibishotel.com*). Doubles from €40 (£27) but book well in advance.

PRIVATE ROOMS

The Tourist Office has a good supply of rooms, some well located, others less so. In peak season, take what you get. As is the case throughout the Algarve during the summer, touts frequently offer rooms at the bus and train stations.

HI HOSTEL

Rua da PSP (tel. 826521). Open all year. Inconveniently located; lacks amenities but cheap. The Tourist Office has details.

CAMPING

Parque de Campismo Municipal da Ilha de Faro, Praia de Faro (tel. 817876). Year-round site. Often full. Very crowded in summer. Camping Carnet required. Bus 16 from the airport or town centre to Praia de Faro. May–Sept. bus runs twice hourly from 7.30am–8pm, hourly the rest of the year. Infrequent service at weekends.

Lisbon (Lisboa) (0)21

TOURIST OFFICES

Turismo, Praça dos Restauradores, Palácio da Foz (tel. 346 3643). Open Mon.–Sat. 9am–8pm, Sun. 10am–6pm. The office distributes a simple plan of the city and lists of accommodation.

Branch offices also operate at the Santa Apolónia station and at the airport. Both can be very busy so you might prefer just to head to the main office.

Lisboa Welcome Centre, Rua do Arsenal 15 (tel. 031 2700, free-phone (inside Portugal) 800 296 296, *www.atl-turismolisboa.pt*, *atl@atl-turismolisboa.pt*).

ARRIVING AND BASIC DIRECTIONS

Most long-distance trains arrive at the Lisboa Santa Apolónia station, by the River Tagus (Rio Tejo), just over 15 minutes' walk from the Tourist Office. Bus 9 or 9A from the side of the station by the Tagus will take you to Praça dos Restauradores. To walk, keep the river on your left and go straight on until you see the broad expanse of Praça do Comércio with the statue of Dom José I on your right, off Terreiro do Paço. Diagonally right across this square is Rua do Ouro, which you can follow into Praça Dom Pedro IV, commonly known as Rossio (the streets to the right of Rua do Ouro are laid out on a grid pattern, an area known as the Baixa). Turning left at the National Theatre brings you to the Rossio train station (services to Queluz and Sintra) at the foot of Praça dos Restauradores. On the left as you walk up Praça dos Restauradores is the Elevador da Gloria, which provides an easy means of reaching the Bairro Alto.

The other two railway stations are within easy reach of the centre. Trains from the Algarve and the south terminate at the Barreiro station across the Tagus, from which there are frequent services to the terminal on Terreiro do Paço, a short walk from Praça do Comércio. The Cais do Sodré station by the Tagus on Praça Duque da Terceira handles traffic from Cascais, Estoril and Oeiras. Walking away from Cais do Sodré with the river on your right you reach Praça do Comércio in about 5 minutes. The terminal for buses of the state-run Rodoviária Nacional is on Avenida Casal Ribiero, close to Praça Saldanha, and linked to Praça dos Restauradores by buses 1, 21, 32 and 36. Arriving at the airport, you can take bus 44 or 45 to Avenida da Liberdade, or the quicker *linha verde* (green line express). (A trip on the *linha verde* costs roughly twice that of the normal service buses.)

TROUBLE SPOTS

Although prostitutes use some of the cheapest hotels around the Rossio station, this area is not really the red light district of the city. The crowds of people in this part of town mean it is quite safe for women to walk around until the early hours. More dangerous (for women especially) are the Bairro Alto (which contains the red light district) and Mouraria (around the castle), quarters which many travellers head for to try to escape the noise and bustle of Rossio. Women are advised not to walk alone here after dusk.

FINDING ACCOMMODATION

At most times of the year finding a cheap room near Rossio should be quite easy. Because of their location, pensions on Avenida da Liberdade fill quickly; those in the streets off the avenue are more likely to have space. In the summer months, however, you may have difficulty finding cheap accommodation as the amount of rooms available just manages to satisfy demand. If you arrive in the afternoon be prepared to pay slightly more than you were hoping to, and then look around early next morning. There is a price ceiling which supposedly prevents pensions from charging ridiculous rates; however, this does not mean that you won't end up paying over the odds. Expect to pay €17.50–27.50 (£11.70–18.50) for a single and €25–47.50 (£16.50–32) for a double, though you can find cheaper rooms. During low season many places drop their rates. The Tourist Office at Praça dos Restauradores will make enquiries for you but does not reserve rooms.

HOTELS

ROSSIO AREA

Ibérica, Praça de Figueira 10-2 (tel. 886 5781). Popular.

Pensão Figueira, Praça da Figueira 9-3 (tel. 342 4323). Breakfast included.

Beira-Minho, Praça da Figueira 6-2 (tel. 346 1846). B&B. All rooms have baths.

BAIXA – THE LOWER TOWN

A roughly rectangular area stretching from Praça Dom Pedro IV and Praça da Figueira down to Praça do Comércio.

Pension Duas Nacoes, Rua August 41 (tel. 346 0710). Doubles from €25 (£16.50). Excellent pension in the heart of Baixa.

Londres, Rua Dom Pedro V 53 (tel. 346 2203, *www.pensao londres.com.pt*). Doubles from €40 (£27). Take funicular by Palácio da Foz to Pr. dos Restauradores.

Arco Bandeira, Rua Arco Bandeira 226-4 (tel. 342 3478). Doubles from €45 (£30). Not cheap, but a very comfortable pension. Just off Rossio.

Moderna, Rua dos Correiros 205-4 (tel. 346 0818). Clean rooms. Doubles around €35 (£23).

Coimbra e Madrid, Praça da Figueira 3-3 & 4 (tel. 342 1760). Doubles from €25 (£16.50). Basic but good value. Cash only.

Norte, Rua dos Douradores 159-1 & 2 (tel. 887 8941). Doubles from €35 (£23).

Santiago, Rua dos Douradores 222-3 (tel. 888 4353). Doubles around €40 (£27).

Hotel Suisso Atlantico, Rua da Gloria 3-19 (tel. 346 1713). Doubles from €50 (£33).

Prata, Rua da Prata 71-3 (tel. 346 8908). Doubles from €30 (£20). Very good.

Globo, Rua do Teixeira 37 (tel. 346 2279). Doubles without bath from €30 (£20).

AROUND SÃO JORGE CASTLE AND CLOSE TO THE ALFAMA

São João da Praça, Rua São João da Praça 97 (tel. 886 2591). Cheap and high quality.

Ninho das Aguias, Rua Costa do Castelo 74 (tel. 885 4070). Doubles from €40 (£27). This is an excellent pension surrounded by a garden and located behind the castle. Highly recommended.

Beira-Mar, Largo Terreiro do Trigo 16-4 (tel. 886 9933). Big, clean rooms. In a square off Av. Infante Dom Henrique. Reserve.

TO THE WEST OF THE BAIXA, AROUND SAN ROQUE AND THE ROSSIO RAILWAY STATION

Residencia Nova Avenida, Rua de Santo Antonio da Gloria 87 (tel. 342 3689). Doubles from €30 (£20). Basic but good value.

Do Duque, Calçada do Duque 53 (tel. 346 3444, *pensao_duque@yahoo.com*). Inexpensive and very clean.

AVENIDA DA LIBERDADE AREA

Residencia Dublin, Rua de Santa Marta 45 (tel. 555 489). Doubles from €45 (£30).

Iris, Rua da Gloria 2A-1 (tel. 3432 3157). A simple pension, but highly recommended for women travelling on their own.

Pemba, Avda da Liberdade 11-3 (tel. 342 5010). Doubles from €40 (£27).

Dom Sancho I, Avda da Liberdade 202-3 & 5 (tel. 354 8648). Popular backpacker haunt.

Flor de Baixa, Rua das Portas de Santo Antão 81-2 (tel. 342 3153). Doubles around €30 (£20).

Floroscente, Rua das Portas de Santo Antão 99 (tel. 342 6609, *www.residenciafloroscente.com*, *geral@residenciafloroscente.com*). Large capacity with some very cheap rooms from €25 (£16.50).

Monumental, Rua da Gloria 21 (tel. 346 9807). Doubles around €30 (£20).

Milanesa, Rua da Alegria 25-2 (tel. 346 6456). Doubles from €30 (£20).

Alegria, Praça da Alegria 53 (tel. 347 5522). Doubles around €30 (£20).

Solar, Praça da Alegria 12-2 (tel. 342 2608). Doubles from €35 (£23).

Dos Restauradores, Praça dos Restauradores 13-4 (tel. 347 5600). Doubles around €40 (£27).

Imperial, Praça dos Restauradores 78 (tel. 342 0166). Doubles around €35 (£23).

AVENIDA ALMIRANTE REIS

A main thoroughfare beginning at Lg. Martin Moniz, close to Praça de Figueira.

Almirante Reis, Avda Almirante Reis 98-2 (tel. 813 8060). Doubles around €30 (£20). Small but good.

Roxi, Avda Almirante Reis 31-3 (tel. 812 6341). Rooms from €40 (£27).

Do Sul, Avda Almirante Reis 34 (tel. 814 7253). Doubles from €30 (£20).

Pombalense, Avda Almirante Reis 67 (tel. 354 5674). Doubles around €30 (£20).

Sara, Avda Almirante Reis 28-1 (tel. 814 8088). Doubles €35 (£23).

HI HOSTELS

'Pousada de Juventude de Lisboa', Rua Andrade Corvo 46 (tel. 353 2696, *lisboa@movijovem.pt*). Dorms in summer from €15 (£10), doubles €33 (£22). Much cheaper in winter: dorms €10

(£6.70); doubles €25. Breakfast included. Metro: Picoas. Bus 1 or 45 from Rossio or Cais do Sodré. 20-minute walk from the centre, off Avda Fontes Pereira de Melo, in the area beyond the Pombal statue. Disabled access.

Parque de Nacoes, Via de Moscavide, 1998 Lisbon Expo (tel. 920890, *lisboaparque@movijovem.pt*). Summer dorms from €11 (£7.30). Winter from €9 (£6). Good hostel, about half an hour from the city centre.

CAMPING

There are around 30 campsites near Lisbon but only one in Lisbon itself. For full listings get hold of a copy of *Portugal: Camping and Caravan Sites*. They are available free from the Tourist Office.

Parque de Campismo Municipal de Lisboa Monsanto (tel. 762 3100). Open all year round. Four-star campsite with a swimming pool and supermarket. Bus 43 runs from Praça da Figueira to the Parque Florestal Monsanto.

There are six sites on the Costa da Caparica. Ask the Tourist Office which metro and/or bus you should take for the different sites. Open all year round unless indicated:

Costa da Caparica, Estrada da Trafaria (tel. 290 0661). Orbitur site. Bungalows available. From Praça de Espanha bus 5 runs right to the site, or take the metro to Palhava.

Um Lugar ao Sol, Estrada da Trafaria (tel. 290 1592).

Costa Velha, Estrada da Trafaria (tel. 290 0100/0374).

Costa do Concelho de Almada, Praia da Saúde (tel. 290 1862).

Costa Nova, Estrada da Costa Nova (tel. 290 3078). Closed Jan.

Piedense, Praia da Mata (tel. 290 2004).

ROMANIA (00)40

Any visit to Romania would be incomplete without seeing Transylvania, home of the infamous Prince Vlad Tepes, also known as Dracula. Some may be disappointed to find that the Carpathians are somewhat different from those depicted in Bram Stoker's book, but the area is very beautiful all the same. Dracula's birthplace is here in the town of Sighisoara, one of the few remaining medieval settlements left virtually untouched by the 20th century. But there is a whole lot more to Romania than the count and his legacy; the Carpathian mountains and the Black Sea coast also boast some of the most impressive landscapes in Europe. In contrast, Bucharest did not survive the onslaught of Communism and still bears the scars of revolution. What will lighten your spirits when you are here, though, is the genuine warmth of the people, who are all very keen to promote tourism.

BACKGROUND

The overthrow of the Ceauşescu regime in 1989 was perhaps Eastern Europe's most dramatic revolution. Although Nikolai and Elena were dead within hours of protests breaking out in Bucharest, Romania has arguably been the slowest country in Eastern Europe to westernise. It was ruled until 1996 by President Iliesceu's National Salvation Front – little more than a cover for former Communists. However, 1996 saw the election of President Constantinescu, the first Romanian leader since the 1930s to be fully committed to liberal democracy and the free market. Economic problems do persist – the closure of numerous state-run industries has produced chronic unemployment and the welfare system is on the point of collapse.

ACCOMMODATION DETAILS

The standard on offer is generally among the worst in Europe. Despite the 1989 revolution, the country is still desperately poor and has yet to adapt to Western-style independent tourism. But it is certainly trying.

A number of Category II **hotels** in Bucharest now offer singles for around £19 ($32), doubles for around £25 ($42). Outside the capital you can look for a 20–25% reduction on these prices for similar accommodation. If these prices seem attractive to you, bear in mind that either you will have to be very fortunate to get one of these rooms on arrival, or you will have to book well in advance. Do not expect too much help from the National Tourist Organisation (ONT) in your quest for a cheap hotel room. ONT supplies hotel lists and books hotels, but old habits die hard and, especially in Bucharest, you may find the staff devote much of their energy to persuading you to stay in a more expensive hotel. Expect to be told that the cheaper hotels are full. If you are not pressed for time, you can try some of the hotels in person.

The Romanian currency is the leu with approximately 60,000 leu to £1 ($1 is 33,000 leu).

Rooms in private homes offer budget travellers a way to avoid paying over the odds in hotels and the efforts involved in trying to book a hostel bed. Many Romanians are keen to let rooms to earn some extra money and, as the problems besetting the country deter many people from visiting Romania, there is a plentiful supply of rooms available. Private rooms can usually be booked through ONT and occasionally through private agencies. Prices are around £10 ($17) per person in Bucharest, £6–8 ($10–13.50) elsewhere. Rooms offered by locals are much cheaper; rarely will their asking price reach £5 ($8.50) per person, and usually it will be considerably less.

Do not be immediately suspicious of anyone offering you a room for free. This is quite a common practice. Your host may well expect some favour in return, such as exchanging money at a rate favourable to all concerned; that is, above the official rate but below the black market norm (this is still illegal). If you do decide to take up an offer of private accommodation, keep an eye on your valuables or leave them at the station.

Youth hostels are controlled by the Romanian youth and student organisation CATT (Compania Autonomă de Turismpentru Tineret – the Independent Youth Tourism Company). Like other East European tourist organisations, CATT has a marked preference for dealing with groups rather than individuals. Most of the beds at the majority of youth hostels are reserved months in advance by school and youth groups. This puts the onus on you to book well ahead of your time of arrival, a major task considering the difficulties of dealing with CATT. Incredibly, when hostels have plenty of space, many simply choose to shut their doors until the next group arrives. Prices are around £8–10 ($13.50–17) per night.

During the university and college summer holidays, CATT lets out student accommodation (*caminul de studenti*) in towns with a sizeable student population. As with youth hostels, these lodgings are frequently filled up by vacationing groups. If you do manage to get a bed, expect to pay £7–8 ($12–13.50). Many towns and university rectorates maintain a surplus capacity of student accommodation, specifically for visiting foreign students. Prices are exceptionally low, around £5 ($8.50). Such accommodation offers an excellent opportunity to meet Romanian students.

There are also a number of **privately run hostels** opening up throughout the country. To find out about the situation in towns not listed here, get talking to your fellow travellers, or the local Tourist Offices.

There are well over 100 **campsites**, most of which are listed on the map *Popasuri Turistice* (text in French). A solo traveller should pay no more than £4 ($7) to pitch a tent for one night. Cabins are available at most sites, with charges of around £3.50 ($6) per person being the norm though, unfortunately, these are usually full in summer. Sites are sometimes located a good distance out of town, and occasionally are none too easy to reach by public transport. Your main complaint may be the quality of the sites. Facilities are very basic, and the toilets and washrooms can be really atrocious. **Camping rough** is technically illegal, but there are few places you are likely to experience any trouble once you get out into the countryside. The authorities outside the towns often ignore freelance campers, as long as you do not light fires, leave litter or damage the natural habitat. Occasionally you may be sent on your way, but it is very rare for the statutory fine to be imposed.

In the countryside, there are well in excess of 100 **cabanas**, simple accommodations for hikers and walkers, many of which are in the more mountainous parts of the country. A booklet, *Invitation to the Carpathians*, gives the location of many *cabanas*, plus suggested itineraries. An overnight stay costs around £5

($8.50). By law, *cabanas* are debarred from refusing entry to any hiker or climber, but it still might be sensible to reserve ahead, either through ONT, or through the regional Tourist Office. Overnight stays are also possible at a number of **monasteries**, but it can be very difficult to gain entrance. An approach has to be made first to ONT, which will do its utmost to convince you to stay in a hotel instead. Persistence is essential on your part and there is still no guarantee of success.

If you can't find a bed in town and face a night sleeping rough, do not attempt to bed down in the town, but rather head for the **train station waiting-room**. If you are disturbed by the police, explain that you are taking a train early in the morning. The chances are that you will have a few Romanians for company in the waiting-room as this is quite a common practice among people setting off on an early morning train. Try to leave your pack in the left luggage store, as theft is quite common.

TOURIST INFORMATION

The quality of tourist information available locally is often very poor, with stocks of pamphlets etc. liable to become exhausted long before the end of the main tourist season. Similarly, the National Tourist Offices abroad are extremely poorly stocked, reflecting the dire state of the national economy. Undoubtedly the best sources of tourist information are those provided in the West.

ADDRESSES

ROMANIAN NATIONAL TOURIST OFFICE
83A Marylebone High Street, London W1M 3DE (tel. 020 7224 3692, *www.romaniatourism.com*). Also see *www.ont.ro*.

HOTELS
Booked in the UK by: Thomas Cook, VIP Travel, 42 North Audley Street, London W1Y 2DU (tel. 020 7499 4221). Or your local Thomas Cook agent.

Alternatively, use the tourist website listed above, or visit *www.hotelsromania.com*, *www.hotels.ro* or *www.inyourpocket. com*.

YOUTH AND STUDENT HOSTELS
See *www.dntcj.ro/yhr/* for full listings of the country's hostels.

Bucharest (Bucureşti) (0)21

TOURIST OFFICES

Gara de Nord: Look for the door marked TOURIST. Staff will provide information on rooms and transport, but do not supply maps or brochures. Open Mon.–Sat. 8am–8pm, Sun. 8am–5pm.

ONT, Carpati Centru, Blvd Magheru 7 (tel. 314 5160, *www.ont.ro*). Changes money, books rooms and transportation. Open Mon.–Fri. 8am–5pm (until 8pm for currency exchange, Sat. 8am–3pm, Sun. 8am–1pm. Tram 87 from the station to Piaţa Romană.

For city information see *www.inyourpocket.com* and *www.bucharest.go.ro*.

ACCOMMODATION AGENCIES

The ONT office (see above) and possibly the Tourist Office at Gara de Nord will arrange accommodation. ONT can arrange beds in student hostels and will inform you of the current locations of these hostels (they tend to change annually).

HOTELS

Most people arrive at the Gara de Nord. Beside the ONT office in the train station there is a board listing all the hotels in the city, with their addresses and telephone numbers.

The prices given below are for double rooms, without baths (unless otherwise stated). Rooms with their own bathrooms tend to cost a few pounds more.

Hotel Cerna, B-Dul Golescu 29 (tel. 311 0535). Doubles from £12.50 ($21).

Bucegi, Str. Witing 2 (tel. 212 7154). Doubles from £14.50 ($24.50). By the Gara de Nord.

Marna, Str. Buzesti 3 (tel. 212 8366). Doubles from £20 ($34).

Muntenia, Str. Academiei 21 (tel. 614 6010, *muntenia@dial.kappa.ro*). Good location but noisy. Doubles from £16 ($27).

Hotel Turist, Poligrafiei 3–5 (tel. 224 2000, *dht@parch.ro*). Doubles from £30 ($51).

Casa Victor, Str. Emanoil (tel. 222 5733, *victor@mediasat.ro*). Doubles around £30 ($51).

Hotel Triumf, Sos Kiseleff 12 (tel. 222 3172). Bus 131 to Arcul de Triumf.

Carpati, Str. Matei Millo 16 (tel. 315 0140, *www.hotelcarpati. compace.ro, carpati@compace.ro*). Doubles from £16 ($27).

Palas, Str. Constantin Mille 18 (tel. 613 6735). Doubles from £25 ($42).

Hanul Lui Manuc Inn, Iuliu Maniu 62 (tel. 313 1415). Metro: Unirii.

PRIVATE ROOMS

Available through ONT main office, or try Peter Express, B-Dul Ana Ipatescu 17 (tel. 650 2567). Expect to pay around £10 ($17) for a centrally located double room.

HOSTELS

Villa Helga, Str. Salcimilor 2 (tel. 610 2214, *helga@rotravel.com*). Open all year, 24 hours. In the centre of the city near Piaţa Galati. Kitchen and laundry facilities available. Run by the real descendants of Dracula ... allegedly ...

Elvis Villa, Avram Iancu 5 (tel. 3155 273, *www.elvisvilla.ro, contact_us@elvisvilla.ro*). Open all year. Excellent cheap hostel with lots of free stuff, like internet access and beer. They also have branches in Brasov and Sighisoara, and details of these can be accessed at their website.

Gellamar Hostel, Sapunari 11 (tel. 313 9118, *www.gellamar.ro, reservations@gellamar.ro*). New hostel. Open all year. Breakfast included, free BBQ on a Sunday. Internet access available too.

CAMPING

Buftea. This is a lakeside campsite 29 km north of Bucharest with dorm-hut accommodation. Open in the summer months only. There is an infrequent train service running from the Gara de Nord train station. It would be advisable to make enquiries there before setting out.

RUSSIA, THE UKRAINE AND BELARUS

Russia is fast becoming one of the world's most fashionable tourist destinations. Fourteen years after the collapse of Communism, the country is in the process of revamping its tourist industry, and things are getting easier all the time for the budget traveller. The country still presents plenty of challenges, with budget accommodation still being thin on the ground, and standards not quite being up to those you'd expect in Western Europe. Don't let that put you off though, as a trip here is still more than rewarding.

Russia is of course the largest country in the world. In 1917, its monarchy was overthrown and replaced by a Communist government. The Communists, under Stalin, defeated Germany in the Second World War and had the distinction of taking Berlin for the Allies. After the war, it was decided, much to Churchill's chagrin, that Russia be given most of Eastern Europe to 'protect'. This led to many years of isolationism and despair. Only in 1989 did these Soviet satellite states begin to break free.

To ensure a successful trip to Russia, the Ukraine and Belarus, you will need a phrasebook (if you intend to communicate with any success), a visa, and plenty of hard currency (in crisp new dollar bills) if you are going to be travelling out of Moscow or St Petersburg. Westerners often worry about crime in the Eastern European cities. Although it is a problem in St Petersburg, tourists are very unlikely to be caught up in it. The main thing is that you enjoy the challenge of these three countries and come away with some exciting and unique experiences.

ACCOMMODATION DETAILS

Though Russia, the Ukraine and Belarus are now individual countries, each requiring a separate visa, the accommodation situation is virtually the same in all three. In the past, visitors were only able to enter under the auspices of Intourist, the notorious official travel agency for the former Soviet Union. Their prices were steep, and so for the budget traveller (with the exception of

Trans-Siberian Express travellers) a trip to Russia was too expensive to contemplate.

With the disintegration of the Soviet Union have come changes in the tourist infrastructure, but still they are not keeping pace with changes elsewhere in the Eastern Bloc. Although it is now much easier to get a visa, especially for the Ukraine and Belarus, and independent travel in these countries has become a viable possibility, they are still not fully equipped for an influx of Western visitors.

Intourist continue to operate, and their prices are gradually dropping: their **hotels** in Moscow and St Petersburg now offer doubles from around £40 ($68). They will also book campsite accommodation, either in tents or chalets. A 2–4 berth chalet without facilities will cost around £16 ($27), while tents and caravans cost about £12 ($20) per person (these prices are for Moscow and St Petersburg; other centres cost £1–5 ($1.70–8.50) less). To book through Intourist, contact them at the address shown below. They may well offer you a group package which will include cheap flights – and only the flights and accommodation are compulsory in order to acquire a visa – other than that you can do what you like, tailoring your itinerary to suit your own taste, provided everything is pre-booked. Intourist will also sort out your visa for you.

This may be a safe and secure way to see Russia, but it's hardly cheap. It's no longer strictly necessary to go through Intourist, because **independent hotels** are starting to materialise which will assist with visa support if you contact them directly. Most Western style hotels tend to arrange domestic and international train tickets, and often offer the best tourist information in Russia. Most importantly, they're friendly and helpful – essential in a place where you might feel completely disorientated, as if you've left the real world behind. Furthermore, most private hotels won't necessarily hold you to the number of nights you've 'booked' in order to secure your visa (although they will charge a booking fee of around £8 ($13.50)), so theoretically you're free to look elsewhere once you arrive.

The local currency is the rouble and £1 is approximately 50 roubles ($1 is roughly 31 roubles).

A network of **youth hostels** is now starting to take shape in

Russia. There are hostels in St Petersburg and Moscow already and there are plans to open more soon. Bookings can be made online at the addresses given below.

Bear in mind that all three countries covered in this chapter are suffering the effects of immense economic turmoil and there is a tendency to assume all Westerners are extremely wealthy. Consequently, you may find hotels increase their prices dramatically (in line with Intourist prices) the moment they become aware of your nationality. For those fluent in Russian this may not be a problem, but the majority of visitors will find that negotiations depend on the mood of the hotel staff on the day, plus their skill at haggling and looking convincingly destitute. Offering hard currency may help. One way or another, it is almost impossible to recommend specific hotels because their attitude (and pricing policy) is so inconsistent. The best advice is to be thick-skinned and keep trying your luck.

Two companies, Sputnik and CCTE (*www.ccte.ru*), specialise in foreign/youth travel, though Sputnik is primarily aimed at groups and may therefore refuse to deal with individuals. It's worth a try, though.

In view of the high cost of hotel accommodation, it makes sense to listen to offers of **private rooms**: some locals ask as little as £5 ($8.50) per night, and you'll usually find them at the station holding cardboard signs advertising their rooms. The accommodation won't be palatial by any standards, but it will usually be fairly central and linked to the city centre by public transport. You have no guarantee of quality or safety, so use your discretion. On the plus side, you may gain a rare and rewarding insight into a lifestyle entirely different from your own (even if you do find yourself watching a Bond movie dubbed in Russian on a flickering black-and-white TV).

In many places – hotel lobbies and stations are the prime locations – you will see an individual sitting at a desk with a pile of handwritten postcards. They're probably acting as an agent for local families or pensioners offering accommodation in their homes to subsidise their income. These private enterprise networks offer a slightly greater guarantee of safety and the promise of a more convenient location, although prices may be slightly higher than you'd expect to pay when dealing direct.

Haggling and impressive body language should get you a room for around £6 ($10) per night.

University dorms are worth a look, especially if you speak the language. Many dorms have spare rooms, and the individuals who supervise each dorm will often take people in (even though they're not supposed to). Again, it's a question of using skilful haggling and quite possibly a little bribery to get in.

A word on bribery: the former Soviet Union is home to a barter system that would not seem out of place in a medieval town. Step out of just about any metro station at midnight and you'll see dozens of women exchanging everything from salami to Reeboks out of sturdy white shopping-bags. The black market is essential to the survival of most citizens, so 'bribery' isn't quite so illicit as it might sound to a Westerner. But be discreet.

If all else fails, an overnight train is always a possibility. Distances in Russia are vast – Moscow to St Petersburg, for example, is an eight-hour train journey, and buying a '*platzcart*' ticket will ensure you a cheap bed. But with as many as eight overnight trains running in each direction – you'll have a range of choices available to you.

USEFUL PHRASES

(Place stress on the syllables in italics)

ENGLISH	RUSSIAN
Yes	Dah
No	Nyet
Please	Pa-*zhol*-sta
Thank you	Spas*ee*ba
Good morning	Dobro *oo*-tram
Goodbye	Do sved*an*-ya
Where is/are	Gd*yeh*
Excuse me	Izven*ee*tye
How much?	Skolko sto-*ee*t?
Can I have ...	Yah hot-*choo*
I don't understand	Yah ne poni*may*-oo
Do you speak English?	Voi govor*eet*-yeh po Angl*ee*skee?
My name is ...	Men-yah za-*voot* ...

ADDRESSES

INTOURIST
Intourist Travel Ltd, 7 Wellington Terrace, London (tel. 020 7727 4100, *www.intourist.co.uk*, *info@intourist.co.uk*).

RUSSIAN YOUTH HOSTELS
Sovetskaya 28, St Petersburg, Russia (tel. (812) 329 8018, *www.ryh.ru*, *ryh@ryh.ru*).

BOB SOPEL UKRAINIAN TRAVEL
Falcon House, Victoria Street, Chadderton, Oldham (tel. 0161 652 5050, *www.ukraine.co.uk*).

USEFUL WEBSITES
www.belarus.org.uk (general information), *www.inyourpocket.com* (general information and booking), *www.russia.direct.dial. pipex.com* (visas for Russia and the Ukraine).

Russia (00)7

Moscow (Moskva) (0)95

TOURIST OFFICES

Central Excursion Bureau, ul. Belinstovo 4A (tel. 203 8271). Two blocks from Red Square. Open daily 9am–9pm. English-speaking staff, but aimed mainly at high-spending, hard-currency tourists.

Moscow Excursion Bureau, ul. Rozhdestvenka 5 (tel. 923 8953). Open daily 10am–2pm and 3–6 pm. Russian-speaking. Accept payment in roubles.

It's advisable to begin your stay at least at the Traveller's Guest House, below, which has information and maps.

Useful websites include: *www.moscowcity.com*, *www.all-moscow. com*, *infoservices.com/moscow*, *www.themoscowtimes.com*.

BASIC DIRECTIONS

Moscow is served by an extensive and efficient metro system. This links all the major railway stations (there are eight) and any accommodation you're likely to find (including the Traveller's Guest House).

HOTELS

Ukraine Hotel, Kutuzovsky Prospekt 2 (tel. 243 3030). Great views. Rooms from £60 ($102) without breakfast.

Tsentralnaya, Tverskaya ulitsa 10 (tel. 229 8957). Doubles around £24 ($40). Metro: Pushkinskaya.

Leningradskaya, Kalanchevskaya ulitsa 21 (tel. 975 1815). Doubles from £30 ($50). Good central location.

Sputnik, Leninsky Prospekt 38 (tel. 938 7106). Doubles from £24 ($40).

Hotel Orlyonok, ul. Kosygina 15 (tel. 939 8884).

Hotel Molodzhnaya, Dimitrovskoe shosse 27 (tel. 210 9311). Bus 227 from Savyolovskaya metro.

Hotel Druzhba, Prospekt Vernadskovo 53 (tel. 432 9631).

Tsentralny Dom Turista, Leninsky Prospekt 146 (tel. 438 5510).

Hotel Salyut, Leninsky Prospekt 158 (tel. 438 0224).

Hotel Turist, ul. Selskokhozayistvennaya 17 (tel. 181 0158). Metro: Botanichesky Sad.

Akademicheskaya Hotel, Leninsky Prospekt 1, korpus 1 (tel. 237 2890). Metro: Oktyabrskaya. This hotel will take anyone who books in advance (it used to be for guests of the Academy of Science only). Singles only but some have kitchens. Expect to pay around £33 ($56).

Arena Hotel, ul. 10-letiya Oktyabrya 11 (tel. 245 2802). Sportivna metro. Three-star hotel near the Novodevichiy Convent. Expensive at over £40 ($68) per person.

PRIVATE ROOMS

Knowledge of Russian will help you considerably, and for a few dollars a night you will find yourself enjoying a unique experience of life in the home of a Russian family or pensioner, within easy reach of the city centre. Look out for people at train stations with cardboard signs advertising their rooms.

HOSTELS

Traveller's Guest House, ul. Bolshaya Pereyaslavskaya 50, floor 10 (tel. 971 4059, *www.tghmoscow.hypermart.net*, *tgh@glasnet.ru*).

Around £20 ($34) per night. It's not easy to find this American-run hostel: take the metro to Prospekt Mira, turn left and then take a right after about 400m. If you're heading towards four chimney stacks, you're going in the right direction. Turn left on Pereyaslavskaya and the building – which hardly advertises itself – is on your right. The hostel will help with visa support, tourist information and domestic/international train tickets (for which there is a small service charge). Kitchen and laundry facilities available.

Sherstone Hostel, Gostinichnyi Proezd 8, Building 1, 3rd floor (tel. 797 8075, *www.sherstone.ru*, *info@sherstone.ru*). Dorms from £10 ($17). Open all year. Provide visa support and registration, as well as train tickets and internet access. Metro: Gostinichnaya Ulitsa, or Vladykino.

Galina's Flat, ul. Chaplygina 8, no. 35 (tel. 921 6038, *galinas.flat@mtu-net.ru*). Metro to Chistye Prudy. Flat on the fifth floor. Only 8 beds, but excellent. Double £13 ($22).

Hostel Tramp, Selskokhozayistvennaya ul. 7, (tel. 551 2876, *www.hostelling.ru*, *hosteltramp@mtu-net.ru*). Provides visa support, and links to other hostels online. Open all year.

CAMPING

At the **Hotel Solnechnaya**, Varshavskoe shosse 21 km (tel. 119 7100). Take bus 679 from Varshavskaya metro. But check with one of the tourist bureaux before leaving that the site is still operating.

St Petersburg (Sankt Peterburg) (0)812

TOURIST OFFICES

The tourist information office is at Nevsky Prospekt 41 (tel. 3311 2843, *www.spb.ru*) and can help you out with maps and so forth.

Hotel service bureaux can advise on travel and entertainment, even if you're not a guest of that hotel.

OST-WEST, Nevsky Prospekt 105 (tel. 327 3416, *www.ostwest. com*, *info@ostwest.com*). Does everything from booking accommodation to fixing theatre tickets.

Also try the RYH hostel. They provide a very useful free map and the most up-to-date guide to the city. There's also a budget travel agency downstairs, Sindbad Travel (tel. 327 8384, *sindbad@sindbad.ru*). A second branch is at Universatetskaya naberezhnaya 11, Vasilevsky Island (tel. 324 0880, *isic@sindbad.ru*).

Also see *www.cityvision2000.com*.

BASIC DIRECTIONS

St Petersburg's metro system efficiently links most points of interest in the city, including the four main stations, the RYH hostel, university dorms and the city centre.

HOTELS

Karelia Hotel, ul. Tukachevsky 27/2 (tel. 118 4048, *www. karelia.spb.ru, b-karelia@online.ru*). Doubles from £45 ($76).

Olgino Hotel, 18 Primorskoye shosse (tel. 238 3671, *www.hotel-olgino.spb.ru, info@hotel-olgino.spb.ru*). Metro: Chernaya Rechka. Singles £30 ($51) including meals.

Russ Hotel, Artilleriyskaya ul. 1 (tel. 273 4683, book through *www.cityvision2000.com*). Doubles from £40 ($68). Metro: Chernyshevskaya.

Sovetskaya, Lermontovsky Prospekt 43/1 (tel. 329 0181, book as above). Metro: Baltiskaya.

Okhtinskaya-Victoria, Bolsheokhtinsky Prospekt 4 (tel. 227 4438, booking as Russ Hotel). Not in town cetnre, but there's a shuttle bus from Nevsky Prospekt.

Moskva, Ploschad Alexandra Nevskovo 2 (tel. 274 3001, booking as Russ Hotel). Near town centre.

Petersburg Hotel, Prigorskaya Naberezhnaya 2 (tel. 542 9411, booking as Hotel Russ). Town centre. Metro: Ploschad Lenina.

Dvorets Molodyozhy, ul. Professora Popova 47 (tel. 234 3484, *ldm@mail.plus.net*). Bus 25 from Nevsky Prospekt. Doubles £29 ($49).

Matisov Domik, Naberezhnaya Reki Priazhki (tel. 218 5445). Doubles from £40 ($68). Near Mariinsky Theatre. Privately run.

Chaika, Serebristi Bulvar 38 (tel. 301 7575, *www.chaika.spb.ru, resp@chaika.spb.ru*). *Banya* (sauna) available.

Vyborgskaya, Torzhkovskaya ul. 3 (tel. 246 9141). Metro:

Chyornaya Rechka. Reserve through the Oktyabrskaya (see below).

Hotel Sputnik, Prospekt Morisa Toreza 34 (tel. 552 5632). Metro: Ploshchad Muzhestva.

Plukovskaya, Ploschad Pobedy (tel. 123 5122). Metro: Moskovskaya.

Mir, ul. Gastello 17 (tel. 108 5166). South of metro Park Pobedy.

Rossiya, pl. Chernyshevskovo 11 (tel. 329 3925). Same metro as the Mir.

PRIVATE ACCOMMODATION

Host Families Association (HOFA), Tavricheskaya ul. 5–25 (tel. 275 1992, *www.hofa.us*). Contact in advance to request visa support. B&B from around £15 ($25). Failing that, you can always rely on the hordes of locals awaiting tourists at the train stations; you will probably be able to negotiate a good deal with them.

HOSTELS

RYH (Russian Youth Hostel), 3rd Sovetskaya ul. 28 (tel. 329 8018, *www.ryh.ru*, *ryh@ryh.spb*). Around £12 ($20) per night, continental breakfast included, plus a £8 ($13.50) reservation fee if you use them for visas and visa support. Kitchen and laundry facilities and English-speaking staff. From Ploshchad Vosstaniya metro station (Moscow station), turn right on to Nevsky Prospekt away from the city centre, then left on to Suvorovski Prospekt and right on to 3rd Sovetskaya ulitsa at the second traffic lights after the Phillips store.

Holiday Hostel, ul. Mikhailova 1 (tel. 327 1017, *www.hostel.ru*, *info@hostel.spb.ru*). B&B around £13 ($22). Metro Ploshchad Lenina, then on Finlandsky Vokzai, left on to ul. Komsomola, then right. Open 24 hours. Good views from the rooftop café.

Puppet Theater Hostel, 12 ul. Nekrasova (tel. 272 5401, *www.hostelling-russia.ru/pth.htm*, *puppet@ryh.ru*). Dorms from £9 ($16). Open all year. Just off Nevsky Prospekt, town centre.

Herzen University Hostel, Kazanskaya ul. 6 (tel. 314 7472). Behind the Kazan Cathedral off Nevsky Prospekt. Good location and decent facilities.

Traveller Hostel, Sadovaya 25 (tel. 319 4462). Open all year.

STUDENT DORMS

Be aware that there's no guarantee you'll get in. If you want to try your luck, the best situated dorm is at **Plekanova 6**, behind the Kazan cathedral on Nevsky Prospekt; the most promising is at **Grazhdansky Prospekt 28**, near the metro of the same name. You may find that this metro station is no longer open due to flooding. If this is the case, get off at Lesnaya, and take one of the taxis marked 'Grazhdansky Prospekt'. This is only advisable if you speak Russian, however. It's also worth checking with the university itself (tel. 218 2000).

CAMPING

Motel-Camping Olgino, Primorskoe shosse 59 (tel. 238 3671). Take the metro to Chyornaya Rechka then bus 411 or 416.

The Ukraine (00)380

If you are planning to visit the Ukraine but don't want the hassle of fixing up your own accommodation, contact Bob Sopel Ukrainian Travel (see Addresses, above). This company can arrange everything, including organising visas, booking hotels, apartments, train tickets and flights. The office is staffed by experts so you may want to discuss certain aspects of your travel plans with them, even if you are planning on taking the independent route.

Kiev (Kyiv) (0)44

For more information about the Ukraine and Kiev, visit *www.kyivpost.com*, *www.uazone.net* and *http://travel.kyiv.org*.

HOTELS

Druzhba, Bulvar Druzhbi Narodiv 5 (tel. 268 3406). Nearest metro: Dzerzhinskaya/Lyubanka. Cheapest hotel in Kiev,

charges £20 ($34) per night in a 3-bed room, though some
travellers claim to have got in for less.

Hotel Ekspres, bulvar Shevchenka 38 (tel. 221 8995). Doubles
around £24 ($40).

Mir, Prospekt 40-Richya Zhovtnaya 70 (tel. 264 9646). South of
the river, nearest metro: Dzerzhinskaya/Lyubanka.

Goloseevskaya, Prospekt 40-Richya Zhovtnaya 93 (tel. 261
4116). See Hotel Mir for directions.

Andrew's Hotel, Vulitsya Vozdvyzhenska 60 (tel. 416 0411,
andrey@economix.kiev.ua). Popular.

Zolotoy Kolos, Prospekt 40-Richya Zhovtnaya 95 (tel. 2614001).
See Hotel Mir for directions.

Lybid Hotel, 3 Peremohy Ploschad (tel. 274 0063). Singles £50
($85), doubles £70 ($120), with breakfast.

Hotel Saint Petersburg, bulvar Shevchenka 4 (tel. 229 7367).
Doubles from £18 ($30).

PRIVATE ROOMS

Locals hang around in the city centre offering private rooms for
around £5 ($8.50) per night in various suburban abodes.

CAMPING

Motel-Camping Prolisok, Prospekt Peremogi 179 (tel. 444
1293). Tent space around £5 ($8.50). A good Intourist
campsite, 12 km from town. Bus 37 from metro Svyatoshino.

Odessa (0)482

TOURIST OFFICE

Intourist, vul. Pushkinska 17 (tel. 258520). In the lobby of Hotel
Krasnaya. Open 9am–1pm and 2–5pm.

HOTELS

Tsentralnaya, ul. Preobrazhenska 40 (tel. 268406). Doubles £40
($68).

Turist, Genuezskaya ul. 24A (tel. 614057). Bus 129 from the
station to the 10 Aprelya stop.

Bolshaya Moskovskaya, Deribasovskaya ul. 29 (tel. 224016). Two blocks back from Ploshchad Potyomkintsev, near the northern shore. Dorms from £15 ($25).

Arkadia, Genuezskaya ul. 24 (tel. 637527). Near Arkadia beach, south of town. From £12 ($20).

Chornoye More, vulitsya Rishelevska 59 (tel. 242028). Cheapest doubles from £24 ($40).

Londonskaya, Primorsky Bulvar 11 (tel. 225019, *londred@ paco.net*). Expensive, but try bargaining at low season.

Pasazh, vul. Preobrazhenska 34 (tel. 224849). Doubles £25 ($42).

Spartak, vul. Deribasivska 25 (tel. 268924). Doubles £22 ($37).

CAMPING

Camping Delphin, doroga Kotovskovo 307 (tel. 555052). 10 km north of Odessa in Luzanovka. Take a ferry to Luzanovka pier, 500m south of the campsite, from the Morskoy Vokzal terminal in the north of the city.

Belarus (00)375

Minsk (0)17

TOURIST OFFICE

Belintourist, pr. Masherava 19 (tel. 226 9056, *www.belarus tourist.minsk.by*). Next to Gastsinitsa Yubileyni. Get the *Minsk in your Pocket* guide, which has accommodation details. Open Mon.–Fri. 9am–6pm. Also see their website at *www.inyour pocket.com*.

HOTELS

Zeloni, Odoysefkogo 52 (tel. 268 5701). Incredibly cheap, but book in advance before you make your way out here.

Academy of Science, Surganova 7 (tel. 284 2701). A very

Belarussian experience. Not new, but very cheap. Book in advance.

Belarus, vul. Starazoskaya 15 (tel. 391705). Doubles around £50 ($85). By the river in the north-west of the city.

Minsk, pr. F. Skaryny (tel. 200132). Doubles around £45 ($76). In the centre of town, 1 km from the station. On Ploshchad Lenina.

Mezhdunarodny Turistky Tsentr Yunost (tel. 362397). Beside the Minsk Sea, 18 km north-west of the city. Take bus 125 from the railway station.

SLOVAKIA (Slovensko) (00)421

The main string to Slovakia's bow is its striking scenery, in particular the High Tatras – a mountain range not dissimilar to the Alps. The interior of the country is largely unspoilt and consists of mountains and forests, making it perfect hiking country, and Bratislava's location makes it an ideal base for day trips to Vienna for those wanting to avoid Austrian accommodation costs.

Western ignorance of Slovakia as a tourist destination means it is an inexpensive country for the budget traveller to visit. The capital, Bratislava, will not give you an impression of the real Slovakia, as it borders Austria, the Czech Republic and Hungary, and you are far more likely to get a true insight into Slovakia by travelling far into the country.

BACKGROUND

In 1918, Slovakia became part of the Czechoslovak republic. From then, it had a brief flirtation with independence for the first time, under a Nazi puppet government during the Second World War. During the following Soviet rule of Czechoslovakia, the Slovaks lived in peaceful coexistence with the Czechs until the 'Velvet Revolution' swept through the country in 1989. Slovakia's subsequent 'Velvet Divorce' from the Czech Republic on 1 January 1993 was fortunately both amiable and bloodless.

Since 1989, Slovakia has endured significant inner turmoil, notably five governments and bitter economic problems. The Czechs got all the industrial and tourist towns when the Czech Republic and Slovakia split. While Bratislava is an interesting and welcoming city, it isn't exactly Prague. But with EU membership, the country is hoping to catch up with its more prosperous neighbour.

ACCOMMODATION DETAILS

Slovakia's emergence as a country separate from the Czech Republic has been a mixed blessing, for the traveller as well as for the nation itself. Bratislava, as already mentioned, is not Prague, but you can nevertheless expect a hard time finding a place to stay in high season. Smaller towns should not present a problem.

CKM (the student travel organisation) professes to operate booking services, but the procedures are time-consuming and elaborate, and in reality there is no regulated accommodation system. If making direct contact with hotels, etc., doesn't appeal, then try to avoid arriving at weekends (when Germans and Austrians flood in for weekend breaks).

The local currency is the Slovak korunen (or crowns) and £1 is approximately 58 Sk ($1 is 32 Sk).

Hotels are divided into five categories: A or deluxe/five-star, A*/four-star, B/three-star, B*/two-star, and C/one-star. Hotels rated in the C/one-star category may be fairly basic but from the budget traveller's point of view they are a real bargain, it's just a shame there are not more of them around. More likely than not, you'll find the only hotels, or the ones with spaces, are two-star hotels. These are still very affordable – on average, a double room will cost around £13 ($22) and a single £10 ($17). No longer have hotel bills to be settled in hard currency, but if you offer dollars rather than Slovakian crowns you're unlikely to be turned away.

It is possible to stay in the homes of local people. Prices for **private rooms** booked through agencies are no longer officially fixed, with the result that they have risen. Expect to pay around £6 ($10) in most towns. Some rooms in the cities can be far from the centre, but as public transport is cheap and efficient, distance should not deter you.

Private rooms offered by individuals will be a similar price to official ones, but standards may vary dramatically. Accessibility is important, but staying one night in the middle of nowhere need not be a disaster if it allows you to get an early start next day to look elsewhere. But take care of your valuables.

Hostelling offers arguably the best value for money out of all the accommodation possibilities, but beds are not easy to find. Although you will find many Slovak hostels listed in the HI handbook very few of them are actually open and those that are are usually full. If you do find an open one with spaces, expect to pay anything from £5–15 ($8.50–25). Booking is definitely advisable, especially in the summer. In Slovakia, permanent hostels are a rarity; most are converted **student dormitories**

which open in July and August. If you're around then, contact CKM, which controls the letting of rooms in student dormitories, often in towns not mentioned in the HI handbook. Many independent hostels are housed in converted student dormitories, and most of these are either unknown or unacknowledged by the official tourist agencies. Apart from relying on word of mouth, advertisements in train and bus stations may be your best guide to new hostels.

Most small towns have very basic dormitory hostels known as *turisticka ubytovna*, where a bunk bed costs around £3 ($5). Facilities seldom extend to anything more than toilets and cold showers. These hostels are meant primarily for workers living away from home, or for groups of workers on holiday, but it is most unlikely you will be turned away if there is room at the hostel. Unfortunately, many such hostels open only when they have a group booking. Nevertheless, enquire at the local CKM offices, as they sometimes offer the only hostel accommodation available in town.

If you are travelling in summer, **camping** *(autokemping)* is a great way to see the country very cheaply (few sites remain open before May or after September). There are several hundred campsites in Slovakia which usually open May–September but some do stay open all year. The price for a solo traveller is around £3 ($5) per night. Sites are usually clean, but few of them have hot water. At many sites it is possible to rent 2- or 4-bed chalets *(chata)*. Standards vary, and be warned: at some sites you may be required to pay for all the beds in the chalet, even if they are not all occupied. Expect to pay around £4–5 ($7–8.50) per person in a fully occupied chalet.

Further off the beaten track, more primitive campsites exist, known as *tborisko*. Facilities are spartan and consequently prices can be as low as £2 ($3.50) per night. Again, these sites may not be open outside the summer months, and even then you may find tourist offices are loath to admit their existence; try asking the locals if there is a *tborisko* in the vicinity. Note, camping on public land is prohibited.

Those with railpasses can take an overnight train. The Bratislava to Prague connection runs nightly, but be warned: this journey has become notorious for the number of thieves operating.

TOURIST INFORMATION

Few cities have tourist offices run along Western lines. If the situation is bleak in the Czech Republic, it is twice as antiquated in Slovakia. In most towns you'll have to rely for information on CKM, which specialises in accommodation and travel. For guides on what to see, it is best to buy a guidebook before setting off. Beware of altered street names; euphoric as the Velvet Revolution was, it did have the side-effect of sending countless weary travellers in search of addresses which have ceased to exist in post-Communist Slovakia.

ADDRESSES

SLOVAK TOURIST BOARD
Namestie L. Stura 1, PO Box 35, Banska Bystrica (tel. (0)48 413 6146, *www.sacr.sk*, *sacr@sacr.sk*). Also see *www.tourist-channel.sk* and *www.inyourpocket.com*.

YOUTH HOSTELS IN SLOVAKIA
Ubytovne Mladych na Slovensku, Prazska 11, Bratislava (tel. (0)2 417 271).

CAMPING
See *www.camping.tourist-channel.sk* for a good list of the country's official campsites.

Bratislava (0)7

TOURIST OFFICES

BIS, Klobucnicka 2 (tel. 5443 3715, *www.bratislava.sk*, *bis@bratislava.sk*). Open June–Sept., Mon.–Fri. 8am–7pm, Sat. 8am–2pm; Oct.–May, Mon.–Fri. 8am–4.30pm. General information, plus advice on the hostel situation. There is also a smaller BIS office at Hlavná Stanica, the train station. These offices will also help you arrange accommodation, and have information on summer hostels.

ACCOMMODATION AGENCIES

Satur, Jesenkého 5–9 (tel. 542 2205, *www.satur.sk*). Open Mon.–Fri. 9am–6pm, Sat. 9am–12pm. Tram 13 from the main train station.

CKM, Vysoka 32 (tel. (0)2 5273 1024, *ckm2000-bts@ckm.sk* or *ckm@ckm.sk*). Open Mon.–Fri. 9am–12pm and 1–4pm.

ARRIVING IN BRATISLAVA

Most trains to Bratislava arrive at Hlavná Stanica, about 15 minutes' walk from the Old Town, or a short trip on trams 1 or 13. Head away from the station past the train terminal and on to Praźka. Turn left down Praźka and go straight ahead, on down Štefánikova until you arrive at the Trinity church. Follow the road round to the left a short distance, then turn right heading for the old St Michael's Gate (Michalská brána). Going through the gate follow Michalská downhill and continue straight ahead to reach Hviezdoslavovo náměstí. Some trains from Slovakia arrive at the Bratislava Nové Mesto station. Trams 6 and 14 link Nové Mesto to the city centre. Most buses arrive at the bus station on Bajkalská. Going right from the bus station for about 100m you reach Vajnorská, from which you can take any tram heading down into the city.

HOTELS/PENSIONS

Krym, Safarikovo náměstí (tel. 325471). B/two-star. Around £12 ($20) for a double. Off Štúrová, close to the Danube.

Hotel Spirit, Vancurova 1 (tel. 5477 7817, *www.univers.host.sk*, *univers@napri.sk*). Near the train station. Unmissable in bright colours. Beds from £15 ($25).

Chez David, Zimocki 13 (tel. 5441 3824). Singles from £26 ($44).

Pension Gremium, Gorkeko 11 (tel. (0)52 5413 1025). Doubles from £17 ($29). In the heart of the Old Town. Book ahead.

Astra, Prievozská 14a (tel. 521 5079). One of the cheapest options; doubles around £15 ($25). 2 km east of the centre. Take tram 218 from the main train station. (Walking distance from the bus station.)

Hotel Taxis, Jaskovy Rad 11 (tel. 5479 3724). Doubles from £18 ($30). Near the train station.

PRIVATE ROOMS

See accommodation agencies listed above, or contact BIS.

HOSTELS

During the summer, Bratislava is well supplied with hostel beds, mostly in converted student dormitories. CKM and BIS are the organisations to approach for information. The bus station and the main train station are favourite places for hostel operators to pin up advertisements.

Mlada Garda, Racianska 103 (tel. 253065, *info@mlada-garda.sk*). University dorms, open July and August only.

Youth Hostel J. Hronca, Bernolákova 3 (tel. 772122). Open July–Aug. Student dorm converted into a temporary HI hostel controlled by CKM. See the Bernolak YH below for directions.

Bernolak Youth Hostel (BIS), Bernolákova 1 (tel. 497721). Lively hostel and cheapest in the city. Reduced prices for ISIC card holders. Open July–mid-Sept. From Hlavná Stanica or the bus station take trolleybus 210 to Račianska myto, or bus 27 or 47 to Zochova, then (in both cases) bus 39 to the terminus. From the bus stop, red footprints signed '*elam*' show the way to the hostel.

YMCA na Slovenska, Karpatská 2 (tel. 5249 8005). Open Apr.–Oct. From Hlavná Stanica walk down past the tram terminus on to Malinovského. Turn left and follow Malinovského until you see Karpatská on the left.

CAMPING

Two sites at Zlaté piesky, both with bungalows, and both pretty awful. But there is a nice lake nearby. Tram 2 from town centre, tram 4 from train station or tram 12 to the Zupka crossroads, then bus 32 to the third stop:

Zlaté piesky camping ground (tel. (0)2 4445 7373, *www.inter camp.sk, kempi@netax.sk*). Cottages as well as bungalows. Open mid-Apr.–mid-Oct. This is the better of the two sites and it is on the lakeside. The other site is nearby (away from the lake).

SLOVENIA (00)386

Slovenia is one of the most successful of the former Eastern European Communist countries. It is as pretty as Austria, but much more affordable. It boasts spectacular mountain scenery (near Lake Bled), and in Ljubljana it has an attractive capital. Travellers are warmly welcomed and there's lots for the tourist to do and see. In the winter the skiing is good and in the summer you can join the Slovenes and head to the coast.

BACKGROUND

Slovenia was part of the Austro-Hungarian Empire until the end of the First World War, when it became part of the 'Kingdom of Serbs, Croats and Slovenes'. This was later incorporated into Tito's Communist Yugoslavia after the Second World War. In 1990, Slovenia became the first Yugoslav Republic to hold free democratic elections. The Slovenes' subsequent declaration of independence on 25 June 1991 led to a ten-day war with the Yugoslav army. Under pressure from the European Community, the Yugoslavs withdrew from Slovenia. Independence was won, and Slovenia was formally recognised by the EU in 1992. It finally gained membership of the EU in 2004.

The Slovenes have always been proud of their national identity, and despite all their troubles, they have retained their own language – a close relation of Serbo-Croat.

ACCOMMODATION DETAILS

The first thing to say about Slovenia is that it's safe. Slovenia's transition into an autonomous country has been relatively painless and undisputed.

Slovenia now offers the full range of budget accommodation in line with Western Europe. Prices are cheaper than Austria and Italy, but don't expect them to be anywhere near as low as in Hungary. The local currency is the tolar and £1 is approximately 350 SIT ($1 is 200 SIT). The tolar is linked to the Deutschmark so prices do not fluctuate madly. You will find however that some hotels, guest houses and campsites still list their prices in Deutschmarks.

Hotels are, for the most part, expensive. Prices range from £30 to £120 ($50–200). Except in Ljubljana, where prices are constant all year, expect to pay considerably more in July and August. Many hotels close in winter.

Motels and **guest houses** (*gostilne*) supplement hotels at prices of around £26 ($44) per double. Small **pensions** are typically better value and solo travellers should opt for these as prices tend to be per person rather than per room. In addition, there is a growing supply of **private accommodation** at about £15–20 ($25–34) per double; authorities prefer longer stays and may impose a surcharge of up to 50% if you only stay for one or two nights. A house bearing a sign saying *sobe* (room) is offering private accommodation. Approach the owner directly and you may get a better rate than the agencies offer.

There are also several **student hotels**, although most are open only in July and August. Many **student dormitories** are converted into hostels in summer. Expect to pay around £10 ($17) per person.

If you want to stay in the countryside you could always stay on a working **farm**. Prices start at around £10 ($17) per person for B&B in the low season. Prices are more expensive in the summer and many of the farms taking part in this programme also offer full board. For more information, and for a list of the farms offering accommodation, contact ABC Farm & Countryside Holidays (see Addresses below).

Slovenia also boasts a number of good **campsites**. They are generally well organised with lots of facilities. Expect to pay £8–12 ($13.50–20) for two people and a tent.

Camping rough without permission is not to be advised – if you're found you will be fined.

There are also **mountain huts** (*planinske koče*) in the Julian Alps for hikers and climbers to stay in. Some are very basic and others are more like hotels. Either arrive early or book a place in advance. (See addresses below for details.)

ADDRESSES

SLOVENIAN TOURIST OFFICE

49 Conduit Street, London W1R 9FB (tel. 020 7734 7131, *www.slovenia-tourism.si*).

SLOVENIAN YOUTH HOSTELS
Pzs Hostelling International, Gosposvetska 83, Maribor, Slovenia (tel. (0)2 2342 137, *www.gaudeamus.si/hostelling*, *pzs@psdsi.com*).
FARM STAYS
ABC Farm & Countryside Holidays, Ulica Jožeta Jama 16, Ljubljana (tel. (0)1 510 4320).
You can also book these stays through the tourist board website listed above.
MOUNTAIN HUTS
Planinska zveza Slovenije, Dvoržakova 9, Ljubljana (tel. (0)1 434 5680, *www.pzs.si*).

Ljubljana (0)1

TOURIST OFFICES
TIC, the Tourist Information Centre, Stritarjeva (tel. 306 1215, *www.ljubljana-tourism.si*, *tic@ljubljana-tourism.si*). Open 8am–7pm every day. Provides information on Ljubljana and the rest of the country.
Information desk at the train station (tel. 433 9475). Open June–Sept. 8am–9pm; Oct.–May 10am–6pm.
The main office of the Alpine Association is at Dvoržakova 9 (tel. 134 3022).

BASIC DIRECTIONS
Ljubljana is a small capital with a good network of buses. Getting around is easy and you can walk to most places of interest. The main bus and railway stations are to the north of town around Trg Osvobodilne Fronte. From there you can walk down Miklošičeva to the centre. The main post office is on Slovenska cesta and buses run from outside the building.

HOTELS, MOTELS AND PENSIONS
Bit Center Hotel, Litijska 57 (tel. 548 0055, *www.bit-center.net*, *hotel@bit-center.net*). Singles from £26 ($44), dorms from £8 ($13.50).
Pri Mraku, Rimska 4 (tel. 421 9600, *mrak@daj-dam.si*). From £33

($56) for a double, £24 ($41) for a single. Breakfast included. Bus 1, 2 or 5, but central.

Hotel Park, Tabor 9 (tel. 433 1306, *www.tabor.si/hotel/hotel.htm*, *hotel.park@siol.net*). Singles from £19 ($32), doubles from £24 ($41). Breakfast included. If you show a student ID card you'll get a 20% discount. Close to the Old Town.

Super Li Bellevue, Pod gozdom 12 (tel. 433 4049, *super.li@ siol.net*). £24 ($41) for a double, £12 ($20) for a single. On the northern edge of Tivoli Park.

Hotel Tivoli, Tivolska 30 (tel. 433 6131). Doubles around £32 ($54). By the park.

City Hotel Turist, Dalmatinova 13 (tel. 234 9130, *www.hotel turist.si*, *info@hotelturist.si*). Central.

PRIVATE ROOMS

Book through Tourist Information Centre (see above). Expect to pay from £10 ($17) for a single and from £15 ($25) for a double. Most of the rooms are out of the centre at Bežigrad.

HOSTELS

Four student dormitories open their doors to travellers in July and August. The first two listed below are HI affiliated:

Dijaški dom Bežigrad, Kardeljeva ploščad 28 (tel. 534 0061, *dd.lj-bezigrad@guest.arnes.si*). From £7 ($12) per person in doubles with bath. Rooms with shared facilities are around £5 ($8.50) per person (10% discount for HI members). Bus 6 from Slovenska cesta to Stadion. Walk a short distance, then go right on to Dimičeva, then left.

Dijaški Dom Tabor, Vidovdanska 7 (tel. 234 8840, *ssljddtals@ guest.arnes.si*). This is the most central hostel. Opposite the Park Hotel. Either walk from the station or take bus 5. From the station go south along Resljeva and then east (left!) on to Komenskega. Beds are around £10 ($17) with breakfast.

Expect to pay around £10 ($17) per person at the other two hostels:

Dijaški dom Ivana Cankarja, Poljanska 26–28 (tel. 474 8600, *www.dic-lj.com*, *dd.lj-ic@guest.arnes.si*). Bus 11 from the train station.

Poljane, Potocnikova 3 (tel. 300 3137, *dd-poljane@guest.arnes.si*).

CAMPING

Autocamp Ježica, Dunajska 270 (tel. 568 3913, *www.gpl.si*, *ac-jezica@gpl.si*). Bus 6 from the train station or bus 8. £4 ($7) per person with tent. Open all year. Also 2-person bungalows to rent, £22 ($37) per night.

Autocamp Smlednik, Dragočajna 14a (tel. 362 7002, *www.dm-campsmlednik.si*, *camp@dm-campsmlednik.si*). 10 km out from Ljubljana.

SPAIN (España) (00)34

Travellers flock to Spain every year by the millions, looking to take advantage of the country's low costs and excellent climate. With mile upon mile of coastline, and the Pyrenees in the North, it is one of the most attractive countries in Europe. Although most people come to Spain for sun, sand and sangria, it is also a country of culture. The works of its famous painters grace the walls of the Prado in Madrid, the Dali gallery in Figueres and the Picasso gallery in Barcelona. A visit to these excellent art houses can be just as fulfilling as a day's inactivity on the beach.

BACKGROUND

Spain is an eclectic country, the result of the many foreign invaders that have come and gone through the centuries – Iberians, Celts, Greeks, Carthaginians and Romans, to name just a few. The Romans called the country 'Hispania', from which we get Spain's modern name.

Spaniards endured civil war in the 20th century (1936–1939), when General Francisco Franco's Nationalists overthrew the new democratic republic with considerable help from Hitler's Nazi Germany. Franco's death in 1975 and the appointment of Juan Carlos as his successor brought dictatorial rule to an end. Spain became a democracy and was admitted to the European Union in 1986.

One or two things may surprise you upon your first visit to Spain. The Spanish, for example, do not sleep in the afternoon. The *siesta* is more of an extended lunch than a lazy afternoon. Also, English is not as widely spoken as many travellers expect. The regional languages of Catalan (in Catalonia), Basque (in Navarra), and Galician (in the north-west) prevail alongside Spanish – so you may well need a phrasebook.

ACCOMMODATION DETAILS

Although prices have risen substantially over the past decade, Spain still offers the budget traveller a plentiful supply of some of the least expensive accommodation in Europe. Virtually all the various types are inspected and categorised by the Secretaria de Estado de Turismo. If you are looking for your own room there is quite an array of officially categorised lodgings to choose from (for the sake of convenience, these are grouped under the heading **pensions** in the city sections below). The intricacies of the rating system detailed below are intended as a rough guide. For the reasons given, do not treat them as hard and fast rules.

Least expensive of all the officially categorised accommodation are *fondas*, denoted by a white 'F' on a square blue sign. Next up the scale are *casas de huespedes* (blue sign with white 'CH'), followed by *pensiónes* ('P'), graded from one up to three stars. Then come *hospedajes*, infrequently seen in the country as a whole, but common in Santiago de Compostela. At this lower end of the market there is little point expecting anything other than basic facilities, but standards of cleanliness are usually perfectly acceptable. *Hostal-residencias* ('HR') and *hostales* ('H'), both graded from one up to three stars, are a bit more expensive, while at the pinnacle of the rating system are *hoteles* ('H') and *hotel-residencias* ('HR'), graded from one up to five stars. The appendage *residencia* indicates that no meals, other than (perhaps) breakfast, are served at the establishment; otherwise a *hostal-residencia* or *hotel-residencia* is similar in every respect to a comparably rated hostel or hotel.

As a rule the singles in any establishment cost around 60–80% of the price of comparable doubles. By law, guests can request that an extra bed be included in a room. This should add no more than 35% to the cost of a double and no more than 60% to the cost of a single. The Secretaria de Estado de Turismo not only categorises establishments but also sets maximum prices for their rooms, according to the facilities available. By law these prices have to be displayed on the door of the room. With certain agreed and stipulated exceptions, it is illegal for owners to charge more than the stated price. The more usual exceptions are the peak season (usually July and August) and, in Seville, during Holy Week and the April Fair, when prices can be raised quite legally. Some owners choose to offer their rooms below the official price, though this can create the impression that the whole system is a bit of a shambles; for example, you can pay more for a room in a *casa de huespedes* than for a similar room in a better category of accommodation such as a *pensión* or *hostal-residencia*. During the quieter period of the year (October to early March) there is scope for bargaining with owners who have not already voluntarily dropped their prices. Understandings can be reached fairly easily with owners who know there are plenty of rooms available just down the street.

Even in peak season there are rooms available in all the types of accommodation mentioned above which fall into the budget category. Your interest in *hoteles* and *hotel-residencias,* however, is likely to be confined to the bottom ranking, as prices for a basic one-star double start at around €35 (£23). A comparable room in a three-star hostel or *hostal-residencia* is usually similar in price, though they can be considerably more expensive. In other types of accommodation, singles for €25 (£16.50) are widely available, as are doubles for €35 (£23). You are more likely to find rooms at the lower end of these price scales outside the main resorts and the more popular tourist towns. On average you can expect to pay around €25 (£16.50) for singles, €40 (£27) for doubles in the main tourist destinations. Although there are some very cheap rooms available in popular places such as Madrid, Barcelona and the Andalucian cities, these tend to fill early in the day during the peak season. Phoning ahead is difficult unless you speak Spanish, as very few owners speak any other language (signs outside their establishment claiming otherwise are often just a ruse to attract your attention) and, in any case, owners seldom accept reservations made by phone. At best, phoning ahead will let you ascertain whether rooms are available, but do not be surprised if they have been filled by the time you arrive. One consolation is that there are generally numerous other accommodation possibilities in the same street, or even in the same building.

Now and again you may also see *camas* (beds), *camas y comidas* (bed and board), or *habitaciones* (rooms) advertised in bars or private homes. These can be the least expensive option of all, with the possible bonus of good, cheap meals thrown in. As always, look at the room before making a firm acceptance. Again, there is probably nothing to be lost by trying to haggle, except in the peak periods when owners can afford to be choosy and may just send you packing.

Hostelling is not a particularly good option in Spain as a whole. There are about 190 hostels of vastly differing quality, at which HI cards are obligatory. Only about 20 hostels remain open all year round, with many operating from July to September only. This means that outside these months hostel accommodation is lacking in a number of places of considerable interest. Even during the period from July to mid-September independent travellers may not be able to get into the temporary hostels in places such as León, Segovia and Avila, as they are frequently filled by school and youth groups.

However, hostelling is not to be dismissed as a way of seeing the main cities, with the possible exception of Seville (with a very small hostel for so popular a city, which is usually full of local students). The question is whether prices, curfews, lack of security and the fact that hostels are rarely centrally located make hostelling worthwhile. The normal hostel curfew of 10.30pm in winter and 11.30pm in summer is extended to 1–2am in Madrid, Barcelona and San Sebastian (no curfew at Madrid 'Richard Schirrmann' but the hostel is a long way from the centre if you miss the last metro). Even a 1am curfew is a bit early for anyone wanting to enjoy the nightlife of the cities, where things do not really begin to get going until around midnight. Charges for an overnight stay at hostels are around €12–18 (£8–12). Most hostels also sell HI cards for €12 (£8).

Camping is not a great option either, and probably not worth considering unless you plan to travel extensively outside the main towns. Sites are frequently situated far from the town centre and ill served by public transport. In effect, this can impose a curfew more restrictive than at any hostel. However, standards at the government-regulated sites are quite high, and although rating makes little difference to price, the facilities at the Class 1 sites do tend to be better. Even in the sites serving the main towns you should pay no more than €7 (£4.70) per person and per tent. However, to this you can add the cost of getting to the site, and, as security is a problem, the cost of leaving your luggage at the train or bus station – usually €3 (£2).

Camping rough outside the official campsites is possible, provided the consent of the landowner is obtained. However, tents must not be pitched in a town; close to roads, military bases or reservoirs; in a dry river bed which may be subject to flooding; or within 1 km of any official site. Camping on publicly owned land is prohibited by some local authorities.

In the remote mountain regions, a network of cheap **refuges** with bunk-bedded dormitories and basic cooking facilities is maintained by the Federacion Español de Montañismo. It may also be possible to stay in some **monasteries**. As the number of inhabitants has fallen, some monasteries have taken to letting vacant cells for about €15 (£10) per night. Some do not charge a set fee, preferring to suggest a donation. Many admit visitors of either sex. Some, especially in Galicia, Catalonia and Majorca, are located in spectacular settings. It is possible simply to enquire about staying the night on arrival, but as there may be no one about, it is advisable to contact the local Tourist Office first. They will arrange a time for you to show up at the monastery.

ADDRESSES
SPANISH TOURIST OFFICE
22–23 Manchester Square, London W1M 5AP (tel. 020 7486 8077, *www.spain.info*).
SPANISH YHA
Red Española de Albergues Juveniles, José Ortega y Gasset 71, Madrid (tel. 91 347 7700, *www.reaj.com*).
CAMPING
Federacion Española de Empresarios de Campings, San Bernardo 97–99, Edificio Colomina 3, Madrid (tel. 91 448 1234).
Maps and information on the official campsites from the above. A map is also available on request from the Spanish Tourist Office, above.
MOUNTAIN REFUGES
Federacion Español de Montañismo, Calle Alberto Aguiler 3, Madrid 15 (tel. 91 445 1382).

Barcelona (0)93

TOURIST OFFICES
Turisme de Barcelona, Pl. Catalunya 17 (tel. for all information; 368 9730, *www.barcelonaturisme.com*). Open 9am–9pm all year.
Barcelona Sants train station. Open daily 8am–8pm.

Barcelona Termino train station. Open Mon.–Sat. 8.30am–9pm.
Plaça Sant Jaume. Open Mon.–Fri. 9am–9pm, Sat. 9am–2pm. In
the Gothic Quarter. Metro: Jaume I, then follow Jaume I.
Airport. Open daily 8am–8pm, except Sun., morning only.
Barcelona Information. Round-the-clock information service (tel.
010). English speakers available.
The youth tourist office, Turisme Juvenil de Catalunya, is at Carrer
Rocafort (tel. 483 8363, *www.tujuca.com*).
All of these offices can help arrange rooms in private homes.

STREET NAMES

Most street signs in Barcelona give the Catalan and Spanish
versions of the street's name. The Catalan version is used in most
of the addresses below.

TROUBLE SPOTS

The Plaça Reial is best avoided after 10/11pm, as is the area
around the docks at the foot of the Ramblas (by the Columbus
monument). During the daytime the crowds which throng the
Ramblas provide an attractive working environment for pickpockets and petty thieves, so be especially careful.

PENSIONS

Expect to pay at least €30 (£20) for a double room, possibly
much more. In summer, prices can reach double the off-peak
rate. There are, however, hundreds to choose from and even if
you choose to search on foot you will find many of the pensions
listed below share a building with similar establishments.

DOUBLES €30–40 (£20–27)

Lourdes, Princesa 14 (tel. 319 3372). Popular. Metro: Jaume I.
Alamar, Carrer de la Comtessa de Sobradiel 1 (tel. 302 5012).
Very quiet and clean. Metro: Liceu.
Mari-Luz, C. Palau 4 (tel. 317 3463). Dorms also available. Metro:
Liceu.
Victoria, C. Comtal 9 (tel. 317 4597). Kitchen on the premises.
Near the Lausanne below.
Hostal-Residencia Europa, C. Boqueria 18 (tel. 318 7620).
Popular. Metro: Liceu.

Residencia Australia, Ronda Universitat 11 (tel. 317 4177). Book in advance.

Roma, Plaça Reial 11 (tel. 302 0366). Metro: Liceu. Right off the Ramblas as you head down to the Columbus monument.

Opera, Sant Pau 20 (tel. 318 8201) Metro: Liceu. Sant Pau runs off the Ramblas near the station, one street closer to the port than the hospital.

Windsor, Rambla Catalunya 84 (tel. 215 1198). Metro: Passeig de Gràcia.

DOUBLES €40–€50 (£27–33)

Lausanne, Av. Portal de l'Angel 24 (tel. 302 1139). Good views!

Levante, Bajada San Miguel 2 (tel. 317 9565, *www.hostal levante.com*).

Palacios, Gran Via Corts Catalanes 629 bis (tel. 301 3792). Metro: Passeig de Gràcia. A short walk from the exit on Via de Corts Catalanes.

Nuevo Colón, Avda. Marqués de la Argentera 19 (tel. 319 5077). One street further up Plaça del Palau from General Castanos.

Goya, Pau Claris 74 (tel. 302 2565). Metro: Urquinaona or Passeig de Gràcia (exit on to Via de Corts Catalanes).

La Palmera, Jerusalem 30 (tel. 317 0997). By the 'La Boqueria' market, also known as the Mercat de Sant Josep, off Rambla de Sant Josep. Metro: Liceu.

Felipe II, Mallorca 329 (tel. 458 7758). Metro: Provença. From Provença turn left down Girona on to Mallorca.

DOUBLES €50–€60 (£33–40)

Mare Nostrum, Carrer Sant Pau 2 (tel. 318 5340). Mare Nostrum is Latin for 'Our Sea'.

Ramos, Carrer Hospital 36 (tel. 302 0723). Old style comfort. Metro: Liceu.

Oriente, Ramblas 45 (tel. 302 2558). Expensive but good.

Toledano, Ramblas 138 (tel. 301 0872, *www.hoteltoledano.com*, *reservas@hoteltoledano.com*).

HI HOSTELS

Hostal de Joves, Passeig de Pujades 29 (tel. 300 3104). 1 or 2am curfew. From €11 (£7.30), including breakfast. Kitchen and laundry facilities. By the Parc de la Ciutadella. Only 300m from the Termino station. Right on leaving the station, left on Passeig de Picasso, then right. Metro: Arc de Triomf on Line 1. From Barcelona Sants take Line 3 to Espana to change to Line 1. Hostel cards are required in July and Aug.

'Mare de Deu de Montserrat', Passeig de Nostra Senyora del Coll 41–51 (tel. 210 5151). This is the biggest and most comfortable hostel. Beds from €12 (£8). Curfew 12am. Laundry facilities. Wheelchair accessible. A 25-minute trip from the centre. Bus 28 from Plaça de Catalunya (Metro: Catalunya).

'Pere Tarres', Numancia 149 (tel. 410 2309, *www.peretarres. org/alberg*). B&B from €10 (£6.70). Numancia runs from Barcelona Sants station in the opposite direction from Tarragona. The hostel is a 15-minute walk along the street. Two metro stops are slightly closer: Les Corts and Maria Cristina.

Studio, Duquesa d'Orleans 58 (tel. 205 0961). Open 1 July–30 Sept. Metro: Reino Elisenda or bus 22, 34, 64 or 66. 24-hour opening. B&B for around €10 (£6.70).

HOSTELS

Gothic Point, Carrer Vigitans 5 (tel. 268 7808, *www.gothic point.com, info@gothicpoint.com*). Dorms from €19 (£12.70). Large breakfast, internet access. Very popular and central.

Kabul, pl. Reial 17 (tel. 318 5190). €15 (£10) per night. Laundry facilities. No curfew. Metro: Drassanes or bus 14 or 18. 24-hour opening. Cannot be booked in advance.

Home, Calle d'Hedila 58 (tel. 427 2479, *www.likeathome.net, home@likeathome.net*). 10 minutes out of town, but one of the best hostels in Spain. Beds from €15 (£10). Internet access, breakfast. Book in advance.

CAMPING

Cala-Gogo-El Prat (tel. 379 4600). Open mid-March–mid-Oct. By the beach in Prat de Llobregat, 8 km from the city. Take bus 605 from Plaça de Espanya to the terminus in Prat, then change to bus 604 to the beach.

La Ballena Alegre (tel. 902 500 256, *www.ballena-alegre.es, ballena1@ballena-alegre.es*). Take bus L95 from the corner of Ronda de la Universitat and Rambla de Catalunya.

Filipinas (tel. 658 2895). Open year round. Also in Vildecans. Buses as above.

Masnou, Canetra N-11 (tel. 555 1503). Near Masnou train station.

Madrid (0)91

TOURIST OFFICES

Información Turistica Oficina Nacional. Various locations. The main office is at Calle del Duque de Medinaceli 2 (tel. 429 4951). Open Mon.–Fri. 9am–7pm, Sat. 9am–1pm. Branch offices operate in the Chamartin train station (tel. 315 9976), near the international arrivals desk at Barajas airport (tel. 305 8656) and at Ronda de Toledo 1 (tel. 364 1876) in the Centro Comercial de la Puerta de Toledo.

Municipal Tourist Office, Plaza Mayor 3 (tel. 366 5477). Metro: Sol. Along Calle Mayor from Puerto del Sol. The office is open Mon.–Fri. 10am–8pm, Sat. 10am–2pm. Great for city and transport maps.

Oficinas de Información, Calle Princesa 1 (tel. 541 2325).

There is also a youth Tourist Information Office in the underground station at Puerta del Sol.

Also see *www.gomadrid.com* and *www.madridtourism.org*.

None of the offices will book rooms, though they will offer advice on accommodation. A private agency called Brujula (see below) will book rooms (office in the underground bus terminal at Plaza de Colón. Metro: Colón).

TROUBLE SPOTS

While Fuencarral and Hortaleza are safe places to stay, you should be wary of the nearby Chuecca quarter (right of Hortaleza as you walk up from Gran Vía). This area, around Plaza de Chuecca including Reina, Utas, San Marcos and the streets in between, is the hard drugs centre of Madrid. Although there is plenty of cheap accommodation in this area (including some listed below), this part of town should be a last resort if you are looking for somewhere to stay.

FINDING ACCOMMODATION

Madrid has a more than adequate supply of cheap rooms, even in summer. The hotels section below offers numerous possibilities which you can telephone or email to see if they have rooms available. If you would prefer simply to head off in search of a room, some areas are particularly good to look in. Gran Vía, the main thoroughfare, has an excellent supply of rooms, but prices are generally higher than elsewhere in the city. Prices are noticeably lower in the streets leading off Gran Vía. Among these Hortaleza and Fuencarral (metro: Gran Vía) and San Bernardo (metro: Noviciado) are especially well supplied with cheap places to stay. The cheapest part of town to stay in is between the Atocha train station and Puerta del Sol. Some of the cheapest establishments around Puerta del Sol are used by prostitutes, which, although the hotels are usually safe enough, hardly makes for a peaceful night. Whichever way you set about looking for a room, read the section on Trouble Spots, above, before you begin.

ACCOMMODATION AGENCY

Viajes Brújula, Torre de Madrid 14, 6th floor (tel. 559 9704). Metro: Plaza España. For a small fee, this office will book accommodation for you. You must go in person and pay a deposit. Open Mon.–Fri. 9am–7pm. There are branch offices at Estacion Atocha (tel. 539 1173), Estacion Charmartin (tel. 315 7894), the AVE terminal and the airport bus terminal (tel. 575 9680).

HOTELS AND PENSIONS

DOUBLES €25–35 (£16.50–23)

Prim, Prim 15 (tel. 521 5495). Metro: Colon.

Victoria, Calle Carretas 7 (tel. 522 9982). Breakfast included. Metro: Sol.

Alonso, Espoz y Mina 17 (tel. 531 5679). Very cheap, excellent location.

Hostal las Murallas, C. Fuencarral 23 (tel. 532 103, *www.hostal murallas.com*, *hostalmurallas@hostalmurallas.com*).

Residencia Abril, C. Fuencarral 39, 4th floor (tel. 531 5338). Metro: Tribunal (closest) or Gran Vía. Fuencarral is off Gran Vía.

Hostal Medieval, C. Fuencarral 56 (tel. 522 2549). Central.

Hostal Villar, C. Principe 18 (tel. 531 6600, *www.villar.arrakis.es*, *hvillar@arrakis.es*). Metro: Sol.

Paz, C. Flora 4 (tel. 547 3047). Very good. Metro: Opera.

Margarita, Gran Vía 50, 5th floor (tel. 547 3549). Metro: Callao. Doubles around €30 (£20). Reserve.

Conchita, Preciados 33 (tel. 522 4923). Metro: Callao or Sol (near the El Corte Inglés department store) to Plaza de Callao (off Gran Vía).

López, Calle de las Huertas 54 (tel. 429 4349, *hostel@ eresmas.net*). Breakfast included.

DOUBLES €35–45 (£23–30)

Mollo, Atocha 104 (tel. 528 7176). Near the train station.

Aguilar, C. San Jeronimo 32 (tel. 429 5926, *www.hostal aguilar.com*). Metro: Sol.

Mondragón, Carrera San Jerónimo 32, 4th floor (tel. 429 6816). **Hostal León** (tel. 429 6778) is in the same building.

La Montaña, Juan Alvarez Mendizábal 44 (tel. 547 1088). Close to the youth hostel (follow the directions below and then, from the hostel, cross Calle Princesa, turn left, go right on Calle Rey Francisco, then left on to Calle J.A. Mendizábal).

Vetusta, Calle de las Huertas 3 (tel. 429 6404). Breakfast included.

Hostal Castilla, C. Santa Teresa 9 (tel. 310 2176). Metro: Alonso Martinez.

Hostal Lauria, Gran Via 50 (tel. 541 9182). Breakfast included.

Sud-Americana, Paseo del Prado 12 (tel. 429 2564). Almost opposite the Prado. Cheap for what you get.

Riosol, Mayor 5 (tel. 532 3142). Just off Puerta del Sol towards Plaza Mayor.

Matute, Plaza de Matute 11 (tel. 429 5585). Central.

Riesco, Calle de Correo 2, 3rd floor (tel. 522 2692).

Hostal Triana, Carrer de la Salud 3 (tel. 532 6812, *www.hostal triana.com*, *triana@hostaltriana.com*).

Hostal Esparteros, Carrer Esparteros 12 (tel. 521 0903). Central.

Hostal Internacional, Carrer Echegaray (tel. 429 6209). Clean and new.

DOUBLES €50 (£33) AND OVER

Cruz Sol, Plaza Santa Cruz 6 (tel. 532 7197). Metro: Sol. No heating in winter.

Odesa, Calle de Hortaleza 38 (tel. 521 0338). The doubles all have private bath and TV. Popular gay hotel.

Hostal Santillan, Gran Via 64 (tel. 548 2328). Top floor. Friendly.

Hostal Valencia, Plaza Oriente 2 (tel. 559 8450). Central.

Hostal Cantabrico, Carrer de la Cruz 5 (tel. 531 0130). Central and very good value.

Hostal Madrid, Esparteros 6 (tel. 522 0600, *www.hostal-madrid.com*).

UNIVERSITY ACCOMMODATION

Available to those wishing to stay five days or more. Ask the Tourist Office for details.

HI HOSTELS

Calle Santa Cruz de Marcenado 28 (tel. 547 4532). B&B around €12 (£8). Metro: Arguelles. Bus 1, 61 and Circular. Open all year.

'Richard Schirrmann', Casa de Campo (tel. 463 5699). B&B from €13 (£8.60). A pleasant hostel, with a well-run lock-up at the reception. 1.30am curfew and far from the centre if you miss the last metro. Set in a large park within easy walking distance of the Lago and Batan metro stops. From Lago the shortest route is to turn left on leaving the station and follow the dirt track along the side of the wire fence. Take bus 33 from Plaza Opera. Open all year.

HOSTELS

Barbieri International Youth Hostel, Calle Barbieri 15 (tel. 531 0258, *www.barbierihostel.com*). Dorms from €15 (£10). Central and very popular.

Los Amigos Hostel, Campomanes 6, 4th floor (tel. 547 1707, *www.losamigoshostel.com, losamigoshostel@yahoo.com*). Dorms from €15 (£10). Near Plaza Mayor. Popular and well run.

CAMPING

Osuna, Avda de Logroño (tel. 741 0510). €5 (£3.30) per tent and per person. About 16 km out of the city beside the Ajalvir to Vicalvaro road. Near the airport. Metro 5 to Canillejas, then bus 105.

Madrid, Iglesia de los Dominicos (tel. 302 2835). Slightly cheaper than Osuna. Good facilities including swimming pool. Located just off the N-11, the main road to Barcelona. Metro to Plaza de Castilla, followed by bus 129 or 151.

Málaga (0)95

TOURIST INFORMATION

Oficinas Municipales de Turismo. There's an office at Av. Cervantes 1 (tel. 213 4734, *www.malagaturismo.com*) and a kiosk in front of the post office on Av. Andalucía. Open Mon.–Fri. 8.15am–2.45pm and 4.30pm–7pm, Sat. 9.30am–1.30pm.

BASIC DIRECTIONS

The main bus and train stations are close to each other on the opposite side of the Guadalmedina river from the historic centre of the city. From Málaga Principal (the main train station) head left from the exit until you reach Paseo de los Tilos. The bus station is a short walk up this street to your left. Bus 3 links both stations to the centre. Otherwise it is a 15- to 20-minute walk.

FINDING ACCOMMODATION

The streets to the north of Alameda Principal (left as you come from the train station) are well supplied with cheap rooms but the quality of the establishments varies considerably, so make a point of checking rooms out before you agree to take them. As a rule, you get what you pay for, so it is probably best to go for a moderately priced room. Streets which are especially well endowed with cheap lodgings include Calle Martínez, Calle Bolsa and Calle San Augustín. Martínez runs between Puerta del Mar and Marqués de Larios. From Marqués de Larios you can turn right down J. Diaz into Bolsa, while San Augustín is reached by going round the cathedral.

TROUBLE SPOTS

Be aware that Málaga is a very large and poor city with high rates of unemployment and crime. It's one of the most dangerous in Spain and independent travellers can stand out as an easy target. If at all possible, leave your pack in the left luggage at the railway station while you look for a hotel, or even while you visit the Tourist Office. Sleeping rough in Málaga would be sheer madness.

HOTELS AND PENSIONS

DOUBLES FROM €30 (£20)

Córdoba, Bolsa 9–11 (tel. 221 4469). From Marqués de Larios turn right down J. Diaz into Bolsa. This hotel has nice rooms with antique furniture and clean shared bathrooms.

Pension Juanita, C. Alarcon Lujan (tel. 221 3586). Breakfast included.

Lis, Cordoba 7 (tel. 222 7300). Town centre.

Rosa, Calle Martinez 10 (tel. 221 2716).

Viena, Strachan 3 (tel. 222 4095). Right off Marqués de Larios.

Venecia, Alameda Principal 9 (tel. 221 3636). Town centre. Friendly and clean.

Hostal Magaña, Rio 11 (tel. 229 3218).

Avenida, Alameda Principal 5 (tel. 221 7729). Central location but noisy.

Las Americas, Cuarteles 66 (tel. 231 9374). Next to the bus station.

DOUBLES FROM €40 (£27)

Hotel Sur, Trinidad Grund 13 (tel. 222 4803, *hotelsur@hotmail.com*). Town centre.

Pedro, Pareo Maritimo La Carihuela 67 (tel. 238 5479). Breakfast included.

Andalucia, Alarcon Lujan 8 (tel. 221 1960).

Hostal Aurora, Muro de Puerta Nueva 1 (tel. 222 4004).

Acapulco, Explanada Estación, Edif. Terminal 3 (tel. 231 8988).

HI HOSTEL

Piaza Pio XII 6 (tel. 230 8500). Beds from around €12 (£8). About 700m from the railway station, or bus 18. Kitchen facilities available. Wheelchair accessible. Close to the beach.

Seville (Sevilla) (0)95

TOURIST OFFICES

Oficina de Turismo de la Junta de Andalucá, Avenida de la Constitución 21B (tel. 422 1404). Open Mon.–Sat. 9am–7pm, Sun. 10am–2pm. A good source of information on the city and the region. Well-informed and helpful staff. Centrally located. A branch office operates at San Pablo airport (tel. 444 9128).

Oficina Municipal de Turismo, Edificio Costurero de la Reina, Paseo de las Delicias 9 (tel. 423 4465). Friendly staff, but the office is less well stocked with pamphlets. On the edge of the Old City by the Guadalquivir river, a short distance from the Glorieta de los Marineros Voluntarios and the Puente del Generalismo.

Also see *www.sevilla5.com* and *www.sol.com*, for further information.

BASIC DIRECTIONS

All mainline trains stop at Estación de Santa Justa, about 30 minutes' walk from the Tourist Offices. The main bus station on Plaza de San Sebastián (just off Menéndez Pelayo) is much closer to the centre; about 10 minutes' walk from the Tourist Offices. From the bus station walk down on to Menéndez Pelayo and head left a short distance until you reach Plaza Don Juan de Austria. At this point you can head straight down to the Glorieta de los Marineros Voluntarios by following Avda del Cid and then Avda de Maria Luisa. Turning right from Plaza Don Juan de Austria you can walk down San Fernando to the Puerta de Jerez, from which the Tourist Office on Avda de la Constitución is just a minute's walk to the left. From the Santa Justa train station you can take bus 70 to the main bus station. The airport bus EA also picks up near Santa Justa and lets you off at Puerta de Jerez, but the service is less frequent than bus 70.

FINDING ACCOMMODATION

Only during Holy Week and around the time of the April Fair are you likely to have difficulty finding cheap accommodation in

Seville. At these times not only do large numbers of visitors converge on the city, but room prices can be raised quite legally, sometimes by as much as 70–100%. Otherwise, even during July and August, there are enough cheap beds to go round. The area around the old Plaza de Armas station on the western fringe of the Old City has a large supply of cheap lodgings, especially San Eloy, which probably has more *fondas* and *casas de huespedes* than any other street in the city. In contrast, the streets around the new Santa Justa station are relatively bare of cheap lodgings, so it is no longer really possible to find a cheap bed within 10–15 minutes of getting off the train. The other area with a good supply of relatively cheap lodgings is the Barrio Santa Cruz, in the heart of the Old City around the Giralda. Although rooms here are slightly more expensive than around the old train station, their location cannot be matched and they are now easier to reach from the main train station.

HOTELS AND PENSIONS

Prices given below are what you can expect to pay in the height of summer; many establishments reduce their rates at other times.

Goya, Mateos Gago 31 (tel. 421 1170). Off the cathedral. Cheapest doubles around €50 (£33).

Capitol, Zaragoza 66 (tel. 421 2441). Just off Plaza Nueva. The rooms vary in price.

Archeros, C. Archeros 23 (tel. 441 8465). Doubles around €40 (£27).

Hotel Madrid, C. San Pedro Martir (tel. 421 4306). Doubles from €50 (£33). Clean and friendly.

Gala, C. Gravina 52 (tel. 421 4503). Doubles around €50 (£33).

San Esteban, Calle San Esteban 8 (tel. 422 2549, *sanesteban@andalunet.com*). Doubles from €30 (£20).

Galatea, C. San Juan de la Palma 4 (tel. 456 3564). Near the Iglesia de San Pedro.

Alfalfa, C. Huelva 34 (tel 620 94 8017, *alfalfa@andalunet.com*). Good views. Doubles from €30 (£20).

Monreal, C. Rodrigo Caro 8 (tel. 421 4166). Central. Doubles around €40 (£27).

Nevada, C. Gamazo 28 (tel. 422 5340, *hostalnevada@telefonica.net*). Doubles from €42 (£28).

Lis I, Escarpin 10 (tel. 421 3088). In the very centre. Around €45 (£30) a double.

Lis II, Olavide 5 (tel. 456 0228). €35 (£23) a double. Lovely house.

Dona Feli, C. Jesus del Gran Poder 130 (tel. 4901 048). Doubles from €40 (£27).

Gravina, Gravina 46 (tel. 421 6414). Doubles from €40 (£27).

El Buen Dormir, C. Farnesio 8 (tel. 421 7492). Doubles from €50 (£33).

Bienvenido, Calle de los Archeros 14 (tel. 441 3655). Doubles around €40 (£27).

Fabiola, Calle de Fabiola 16 (tel. 421 8346). Doubles from €35 (£23).

Plaza Sevilla, C. Canalejas 2 (tel. 421 7149). Centre. Doubles from €40 (£27).

Hotel Duque, Calle de Trajano 15 (tel. 438 7011). Doubles from €35 (£23).

Paris, Calle san Pedro Mártir 14 (tel. 422 9861). Off Calle Gravina. Rooms have bath, A/C, TV and phone. One of the best places to stay in town and it's affordable. Doubles from €50 (£33); it's worth asking about student discounts.

HI HOSTEL

Sevilla, Isaac Peral 2 (tel. 505 6500). Beds from €10 (£6.70). Non-members can stay for an extra €3 (£2) per night. Bus 6 or 34 from Plaza Nueva. Reservation required. Wheelchair accessible.

CAMPING

Buses to the three sites below depart from the main bus station on Plaza de San Sebastián.

Sevilla (tel. 451 4379). Around €3 (£2) per tent and per person. Grade 2 site, open all year. Swimming pool, supermarket and hot showers. About 12 km out on the road to Madrid (near the airport). There's a site shuttle bus which runs daily, apart from on Sun. Alternatively, catch bus 70 which stops near the site.

Villsom (tel. 472 0828). €4 (£2.70) per tent and per person. Grade 2 site, open year round. In Dos Hermanas, 18 km out on the road to Cádiz. The Los Amarillos bus runs about every 45 minutes 6.30am–12am.

Club de Campo, Avda de la Liberdad 13 (tel. 472 0250). Around €4 (£2.70) per tent and per person. Swimming pool. 10 km out on the road to Dos Hermanas. Same bus as for Villsom above. Grade 1 site, open year round.

SWEDEN (SVERIGE) (00)46

BACKGROUND

Sweden emerged as a fully independent nation in 1523 when Gustav Vasa defeated the Danes, thus breaking up the Danish-dominated Union of Kalmar – originally a Scandinavian alliance to resist Germanic influence. The country's influence grew significantly in the 17th century when under King Gustavus Adolphus it became the dominant power in the Baltic region. The cost of successive wars to defend its pre-eminence eventually proved too much and since the 1800s, Sweden has been a neutral country.

Today, Sweden is known primarily for its automobile industry (Volvo and Saab), generous welfare provision, and cultural figures such as Alfred Nobel, Ingmar Bergman, Greta Garbo and the squeaky-clean 70s pop foursome ABBA. The countryside, especially the north, is exceptionally beautiful and is well suited to those who enjoy outdoor pursuits.

More than a century of sustained peace in Sweden has created one of the world's highest standards of living. The drawback of this is that Sweden, like the rest of Scandinavia, is notoriously expensive for the budget traveller. You will certainly need a lot of 'Money, Money, Money'.

ACCOMMODATION DETAILS

As with the other Scandinavian countries, the best advice to the budget traveller in Sweden is to prepare for hostelling and camping. The currency is the Swedish krona (kr) and £1 is approximately 13 kr ($1 is roughly 7 kr). While many **hotels** cut their prices substantially during the summer, even this, unfortunately, does not bring them into our accommodation price range, as you can still expect to pay from 340 kr (£26; $44) for singles and 560 kr (£43; $73) for doubles. However, Stockholm, Gothenburg and Malmö do offer cut-price packages which include a hotel room, free entry to the main attractions in the city and free local transport – plus an optional reduced return rail ticket. Visit the city Tourist Offices for more information. Tourist Offices will also book **private rooms** for you where these are available, costing around 260 kr (£20; $34) for singles, 330 kr (£25; $42) in doubles or larger rooms. In villages and small towns look out for the *Rum* sign, because approaching the owner directly will save you paying the booking fee charged by the Tourist Offices.

Most towns that you are likely to visit will have an **HI hostel**. Of the 280 HI hostels (*vandrarhem*) in Sweden, about 130 stay open all year round, while others open only during the main tourist season (June to late August). Most are located in the southern and central regions. Prices vary from 80 to 150 kr (£6–11.50; $10–19.50) according to location and standard. Non-members are charged an extra 50 kr (£3.80; $6.50) per night, though International Guest Cards can be bought at most hostels. Outside the main towns superior-grade hostels are very popular with families, so no matter where you are heading, it makes sense to book a bed in advance. If you expect to arrive after 6pm you should inform the hostel, otherwise your reservation will not be held beyond that time. In university towns, it is often possible to find a bed in a student hostel during the summer. The local Tourist Office will advise you.

Almost every town or village of any size has a **campsite** and quite often you will have a choice. There are some 750 sites officially approved and classified by the Swedish Camping Association, rated from one star up to five stars. A one-star site has everything you would expect, while five-star sites tend to offer a whole range of facilities you will use rarely, if at all. Most sites operate with all their facilities between June and September, while in those which are also open in April and May, certain supplementary facilities may not be available. The Tourist Office boasts that the overnight charge for a family is one of the lowest in Europe, and this is hard to refute. But, as the fee for a tent is the relatively high 50–100 kr (£3.80–7.60; $6.50–12.50), and some sites also make a nominal charge per person, this means that solo travellers do not benefit from the pricing system, whereas three or four people sharing a tent certainly do. There are very few sites at which a camping pass is not required, so unless you have an International Camping Carnet you will be obliged to buy a Swedish camping pass at the first site you visit. This costs 50 kr (£3.80; $6.50) and is valid for the rest of the camping season. For a free card, apply at least one month before your journey to Sveriges Campingvardars Riksförbund, Box 255, 45117 Uddevalla (fax 0522 64 2430).

There are also 4,500 **cabins** for rent, spread over 350 sites. Cabins sleep between two and six people, are usually equipped with a kitchen and their overnight charges vary from 80 to 110 kr (£6–8.50; $10–14.50) per person.

Under the ancient law of Allemannsrätt it is possible to **camp for free**, with certain restrictions. It is permissible to erect a tent for a day and a night on land that is not used for farming, providing you are some distance from habitation. You must obtain the consent of the landowner before pitching your tent near any dwelling place or if you are camping in a group. Avoid lighting any potentially dangerous fires, and make sure you leave no rubbish behind on your departure. In more sparsely populated areas, such as the mountains, it is perfectly acceptable to stay longer than a day and a night. As with neighbouring Norway, the two problems facing campers are the cold nights and mosquitoes, so prepare yourself accordingly.

The Swedish YHA operates two other types of accommodation in the mountains. **Mountain centres** can be expensive, with the cost of a bed 80–350 kr (£6–27; $10–46). **Mountain huts**, however, offer beds for around 100 kr (£7.60; $12.50), in areas where any accommodation can be hard to find. These huts are normally sited far from either roads or railways, so they are likely to appeal only to those planning on doing some hiking.

ADDRESSES

SWEDISH TRAVEL AND TOURISM COUNCIL
11 Montagu Place, London W1H 2AL (tel. 020 7870 5600, *www.visit-sweden.com*, *info@swetourism.org.uk*).

CAMPING
See the tourist information website listed above for details of campsites nationwide. They are associated with the Swedish Campsite Owners Association, and carry all their listings. Also see *www.camping.se* for further lists.

SWEDISH YHA
Svenska Turistföreningen (STF), Box 25, S-101 20 Stockholm (tel. (0)8 463 2100, *www.stfturist.se*, *info@stfturist.se*).

MOUNTAIN HUTS AND MOUNTAIN CENTRES
Contact the Swedish YHA Information Office.

Stockholm (0)8

TOURIST OFFICES

Stockholm Information Service, Hamngatan 27 (tel. 789 2490, *www.stockholmtown.com*). Open mid-June–late Aug., Mon.–Fri. 8.30am–6pm, weekends 8.30am–5pm; rest of the year, Mon.–Fri. 9am–5pm, weekends 9am–2pm. In the Sverigehuset in the Kungsträdgården on Hamngatan. T-bana (underground): Kungsträdgården.

ACCOMMODATION AGENCIES

From June to August, finding somewhere reasonably cheap to stay in Stockholm can be difficult. If you have not booked ahead consider using the services of the Tourist Offices for a hostel bed. The charge for this service is 15 kr (£1.10; $1.80). The Tourist Offices will also find you a hotel room for about 40 kr (£3; $5), but this option needs to be avoided as even the cheapest hotels are outside the budget-travel category.

Hotellcentralen (tel. 289 2425). In Stockholm Central train station on the lower floor. Open June–Aug., daily 8am–9pm; May and Sept., 9am–7pm; at other times 9am–5pm. 15 kr (£1.10; $1.80) charged for booking a hostel and 40 kr (£3; $5) fee for booking a hotel.

Hotelljänst, Vasagatan 15–17 (tel. 104437, *www.hotelltjanst.com*). Open Mon.–Fri. 9am–5pm. Accommodation found free of charge, provided you stay at least two days. Close to Central station.

HOTELS

Many hotels lower their prices in summer. At other times, prices can be much higher.

CHEAPEST DOUBLES AROUND 400 KR (£31; $53)

Tre Små Rum, Högbergsgatan 81 (tel. 641 2371, *www.tresma rum.se*, *info@tresmarum.se*). In the Södermalm area, close to the Old Town.

Good Night Hotel Danielsson, Vastmanngatan 5 (tel. 411 1065). Near the train station.

CHEAPEST DOUBLES FROM 550 KR (£42; $71)

Bed and Office Hotel, Vretenborgsvagen 14 (tel. 196100). Clean and comfortable.

Haverdorals Hotell, Edebovagen 9 (tel. 0175 22425). Popular and good value.

Hotell Ostermalm, Karlavagen 57 (tel. 660 6996). Small and friendly.

PRIVATE ROOMS

Book at either of the Tourist Offices, or one of the Accommodation Agencies listed above. Expect to pay around 450 kr (£34.50; $50) for a double in and around Stockholm. Hotelltjänst will find you a double from 500 kr (£38; $64.50).

HI HOSTELS

Långholmen, Gamla Kronohäktet (tel. 668 0510, *www.langholmen .com*, *vandrarhem@langholmen.com*).This hostel is the former prison on Långholmen Island. Dorm beds around 150 kr (£11.50; $19.50). There are also expensive hotel rooms: doubles 800 kr (£61; $104). T-bana: Hornstull. There is also a ferry service from Stadshubron to Långholmen during the summer. Booking essential. Open all year.

Zinkensdamm, Zinkensväg 20 (tel. 616 8100, *www.zinkensdamm .com*, *mail@zinkensdamm.com*). Open all year. No curfew, Breakfast available. T-bana: Zinkensdamm, then right on to Hornsgatan. Follow the street to no. 103, then go left down the steps at the hostel sign.

Chapman/Skeppsholmens Vandrarhem (tel. 463 2266, *info@chapman.stfturist.se*). Open all year. This is the popular boat hostel. Bunks from 130 kr (£10; $17), breakfast extra. Beside the boat hostel, on dry land is the Skeppsholmen hostel which has the same reception and charges the same prices. Bus 65 from T-Centralen.

Backpackers' Inn, Banergatan (tel. 660 7515, *backpackersinn@ telia.com*). T-bana: Karlaplan. Open June to Aug. only. 100 kr (£7.60; $12.50) for members, more for non-members.

Jakobsberg, Kaptensvagen 7 (tel. 445 7270, *vandrarhemmet* *.majorskan@swipnet.se*). Beds from 180 kr (£15, $23). Closed January.

HOSTELS

Hostel Bed and Breakfast, Rehnsgatan 21 (tel. 152838, *www.hostelbedandbreakfast.com*, *hostelbedandbreakfast@chello.se*). Town centre. Open all year.

Hostel Mitt i City, Västmannagatan 13 (tel. 217630, *www.stores.se/hostal.htm*). A pleasant Swedish-Japanese hostel. Short walk from the Central station. Open all year. No curfew. Beds from 140 kr (£11; $19).

Columbus Hotell-Vandrarhjem, Tjarhovsgatan 11 (tel. 503 11200, *columbus@columbus.se*). 130 kr (£10; $17). No curfew and 24hr reception. 2- to 6-bedded rooms. T-bana: Medborgarplatsen.

Brygghusest, Nortullsgatan 12N (tel. 312424). Open June–Sept. In a converted brewery. Nice, quiet hostel.

Gustaf af Klint, Sladsgårdskajen 153 (tel. 640 4077). Dorm beds from 100 kr (£7.60; $12.50). Beds in two-berth cabins from 150 kr (£11.50; $19.50). In an old navy ship. 24hr reception. T-bana: Odenplan.

City Backpackers' Hostel, Upplandsgatan 2 (tel. 206920, *www.citybackpackers.se*, *info@citybackpackers.se*). 150 kr (£11.50; $19.50) p.p. per night. Near the Old Town and the train station. Open all year. Well-equipped hostel with sauna, kitchen and laundry.

Red Boat Malaren, Soder Malarstrand, Kajplats 6 (tel. 644 4385, *www.theredboat.com*, *info@theredboat.com*). In a boat in the centre of town. Popular and very good, so book in advance. Open all year.

CAMPING

Ostermalms Citycamping, Fiskartorpsvagen 32 (tel. 411 7020). Open June–Aug. 1 mile from the town centre.

Bredäng, Stora Sallska, Sallskapetsveg (tel. 977071). Open all year. Expensive. About 10 km south on Lake Mälaren. There's also a youth hostel and restaurant on site. T-bana: Bredäng (line 13 or 15). 10-minute walk signposted from the station.

Ångby, Blackebergsvagen 24, Bromma (tel. 370420). Open June–Aug. On Lake Mälaren. T-bana: Angbyplan (line 18 or 19).

Flatenbadens Camping, Flatenvagen, Skarpnack (tel. 773 0100). Open May–Sept. Bus 401 from Slussen.

Klubbensborg (tel. 646 1255). On a small peninsula on Lake Mälaren. There is a youth hostel, cafe and bakery on site. T-bana: Mälarhöjden (line 13 and 18) and then a 10-minute walk. Open June–Sept.

SWITZERLAND (HELVETIA) (00)41

This land-locked nation is a land of contrasts: four different languages (French, German, Italian and Romansch); clean, efficient cities; stunning Alpine scenery; a neutral country with an army of half a million.

BACKGROUND

Central referendums on a variety of issues are common and outdoor public votes still take place in rural areas. The Swiss central government in Berne, therefore, has little power domestically and deals primarily with international affairs.

Today, Switzerland is known for its secretive banking system and its watch-making industry. On a per capita basis, it remains the world's richest country, with the Swiss franc (Sfr) one of the strongest currencies (£1 is approximately 2.4 Sfr; $1 is roughly 1.2 Sfr.). This makes Switzerland one of Europe's most expensive destinations, but a visit there is certainly worth the investment. There is virtually no unemployment or crime and everyone is always on time. In addition, the Swiss people themselves are friendly and their knowledge of languages makes it easy for them to help you. If your idea of heaven is cleanliness, efficiency and beauty, you would have to be cuckoo not to love Switzerland.

ACCOMMODATION DETAILS

Despite being widely regarded as one of the most expensive countries in Europe, it is quite possible both to eat well and to sleep cheaply in Switzerland. **Hotels** are likely to be outside your budget and probably only to be considered in emergencies. Even the very cheapest hotels cost from 55 Sfr (£23; $39) in singles, 85 Sfr (£35; $59.50) in doubles. In country areas, **B&Bs** or **private rooms** can be more reasonable but, in the main, your choice is between hostelling or camping. In some ways, this is quite lucky because both of these give you the opportunity of meeting other travellers and also vastly increase your chances of meeting young Swiss holidaymakers. In a country where the cost of a night out can limit your visits to pubs and clubs, these opportunities to make friends can be invaluable.

There are about 75 **HI hostels**, the vast majority of which are open to members only. However, hostels in the larger towns may admit non-members (not Lucerne). If this is the case it is compulsory to pay a 'guest fee' of 6 Sfr (£2.50; $4.60); six of these guest fees add up to a full international membership card – or you could buy a membership card for 33 Sfr (£13.75; $24). In the main towns, hostels are open all year, except perhaps for a couple of weeks around Christmas and the New Year. Elsewhere, hostels shut for differing periods at no specific time of the year. In the larger cities a midnight or 1am curfew is normal in summer, but you can expect a 10pm closing time at the others. Prices vary according to the grading: the top-rated ones cost up to 45 Sfr (£18; $30), mid-range hostels up to 35 Sfr (£14.50; $24.50), and the lower grade up to 20 Sfr (£8; $13.50). Many do, though, offer a reduction of around 3 Sfr (£1.25; $2) for the second night. The average you should expect to pay in a hostel is 25 Sfr (£10; $17) per night. Facilities in the lower-grade hostels tend to be quite basic, but are perfectly adequate. In the top-rated hostels you will have no access to kitchen facilities, though these are available in many of the lesser-rated establishments. Breakfast is usually included in the price. Except in the main towns, where a three-night maximum stay operates in summer, there is no limit to how long you can stay. During the summer it is advisable to reserve hostels in the larger towns, either by letter, phone or fax. You can also make email bookings through the Swiss Youth Hostel Association (SJH). If you find a hostel full, you might consider staying in one in a nearby town if you have a railcard, rather than having to pay for a hotel. In summer, some **student dorms** are converted into hostel accommodation, with beds going for anything from 20–35 Sfr (£8–14.50; $13.50–24). You don't have to be a student to use these dorms. An excellent leaflet, *Student Lodgings in University Cities*, is available from the SNTO (address below).

There is no shortage of **campsites**; around 1,200 in all. Unfortunately, there are three camping organisations, which makes advance planning slightly more complicated. Swiss campsites rank among the best Europe has to offer, being particularly clean and well run. Prices can vary quite substantially, starting at around 7 Sfr (£2.80; $4.50) per person plus 3–10 Sfr (£1.25–4; $2–7) per tent, but rising to 15 Sfr (£6; $10) per tent and 9 Sfr (£3.65; $6.50) per person charged at one site in Interlaken. One drawback to camping is that some of the large towns, such as Berne, have no central or easily reached site. In other places, however, you may have a choice. Some campsites also offer dormitory accommodation.

Tourist Offices will also have information on whether you can **camp rough** in the area. Most cantons allow freelance camping on uncultivated land, but the permission of the landowner is required on privately owned land. Camping in public places or along the roadside is expressly forbidden. Whether you camp or sleep rough, a good quality sleeping bag is recommended as it gets very cold at night, even in summer, and especially in the more mountainous areas. Hikers and climbers might wish to take advantage of the chain of **mountain refuges** run by the Swiss Alpine Club.

ADDRESSES

SWISS NATIONAL TOURIST OFFICE (SNTO)
Swiss Centre, 10 Wardour Street, London (tel. freephone 0800 100 20031, *www.switzerlandtourism.ch*).

HOTELS
Swiss Hotels Association, Montbijoustraße 130, CH-3001 Bern (tel. 031 370 4111, *www.swisshotels.ch* – not in English).

E&G Swiss Budget Hotels, Route des Layeux, case Postale 160, Villars (tel. (0)848 805 508, *www.rooms.ch*, *info@rooms.ch*).

B&B
Visit *www.bnb.ch*, or email *info@bnb.ch* for full listings and booking facilities throughout the country.

SWISS YHA
Schweizerischer Bund für Jugendherbergen, Schaffhauserstraße 14, Zurich (tel. (0)1360 1414, *www.youthhostel.ch*, *marketing@ youthhostel.ch*).

CAMPING
Visit the excellent *www.swisscamps.ch* for a fully searchable database of all kinds of campsites.

Schweizerischer Camping und Caravanning-Verband, Postfach, Basel (tel. (0)61 302 2626, *www.sccv.ch* – not in English).

MOUNTAIN HUTS

Schweizer Alpine Club (SAC), Montbijoustraße 61, Bern (tel. (0)31 370 1818, *www.sac-cas.ch* – not in English, *info@sac-cas.ch*).

Geneva (Genève) (0)22

TOURIST OFFICES

Office du Tourisme de Genève, Rue du Mont-Blanc 18 (tel. 909 7000, *www.geneve-tourisme.ch*). One minute from the Mont-Blanc bus station. Open 9am to 6pm Mon.–Fri. (Open daily July to mid-Sept.) Will book accommodation for a small fee.

Office du Tourisme de Genève, Pont de la Machine 1 (tel. 311 9827). Open Mon. 1–6pm, Tues.–Fri. 9am–6pm, Sat. 10am–5pm. Closed Sundays.

ARRIVING BY TRAIN

The main train station in Geneva is the Gare de Cornavin, which receives trains from Spain, Italy, Nice and Paris, as well as from all over Switzerland. Coming from Chamonix or Annecy (via La Roche-sur-Foron) you arrive at the Gare des Eaux-Vives. There is no connecting train service between the stations, but you can easily get between them by bus. The simplest way to get from Eaux-Vives to Cornavin is to walk down av. de la Gare, turn right down Route de Chêne, then right again at av. Pictet-de-Rochemont which leads into pl. des Eaux-Vives, from which you can take bus 9 to Cornavin. Alternatively, walk left a short distance up Route de Chêne to the bus stop, then take bus 12 to pl. Bel-Air, from which you can take bus 1, 4 or 5 to Cornavin. If you fly into Cointrin Airport there are trains about every six minutes to Cornavin (railpasses valid).

BASIC DIRECTIONS

From pl. de Cornavin in front of the train station rue des Alpes runs from the left-hand end of the square down to Lake Geneva (Lac Léman). At the right-hand end of the square rue du Mont-Blanc leads to the Pont du Mont-Blanc which crosses the River

Rhône just as it flows out of the lake. Going straight ahead you arrive at pl. du Port from which pl. Longmalle and then rue de la Fontaine lead into the picturesque pl. du Bourg-de-Four, in the heart of the Old Town, beneath the cathedral. The walk from Cornavin to pl. du Bourg-de-Four takes 10–15 minutes.

HOTELS

If you want a hotel room but cannot afford the prices quoted below, those with railpasses can stay in the French town of Bellegarde, a half-hour train trip from Cornavin.

CHEAPEST DOUBLES AROUND 75 SFR (£29; $49)

Centre St Boniface, av. du Mail 14 (tel. 322 2600, *www.cstb.ch*, *acceuil@cstb.ch*). Bus 1, 4 or 44 from Cornavin to place du Cirque, or tram 1c3 or a 20-minute walk from the station. Right from Cornavin along blvd James-Fazy to the Rhône. Cross the river and go straight on, along blvd Georges-Favon to place du Cirque, then right on the other side of the square down av. du Mail. Doubles around 65 Sfr (£27; $46) (mid-July to late Sept.).

Jean-Jacques Rousseau, rue Rousseau 13 (tel. 731 5570). Right in the centre of town. Basic but good value.

CHEAPEST DOUBLES AROUND 85 SFR (£32.50; $55)

Hôtel Luserna, av. Luserna 12 (tel. 345 4676). A 20-minute walk from Cornavin. Right down rue de la Servette, left at av. Wendt, right at av. Luserna. Buses 3, 10 and 15 from Cornavin stop at Servette École, just before av. Wendt.

Hôtel Beau Site, place du Cirque 3 (tel. 328 1008). Doubles from 80 Sfr (£33; $56), triples from 95 Sfr (£39.50; $67), quads from 107 Sfr (£44.50; $75.50). 10% student discount. Breakfast included. These rooms all have sink and radio. There are 6 rooms without sinks and these cost around 48 Sfr (£18.50; $31) per night. However, you'll be lucky to get one of these as they are usually occupied by long-term guests. Phone ahead. A 15-minute walk from Cornavin or bus 1, 4 or 44.

Hôtel du Lac, rue des Eaux-Vives 15 (tel. 735 4580). Slightly cheaper per person in triples. Bus 9 from Cornavin to pl. des Eaux-Vives, then a short walk along rue des Eaux-Vives. A 15-

to 20-minute walk from Cornavin. Left along quai Général Guisan after crossing the Pont du Mont-Blanc and straight on along rue Versonnex into pl. des Eaux-Vives.

Carmen, rue Dancet 5 (tel. 329 1111). Doubles without shower from 85 Sfr (£35; $60). Central.

Hôtel de la Cloche, rue de la Cloche 6 (tel. 732 9481). Singles for 55 Sfr (£23; $39), doubles from 85 Sfr (£35; $60). Breakfast extra. About 10 minutes' walk from Cornavin. Left off rue des Alpes along rue Philippe-Plantamour at place des Alpes, then right at rue Cloche. Always popular so call ahead.

Le Clos Voltaire, rue de Lyon 49 (tel. 344 7014). Beautiful old hotel.

Hôtel St-Gervais, rue des Corps-Saints 20 (tel. 732 4572). 5 minutes from Cornavin – a continuation of rue Cornavin, one block past Notre Dame church. Doubles around 80 Sfr (£33; $56). Breakfast included. Reserve if possible.

CHEAPEST DOUBLES AROUND 95 SFR (£39.50; $67)

Central, rue de la Rotisserie (tel. 818 8100). Very central, and very good value.

International et Terminus, rue des Alpes 20 (tel. 732 8095). Good value and location.

Le Prince, rue des Voisins 16 (tel. 807 0500, www.hotel-le-prince.ch). Town centre.

Rio, place Isaac Mercier 1 (tel. 732 3264, www.hotel-rio-geneve.ch, hotelrio@vtx.ch). This hotel is a few minutes' walk from Cornavin, right along blvd James-Fazy into pl. Isaac Mercier.

Bernina, place Cornavin 22 (tel. 908 4950, www.bernina-geneve.ch, info@bernina-geneve.ch). Doubles from 150 Sfr (£62.50; $106).

Des Tourelles, blvd James-Fazy 2 (tel. 732 4423). Great place, and excellent views.

HI HOSTEL

Auberge de Jeunesse, rue Rothschild 28–30 (tel. 732 6260, www.yh-geneva.ch, geneve@youthhostel.ch). Midnight curfew in summer, 11pm at other times. HI members pay 25 Sfr (£10; $17) in dorms, breakfast included. B&B from 60 Sfr (£25; $42) for doubles with shower and WC. Wheelchair accessible. Family rooms. About 10 minutes' walk from Cornavin, left out of the station along rue de Lausanne, then right. Or tram 1 to Palais Wilson stop. The hostel is closed 10am–5pm (4pm in summer) Open all year.

HOSTELS/FOYERS/STUDENT ACCOMMODATION

City Hostel, rue Ferrier 2 (tel. 901 1500, *www.cityhostel.ch*). Dorms from 25 Sfr (£10; $17). Central, friendly and very popular.

Hôme St-Pierre, cours St-Pierre 4 (tel. 310 3707, *www.home stpierre.ch*). Women only. Dorms start at around 25 Sfr (£10; $17), doubles 60 Sfr (£25; $42) and singles 42 Sfr (£16; $27). Breakfast included. No curfew. Excellent location by the cathedral. Very popular so ring ahead.

Cité Universitaire, av. Miremont 46 (tel. 839 2222, *cite-uni@unige.ch*). Good facilities: restaurant, disco, ping pong, tennis, shop, internet access. Dorms 20 Sfr (£8; $13.50) (there are only four dorms and they are only available July–Sept.), doubles start around 62 Sfr (£25.80; $43), singles around 48 Sfr (£18.50; $31) (prices are cheaper for students). Curfew 11pm for dorm residents only. From place de 22 Cantons by Cornavin station take bus 3 to the Crêts de Champel terminus.

Centre St Boniface, av. du Mail 14 (tel. 322 2600, *www.cstb.ch*, *acceuil@cstb.ch*). Dorm beds. See directions for Centre St Boniface, above.

Bureau Logements Université, rue de Candolle 4 (tel. 705 7720). Three-day minimum stay. See directions for Cité Universitaire hostel above.

Evangelische Stadtmission, rue Bergalonne 7 (tel. 321 2611). Dorms, triples, doubles and singles available. Curfew 11pm. Bus 1, 4 or 44 from Cornavin to École-Médecine (rue Bergalonne is to the rear of the Musée d'Ethnographie), or a 15- to 20-minute walk. Rue Bergalonne runs right off av. du Mail (see directions for Centre St Boniface, above.

Centre Masaryk, av. de la Paix 11 (tel. 733 0772). B&B in dorms 30 Sfr (£12.50; $21). Smaller rooms also available. 11pm curfew. Near the Palace of the United Nations. Bus 5 or 8 from Cornavin to the Nations terminus, or a 20-minute walk.

Foyer St-Justin, rue du Prieuré 15–17 (tel. 731 1135). A 5-minute walk from Cornavin, left along rue de Lausanne, then right.

Forget-Me-Not, rue Vignier 8 (tel. 320 9355). Dorms 27 Sfr (£11.25; $18), singles 57 Sfr (£22; $37) and doubles 87 Sfr (£36.25; $61). Breakfast and showers included. Great facilities: rooftop terrace, kitchen, laundry, TV/video room, phones, food and drink machines. No curfew.

Centre Universitaire Zofingien, rue des Voisins 6 (tel. 329 5113). Triples 105 Sfr (£41; $69), doubles 85 Sfr (£35; $59.50), singles 62 Sfr (£25.80; $43). Breakfast included. During the university year only.

CAMPING

Pointe-à-la-Bise, Chemin de la Bise (tel. 752 1296, *pointealabise@ swisscamps.ch*). 14 Sfr (£5.40; $9) for one person, two people 20 Sfr (£8; $13.50). No tents provided. Open Apr.–Oct. About 8 km out from the centre, close to Lake Geneva. From Cornavin take bus 9 to Rive, then change to bus E.

D'Hermance, rue de Nord 44 (tel. 751 1483). One person 10 Sfr (£4; $7), two people 18 Sfr (£7.25; $12.50). Open Apr.–Sept. About 14 km from the city centre, close to Lake Geneva. Bus 9 from Cornavin to Rive, then take bus E to the terminus.

Lucerne (Luzern) (0)41

TOURIST OFFICE

Tourist Information, Bahnhofstrasse 3 (tel. 227 1717, *www.luzern. org*). Open Mon.–Fri. 8am–6pm, Sat. and public holidays 9am–5pm.

HOTELS

Pension Panorama, Kapuzinerweg 9 (tel. 420 6701, *www.pensionpanorama.com*). Singles 50 Sfr (£19.25; $32), doubles 82 Sfr (£34; $58). Breakfast included. Near Old Town. Bus 5 or 7 takes you to the street. (For a small fee the owner will pick you up from the station.) Great views.

Hotel Pickwick, Rathuasquai 6 (tel. 410 5927, *www.hotel pickwick.ch, hotelpickwick@gastrag.ch*). Doubles from 82 Sfr (£34; $58).

Hotel Villa Maria, Haldenstraße 36 (tel. 370 2119, *villamaria@ bluewin.ch*). Doubles around 105 Sfr (£44; $75). Overlooks the lake. A 25-minute walk from the train station (follow the directions for Camping Lido, below), or take bus 2 to the stop near the Hotel Europe.

Linde, Metzgerrainle 3 (tel. 410 3193). Off Weinmarkt. Basic doubles for 90 Sfr (£37.50; $64) without breakfast. Rooms available from April to Oct. only. Note, there is no check-in on a Sunday.

Alpha (tel. 240 4280, *www.hotelalpha.ch*, *info@hotelalpha.ch*). At the corner of Pilatusstraße and Zahringerstraße 24. Doubles from 95 Sfr (£39.50; $67), breakfast included. Prices are slightly cheaper in winter.

HI HOSTEL

Am Rotsee, Sedelstraße 12 (tel. 420 8800, *luzerne@youth hostel.ch*). Dorm beds are 30 Sfr (£12.50; $21) with breakfast included. Doubles available for around 75 Sfr (£31; $53). 11.30pm curfew. Not central. A 30-minute walk from the train station. Bus 18 to Goplismoos/Friedental leaves you with a couple of minutes' walk. Last bus 7.30pm. The more frequent bus 1 to Schloßberg leaves you a 10-minute walk down Friedentalstraße. Reception opens 4pm, and 1-hour queues are not uncommon during the summer, with no guarantee of getting in. Open all year.

HOSTELS

Backpackers' Hostel, Alpenquai 42 (tel. 360 0420, *www.back packerslucerne.ch*). South-east of the station, 15-minute walk. Around 22 Sfr (£9.15; $15.25) p.p. in quads, 27 Sfr (£11.25; $19) per person in doubles. Breakfast extra. Great views of the lakes and mountains.

Tourist Hotel, Kaihquai 12 (tel. 410 8414, *www.touristhotel.ch*, *info@touristhotel.ch*). Both dorms and private rooms available. Good value but popular, so book in advance.

CAMPING

Lido, Lidostraße 8 (tel. 370 2146). From 3 Sfr (£1.25; $2) per tent, 8 Sfr (£3.50; $6) per person. Also dorm beds in bungalows available (nonreservable). Mini-golf, tennis and swimming nearby. Near the beach and the lake. A 35-minute walk from the train station, over the Seebrücke, then right along the lakeside. Bus 2 to Verkehrshaus. Site open mid-Mar.–Oct.

Howr (tel. 340 3558). Open Apr.–Sept. Bus 20 for a 20-minute trip to Horw Rank. Quiet campsite by a lake. 11 Sfr (£4.60; $7.50) per person and 6 Sfr (£2.50; $4) per tent. Showers included.

HI HOSTEL NEARBY

Allmendstraße 8, Sportstadion 'Herti', Zug (tel. (0)41 711 5354, *zug@youthhostel.ch*). 11.30pm curfew. There are frequent trains from Lucerne to the nearby town of Zug (*www.zug.ch*) where this hostel is located. The journey takes 30 minutes.

Zürich (0) I

TOURIST OFFICE

Offizielles Verkehrsbüro Zürich, Bahnhofplatz 15 (Hauptbahnhof) (tel. 215 4000, *www.zurichtourism.ch*). Just outside the train station. To book hotels call 215 4040, or email *hotel@ zuerich.com*.

Switzerland Tourism, Tödistraße 7 (tel. 288 1111). This office has information on the whole of Switzerland.

TROUBLE SPOTS

The city authorities once operated a controversial needle exchange in one of the city's parks. It has been claimed that this attracted drug users from all over the country (and even from Germany) to the city. In late 1991, the authorities halted the scheme and closed the park. The result was that addicts began to gather on the city's streets, particularly around the main train station. Although there have been no reports of violence around the station at the time of writing, the sight itself is harrowing (particularly as drugs are injected quite openly) and you are likely to be pestered for money.

HOTELS

St Josef, Hirschengraben 64–68 (tel. 251 2757, *www.st-josef.ch*, *info@st-josef.ch*). Singles 72 Sfr (£30; $51), doubles 105 Sfr (£45; $75). Breakfast included.

Justinus heim, Freudenbergstraße 146 (tel. 361 3806). Singles around 35 Sfr (£14.50; $24.50), doubles from 85 Sfr (£35; $60). Breakfast included. Open July–Oct. and Mar.–Apr. Few vacancies. Tram 9 or 10 to the junction of Winterthurerstraße and Langensteinerstraße, then bus 39 to Freudenbergerstraße. You can also catch bus 39 from the terminus of trams 5 and 6 near the zoo, though this is a longer journey.

Regina, Hohlstraße 18 (tel. 298 5555). Doubles from 130 Sfr (£54; $92). A 10-minute walk from Zürich Hbf. Diagonally right across Bahnhofplatz, along Gessnerallee, right over the Gessnerbrücke, left along the River Sihl, then right down Zeughausstraße.

St Georges, Weberstraße 11 (tel. 241 1144, *www.hotel-st-georges.ch*, *st-georges@bluewin.ch*). Doubles from 95 Sfr (£39.50; $67). Just over 10 minutes' walk from Zürich Hbf. Diagonally right across Bahnhofplatz, along Gessnerallee, right over Gessnerbrücke then left along the River Sihl until you see Webergasse on the right after the second bridge.

Splendid, Rosengasse 5 (tel. 252 5850, *www.hotelsplendid.ch*). Doubles from 95 Sfr (£39.50; $67). A 5-minute walk from Zürich Hbf. Cross the River Limmat by the Bahnhofsbrücke, then right along the Limmatquai until you see Rosengasse on the left after Mühlegasse.

Zic-Zac Rock Hotel, Marktgasse 17 (tel. 261 2181, *www.ziczac.ch*). In the Old Town. Doubles from 100 Sfr (£41.65; $71).

Goldenes Schwert, Marktgasse 14 (tel. 266 1818). Doubles for 160 Sfr (£66.50; $113) with bath. Gay-friendly hotel.

Seefeld, Seehofstraße 11 (tel. 387 4141, *www.hotel-seefeld.ch*, *info@hotel-seefeld.ch*). Tram 4 along Seefeldstraße until you see Seehofstraße on the right after the tram turns off Ramistraße along Theaterstraße, or a 15-minute walk from Zürich Hbf. Follow the directions for Hotel Hinterer Sternen, above, to Ramistraße, then turn right along Theaterstraße and keep going until you see Seehofstraße on the right.

HI HOSTEL

Mutschellenstraße 114, Zürich-Wollishofen (tel. 482 3544, *www.youthhostel.ch, zuerich@youthhostel.ch*). Dorm beds for around 29 Sfr (£12; $20), non-members pay more. There are also double rooms. Cheaper if you stay more than one night. Breakfast included. 1am curfew. Tram 7 to Morgental, then a well-signposted 5-minute walk. There is a local train station, Zürich-Wollishofen, if you have a railpass and want to save some money on transport. Wheelchair accessible. Open all year.

HOSTELS

City Backpacker, Niederdorfstraße 5 (tel. 251 9015, *www.city-backpacker.ch, sleep@city-backpacker.ch*). Dorm beds from 32 Sfr (£13.30; $22.50), private rooms from 65 Sfr (£27; $46). In the heart of the Old Town.

Hotel Martahaus, Zähringerstraße 36 (tel. 251 4550, *www.martahaus.ch, info@martahaus.ch*). Six-bed dorms from 33 Sfr (£13.75; $23.50). Doubles around 100 Sfr (£42; $71). A 5-minute walk from Zürich Hbf. Cross the River Limmat by Bahnhofsbrücke. Limmatquai runs away to the right along the river. Zähringerstraße runs parallel to the Limmatquai, two streets back from the river.

Foyer Hottingen, Hottingerstraße 31 (tel. 256 1919, *www.foyer-hottingen.ch, info@foyer-hottingen.ch*). Dorms 28 Sfr (£11.65; $19.50) (more expensive if you opt for a dorm with partitions). Doubles around 90 Sfr (£37.50; $64). Breakfast and kitchen access included. This one-star hostel is run by nuns. Only women can stay in the larger dorms but men can stay in the 3- and 4-bedded rooms. Tram 3 to Holtingerplatz from Bahnhofplatz.

CAMPING

'Seebucht', Seestraße 559, Zürich-Wollishofen (tel. 482 1612, *www.camping-zurich.ch*). 9 Sfr (£3.65; $6.50) per person, 12 Sfr (£5; $8.50) per tent. Showers extra. Shop, terrace and café on site. Open May–Sept. Excellent site on the Zürichsee. Local train to Zürich-Wollishofen, then a 10-minute walk. Alternatively, take bus 161 or 165 from Bürkliplatz.

HI HOSTELS NEARBY

Kanalstraße 7, Baden (tel. (0)56 221 6736, *baden@youth hostel.ch*). Open 16 Mar.–23 Dec. Frequent trains, a 30-minute trip.

Allmendstraße 8, Sportstadion 'Herti', Zug (tel. (0)41 711 5354, *zug@youthhostel.ch*). Frequent trains, a 45-minute trip. Wheelchair accessible.

Schloß Hegi, Hegifeldstraße 125, Winterthur (tel. (0)52 242 3840). Open Mar.–Oct. 20 minutes by train from Zürich. From Winterthur, take bus 1 to Oberwinterthur. Situated within a 15th-century castle.

TURKEY (Türkiye) (00)

BACKGROUND

Turkey borders Syria, Iran and Iraq, but its main rival is Greece. Poor relations between the countries hark back hundreds of years. They were brought to the fore again in 1998 over the ownership of Cyprus – the island Turkey invaded in 1974.

The Ottoman Empire dominates Turkish history. Its reign as one of the world's principal powers lasted 700 years. Its decline during the 18th and 19th centuries resulted in the British, French and Italians sharing control of Turkey after the latter's defeat in the First World War. However, during their disastrous campaign, Turkey produced a gem in General Mustafa Atatürk. It was under his leadership that Turkey regained its independence in 1923. Atatürk then began a process of modernisation, founding the modern Turkish republic and giving Turkish women the right to vote.

Present-day Turkey is a European nation, despite only 3% of it being in Europe. The rest lies in Asia. The Asian influence ensures that everything seems new for the first-time visitor, from the sights and the sounds to the people and their fascinating way of life. The people themselves are friendly and pride themselves on being polite. Some parts of Turkey, however, can be dangerous, and it is always worth checking with the Foreign Office before you go (*www.fco.gov.uk*).

ACCOMMODATION DETAILS

As a rule, budget travellers will seldom encounter any difficulty finding suitably priced accommodation in Turkey, with the notable exceptions of the coastal resorts and the capital at the height of the summer season. While Ankara is not really a tourist town (and is correspondingly short on budget accommodation), it seems to attract many travellers on the basis of its status as the national capital. Otherwise, it is usually quite simple to find a place to stay for about £7 ($12) per person along the Aegean coast, £6 ($10) along its Mediterranean counterpart, or from £5 ($8.50) per person in the very east of the country.

The Turkish currency is the lira and £1 is approximately 2,470,000 TL ($1 is 1,540,100 TL).

In any town with a reasonable tourist trade you will have the option of staying at one of the **hotels** which are registered with the Ministry of Tourism. These hotels are rated from one star up to five stars. Standards of cleanliness and comfort are rigorously enforced by the authorities. You can expect to pay from £10 to £19 ($17–32) for a double in a one-star hotel, rising to £12–22 ($20–37) in Istanbul. The cost of a double in a two-star hotel starts around £16 ($27), again being slightly higher in Istanbul.

Locally licensed hotels are usually a good bit cheaper than those registered with the Ministry of Tourism; expect to pay in the region of £3.25–6.25 ($5.50–10.50) per person in singles or doubles.

Alternative to hotel accommodation is a **guest house**, known as a *pansiyon* (or in ski resorts known as *oberj*). Guest houses, often small, family-run establishments providing good-value meals are plentiful throughout the country. A few are registered with the Ministry of Tourism. The standard of accommodation in these establishments is uniformly high. Doubles cost £10–19 ($17–32), depending on the facilities available. At other guest houses you can expect to pay from £5 ($8.50) per person in singles or doubles. As with locally licensed hotels, check rooms at unregistered guest houses before making a firm acceptance.

Another cheap accommodation option is **private rooms**, though these are much less common than guest houses. Look out for the sign *Oda Var* indicating rooms are available (sometimes also advertised in German: *Zimmer frei*). Prices for private rooms are unlikely to be above £5 ($8.50) per person.

There are 45 **youth hostels** in Turkey, only one of which is affiliated to the HI. Some student residences also serve as hostels (mainly during July and August, though some operate all year round). Normally a student ID card guarantees entrance, but it makes sense to have an HI card as, for some strange reason, even some of the non-affiliated hostels sometimes ask. Hostel dormitories are called *Yurtkur*. A booklet, *Youth Tourism in Turkey*, available from Tourist Offices, lists over 100 as well as nearly 50 youth and forest camps. Converted **student dorms** usually cost around £5 ($8.50) per person.

Camping is popular in Turkey, and the number of sites is growing annually. Campsites are generally open from April/May to October. Although facilities are still on the whole exceptionally basic, you nevertheless get reasonable value for money as prices are normally around £3 ($5) per person (tent included) for an overnight stay. At the network of BP *mocamps*, prices are around £5 ($8.50) per person per night, again including tent (a 20% surcharge is added in July and August). Some campers have cast doubt upon whether BP *mocamps* offer good value for money, but on a European scale it is fair to say that they do. Unless you are going to be travelling widely outside the main towns, it may not be worth taking a tent: the sites serving the cities can be inconveniently located far out of town and not always well served by public transport. In the cities, your best bet can be to make enquiries as to any hotels which allow camping in their gardens for a small charge.

ADDRESSES

TURKISH INFORMATION OFFICE
1st Floor 170/173 Piccadilly, London W1V 9DD (tel. 020 7629 7771, *www.gototurkey.co.uk*, *info@gototurkey.co.uk*).

GENÇTUR TURIZM VE SEYAHAT ACENTASI
Istiklal Cad. 15, Istanbul (tel. (0)212 249 2515, *www.genctur. com*). Information on youth and student travel and accommodation possibilities.

YOUTH HOSTELS
Visit *www.youthhostelturkey.com* for full listings of the country's hostels, as well as an online booking service.

TURKISH CAMP AND CARAVAN ASSOCIATION (TURKIYE KAMP VE KARAVAN DERNEGI)
Bestekar Sok 62/12 Kavakhdere, Ankara (tel. (0)312 466 1997).

Antalya (0)242

TOURIST OFFICE

Turizm Danisma Burosu, Cumhuriyet Caddesi 2 (tel. 241 1747). Open Mon.–Fri. 8am–6pm, weekends 9am–5pm. The office distributes small plans of the city and lists of local accommodation registered with the Ministry of Tourism, but no lists of locally licensed accommodation. As you walk along Cumhuriyet Caddesi from Kazim Özalp Caddesi, the office is about 250m beyond the Atatürk statue, set back a little off the right-hand side of Cumhuriyet Caddesi.

Also see *www.antalyaguide.org* and *www.antalya-ws.com*.

BASIC DIRECTIONS

Walking down Kazim Özalp Caddesi (also known as Sarampol) from the bus station, you arrive at the junction with Cumhuriyet Caddesi, at which point you should turn right to reach the Tourist Office.

FINDING ACCOMMODATION

Over the past decade, many town houses in the Old Town (Kaleiçi, the area roughly bounded by Cumhuriyet Caddesi and Atatürk Bulvarı) have been converted into guest houses. Hıdırlık Sokak and Hesapçı Sokak are particularly well supplied with guest houses. There are cheap hotels near the bus station, but this area is much noisier than the Old Town.

You should be able to find somewhere to suit you, and somewhere with spaces, from the list below. Failing that, ask at the Tourist Office for a list of guest houses and hotels which are registered with the Ministry of Tourism and for a list of hotels which are locally licensed.

GUEST HOUSES

LOCALLY LICENSED GUEST HOUSES. DOUBLES AROUND £8–14 ($13.50–24)

Kilim Pansiyon, Tabakhane Sokak 3 (tel. 248 2111). In the Old Town.

Senem Family Pansiyon, Zeytin Geçidi Sokak 9 (tel. 247 1752). Popular.

Beyaz Cül Pansiyon, Barbaros Mahalle Civelek Sokak 4 (tel. 247 3951). Recommended.

Adler Pansiyon, Barbaros Mahalle Civelek Sokak 16 (tel. 321 7818 or 241 7818).

Antique Pansiyon, Tuzcular Mah, Pasa Cami Sokak 28 (tel. 242 4615).

Ozmen Pansiyon, Zeytin Çıkmaı 5 (tel. 241 6505, ozmen@ozmenpension.com). Good value. Internet access.

Sabah Pansiyon, Hesapçı Sokak 60A (tel. 247 5345, *sabahpansiyon@yahoo.com*). Dorms also available. Breakfast included. Popular.

Lazer Pansiyon, Hesapçı Sokak 60 (tel. 242 7194, *ercument_ozturk@hotmail.com*). Welcoming.

White Garden, Hesapçı Geçidi 9 (tel. 241 9115, *garden@mail.koc.net*). Very clean.

Erken Pansiyon, Hıdırlık Sokak 5 (tel. 247 9801). Breakfast included.

Erkal Pansiyon, Kandiller Geçidi 5 (tel. 241 0757).

HOSTELS

Kadir's Top Treehouses, Olympos (tel. 892 1250, *www.kadirstreehouses.com*, *info@olympostreehouses.com*). Dorms from £5 ($8.50). Beds in actual tree houses, cabins or bungalows in the woods. Book in advance, it's very popular (and slightly surreal).

Ask at the Tourist Office for details of **summer hostels** in Antalya itself.

CAMPING

Freelance camping within Antalya itself is not to be recommended.

Camping Bambus, Lara Yolu (tel. 321 5263, fax 321 3550). By the beach at the Bambus Motel, 3 km out of town along the road to Lara. Although the site is expensive by Turkish standards, the facilities available are of a good standard.

Istanbul (0)212

TOURIST OFFICES

On arrival, head for one of the several offices the Tourist Board operates in the city. Arriving by train from Europe, the most conveniently located office is actually at the station (tel. 511 5888, *www.istanbul.com*). After that the nearest office is at Divanyolu Caddesi 3 (tel. 518 1802), in the Sultanahmet district (open daily 9am–5pm).

The offices at the Karaköy ferry terminal (tel. 249 5776) and at Atatürk airport (tel. 663 0793) keep the same hours as the Sultanahmet office.

Another office operates in the Hilton Hotel Arcade, off Cumhuriyet Caddesi, in the Harbiye district (tel. 233 0592).

BASIC DIRECTIONS

Trains from Europe arrive at the train station in Sirkeci, a short distance from the main sights in the Sultanahmet district. Going left from the exit of the station, you cross two main roads before arriving at the junction with Aşirefendi Caddesi (right) and Ebussuut Caddesi (left). Go straight across and follow the winding Ankara Caddesi into Yerebatan Caddesi. Go right and follow the street down to the magnificent Aya Sofya church. The Tourist Office is just a short walk to the left at the start of Divan Yolu Caddesi. The walk from the train station to the Tourist Office takes about 10 minutes.

Divan Yolu Caddesi runs into Yeniçeriler Caddesi, which subsequently becomes Ordu Caddesi. The Lâleli Mosque, about halfway along Ordu Caddesi, is about 20 minutes' walk from the Tourist Office. Many of the Tourist Board registered hotels listed below are in the streets off Ordu Caddesi around the mosque.

FINDING ACCOMMODATION

Due to its proximity to the major sights, the Sultanahmet district is a particularly popular place to stay. The area has the largest concentration of cheap rooms in the city, so outside peak season you are virtually assured a room here. Although there are few one-star hotels in the district, the standard of locally licensed accommodation is generally fine, but check thoroughly before accepting a room as there are some very poor establishments in Sultanahmet. There is quite a choice of one-star hotels in the Lâleli and Aksaray districts (a 20-minute walk from Sultanahmet), as well as a host of hotels licensed by the municipal authorities.

SULTANAHMET DISTRICT

Cordial House, Feykhane Sokak (tel. 516 108, *www.cordial house.com*, *reservations@cordialhouse.com*). Doubles from £13 ($22), dorms from £4 ($7). Cheaper if you book online.

Side Hotel, Utangaç Sokak 20 (tel. 517 6590, *www.sidehotel. com*). Near the entrance of the Four Seasons Hotel. Doubles from £16 ($27) in the *pansiyon*. In the hotel part doubles are £29 ($49). Prices are cheaper in winter.

Hotel Sebnem, Adliye Sokak (tel. 517 6623, *www.sebnem hotel.com*). Doubles from £23 ($40).

Hotel Poem, Terbiyik Sokak 12 (tel. 517 6836, *www.istanbul hotels.com/hotelpoem*. Doubles from £30 ($50).

Optimist Guest house, Atmeydani 68 (tel. 516 2398). Spotlessly clean, with superb views from the roof. Understandably popular, so advance reservation is recommended.

Terrace Guesthouse, Kutlugun Sokak 39 (tel. 638 9733). Doubles from £23 ($40). Very small and friendly.

Celik Guest house, Mimar Mehmetaga Caddesi 22 (tel. 518 9675). Doubles from £18 ($30).

Hotel Antique, Küçük Ayasofya Caddesi, Oğul Sokak 17 (tel. 516 4936). Looking at the Sultan Ahmet mosque from the Hippodrome, Küçük Ayasofya Cad. runs from the rear of the mosque, to the right.

Hanedan, Akbiyik Caddesi, Adliye Sokak 3 (tel. 516 4869). Doubles £16 ($27). Breakfast included.

Hotel Ema, Salkim Söğüt Sokak 18 (tel. 511 7166). Dorm beds available as well as the usual singles and doubles. Off Yerebatan Caddesi.

Nayla Paris Pansion, Kutlugun Sokak 22 (tel. 516 3567, *nayla@ superconline.com*). Charming hotel. Doubles from £15 ($25).

Star Guesthouse, Akbiyik Caddesi 18 (tel. 638 2302). Doubles from £18 ($30). Lively.

Alp Guest house, Adliye Sokak 4 (tel. 517 9570, *www.alpguest house.com, reservation@alpguesthouse.com*). £32 ($54) for a double.

Rose Pansiyon, Ishakpasha Mah Aksakal Sokak 20 (tel. 518 9705). In a quiet quarter off the Hippodrome.

Berk Guesthouse, 27 Kutlugun Sokak 27 (tel. 517 6561, *www.berkguesthouse.com, reservations@berkguesthouse.com*). Small, family run pension.

Empress Zoe, Adliye Sokak 10 (tel. 518 2504, *www.emzoe.com*). Cheap but plush.

AKSARAY DISTRICT

Dorms and roof space, as well as comparably priced smaller rooms, are available at several of the locally licensed hotels and guest houses listed below.

Hotel Burak, Fethibey Caddesi, Ağa Yokusu 1 (tel. 511 8679). Decent one-star hotel.

Nobel, Aksaray Caddesi 23 (tel. 522 0617). Breakfast included.

Okey, Fethi Bey Caddesi 65 (tel. 511 2162). Good value.

Uzay, Şair Fitnat Sokak 30 (tel. 526 8776). Off Ordu Caddesi, near Koska Caddesi.

Selim, Koska Caddesi 39 (tel. 511 9377).

Oran, Harikzadeler Sokak 40 (tel. 528 5813).

Babaman, Lâleli Caddesi 19 (tel. 526 8238).

Geçit, Aksaray Caddesi 5 (tel. 516 8828).

Tebriz, Muratpaşa Sülüklü Sokak (tel. 524 4135).

TAKSIM DISTRICT

Gezi, Mete Caddesi 42 (tel. 521 7430). Good value and location.

Plaza, Aslanyataga Sokak 19, Siraselviler Caddesi (tel. 274 1313). A real bargain, and with excellent river views.

Dünya, Mesurityet Caddesi 79 (tel. 244 0940). Dirt cheap.

Hotel Yonca, Tarlabasi Bulvari, Toprak Lule Sokak 5 (tel. 293 9391). Doubles from £12 ($20).

Vardar Palace Hotel, Siraselvier Caddesi 54 (tel. 252 2888, *www.vardarhotel.com.tr*). Doubles from £36 ($60). Not great value.

SIRKECI TRAIN STATION AREA

Ağan, Saffetinpas Sokak 6 (tel. 527 8550).

Hotel Engin, Riktin Caddesi, Recaizade Sokak 1 (tel. 512 2730).

Hotel Silviya, Asmahmescit Sokak 54, Tepebasi (tel. 0121 292 7749). Doubles from £12 ($20). Clean and new.

Eriş, Istasyon Arkasi 9 (tel. 511 5906). The street runs down the side of the station.

Yaşmak, Ebussuut Caddesi 18 (tel. 526 3155). Great hotel with great views.

HI HOSTEL

Interyouth Hostel, Caferiya Sokak 6/1 (tel. 513 6150, *www.yucelt hostel.com*, *info@yucelthostel.com*). Doubles £12 ($20); dorm beds from £4 ($7). HI membership compulsory, but cards are sold at the hostel. Best reserved in advance. The street runs from the foot of Yerebatan Cad. along the side of Aya Sofya.

HOSTELS

Hotel Büyükayasofya, Caferiya Sokak 5 (tel. 522 2981). Next door to the HI hostel.

Arsenal Youth Hostel, Dr Emin Paşa Sokak 12 (tel. 513 6407). Off Divan Yolu by the Tarihi Park Hamani. Dorm beds from around £4 ($7), doubles from £12 ($20).

True Blue Hostel, Akbıyık Caddesi 2. Akbıyık Cad. runs parallel to Kutluğun Sok.

Orient International Youth Hostel, Akbıyık Caddesi 13 (tel. 516 0171, *orienthostel@superonline.com*). Dorms from £4.60 ($7.50). Breakfast included. Email access, cable TV, 24hr hot water. Along the street from the True Blue Hostel, above.

Konyali Youth Hostel, Akbıyık Caddesi 15/2, Terbiyik.

Istanbul Hostel, Kutlu Gün Sokak 35 (tel. 516 9386, fax 516 9384). New and clean. Dorm beds £5 ($8.50), singles £16 ($27). Breakfast extra. South-east of the Grand Bazaar, next to the Blue Mosque.

STUDENT ACCOMMODATION

The Tourist Offices will be able to tell you about student accommodation which is converted into temporary hostels during July and August.

CAMPING

EXPECT TO PAY AROUND £5 ($8.50) FOR TWO PEOPLE AND A TENT PER NIGHT.

Londra Mokamp, Eski Londra Asfalt, Bakırköy (tel. 559 4200/560 4200). Very crowded site, about 1 km from the airport. Linked to Aksaray by buses and *dolmuses*. Bungalows available.

Ataköy Tatil Köyü, Rauf Orbay Caddesi, Ataköy (tel. 559 6000). Just south-east of the airport, between the main road and the Marmara Sea. 16 km from the city centre. Take bus 82 to the centre. Good facilities. Only £4 ($7) a night for two people and a tent.

Yeşilyurt (tel. 573 8408/574 4230). By the Marmara Sea, close to the village of Yeşilköy.

Kervansaray Kartaltepe Mokamp, Çobançeşme Mevkii, Bakırköy (tel. 575 4721).

UNITED KINGDOM

Four nations make up the United Kingdom of Great Britain and Northern Ireland, with four very different cultures: English, Welsh, Scottish and Irish. There is arguably more history and legend crammed into these small islands than in any other country in Europe.

BACKGROUND

England, the largest of the four countries, is dominated by the capital, London, which has recently been voted one of the 50 'places of a lifetime' to visit by the National Geographic Society. It is also one of the world's most fashionable cities. While this may be the case, London is pricey even for the British. Although the capital has a fair bit of history and many famous sites to see, you will only get a true impression of Britain if you travel further afield.

The history of Britain is characterised by a number of pivotal dates: 1066 and the Battle of Hastings, 1215 and the Magna Carta, the 17th century and the Civil War, and 1966, when England won the World Cup! Most important, though, to Britain's development as a world power, was the Industrial Revolution. By this time, Scotland, England and Wales were united as one nation, and soon began to take on the role of 'workshop of the world', such was their productivity and success at industry. With its enormous empire, Britain continued to dominate into the 20th century, until the strain of stepping head-first into two world wars gradually led to its decline.

In recent years, the perennial Scottish and Welsh rumblings for independence from the English government in Westminster have finally borne fruit. The Scots and the Welsh now have their own parliaments and assemblies after referendums in their countries. The situation in Northern Ireland is still fragile but progress is being made there too and things are looking more optimistic.

ACCOMMODATION DETAILS

If, as is probable, London is your first stop in the UK, you might well wonder just how long your budget will survive, given that hostels cost £15–25 ($25–42), B&B is rarely available for under £25 ($42) per person and the Tourist Information Centre charges a staggering £5 ($8.50) to find rooms that are well outside the budget category. Certainly a trip to the UK is likely to put some strain on your budget, as there is a shortage of accommodation possibilities under £13 ($22) per night.

Bed and breakfast accommodation in guest houses and B&Bs is available throughout the UK, with prices starting at around £15–17 ($25–29) per person. In most towns, including popular destinations such as Edinburgh and York, you should be able to find a bed in the £15–18 ($25–30) price range without much difficulty, except at the height of the season or during special events. However, in some of the more popular small cities, such as Bath and Oxford, you can consider yourself lucky if you find a bed for under £20 ($34).

Tourist Information Centres distribute free lists of local guest houses and B&Bs, so unless the town is very busy you can normally find a bed quite easily by trying a few telephone numbers; however, many offices operate a free local room-finding service. Many run a system whereby you pay a deposit (not a commission) at the office, which is then deducted from your final bill. A few offices do charge for finding a room, normally £1.50–3 ($2.50–5). One really useful service provided by Tourist Information Centres is the Book-a-Bed-Ahead facility, which costs £2.50 ($4.25) and lets you make a reservation at your next destination. This can save you a great deal of time, aggravation and even money.

The **HI hostel** network in the UK is extensive, although there are several important gaps, notably some of the larger English cities such as Birmingham and Leeds. There are three youth hostel associations in the UK: the Youth Hostels Association of England and Wales, the Youth Hostel Association of Northern Ireland and the Scottish Youth Hostels Association. Curfews are normally 11pm in England and Wales (later in London; some London hostels have no curfew), 11.30pm in Northern Ireland and 11.45pm in Scotland (2am in Glasgow, Edinburgh, Aberdeen and Inverness). Prices vary according to the standard of facilities and the age of the user. Those aged 18 and over are referred to as 'seniors', while visitors aged under 18 are classed as 'juniors'.

Annual membership costs £13.50 ($22) for seniors and £6.75 ($11.50) for under 18s in England and Wales, £7 ($12) and £3 ($5) in Ireland and £6 ($10) for seniors, £2.50 ($4.25) for juniors in Scotland.

Advance booking of hostels in the main places of interest is advisable from May to September and around Easter, preferably in writing, with payment enclosed. Telephone reservations are accepted on the day, but you must turn up by 6pm to claim your bed. A scheme covering all eight hostels in London, as well as several other major tourist centres, exists: callers can ring 020 7373 3400 or fax 020 7373 3455 and receive an instant confirmation of their booking. Hostels in 26 popular destinations in England and Wales are also part of a Book-a-Bed-Ahead scheme for which a small fee is charged (the An Óige hostels in Dublin are also included in the network). Full details are available at hostels or in the Youth Hostels Association of England and Wales handbook. A similar system operates at 20 of the most visited Scottish hostels. Beds reserved through the Book-a-Bed-Ahead system can be claimed up until 10pm.

There are some **independent hostels** in the main places of interest. Standards are generally on a par with the local HI hostels but the 'rules' are slightly more relaxed; usually there is no lock-out or curfew and you do not have to be a member. Prices do tend to be slightly higher and it is rare to get a bed for under £11 ($19). For more information, either pick up a list of hostels from the local TIC or buy a copy of the *Independent Hostel Guide* (£3.95, $7), which covers England, Scotland, Wales and the whole of Ireland. The YMCA and YWCA operate hostels in several cities; accommodation is usually in singles or doubles. However, prices can be as high as for bed and breakfast accommodation.

During the Easter and summer vacations (normally mid-March to mid-April and July to early September) many universities let rooms (mostly singles) in student residences. Contact the Venue Masters for more information (see Addresses). The universities are primarily concerned with attracting groups, so book well in advance. Overnight prices are generally in the £15–25 ($25–42) price range. If there are any spare beds available, some universities will let rooms on the day for around £12 ($20) to students with ID. If there are several of you travelling together, renting a furnished student flat from a university is better value. The Tourist Information Centre will inform you about individuals and organisations letting self-catering accommodation in the locality. The one hitch to renting a flat may be an insistence on a minimum stay of up to one week, although this is not always the case.

There are campsites in, or just outside, most of the main places of interest (Glasgow is a notable exception). Standards, and prices, vary dramatically but, short of sleeping rough, **camping** is the best option for keeping accommodation costs low. That said, in comparison to other European countries, prices are high. In popular tourist destinations it is not unusual for a solo traveller to pay £9–12 ($15–20) for an overnight stay. Elsewhere it is unusual for prices to rise above £7 ($12). In smaller towns and villages, local farmers will usually let you pitch a tent on their land if you ask permission first. In the more remote areas, there will seldom be any objection to your camping rough, provided you do not leave litter lying about or light any potentially dangerous fires. As the nights can be very cold in the hilly parts of the country, a good-quality sleeping bag is essential, especially in the Scottish Highlands (anyone visiting the Highlands in summer would also be well advised to invest in an effective insect repellent). The one main drawback to camping is the damp climate, so be sure that your tent really is waterproof.

ADDRESSES

NATIONAL TOURIST BOARDS

www.visitbritain.com.

English Tourism Council, Thames Tower, Black's Road, Hammersmith, London (tel. (0)208 563 3000, *www.english tourism.org.uk*).

Northern Ireland Tourist Board, St Anne's Court, 59 North Street, Belfast (tel. (0)28 9023 1221, *www.discovernorthernireland.com*).

Scottish Tourist Board, 23 Ravelston Terrace, Edinburgh (tel. (0)131 332 2433, *www.visitscotland.com*).

Bwrdd Croeso Cymru (Welsh Tourist Board), Ty Brunei, 2 Ffordd Fitzalan, Caerdydd (tel. (0)29 2049 9909, *www.visitwales.com*).

B&B

Bed and Breakfast (GB), 94–96 Bell Street, Henley-on-Thames, Oxon (tel. (0)1491 578803). This is a reservation service which covers England, Ireland, Scotland and Wales. There is a minimum deposit of £30 ($51) which is non-refundable but can be deducted from the total price of your stay.

In Northern Ireland, pick up a copy of *Where to Stay in Northern Ireland*. It can be bought from most Tourist Offices for £4 ($7).

HI HOSTELS

Youth Hostels Association of England and Wales, Trevelyan House, Dimple Road, Matlock, Derbyshire (tel. (0)1629 592600 for the switchboard or 0870 770 8868 (inside the UK) for customer services, *www.yha.org.uk*).

Youth Hostel Association of Northern Ireland, 22–32 Donegal Road, Belfast BT12 5JN (tel. (0)28 9032 4733, *www.hini.org.uk*, *info@hini.org.uk*).

Scottish Youth Hostels Association, 7 Glebe Crescent, Stirling FK8 2JA (tel. (0)871 330 8560, *www.syha.org.uk*).

UNIVERSITY ACCOMMODATION

Venue Masters, The Workstation, Paternoster Row, Sheffield (tel. 0114 249 3090, *www.venuemasters.co.uk*, *info@venuemasters. co.uk*).

Bath (0)1225

TOURIST OFFICE

Tourist Information Centre, Abbey Chambers, Abbey Church Road (tel. 477101, *www.visitbath.co.uk*). Open June–Sept., Mon.–Sat. 9.30am–6pm, Sun. 10am–4pm; Oct.–May, Mon.–Sat. 9am–5pm, Sun. 10am–4pm. The small city plan sold at the office is useful for sightseeing and for finding your way to accommodation. Local accommodation service and walking tours. There's a £2.50 ($4.25) booking service and you pay a 10% deposit at the office, which is subtracted from your final bill. Book-a-Bed-Ahead service available.

FINDING ACCOMMODATION

The popularity of the town, especially with more affluent, middle-aged tourists, means that prices in local B&Bs are slightly higher than normal. You can expect to pay about £15–20

($25–34) per person to share a room in one of the cheaper establishments.

Finding a bed in one of the cheaper B&Bs can be difficult in summer as the city attracts large numbers of visitors. At this time of year, you are as well heading straight for the Tourist Information Centre and asking them for the cheapest B&B available. If you arrive early in the morning there are a few areas of the city you can look in before the office opens, all within 15 minutes' walk of the bus and train stations. The best area to look is around Pulteney Road, as this has the highest concentration of the cheaper B&Bs. After that the area around Wells Road is probably just slightly better than that around the start of Upper Bristol Road.

GUEST HOUSES AND BED AND BREAKFAST

DOUBLES FROM £30 ($51)

Siena Guest House, 25 Pulteney Road (tel. 425495, *siena.hotel@dial.pipex.com*).

The Albany Guest House, 24 Crescent Gardens (tel. 313339, *the_albany@lineone.net*).

Koryu Guest House, 7 Pulteney Gardens (tel. 337642, *japanese koryu@aol.com*).

Glan Y Dwr, 14 Newbridge Hill (tel. 317521, *glanydwr@ hotmail.com*).

DOUBLES FROM £35 ($59.50)

Henry Guest House, 6 Henry Street (tel. 424052, *cox@thehenry bath.freeserve.co.uk*).

Hollies Guest House, Hatfield Road, Wellsway (tel. 313366, *davcartwright@lineone.net*). This guest house is 15 minutes' walk from the train station. Wellsway is a continuation of Wells Road.

The Belmont, 7 Belmont, Lansdowne Road (tel. 423082).

Toad Hall Guest House, 6 Lime Grove (tel. 423254).

DOUBLES FROM £40 ($68)

Della Rosa Guest House, 59 North Road (tel. 837193, *della@rosa.totalserve.co.uk*).

Leighton House, 139 Wells Road (tel. 314769, *www.leighton-house.co.uk*, *welcome@leighton-house.co.uk*).

Holly Villa Guest House, 14 Pulteney Gardens (tel. 310331, *hollyvilla.bb@ukgateway.net*).

St Leonard's Guest House, Warminster Road (tel. 465838, *stleon@dircon.co.uk*).

Oakleigh Guest House, 19 Upper Oldfield Park (tel. 315698, *oakleigh@which.net*).

Highways House, 143 Wells Road (tel. 421238, *www.highway house.co.uk, info@highwayhouse.co.uk*).

Cheriton House, 9 Upper Oldfield Park (tel. 429862, *www. cheritonhouse.co.uk, cheriton@which.net*).

Brocks Guest House, 32 Brock Street (tel. 338374, *www.brocks guesthouse.co.uk, marion@brocksguesthouse.co.uk*).

HI HOSTEL

Bath Youth Hostel, Bathwick Hill (tel. 465674 or freephone 0870 770 5688, *bath@yha.org.uk*). Juniors £8.25 ($14), seniors £11.50 ($19.50) – bed only. Breakfast, lunch and dinner are available, but cost extra. A 15- to 20-minute walk from the train station. From the roundabout on Pulteney Road by St Mary's church turn down Raby Place, which becomes George Street and then Bathwick Hill. Alternatively, take Badgerline bus 18 from the bus station.

HOSTELS

Bath Backpackers' Hostel, 13 Pierrepont Street (tel. 446787, *www.backpackers.co.uk, info@backpackers-uk.demon.co.uk*). Dorm beds £10 ($17). Breakfast £1.50 ($2.50). Close to the bus and train stations. Caters to a young, fun-loving crowd.

YMCA International House, Broad Street Place (tel. 325900, *www.bathymca.co.uk, reservations@bathymca.co.uk*). Dorms £12 ($20), doubles £16 ($27) per person, singles £18 ($30). Breakfast included. Open to men and women. No curfew. Central (about 300m from the Tourist Information Centre). Very popular, so reserve in writing well in advance.

HI HOSTEL NEARBY

Bristol International YHA Centre, Hayman House, 14 Narrow Quay, Bristol (tel. 0117 922 1659, *bristol@yha.org.uk*). 2- to 6-bed rooms. Juniors £12 ($20), seniors £16 ($27) – bed only.

Meals available. About 8 minutes' walk from Bristol Temple Meads train station. Bristol is 22.5km from Bath; the two towns are linked by frequent trains.

CAMPING

Newton Mill Camping Park, Newton Road (tel. 333909, *www.campinginbath.co.uk*, *newtonmill@hotmail.com*). 5 km from the centre. Take bus 5 from the bus station to Newton Road (every 12 minutes). Open all year. Around £4.50 ($7.50) per person if you just turn up with a tent. It costs £10 ($17) for a tent, car and two people. If you are coming by car you need to reserve at least a week in advance. At this centre there are good facilities: shop, laundry, bar, restaurant and free showers.

Cambridge (0)1223

TOURIST OFFICE

Tourist Information Centre, Wheeler Street (tel. 322640, *www.tourismcambridge.com*, *tourism@cambridge.gov.uk*). Open Apr.–Sept., Mon.–Sat. 9am–6pm, Sun. 11am–4pm; Oct.–Mar., Mon.–Fri. 10am–5.30pm, Sat. 10am–5pm. Room-finding service for £3 ($5) fee plus 10% deposit. The office sells a list of local accommodation, a copy of which is displayed in the office window. Book-a-Bed-Ahead service available (tel. 457581).

BASIC DIRECTIONS

The train station is just under 20 minutes' walk from the centre of the town. Head down Station Road, turn right at the end of the street along Hills Road (A604), and keep going straight ahead until you see Downing Street running left off St Andrew's Street. Turning right off Downing Street along Corn Exchange Street takes you into Wheeler Street. Buses 1, 5 and 9 link the train station with the centre. The Drummer Street bus station is right in the heart of the city. The lane running down the side of Christ's College brings you on to the main street opposite the post office. Cross the road, then head right and take the lane on your left to reach Wheeler Street.

FINDING ACCOMMODATION

Cambridge has a plentiful supply of rooms, so only during the peak season (late June to the end of August) are you likely to have any difficulty finding a room, at which time it is advisable to try to reserve a bed in advance. Tenison Street, near the train station, is a good place to look for one of the cheaper B&Bs at any time of year. Outside university term-time in and around Jesus Lane, near Jesus College, is another good area to look in. Many of the establishments in this part of town are only open to visitors during the university vacations (mid-June–end Sept., and possibly Easter and Christmas), because they are filled with students during the university year.

GUEST HOUSES AND BED AND BREAKFAST

DOUBLES FROM £30 ($51)

Antony's Guest House, 4 Huntingdon Road (tel. 357444). Singles, doubles and triples.

Abbeyfield Guest House, 2 Rustat Road (tel. 246474, *www.abbeyfieldguesthouse.co.uk, stay@abbeyfieldguesthouse.co.uk*).

The Old Rosemary Branch, 67 Church End, Cherry Hinton (tel. 247161, *s.anderson@constructionplus.net*).

Carolina B&B, 148 Perne Road (tel. 247015, *carolina.amabile@ntlworld.com*).

DOUBLES FROM £36 ($61)

Bon Accord House, 20 St Margaret's Square (off Cherry Hinton Road) (tel. 246568).

Dykelands Guest House, 157 Mowbray Road (tel. 244300, *www.dykelands.com, dykelands@fsbdial.co.uk*).

Victoria Guest House, 57 Arbury Road (tel. 350086, *victoriahouse@ntlworld.com*).

The Ark, 30 St Matthews Street (tel. 311130, *bartow.wylie@friendsinternational.org.uk*).

DOUBLES FROM £40 ($68)

Ashtrees Guest House, 128 Perne Road (tel. 411233, *ashtrees@csuk.net*).

Lantern House, 174 Chesterton Road (tel. 359980, *lanternhouse@talk21.com*).

Lynwood House, 217 Chesterton Road (tel. 500776, *lynwood. house@talk21.com*).

Oakley Lodge, 627–631 Newmarket Road (tel. 506007, *www.oakleylodge.co.uk*, *oakleylodge@talk21.com*).

Somerset House, 107 Milton Road (tel. 505131, *somersethouse@ amserve.net*).

El Shaddai, 41 Warkworth Street (tel. 327978, *www.droy. freeserve.co.uk*, *pauline@droy.freeserve.co.uk*).

Fairways, 141–143 Cherry Hinton Road (tel. 246063, *www. fairwaysguesthouse.com*, *mike.slatter@btinternet.com*).

Brooklands, 95 Cherry Hinton Road (tel. 242035, *www.brook landsguesthouse.co.uk*, *brooklands@cscuk.net*).

HI HOSTEL

Cambridge Youth Hostel, 97 Tenison Road (tel. 354601, or free-phone 0870 770 5742, *cambridge@yha.org.uk*). Juniors £12 ($20), seniors £16 ($27). Open year round. From 2- to 8-bed rooms. No curfew or lockout. Described by the YHA England and Wales as one of their busiest hostels, so try to reserve well in advance. Kitchen facilities and laundry room provided. Breakfast, lunch and dinner available. A few minutes' walk from the train station, right along Tenison Road from Station Road.

HOSTEL

Cambridge YMCA, Queen Anne House, Gonville Place (tel. 356998, *www.theymca.org.uk*, *admin@camymca.org.uk*). Open to men and women. B&B available in both singles and doubles. Clean and bright, with a buzzing social scene. Contact the YMCA for up to date prices and reservations.

CAMPING

There is no shortage of sites in the Cambridge area. Details of these sites are contained in the list sold by the Tourist Information Centre.

Cherry Hinton Caravan Club Site, Lime Kiln Road (tel. 244088). Open Mar.–Jan. Approximately 10 minutes from the centre of town. From £8 ($13.50) for 2 people. Some tent pitches available.

Highfield Farm Camping Park, Long Road, Comberton (tel. 262308, *www.highfieldfarmtouringpark.co.uk*). Open Apr.–Oct.

About 6.5 km from town, on the B1046 (turn off the A603 at Barton). Bus 118 or 119 from the Drummer Street bus station. From £6.75 ($11.50) for 2 people.

The Lake District

Keswick (0)17687

Keswick is about 55 km from Carlisle, and 19 km from Grasmere. The Tourist Information Centre in the Moot Hall on the Market Square (tel. 72645, *www.keswick.org, keswicktic@lake-district.gov.uk*) books local accommodation free of charge. Book-a-Bed-Ahead service available.

BED AND BREAKFAST

DOUBLES FROM £33 ($56)

Birch How, 41 Brundholme Terrace, Station Road (tel. 73404, *www.birchhow.com, info@birchhow.com*).

Bonshaw Guest House, 20 Eskin Street (tel. 73084, *www.bonshaw.co.uk, info@bonshaw.co.uk*).

Lindisfarne Guest House, 21 Church Street (tel. 73218, *www.lindisfarnehouse.com, lindisfarnehouse@tinyworld.co.uk*).

Badgers Wood, 30 Stanger Street (tel. 72621, *www.badgers-wood.co.uk, enquiries@badgers-wood.co.uk*).

Squirrel Lodge, 43 Eskin Street (tel. 71189, *www.squirrel lodge.co.uk*).

HI HOSTELS

Juniors £8.25 ($14), seniors £11.50 ($19.50) for the hostels below (bed only):

Keswick YH, Station Road (tel. 72484, or freephone 0870 770 5894, *keswick@yha.org.uk*). Off the Market Place, down towards the River Greta (some rooms have balconies overlooking the river). Station Road runs from the TIC. Curfew

11pm. Nice hostel with good facilities including kitchen, laundry and a games and TV room. Open all year.

Derwentwater YH, Barrow House, Borrowdale (tel. 77246, or freephone 0870 770 5792, *derwentwater@yha.org.uk*). Curfew 11pm. Fantastic old house, brimming with character. About 3 km out. Hourly bus 79 to Seatoller. Open Feb.–Nov. and every weekend.

CAMPING

Castlerigg Hall (tel. 74499, *www.castlerigg.co.uk*). From £7.60 ($13) for 2 people (no groups). About 1.5 km out of town to the south-east. Open Mar.–Nov.

Hutton Moor Caravan & Camping Site, The Stable, Hutton Moor End, Troutbeck (tel. 79615). 7 miles out of town. Prices from £7 ($12).

Ambleside (0)15395

About 8 km from Grasmere, 9.5 km from Hawkshead, 6.5 km from Windermere. The Tourist Information Centre in the Old Courthouse on Church Street (tel. 32582, *www.ambleside.u-k.org*, *amblesidetic@southlakeland.gov.uk*) charges £3 ($5) to book local accommodation. You also pay 10% of the bill at the office as a deposit and the remainder to the proprietor. Book-a-Bed-Ahead service also available.

BED AND BREAKFAST

Try Church Street or the Compston Road. The road leading out to Windermere, Lake Road, is particularly well supplied with B&Bs.

DOUBLES FROM £35 ($59.50)

Wanslea Guest House, Lake Road (tel. 33884, *www.wanslea guesthouse.co.uk*, *wanslea.guesthouse@virgin.net*).

Lattendales, Compston Road (tel. 32368, *www.latts.freeserve. co.uk*, *info@lattendales.co.uk*).

Broadview Guest House, Lake Road (tel. 32431, *www.broad viewguesthouse.co.uk*, *enquiries@broadviewguesthouse.co.uk*).

Melrose Hotel, Church Street (tel. 32500, *www.melrose-guesthouse.co.uk*, *enquiries@melrose-guesthouse.co.uk*). Opposite the Tourist Office.

HI HOSTEL

Ambleside YH, Waterhead (tel. 32304, or freephone 0870 770 5672, *ambleside@yha.org.uk*). Juniors £10 ($17), seniors £14 ($24) – bed only. Open all year. Curfew 12am. By Lake Windermere. Kitchen facilities, laundry room and luggage store.

CAMPING

Both campsites below are run by the National Trust (*www.nationaltrust.org.uk*) and only take bookings for families or groups.

Low Wray (tel. 32810, *rlwcam@smtp.ntrust.org.uk*). From £8 ($13.50) for 2 people. About 5.5 km from town, on the road to Hawkshead. The 505/506 bus services stops nearby. Open Easter–Oct.

Langdale, (tel. 37668, *rlcenq@smtp.ntrust.org.uk*). From £7 ($12) for 2 people. Approximately 6 miles from town. The 516 bus service runs out to the site. Open all year.

Windermere and Bowness (0)15394

About 6.5 km from Ambleside and 14.5 km from Hawkshead (by ferry). Another of the major gateways to the Lake District, thanks to the town's train station. Windermere's Tourist Information Centre is in Victoria Street (tel. 46499), close to the railway station. The office books local accommodation for free: a 10% deposit is paid at the office, the remainder to the owner. Book-a-Bed-Ahead service also available. In summer, similar services are available at the Bowness Tourist Information Centre in Glebe Road (tel. 42895).

BED AND BREAKFAST

DOUBLES FROM £35 ($59.50)

Ashleigh House, 11 College Road (tel. 42292, *www.ashleighhouse.com*, *enquiries@ashleighhouse.com*).

High Street House, 5 High Street (tel. 46930, *www.highstreethouse windermere.co.uk*, *nazray@highstreethousewindermere.co.uk*).

Elim House, Biskey Howe Road (tel. 43430, *elimhouse@ btopenworld.com*).

Meadfoot Guest House, New Road (tel. 42610, *www.meadfoot-guesthouse.co.uk*, *queries@meadfoot-guesthouse.co.uk*).

HI HOSTEL

Windermere YH, High Cross, Bridge Lane, Troutbeck (tel. 43543, or freephone 0870 770 6094, *windermere@yha.org.uk*). Juniors £8.25 ($14), seniors £11.50 ($19.50) bed only. 11pm curfew. Meals available. Troutbeck village is 3 km to the north of Windermere, off the A591. The bus to Ambleside stops in Troutbeck Bridge, about 10 minutes' walk from the hostel. There's also a YHA shuttlebus from the train station. Open Feb to Dec.

HOSTELS

Lake District Backpackers' Lodge, High Street (tel. 46374, *www.lakedistrictbackpackers.co.uk/lodge/home.htm*, *lodge@ backpackjobs.com*). Opposite the Tourist Information Centre. Friendly and relaxed hostel, with beds available from £10 ($17) a night.

CAMPING

Limefitt Park (tel. 32300, *www.limefitt.co.uk*). From £9.50 ($16) for 2 people. Couples and families only. On the A592 6.5 km south of Bowness.

Kendal (0)1539

About 18 km from Windermere, Kendal's train station and its proximity to the M6 mean it is likely to be on your route if you are coming from the south. The Tourist Information Centre is in the Town Hall on Highgate (tel. 725758). Local accommodation and Book-a-Bed-Ahead services available.

HI HOSTEL

Kendal YH, 118 Highgate (tel. 724066, or freephone 0870 770 5892, *kendal@yha.org.uk*). Juniors £10.50 ($18), seniors £14 ($24) – bed only. Meals available. 11pm curfew. In the town centre, close to the bus and rail stations. Open mid-Feb.–Oct. Closed Sun./Mon. in Feb.–Mar. and Sept.–Oct.

London (0)20

TOURIST OFFICES

London Tourist Board & Convention Bureau, 1 Warwick Row, London SW1E 5ER (tel. 09068 663344, *www.visitlondon.com*). The phone number is a centralised one as the offices below only handle walk-in enquiries.

There are eight/nine Tourist Information Centres operating in central London, according to the time of year. All these offices will book accommodation in London for a hefty £5 ($8.50) commission. The Book-a-Bed-Ahead service is also available, unless otherwise stated.

Victoria Station Forecourt, SW1. Open Mon.–Sat. 8am–7pm, Sun. 8am–4pm.

Liverpool Street underground station, Liverpool Street, EC2. Open Mon.–Fri. 8am–6pm, Sat.–Sun. 8.45am–5.30pm.

Waterloo International Arrivals Hall, Waterloo station, SE1. Open 8.30am–9pm.

Heathrow Terminals 1, 2, 3, Underground station concourse, Heathrow Airport. Open daily 8am–6pm.

British Travel Centre, 12 Regent Street, Piccadilly Circus, SW1. Open Mon. 9.30am–6.30pm, Tue.–Fri. 9am–6.30pm, weekends 10am–4pm. Saturday hours in June–Oct. are 9am–5pm.

Tower of London, West Gate. Open during the summer only.

Clerkenwell Heritage Centre, 33 St John's Square.

Bloomsbury Tourist Information Centre, 35–36 Woburn Place. Open 9.45am–7pm.

The City of London Corporation has an information centre in St Paul's Churchyard, opposite St Paul's Cathedral (tel. 7332

1456). It will not book accommodation. Open 9.30am–5pm. (Closed Sat. pm and Sun. from Oct. to Mar.)
Another possible resource is *www.londontown.com*.

FINDING ACCOMMODATION

There is a serious shortage of cheap places to stay in London throughout most of the year, but especially in the summer. If you plan to arrive then, it is advisable to book a bed as far in advance as you possibly can as you will struggle to find a place on arrival. Outside the HI hostels and a few independent hostels it is difficult to find a bed for under £18 ($30). You can expect to pay from £24 ($41) for a single in a guest house, with doubles rarely available for under £38 ($64.50). There are cheaper guest houses, but they are invariably filled with homeless families, temporarily boarded by the Department of Social Security.

HOTELS AND GUEST HOUSES

The cheapest singles at the establishments listed below are generally around two-thirds of the price of the cheapest doubles. All hotels and guest houses listed are in central London, unless stated otherwise (the phone numbers of those which are not in central London generally start with an 8 rather than with a 7).

DOUBLES FROM £36 ($61)

Colliers Hotel, 97 Warwick Way (tel. 7834 6931, *colliershotel@ aol.com*). Underground: Victoria (Circle, District and Victoria lines). BR mainline station.

Windsor House, 12 Penywern Road (tel. 7373 9087, *www.windsor-house-hotel.com*, *bookings@windsor-house-hotel. com*). Underground: Earls Court (District and Piccadilly lines). As well as private rooms, there are some cheaper dorm rooms available.

St Athan's Hotel, 20 Tavistock Place, Russell Square (tel. 7837 9140, *www.stathanshotel.com*, *stathans@ukonline.co.uk*). Underground: Russell Square (Piccadilly line).

Holly House Hotel, 20 Hugh Street (tel. 7834 5671, *www.hollyhousehotel.co.uk*, *hhhotel@ukgateway.net*). Underground: Victoria (Circle, District and Victoria lines). BR mainline station.

Fairway Hotel, 13/15 Argyle Street (tel. 7278 8682, *www.cyber lobby.com/fairway*, *fairway@cyberlobby.com*). Underground: Kings Cross, St Pancras (Circle, District, Piccadilly and Victoria lines).

The Queens Hotel, 33 Anson Road (tel. 7607 4725, *queens@stavrouhotels.co.uk*). North London. Underground: Tufnell Park (Northern line).

Grangewood Lodge Hotel, 104 Clova Road, Forest Gate (tel. 8534 0637,*www.grangewoodlodge.co.uk, info@grangewoodlodge. co.uk*). East London. Close to British Rail's Forest Gate station.

DOUBLES FROM £42 ($71)

Sass House Hotel, 10–11 Craven Terrace (tel. 7262 2325, *www.sasshotel.com*, *info@sasshotel.com*). Underground: Paddington (Circle, District, Bakerloo and Hammersmith & City lines) or Lancaster Gate (Central line). BR mainline station.

Shellbourne Hotel, 1 Lexham Gardens (tel. 7373 5161, *www.eol.net.mt/shellbourne, shellbourne@dial.pipex.com*). Underground: Gloucester Road (Circle, District and Piccadilly lines).

Alhambra Hotel, 17–19 Argyle Street (tel. 7837 9575, *www.alhambrahotel.com*, *postmaster@alhambrahotel.com*). Underground: Kings Cross, St Pancras (Circle, District, Piccadilly and Victoria lines).

Langland Hotel, 29–31 Gower Street (tel. 7636 5801, *www.langlandhotel.com*, *langlandhotel@lineone.net*). Underground: Goodge Street (Northern line).

Rasool Court Hotel, 19–21 Penywern Road, Earls Court (tel. 7373 8900, *www.rasoolcourthotel.com*, *rasool@rasool.demon. co.uk*). Underground: Earls Court (District and Piccadilly lines).

Ramsees Hotel, 32–36 Hogarth Road (tel. 7370 1445, *www.ramseeshotel.com*, *ramsees@rasool.demon.co.uk*). Underground: Earls Court (District and Piccadilly lines).

Charlotte Guest House, 195–197 Sumatra Road (tel. 7794 6476, *www.charlotteguesthouse.co.uk, charlotteguesthouse@ fax.co.uk*). North London. Underground: West Hampstead (Jubilee line).

Manna House, 320 Hither Green Road (tel. 8461 5984, *mannahouse@aol.com*). BR mainline station: Hither Green Road.

DOUBLES FROM £48 ($81)

Dillons Hotel, 21 Belsize Park, Hampstead (tel. 7794 3360, *www.dillonshotel.com, desk@dillonshotel.com*). North London. Underground: Belsize Park (Northern line).

Brindle House Hotel, 1 Warwick Place North (tel. 7828 0057, *www.brindlehousehotel.co.uk, info@brindlehousehotel.co.uk*). Underground: Victoria (Circle, District and Victoria lines). BR mainline station.

Hotel Cavendish, 75 Gower Street (tel. 7636 9079, *www.hotelcavendish.com, bookings@hotelcavendish.com*). Underground: Goodge Street (Northern line).

Dolphin Hotel, 32–34 Norfolk Square (tel. 7402 4943, *www.dolphinhotel.co.uk, info@dolphinhotel.co.uk*). Underground: Paddington (Circle, District, Bakerloo and Hammersmith & City lines). BR mainline station.

Georgian House Hotel, 35–39 St George's Drive (tel. 7834 1438, *www.georgianhousehotel.co.uk, reception@georgianhousehotel.co.uk*). Underground: Victoria (Circle, District and Victoria lines). BR mainline station.

Falcon Hotel, 11 Norfolk Square (tel. 7723 8603, *www.central-london-hotel.com, info@aafalcon.co.uk*). Underground: Paddington (Circle, District, Bakerloo and Hammersmith & City lines). BR mainline station.

Grange Lodge Hotel, 48–50 Grange Road, Ealing (tel. 8567 1049, *www.londonlodgehotels.com, enquiries@londonlodgehotels.com*). West London. Underground: Ealing Broadway (Central and District lines).

Martel Guest House, 27 The Ridgeway, Golders Green (tel. 8455 1802, *www.martelguesthouse.co.uk, reservations@martelguesthouse.co.uk*). North London. Underground: Golders Green (Northern line).

PRIVATE ROOMS

London Homestead Services, Coombe Wood Road, Kingston-upon-Thames, Surrey (tel. 8949 4455, *www.lhslondon.co.uk, lhs@netcomuk.co.uk*). Rooms available in central London and in the suburbs from £16 ($27) per person per night. Deposit required.

Host and Guest Service, 103 Dawes Road (tel. 7385 9922,

www.host-guest.co.uk, *info@host-guest.co.uk*). Rooms available from £16.50 ($28) per person per night. Booking fee required.

London Bed & Breakfast Agency, 71 Fellows Road (tel. 7586 2768, *www.londonbb.com*, *stay@londonbb.com*). Rooms available from £22 ($37) per person per night. No one-night stays.

HI HOSTELS

London's seven HI hostels are frequently filled to capacity around Easter and from June to September, so advance reservation is highly recommended. All seven hostels are open year round and operate no curfew although, with the exception of the City of London and Earls Court hostels, the reception closes at 11pm. The price listed, unless otherwise stated, is for bed and breakfast. Full details for all the hostels can be found on *www.yha.org.uk*.

City of London YH, 36 Carter Lane (tel. 7236 4965, or freephone 0870 770 5764, *city@yha.org.uk*). Juniors £20 ($34), seniors £24 ($41). 24hr reception. About 300m from St Paul's underground station (Central line) and Blackfriars underground (Circle and District lines) and BR station.

Earls Court YH, 38 Bolton Gardens (tel. 7373 7083, or freephone 0870 770 5804, *earlscourt@yha.org.uk*). Juniors £16.75 ($28.50), seniors £19 ($32) – bed only. 24hr reception. 300m from Earls Court underground station (District and Piccadilly lines), off the Earls Court Road.

Hampstead Heath YH, 4 Wellgarth Road (tel. 8458 9054, or freephone 0870 770 5846, *hampstead@yha.org.uk*). Juniors £18 ($30), seniors £20.40 ($35). About 400m from the Golders Green underground station (Northern line), off North End Road.

Holland House YH, Holland Walk, Kensington (tel. 7937 0748, or freephone 0870 770 5866, *hollandhouse@yha.org.uk*). Juniors £18.75 ($32), seniors £21 ($36). About 400m from both the Holland Park underground station (Central line) and the High Street Kensington underground station (District and Circle). Holland Walk cuts through Holland Park between Holland Park Avenue and Kensington High Street.

Oxford Street YH, 14 Noel Street (tel. 7734 1618, or freephone 0870 770 5984, *oxfordst@yha.org.uk*). Juniors £17.75 ($30), seniors £22 ($37) – bed only. About 400m from both the Oxford Circus (Central, Bakerloo and Victoria lines) and Tottenham Court Road (Central and Northern lines) underground stations. From Oxford Street, turn down Poland Street or Berwick Street.

Rotherhithe YH, Island Yard, 20 Salter Road (tel. 7232 2114, or freephone 0870 770 6010, *rotherhithe@yha.org.uk*). Juniors £20 ($34), seniors £24 ($41). 300m from Rotherhithe underground station on the East London line. Join the East London line at Whitechapel (District and Metropolitan lines). Bus P105 from Waterloo BR station runs straight to the hostel.

St Pancras International YH, 79–81 Euston Road (tel. 7388 9998, or freephone 0870 770 6044, *stpancras@yha.org.uk*). Juniors £20 ($34), seniors £24 ($41). From King's Cross/St Pancras stations turn right on to Euston Road. Continue up the road over the crossroads with Judd Street and the hostel is the second building on the left-hand side. From Euston station turn left on to Euston Road.

HOSTELS/STUDENT RESIDENCES

Venue Masters, The Workstation, Paternoster Row, Sheffield S1 2BX (tel. 0114 249 3090, *www.venuemasters.co.uk*, *info@venue masters.co.uk*). This company is the result of a recent merger between the British Universities Accommodation Consortium (BUAC) and Connect Venues. The website provides details and links to 11 universities in London that offer accommodation during the summer months, as well as to several other universities around the country.

The **Astor Hostel Group** runs five separate hostels. Their website, *www.astorhostels.com*, has complete details.

Astor Hyde Park Hostel, 2–6 Inverness Terrace (tel. 7229 3170, *hydepark@astorhostels.com*). Dorm beds from £11 ($19). Underground: Bayswater (District line).

Astor Leinster Inn, 7–12 Leinster Square (tel. 7229 9641, *leinster@astorhostels.com*). Dorm beds from £14 ($24). Underground: Bayswater (District line).

Astor Quest Hotel, 45 Queensborough Terrace (tel. 7229 8106, *astorquest@astorhostels.com*). Dorm beds from £12 ($20). Underground: Bayswater (District line).

Astor Victoria Hotel, 71 Belgrave Road (tel. 7834 3077, *astorvictoria@astorhostels.com*). Dorm beds from £14 ($24). Underground: Victoria (Circle, District and Victoria lines). BR mainline station.

Astor Museum Inn, 27 Montague Street (tel. 7580 5360, *astormuseuminn@astorhostels.com*). Dorm beds from £14 ($24). Underground: Russell Square (Piccadilly line).

Astor College, 99 Charlotte Street (tel. 7580 7262/7263/7264). Singles and doubles, £18–25 ($30–$42) per person. Underground: Goodge Street (Northern line).

Bryanston Residence, 16 Bryanston Square (tel. 7402 8608/796 3889). Singles, doubles and larger rooms. Underground: Marble Arch (Central line).

Carr-Saunders Hall, 18–24 Fitzroy Street (tel. 7323 9712). Open Dec.–Jan., Mar.–Apr. and July–Sept. Singles and doubles. B&B from £21 ($36) p.p. Underground: Goodge Street (Northern line) or Great Portland Street (Circle, Hammersmith & City lines).

International Students' House, 229 Great Portland Street (tel. 7631 8300). Singles, doubles and larger rooms. Dorm beds from £15 ($25), doubles from £44 ($75), including breakfast. Underground: Great Portland Street (Circle and Hammersmith & City lines). (You don't have to be a student to stay here.)

Allen Hall Summer Hostel, Allen Hall, 28 Beaufort Street (tel. 7351 1296/1297). Open July–Aug. Singles and doubles. B&B from £24 ($41). Underground: Sloane Square (Circle and District lines).

Anne Elizabeth House Hotel, 30 Collingham Place (tel. 7370 4821). Doubles and larger rooms. Underground: Earls Court (District and Piccadilly lines).

Crofton Hotel. 13–16 Queen's Gate (tel. 7584 7201). Singles, doubles and larger rooms. £16–38 ($27–$64.50). Underground: Gloucester Road (Circle, District and Piccadilly lines).

Culture Link International Student Residence, 161 Old Brompton Road (tel. 7373 6061). Singles, doubles and larger rooms. Underground: West Brompton (District line).

Curzon House Hotel, 58 Courtfield Gardens (tel. 7581 2116). Singles, doubles and larger rooms, £15–40 ($25–$68) for B&B. Underground: Earls Court (District and Piccadilly lines).

Queen Alexandra's House, Bremner Road, Kensington Gore (tel. 7589 1120). B&B from £26 ($44). Open May–Aug. Women only. Singles and doubles. Underground: South Kensington (Circle, District and Piccadilly lines).

Palace Court Hotel, 12–14 Pembridge Square (tel. 7727 4412). Singles, doubles and larger rooms. Underground: Bayswater (Circle and District lines).

Palace Hotel, 31 Palace Court (tel. 7221 5628). Dorm beds £14 ($24). Underground: Notting Hill Gate (Central, Circle and District lines).

C/E/I International Youth Hotel (Centre Française), 61 Chepstow Place, Notting Hill Gate (tel. 7221 8134). £15–20 ($25–$34) in dorms, £26 ($44) in singles. Singles, doubles and larger rooms. Underground: Bayswater (Circle and District lines).

Glendale Hotel, 8 Devonshire Terrace (tel. 7262 1770). £26.50 ($45) for B&B. Singles, doubles and larger rooms. Underground: Paddington (Circle, District, Bakerloo and Hammersmith & City lines). BR mainline station.

Lord's Hotel, 20–22 Leinster Square (tel. 7229 8877). Singles, doubles and larger rooms. Underground: Bayswater (Circle and District lines).

Ifor Evans Hall/Max Rayne House, 109 Camden Road (tel. 7485 9377). Open Mar.–Apr. and June–Sept. Singles and doubles. Underground: Camden Town (Northern line).

John Adams Hall (Institute of Education), 15–23 Endsleigh Street (tel. 7387 4086/7307 4796). B&B from £23 ($39) per person. Open Dec.–Jan., Mar.–Apr. and July–Sept. Singles and doubles. Underground: Russell Square (Piccadilly line) or Euston (Northern and Victoria lines). BR mainline station.

Passfield Hall, 1 Endsleigh Place (tel. 7387 7743/3584). Open Mar.–Apr. and July–Sept. Singles, doubles and triples. Underground: Euston (Northern and Victoria lines).

Regent's College, Inner Circle, Regent's Park (tel. 7487 7483). £35–50 ($59.50–$85). Open Dec.–Jan. and May–Aug. Singles, doubles and triples. Underground: Baker Street (Jubilee, Northern, Metropolitan, Bakerloo and Hammersmith & City lines).

Rosebery Avenue Hall, 90 Rosebery Avenue (tel. 7278 3251). Open Mar.–Apr. and July–Sept. Singles and doubles. Underground: Angel (Northern line).

Queen Mary and Westfield College Halls of Residence, 98–110 High Road, South Woodford (tel. 8504 9282). B&B. Open Mar.–Apr. and July–Sept. Singles and doubles. Underground: South Woodford (Central line).

Finsbury Hall, City University, Bastwick Street (tel. 7477 8811). Open Mar.–Apr. and July–Sept. Singles and doubles. Underground: Barbican (Circle and Metropolitan lines).

King's Campus Vacation Bureau, 552 Kings Road, SW1 (tel. 7351 6011). King's College has residences on several campuses in central London. Singles from £22 ($37) in Kensington, Chelsea and Westminster areas, and from £16 ($27) in Hampstead and Wandsworth.

London Student Hotel, 14 Penywern Road (tel. 7244 6615). Dorms from £12 ($20). Underground: Earls Court (District and Piccadilly lines).

Airton House Youth and Student Hotel, 8 Philbeach Gardens (tel. 7244 7722). Underground: Earls Court (District and Piccadilly lines).

Kent House, 325 Green Lanes (tel. 8802 0800/9070). Singles from £22 ($37). Doubles also available. Underground: Manor House (Piccadilly line).

Northampton Hall, City University, Bunhill Row (tel. 7628 2953). Open Mar.–Apr. and July–Sept. Singles and doubles. Underground: Old Street (Northern line).

University of North London, James Leicester Hall, Market Road (tel. 7606 2789). Open April and July–Sept. Underground: Caledonian Road (Piccadilly line).

University of North London, Tufnell Park Hall, Huddleston Road (tel. 7606 2789). Open Mar.–Apr. and July–Sept. Underground: Tufnell Park (Northern line).

Driscoll House Hotel, 172 New Kent Road (tel. 7703 4175). Full board around £165 ($280) per week. Underground: Elephant & Castle (Bakerloo and Northern lines).

Milo Guest House, 52 Ritherdon Road, Balham (tel. 8767 7225). From £16 ($27). Singles, doubles and larger rooms. Underground: Tooting Bec (Northern line). Advance bookings contact: Ms H. Milo, Kismet, Poynders Road, Clapham Park, London SW4 8PS (tel. 8671 3683).

Imperial College Reservations, 15 Prince's Gardens (tel. 7594

9494 or 7594 9525). B&B £35–46.50 ($59.50–79) in singles. Open Easter and summer. Underground: South Kensington (District, Circle and Piccadilly lines).

Expect to pay in the region of £22–£40 ($37–68) for a single/double in London's YWCAs and YMCAs. They are always popular so book as far in advance as possible:

YWCA, 2 Devonshire Street (tel. 7580 5323). Central London.

YWCA, 31 Draycott Avenue, Chelsea (tel. 7589 6017).

YWCA, 14 Endsleigh Gardens, Euston (tel. 7387 3378).

YMCA (Barbican), 2 Fann Street, EC2 (tel. 7628 0697). Underground: Barbican (Circle and Metropolitan lines).

YMCA (London City Hostel), 8 Errol Street (7628 4080/8832). Central London (Barbican).

YMCA, 10–12 West Cromwell Road (tel. 7373 0787).

CAMPING

Lee Valley Camping & Caravan Park, Meridian Way, Edmonton (tel. 8803 6900, *www.leevalleypark.co.uk*, *leisurecentre@lee valleypark.co.uk*). Open all year round. £11.20 ($19) for 2 people. About 16 km from the centre. British Rail train from Liverpool Street to Lower Edmonton, then bus W8. Alternatively take the underground (Victoria line) to Seven Sisters, then take a BR train to Lower Edmonton, followed by bus W8.

Lee Valley Campsite, Sewardstone Road, Chingford (tel. 8529 5689, *www.leevalleypark.co.uk*). Open Mar.–Oct. £11.20 ($19) for 2 people. About 19.5 km from the centre. British Rail train from Liverpool Street to Chingford, then take bus 505 or 379, both of which stop about 800m from the site. Alternatively, take the underground (Victoria line) to Walthamstow Central, then bus 505 or 215 to Chingford, 800m from the site. In peak season, bus 215 runs right to the site.

The Caravan Club (*www.caravanclub.co.uk*) has two sites close to the centre of London. The prices listed below are for non-members.

Crystal Palace Caravan Club Site, Crystal Palace Parade (tel. 8778 7155). Open year round. From £17 ($29) for 2 people. About 19.5 km from the centre. British Rail train from Victoria to Crystal Palace. Buses 2A, 3 and 3A stop close to the site.

Abbey Wood Caravan Club Site, Federation Road, Abbey Wood (tel. 8311 7708). Open year round. From £18 ($30) for 2 people. British Rail train from Charing Cross to Abbey Wood.

SLEEPING ROUGH

It is not possible to sleep in the train stations, nor is it safe to sleep in the surrounding areas. Sleeping rough is not to be advised in London as a whole, but if you must sleep rough, at least try to bed down beside other people (travellers, preferably). The Embankment at Westminster Bridge, or Hyde Park, are the most obvious places to try.

Manchester (0)161

TOURIST OFFICE

Tourist Information Centre, Town Hall Extension, Lloyd Street (tel. 234 3157, *www.manchester.gov.uk/visitorcentre*, *manchester. visitor.centre@notes.manchester.gov.uk*). Open Mon.–Sat. 10am–5.30pm, Sun. 10.30am–4.30pm. Rooms found in local accommodation for £2.50 ($4.25) fee. Book-a-Bed-Ahead service also available. Also see *www.manchester.com*, and *www.explore.destinationmanchester.com*, for more information.

FINDING ACCOMMODATION

Local B&Bs start around £15–16 ($25–$27) per person, but it is very difficult to find a centrally located B&B at those prices. The most reasonable terms for B&B in the city centre are offered by some of the pubs along Chapel Street. Apart from these, you are going to have to base yourself outside the centre. One of the better areas to look is the Chorlton district of the city, a 15- to 20-minute trip from the centre by bus 85, 86, 102 or 103.

BED AND BREAKFAST
DOUBLES FROM £35 ($59.50)
White Lodge Hotel, 89 Great Cheetham Street West (tel. 792 3047, *wlh.man@orbix.uk.net*). In Salford.

Cleveland Lodge, 117 Cleveland Road (tel. 795 0007, *michael. musgrove@ntlworld.com*). In Crumpsall.

Oakhill B&B, 75 Hill Lane (tel. 795 9441, *john@city53. fsnet.co.uk*). In Blackley.

Clydemount Guest House, 866 Hyde Road, Debdale Park (tel. 231 1515, *clydemount.e.h@amserve.net*). In Gorton.

The Copperheads, 187–189 Chapel Street (tel. 278 7000, *copperheadshotel@aol.com*).

STUDENT RESIDENCES

For more information on these and other student halls, contact the University Accommodation Office, Precinct Centre, Oxford Road, Manchester M13 9RS (tel. 275 2888).

University of Manchester, Woolton Hall (tel. 224 7244). Mainly singles, with only a limited number of doubles. B&B £17 ($29). Highly popular with groups. Buses 40–46 and bus 49 to Owens Park. Also **St Gabriels Hall**, 1–3 Oxford Place (tel. 224 7061). Dorm accommodation available during the summer holidays. Around £12 ($20) for singles (£8 ($13.50) for students). Reserve a week or more in advance with deposit. Three-day minimum stay.

The Student Village, Lower Chatham Street (tel. 237 6045). Masses of singles available in the summer for around £17 ($29) including breakfast. A short walk from St Peter's Square.

St Anselm Hall, Kent Road East, Victoria Park (tel. 224 7327). Around £17 ($29). Hall of residence with single study bedrooms, all with washbasins. 25 rooms.

HI HOSTEL

Manchester Youth Hostel, Potato Wharf, Castlefield (tel. 839 9960, or freephone 0870 770 5950, *manchester@yha.org.uk*). Juniors £14 ($24), seniors £19 ($32) – bed and breakfast. Open all year, 24-hour access. The hostel is about 800m from Manchester Piccadilly station, opposite the Museum of Science and Industry.

HOSTEL

Peppers, 17 Great Stone Road, Stretford (tel. 848 9770, *peppers59@hotmail.com*). Beds £9 ($15) per night. Self-catering accommodation 10 minutes from Manchester city centre by Metrolink. Close to Manchester United's football ground. Limited space.

WALES (CYMRU)

Cardiff (Caerdydd) (0)29

TOURIST OFFICE

Tourist Information Centre, Central Station, Central Square (tel. 2022 7281). Apr.–Sept. open Mon., Wed.–Sat. 9am–6.30pm, Tue. 10am–6.30pm, Sun. 10am–4pm; Oct.–Mar. closes at 5.30pm. Local accommodation service and Book-a-Bed-Ahead available. Free guide to the city's sights.

GUEST HOUSES AND BED AND BREAKFAST

DOUBLES FROM £35 ($59.50)

Briars Hotel, 126–128 Cathedral Road (tel. 2034 0881, *john.pottingerbriarshotel@ukgateway.net*).

Princes Guest House, 10 Princes Street (tel. 2049 1732, *info@ princesguesthouse-cardiff.co.uk*).

St Hilary Hotel, 144 Cathedral Road (tel. 2034 0303, *sthilary. hotel@virgin.net*).

Domus Guest House, 201 Newport Road (tel. 2047 3311, *www.nebsweb.co.uk/domusguesthouse, tonymurf@btinternet.com*). 10 minutes from town, or take bus 44 or 45.

Austin's Hotel, 11 Coldstream Terrace (tel. 2037 7148, *www. hotelcardiff.com, austins@hotelcardiff.com*). Doubles from £30 ($51). Great location, 400m from the castle.

HI HOSTEL

Cardiff YH, 2 Wedal Road, Roath Park (tel. 2046 2303, or freephone 0870 770 5750, *cardiff@yha.org.uk*). Juniors £10.50

($18), seniors £14.50 ($24.50) – bed only. Open all year. 11pm curfew. About 3 km from the city centre, near the Roath Park Lake at the junction of Wedal Road and Lake Road West. Bus 28, 29 or 29B from Central Station.

HOSTEL

Cardiff Backpackers' Hostel, 98 Neville Street (tel. 2034 5577, *www.backpackers.co.uk/cardiff*, *cardiffbackpacker@hotmail.com*). Prices for B&B in dorms start at £14 ($24) per person. The price goes down for stays of more than 3 nights, and the weekly rate is lower still. There are also some double and triple rooms available.

CAMPING

Acorn Camping and Caravanning, Rosedew Farm, Ham Lane South, Llantwit Major (tel. 01446 794024, *www.campingand caravansites.co.uk*, *acorncampsite@aol.com*). Not very convenient. It's an hour's bus ride away. Take bus 92 from the central station. When you get out of the bus it's still a 15-minute walk. Around £8 ($13.50) for two people and a tent in high season.

SCOTLAND

Edinburgh (Dun Eid Eann) (0)131

www.visitscotland.com (tel. 0845 225 5121 inside the UK, (0)1506 832121 from outside the UK, *info@visitscotland.com*).

TOURIST OFFICES

Edinburgh & Scotland Information Centre, 3 Princes Street (*www.edinburgh.org*). All phone enquiries are handled by the national contact centre (see above). July–Aug. open Mon.–Sat., 9am–8pm, Sun. 10am–8pm; Sept.–June Mon.–Sat. 9am–6pm,

Sun. 10am–6pm. Book-a-Bed-Ahead and local accommodation services. £4 ($7) fee for finding rooms in local guest houses and B&Bs; the only town in Scotland charging for this service (see Finding Accommodation, below). You pay 10% of the bill at the office as a deposit and the remaining 90% to the proprietor. Free lists of local guest houses and B&Bs, and hostels. The staff will check the availability of beds in local hostels, but cannot make bookings. Good range of information on the city. Very helpful staff. Set back off Princes Street, by the Waverley Steps, right above the Waverley Market shopping centre.

Tourist Information Desk, Edinburgh International Airport (tel. 0900 992244). Open Apr.–Oct., Mon.–Sat. 8.30am–9.30pm, Sun. 9.30am–9.30pm; Nov.–Mar., Mon.–Fri. 9am–6pm, weekends 9am–5pm. Opposite Gate 5 in the main hall.

BASIC DIRECTIONS

All trains to Edinburgh stop at the main Waverley station, just off Princes Street. With the exception of express services running on the East Coast line (through Newcastle and Berwick-upon-Tweed) all trains also pass through the Haymarket station, about 2 km from Waverley Station along Princes Street, Shandwick Place and West Maitland Street. To reach the Tourist Office from Waverley station either go up the Waverley Steps (beginning near platforms 1 and 19) and turn left at the top, or go out of the rear exit used by taxis, turn right up Waverley Bridge towards Princes Street, then right again across the pedestrian concourse. Some long-distance coaches drop passengers on Waverley Bridge, but most use the nearby St Andrew's Square Bus Station. From the bus station, walk out on to the open space of St Andrew's Square, turn left and follow South St Andrew's Street on to Princes Street, at which point the Tourist Office is diagonally left across the street. The shuttle buses which serve the airport run from/to Waverley train station or Waverley Bridge.

FINDING ACCOMMODATION

Despite the fact that the Scottish capital has more guest houses and B&Bs than any other city in the UK save London, plus a relatively large hostel capacity in peak season, you will toil to find a bed in a hostel or one of the cheaper guest houses or B&Bs if you arrive without reservations during the annual Edinburgh Festival (a three-week period in August). If you are arriving from another Scottish town at this time it is a good idea to try to fix up one of the cheaper B&Bs in advance using the Book-a-Bed-Ahead service; you pay roughly the same fee (or even slightly less) as the local Tourist Office charges to find a bed, but will avoid the queues, which can be horrendous. There is a free accommodation service in the Waverley train station (by platforms 1 and 19) but they have a limited supply of rooms, while phoning around on your own during the Festival period can be both soul-destroying and expensive. If you arrive without reservations and find all the affordable accommodation gone, those with railpasses might consider staying in the surrounding counties of East Lothian, Midlothian and West Lothian for the first night, while trying to make a reservation in the city for subsequent nights. Fortunately, the accommodation situation improves dramatically outside the Festival period: even in July it is not too difficult to find one of the cheaper beds, provided you arrive reasonably early in the day. The exception is in the week leading up to one of the Six Nations rugby internationals (played Jan.–Mar.), when hordes of visiting fans descend on the city. The situation is at its worst when the Welsh are the visitors, as they not only fill up the cheaper accommodation in the capital but in most of the towns within 50 km south and east of the city. If you want to look for guest houses and B&Bs on your own, particularly good areas to search in are Bruntsfield, and Newington/Mayfield (between the Royal Commonwealth Pool and the Cameron Toll shopping centre). LRT buses running up Lothian Road will take you into Bruntsfield, while those heading up The Bridges will take you into Newington/Mayfield.

TROUBLE SPOTS

If you are staying in Bruntsfield, Newington or Mayfield, the tree-lined park known as the Meadows can be a useful short-cut to the centre if you are on foot. The Meadows should, however, be avoided after dark. In recent years there have been a number of rapes here and numerous instances of women being subjected to severe sexual harassment. Unprovoked assaults on men by gangs of youths have also become regrettably common over the last few years.

GUEST HOUSES AND BED AND BREAKFAST

Expect to pay more during the festival.

DOUBLES FROM £30 ($51)

Falcon Crest Guest House, 70 South Trinity Road (tel. 552 5294, *falconcrest@btinternet.com*).

Rosevale Guest House, 15 Kilmaurs Road (tel. 667 4781, *rosevale1@clara.co.uk*).

Menzies Guest House, 33 Leamington Terrace (tel. 229 4629, *www.menzies-guesthouse.co.uk, info@menzies-guesthouse.co.uk*).

Harvest Guest House, 33 Straiton Place (tel. 657 3160, *www.harvestguesthouse.co.uk, sadol@blueyonder.co.uk*).

Clashaidy B&B, 21 Kilmaurs Road (tel. 667 2626, *clashaidy@lineone.net*).

McKay B&B, 121 Captains Road, Liberton (tel. 658 1578, *dorothy_mckay@lineone.net*).

Villa Nina Guest House, 39 Leamington Terrace (tel. 229 2644, *villanina@amserve.net*).

DOUBLES FROM £35 ($59.50)

Priestville Guest House, 10 Priestfield Road (tel. 667 2435, *priestville@hotmail.com*).

Edinburgh Thistle Guest House, 10 East Hermitage Place (tel. 554 8457, *www.edinburghthistle.com, edinburghthistle@blueyonder.co.uk*).

Gilmore Guest House, 51 Gilmore Place (tel. 229 5008, *gilmoregh@hotmail.com*).

Tiree Guest House, 26 Craigmillar Park (tel. 667 7477, *www.tireeguesthouse.com, reservations@tireeguesthouse.com*).

Aeon-Kirklands Guest House, 128 Old Dalkeith Road (tel. 664 2755, *www.jimkirklands.co.uk, jimkirklands@aol.com*).

Kariba Quest Guest House, 10 Granville Terrace (tel. 229 3773, *karibaquest@hotmail.com*).

Kaimes Guest House, 12 Granville Terrace (tel. 229 3401, *kaimeshouse@hotmail.com*).

Adam Drysdale House B&B, 42 Gilmore Place (tel. 228 8952, *addrysdale@drysdale57.fsnet.co.uk*).

Blackfriars B&B, 47/1 Blackfriars Street (tel. 556 8302, *katie.millar@tesco.net*).

Corner House B&B, 1 Greenbank Place (tel. 447 1077, *keith_t@ lineone.net*).

Divine B&B, 116 Greenbank Crescent (tel. 447 9454, *mary@ greenbank.fsnet.co.uk*).

Mitchell B&B, 19 Meadow Place Road, Corstorphine (tel. 334 8483, *nancymitchell@beeb.net*).

South Lodge B&B, 2A Dovecot Road (tel. 334 4651, *southlodge2a@yahoo.co.uk*).

Diggins B&B, 4 St Marks Place, Portobello (tel. 669 5018, *shaydiggin@compuserve.com*).

DOUBLES FROM £40 ($68)

Aros House B&B, 1 Salisbury Place (tel. 667 1585, *aros.house@ virgin.net*).

Kenvie Guest House, 16 Kilmaurs Road (tel. 668 1964, *www.kenvie.co.uk, dorothy@kenvie.co.uk*).

Portobello House, 2 Pittville Street (tel. 669 6067, *portobello. house@virgin.net*).

AmarAgua Guest House, 10 Kilmaurs Terrace (tel. 667 6775, *www.amaragua.co.uk, reservations@amaragua.co.uk*).

Granville Guest House, 13 Granville Terrace (tel. 229 1676, *www.granvilleguesthouse.com, enquiries@granvilleguesthouse.com*).

Hamilton House B&B, 22 Craigmillar Park (tel. 662 9324, *dwwren@aol.com*).

Ross B&B, 5 Linn Mill, South Queensferry (tel. 331 2087, *www.drossco.com, b&b@drossco.com*).

Lindenlea B&B, 6 St Marks Place (tel. 669 6490, *betty@ lindenlea6.freeserve.co.uk*).

Alloway Guest House, 95 Pilrig Street (tel. 554 1786, *alloway@eh65ay.fsnet.co.uk*).

Morningside Guest House, 7 Hermitage Terrace (tel. 447 4089, *www.heather_giorgio.pwp.blueyonder.co.uk, heather_giorgio@ hotmail.com*).

Belford Guest House, 13 Blacket Avenue (tel. 667 2422, *www.belfordguesthouse.com, mailbox@belfordguesthouse.com*).

Rosebank Guest House, 161 High Street, Tranent (tel. 01875 610967, *rosebankdavie@aol.com*).

Newington Lodge B&B, 222 Dalkeith Road (tel. 667 0910, *cmackay@aol.com*).

Granville B&B, 1 Britwell Crescent (tel. 669 8426, *granville.britwell@tinyworld.co.uk*).

McDonald Guest House, 5 McDonald Road (tel. 557 5935, *www.5mcdonaldroad.co.uk*, *white@5mcdonaldroad.co.uk*).

Darlington B&B, 7 Argyle Place, off Melville Drive (tel. 667 5578, *catherine@darlington496.freeserve.co.uk*).

Laurie B&B, 59 Craigcrook Avenue (tel. 467 4284, *ellalaurie@aol.com*).

Abacus B&B, 7 Crawfurd Road, Newington (tel. 667 2283, *abacus1@blueyonder.co.uk*).

STUDENT RESIDENCES

Prices in local student residences are expensive, although if there are any beds which have not been pre-booked by groups, they may be let out to students with ID for about half the normal price.

Pollock Halls of Residence (University of Edinburgh), 18 Holyrood Park Road (tel. 0800 028 7118 inside the UK, (0)131 651 2184 from outside the UK, *www.edinburghfirst.com/accommodation*). Open Easter and July–Sept. B&B from £30 ($51) per person. By the Royal Commonwealth Pool.

Queen Margaret University College, 36 Clerwood Terrace (tel. 317 3317, *www.qmuc.ac.uk/hospitality/holiday_accommodation.htm*, *capitalcampus@qmuc.ac.uk*). Open July–Sept. B&B from £32 ($54) for 2 people.

HI HOSTELS

Edinburgh has five youth hostels. Two of these, Eglinton and Bruntsfield, are open year round. The prices listed for these below are for low season (bed only) but go up by about £3 ($5) in high season – during the Edinburgh Festival (Aug.), at Christmas & New Year, and during the Six Nations (Jan.–Mar.). The other three hostels, Central, Pleasance, and International, are only open in the summer. All three offer single rooms with 24hr access and charge a flat rate for both juniors and seniors. To book any of the hostels, call the Central Reservations line (0870 155 3255).

Eglinton Youth Hostel, 18 Eglinton Crescent (tel. 0871 330 8516). Juniors £10.50 ($18), seniors £12 ($20). Curfew 2am. A 20-minute walk from Waverley train station but only 5 minutes from Haymarket station. From West Maitland Street, turn down Palmerston Place and watch for Eglinton Crescent on your left. Buses 3, 4, 12, 13, 22, 26, 28, 31, 33 and 34 run along Princes St to Palmerston Place. 158 beds.

Bruntsfield Youth Hostel, 7 Bruntsfield Crescent (tel. 0871 330 8515). Juniors £10.25 ($17.50), seniors £11.50 ($19.50). Curfew 2am. Check in from 11.30am (no earlier). About 30 minutes' walk from either train station. Buses 11, 15, 16 and 17 run down Lothian Road into Bruntsfield.

Central Youth Hostel, Robertson's Close, Cowgate (tel. 0871 330 8517). July £17.50 ($29.50), Aug. £20 ($34).

Pleasance Youth Hostel, New Arthur Place (tel. 0871 330 8518). Aug. only £20 ($34).

International Youth Hostel, Kincaid's Court, Cowgate (tel. 0871 330 8519). July £17.50 ($29.50), Aug. £20 ($34).

HOSTELS

Scotland's Top Hostels (*www.scotlands-top-hostels.com*) runs three hostels in Edinburgh. All three are open all year and offer dorm beds from £11 ($19) per night, £13 ($22) in July and August:

High Street Hostel, 8 Blackfriars St (tel. 557 3984, *high-street@scotlands-top-hostels.com*). Turn left down the High Street from the Bridges, then right down Blackfriars Street. From Waverley train station, go out by the exit the taxis use, then left up Waverley Bridge. At the mini-roundabout go uphill on Cockburn Street, then turn left down the High Street to the junction with the Bridges. Go straight ahead, then turn right at Blackfriars Street.

Royal Mile Backpackers, 105 High Street (tel. 557 6120, *royal-mile@scotlands-top-hostels.com*). Close to the High Street Hostel.

Castle Rock Hostel, 15 Johnstone Terrace (tel. 225 9666, *castle-rock@scotlands-top-hostels.com*).

Hoppo (*www.hoppo.com*) have two hostels in Edinburgh. Both are open all year, with no curfew:

Edinburgh Backpackers' Hotel, 65 Cockburn Street (tel. 220 1717, *info@hoppo.com*). Dorm beds from £13.50 ($23) per night, £15.50 ($26) in August.

Belford Youth Hostel, 6–8 Douglas Gardens (tel. 225 6209, *info@hoppo.com*). Dorm beds from £12 ($20) per night, £15.50 ($26) in August. In a converted church, choose between sleeping in the Great Hall or a private room. A lovely hostel with great facilities. From Princes Street go to Queensferry Street, bear left to Belford Road. Hostel is at intersection with Douglas Gardens.

Princes Street Backpackers, 5 West Register Street (tel. 556 6894, *www.edinburghbackpackers.com*, *reception@edinburghbackpackers.com*). Dorm beds £11 ($19) per night. Open all year. No curfew. Behind Princes Street, close to the bus station.

A1-Playfair House Hostel, 8 Blenheim Place, Royal Terrace (tel. 478 0007, *www.a1-playfairhousehostel.com*, *info@a1-playfairhousehostel.com*). Dorm beds £11 ($19) per night, with a cheaper rate for weekly stays.

CAMPING

Mortonhall Park Caravan Park, 38 Mortonhall Gate, Frogston Road East (tel. 664 1533, *mortonhall@meadowhead.co.uk*). From £9.50 ($16) for 2 people per night. Open Mar.–Oct. Take the number 11 bus. Meadowhead (*www.meadowhead.co.uk*) also run three other campsites around Edinburgh.

Gisland Caravan and Camping Park, Grange Road, North Berwick (tel. 01620 892205, *bmcnair@gilnbscot.freeserve.co.uk*). From £3.50 ($6) per person per night. North Berwick is a town close to Edinburgh. It can be reached by train from Waverley station or by bus.

NORTHERN IRELAND (0)28

Belfast

TOURIST OFFICE

Northern Ireland Tourist Board, St Anne's Court, 59 North Street, Belfast (tel. 9023 1221, *www.gotobelfast.com*). Head office of the Tourist Board. Very helpful if you want information to help you plan your trip. On arrival, head for their Tourist Information Centre at the same address (tel. 9024 6609). Open June–Sept., Mon.–Fri. 9am–5.15pm, Sat. 9am–2pm; Oct.–May, closed on Sat. Courteous and knowledgeable staff. Room-finding service (a small fee is charged). The office distributes a good map, complete with bus routes, and a pamphlet detailing an enjoyable walking tour of the city. From the central railway station, go left along East Bridge Street, right at Victoria Street, left along Chichester Street into Donegal Square, then right along Donegal Place and straight on down Royal Avenue into North Street.

FINDING ACCOMMODATION

No matter when you arrive in Belfast, you should be able to fix yourself up without too much difficulty. The bulk of the accommodation possibilities are about 3 km south of the centre, around the Botanic Gardens and the university, along or just off the Lisburn Road and Malone Road. There is also a reasonable supply of B&Bs to the east of the River Lagan, around Belmont Road and Upper Newtownards Road.

PUBLIC TRANSPORT

Although most of the accommodation is out from the centre, regular buses run all over the city. Most depart from Donegal Square, or from the streets off it. To get to the area around the Botanic Gardens and the university take bus 69, 71, 84 or 85 from the City Hall on Donegal Square. Bus 16 runs along Upper Newtownards Road, while Belmont Road is served by buses 20, 22 and 23. Those with a railpass staying around the Botanic Gardens area can take a train to the Botanic Rail Station or the City Hospital station. The Adelaide, Balmoral and Finaghy stations may be useful if you are staying around Lisburn Road and Malone Road.

TROUBLE SPOTS

Do not be deterred from visiting Northern Ireland because of fears about your safety. Tourists have nothing to worry about, either in or outside the capital, provided they are sensible. A bonus is that the incidence of petty crime is actually considerably lower than in mainland Britain. Another plus point is that there are few places in the United Kingdom where visitors are as warmly received by the local people as in Belfast. For obvious reasons, however, you should avoid talking about politics, religion and Irish history.

GUEST HOUSES AND BED AND BREAKFAST

DOUBLES FROM £36 ($61)

Rockbank, 40 Belfast Road (tel. 9335 2261, *phildapark@aol.com*).
Windermere Guest House, 60 Wellington Park (tel. 9066 2693).
Ashberry Cottage, 19 Rosepark Central (tel. 9028 6300).

DOUBLES FROM £42 ($71)

Bienvenue Guest House, 8 Sans Souci Park (tel. 9066 8003, *bienvenueguesthouse@hotmail.com*).
Pearl Court, 11 Malone Road (tel. 9066 6145, *pearlcourtgh@ hotmail.com*).
Hazelville B&B, 116 Upper Newtownards Road (tel. 9065 2802, *hazelville@amserve.net*).
All Seasons, 365 Lisburn Road (tel. 9068 2814, *www.allseasons belfast.com, allseasons@fsmail.net*).

STUDENT RESIDENCE

Queen's Elms, Queen's University, 78 Malone Road (tel. 9038 1608, *www.qub.ac.uk*). £9–16 ($15–$27) per person in singles or doubles. (Students pay less than non-students.) Open mid-June–mid-Sept. No curfew. Bus 71 from Donegall Square East. The closest rail station is Adelaide.

HI HOSTEL

Belfast International Youth Hostel, 22–23 Donegal Road (tel. 9031 5435, *www.hini.org.uk*). Dorm beds from £8.50 ($14.50) per person. Private rooms also available. No kitchen facilities. Open all year. No curfew. Wheelchair access.

HOSTEL

Paddy's Backpackers, The Linen House, 18–20 Kent Street (tel. 9058 6400, *www.belfasthostel.com, info@belfasthostel.com*). Dorm beds from £6.50 ($11) per person. Just off North Street.

Index